Smart Life and Smart Life Engineering

Elena Kornyshova • Rébecca Deneckère •
Sjaak Brinkkemper
Editors

Smart Life and Smart Life Engineering

Current State and Future Vision

Springer

Editors
Elena Kornyshova
Centre d'Etudes et de Recherche en
Informatique et Communications
Conservatoire National des Arts et Métiers
Paris, France

Rébecca Deneckère
Centre de Recherche en Informatique
Université Paris I Panthéon-Sorbonne
Paris, France

Sjaak Brinkkemper
Department of Information and Computing
Sciences
Utrecht University
Utrecht, The Netherlands

ISBN 978-3-031-75889-8 ISBN 978-3-031-75887-4 (eBook)
https://doi.org/10.1007/978-3-031-75887-4

This work was supported by Conservatoire National des Arts et Métiers and Utrecht University.

This Springer imprint is published by the registered company Springer Nature Switzerland AG
The registered company address is: Gewerbestrasse 11, 6330 Cham, Switzerland

Preface

Welcome to the world of Smart Life Engineering! In this book, we look into the fascinating domain of Smart technologies and their impact on our daily lives. From Smart homes to Smart cities, from advanced algorithms to ethical considerations, this book explores the multifaceted dimensions of Smart Life Engineering.

Our main motivation for writing this book on Smart Life Engineering is to identify and define the field of Smart Life, providing a clear scope of what constitutes "Smart" in the context of digital technologies. We aim to develop a cross-field perspective, provide insights on various disciplines within Smart Life, and offer illustrative examples of existing works in the field.

This book results from the scientific collaborations created during a serie of three workshops called "Information System Engineering for Smarter Life" (ISESL) collocated with the International Conference on Advanced Information Systems Engineering (CAiSE). This workshop, initiated in 2020, aimed at bringing together researchers and practitioners interested in the application of disruptive technologies to Smarter Life. During three editions in 2020, 2022, and 2023, the participants of this workshop worked on topics emerging from the application of the expanding digital technologies to different fields of life through the perspective of information systems. The last edition of this workshop was focused on the elaboration of the different chapters of the given book.

The book contains 13 chapters divided into 4 parts, including (I) Fundamentals of Smart Life and Smart Life Engineering, (II) Conceptual Contributions to Smart Life, (III) Smart Life Applications, and (IV) Experience Reports on Smart Life Applications.

Fundamentals of Smart Life and Smart Life Engineering

The first part of this book focuses on the foundational aspects of Smart Life and Smart Life Engineering. This part begins with an exploration of the concept of Smart Life, examining its various dimensions and implications (Chap. 1). Then a taxonomy of Smart applications (Chap. 2) and evolution of the scientific domain of Smart Life (Chap. 3) reveal its development and key areas of research. Additionally, a comprehensive review of social, behavioral, and ethical considerations for Smart Life Engineering, highlighting the importance of responsible and ethical innovation in this field, is conducted in Chap. 4.

Conceptual Contributions to Smart Life

The second part of the book investigates conceptual contributions to Smart Life, exploring innovative ideas and approaches that shape the future of Smart technologies. The implications of Smart environments for environmental governance are examined in Chap. 5 with a discussion on how these technologies can contribute to sustainability efforts. Common misconceptions about Smart homes are addressed in Chap. 6. Chapter 7 explores the stakeholders involved in Smart city standardization, shedding light on the complex ecosystem of Smart urban development. In Chap. 8, the concept of Smart tourism and Smart tourism tools are discussed.

Smart Life Applications

The third part focuses on reviewing three Smart Life applications, examining real-world implementations and their impact on various domains. The application of deep learning in Smart viticulture and recent advancements in yield prediction are explored in Chap. 9. Passengers' in-cabin behavior in Smart elevators is analyzed in Chap. 10. Finally, a wireless crowd detection technique for Smart overtourism mitigation is highlighted in Chap. 11.

Experience Reports on Smart Life Applications

Finally, we look into real-world experience reports of Smart Life applications in this part. Chapter 12 focuses on the Smart city experience of Leuven. Another case concerns the case study of Monserrate, where immersive technologies and gaming are utilized to enhance the visitor experience (Chap. 13).

Through these themes and chapters, this book provides a comprehensive overview of Smart Life Engineering, from its foundational principles to its practical applications and theoretical advancements. Whether you are a researcher, practitioner, or enthusiast, we invite you to embark on this journey into the exciting world of Smart technologies and their impact on our lives.

Acknowledgments

We would like to express our deepest gratitude to the participants of the ISESL workshops. It is thanks to their commitment, innovative ideas, and enthusiasm that this book became a reality. Their contributions were essential in enriching the discussions and guiding the reflections presented in these pages.

We also wish to thank the organizers of the three editions of the CAISE conference (2020, 2022, 2023) for making these workshops possible. Their logistical support was crucial in creating an environment beneficial to exchange and collaboration.

Finally, we extend our sincerest thanks to the authors and reviewers of this book. Twenty-eight authors, spread across 14 chapters, have generously shared their expertise and knowledge. The reviewers, with their rigor and insightful advice, have helped enhance the quality and coherence of the entire work. Without their hard work and dedication, this book would not have achieved the level of excellence we hoped for.

Thank you all for your invaluable contributions.

Paris, France Elena Kornyshova
Paris, France Rébecca Deneckère
Utrecht, The Netherlands Sjaak Brinkkemper

Contents

Part I
Fundamentals of Smart Life and Smart Life Engineering

Chapter 1
Exploring Smart Life

Elena Kornyshova, Rébecca Deneckère, Kamal Mustapha Benramdane, and Sjaak Brinkkemper

Abstract In the contemporary landscape of technological advancement, the concept of Smart Life has emerged as a multifaceted domain, encapsulating a myriad of interconnected elements that deeply influence our daily experience. A lot of research works are published on this topic each month, and new devices continue to appear. However, after examining the existing literature, we found out the need for a consistent definition of Smart Life. This chapter addresses this limitation by providing a more precise definition of the Smart Life concept. We present various terms related to "Smart," characterize in detail the concept of Smart Life, present a systemic view on this topic, and, finally, introduce the basic elements for Smart Life governance.

Keywords Smart Life · Smart artifact · Smart application · Smart domain · Governance

1.1 Introduction

The term *Smart* has its roots in Old English, dating back to the thirteenth to fourteenth century, originally connoting quick, active, and clever in relation to sharp humor or words (Online Etymology Dictionary 2024). Over time, it evolved to become synonymous with intelligent, quick, and fashionable (Oxford Dictionary

E. Kornyshova (✉) · K. M. Benramdane
Centre d'Etudes et de Recherche en Informatique et Communications, Conservatoire National des Arts et Métiers, Paris, France
e-mail: elena.kornyshova@cnam.fr; mustapha-kamal.benramdane@lecnam.net

R. Deneckère
Centre de Recherche en Informatique, Université Paris 1 Panthéon-Sorbonne, Paris, France
e-mail: rebecca.deneckere@univ-paris1.fr

S. Brinkkemper
Department of Information and Computing Sciences, Utrecht University, Utrecht, the Netherlands
e-mail: s.brinkkemper@uu.nl

E. Kornyshova et al. (eds.), *Smart Life and Smart Life Engineering*,
https://doi.org/10.1007/978-3-031-75887-4_1

2024). In the early 1970s, the term "Smart" took on a new dimension, referring to devices behaving as they were guided by intelligence. With the widespread adoption of Internet of Things (IoT), the concept of smartification arises in many domains (Schuh et al. 2019), where both devices and human activities incorporate computational and intelligent features. This is peculiar to a lot of areas, such as Smart cities, Smart energy, Smart homes, Smart manufacturing, etc.

Various Smart applications take more importance continuously. However, there is still a lack of understanding of what is Smart Life. Even the term "Smart" is to some extend ambiguous:

- *Subjectivity of intelligence*: The term "Smart" can mean different things to different people. What one considers as Smart might not align with someone else's perspective. This subjectivity can lead to debates and disagreements, particularly when applied to technologies and systems in different user circumstances.
- *Ambiguity in technology*: In the context of technology, there might be ambiguity about what features or capabilities make a device or system truly "Smart." This lack of clarity can lead to misunderstandings and misinterpretations.
- *Rapid technological evolution:* As technology evolves rapidly, what was considered Smart yesterday might be outdated or commonplace today. This fast-paced evolution can make it challenging to establish a fixed definition.
- *Overuse and marketing:* "Smart" has been widely used in marketing to promote various products and technologies, usually without a clear definition or standard. This overuse has diluted its meaning and contribute to skepticism or confusion about what truly qualifies as "Smart."

In summary, the term "Smart" is controversial due to its subjective nature, ambiguity in technology, the rapid evolution of technology, and its overuse in marketing. It is therefore essential to lead scientific debates around "Smart" to establish a set of clear definitions, which will serve for a uniform understanding.

In our previous works (Kornyshova et al. 2022a, b), we started to develop and formalize the concept of Smart Life. This chapter gives a more detailed vision by detailing the layers of Smart Life and its core components—Smart artifacts, Smart applications, Smart domains, Smart Life Engineering, and other related concepts—and unveiling the systemic nature that underpins this paradigm.

Section 1.2 overviews the concept "Smart" and other similar terms. Our detailed vision of the concept "Smart" is explained in Sect. 1.3. In Sect. 1.4, we present our systemic vision of Smart Life. We discuss the aspects related to Smart Life governance in Sect. 1.5. We conclude this chapter in Sect. 1.6.

1.2 Concept of "Smart"

The idea of Smart Life is often associated with the Internet of Things in the existing literature, especially within various Smart devices. IoT has brought significant changes in human life by enabling the exchange of information in various applications such as Smart cities, Smart homes, Smart health, Smart transport, etc. In Lee et al. (2021), the authors characterized Smart Life applications based on IoT as a new lifestyle. Smart Life connects all IoT microdevices and microsensors through wireless communication grids, as described in Cho et al. (2018). This concept of connecting all embedded devices to the Internet has the potential to change our lives and the world, making it possible for us to live a Smart Life in a Smart world, as stated in Mizintseva (2021). IoT is an essential technology to enhance the quality of human life (Ho et al. 2015; Sharma and Tayal 2019). IoT objects and devices collect user data, and their final goal is an intelligent use of these data to provide meaningful support to the user (Fu 2016). These intelligent devices are leading the way to Smart Life, pointing toward a fresh and innovative direction for the Internet (Gonzales Garcia et al. 2017).

However, Smart Life is not restricted to the concept of IoT. The main idea behind Smart Life is using and processing data to improve the conditions of our lives. Any artifact that processes data in an autonomous way can be considered as "Smart," independently of its connectivity status. In addition, the understanding of the term "Smart" varies not only between sub-fields but also within specific fields. For example, Liu and Baiocchi (2016) and Thagard (1993) present different perspectives on the concept of Smart objects, but a unanimous agreement on the definition of a Smart object is absent.

Many terms exist that are closely related to this concept. Most notably, in scientific literature, this is the case for "intelligent," "autonomous," "stand-alone," and "sentient."

Intelligent Merriam-Webster (2024a) gives several definitions of the term "intelligent." The definition, the most adapted to our context, is "something guided or controlled by a computer." Morris and Langari (2016) propose to define the term "intelligent device" as "a package containing either a complete measurement system, or else a component within a measurement system, which incorporates a digital processor."

Autonomous Merriam-Webster (2024b) defines autonomous as "(a) having the right or power of self-government (b) is undertaken or carried on without outside control (c) existing or capable of existing independently (d) responding, reacting, or developing independently of the whole." An example of Smart systems that are defined as autonomous represents the autonomous vehicles. Faisal et al. (2019) propose a state of the art on autonomous vehicles, aka automated car, self-driving car, or driverless car (Spyropoulou et al. 2008; Chong et al. 2013; Olaverri-Monreal 2016).

Stand-alone Merriam-Webster (2024c) defines stand-alone as "intended, designed, or able to be used or to function alone or separately : not connected to or requiring connection to something else in order to be used or to function." Nawandar et al. (2021) describe a stand-alone device as "having numerous capabilities: (i) interaction with user, (ii) required application selection, (iii) data sensing, (iv) data publish, and (v) decision making and actuation."

Sentient Merriam-Webster (2024d) gives a definition of "sentient" as being "capable of sensing or feeling: conscious of or responsive to the sensations of seeing, hearing, feeling, tasting, or smelling." Applied to the context of artificial intelligence (AI), A. Husain (2017) defines the term of "sentient machine." He promotes sentience as the path from artificial narrow intelligence (e.g., drones) to artificial generalized intelligence (achievement of machine consciousness). In Kornyshova and Gressier-Soudan (2021), this term is used to introduce sentient requirements for ICT. These requirements aim to improve and protect the well-being of ICT users and to contribute to the maintenance of the human sovereignty with regard to digital technologies.

All these definitions are tightly linked and represent nearly the same ideas. Our definition of Smart also introduces some different degrees, called "smartness degrees," detailed in the following section.

1.3 Characterization of Smart Life

To gain a deeper understanding of the Smart Life domain, we established a two-dimensional framework that we explain through the notion of an artifact. The first dimension encompasses the different levels of smartness, and the second dimension considers the connectivity of devices.

We identify three degrees of smartness: *Smart*, *intelligent*, and *sentient.*

- *Degree 1 of Smartness—Smart:* is the ability of an artifact to process data and adapt its functioning accordingly. The device should be able to trigger further action depending on the context characteristics.
- *Degree 2 of Smartness—Intelligent:* is the ability of an artifact to process data and adapt its functioning using artificial intelligence. At this degree, AI algorithms are involved in deciding about the next action.
- *Degree 3 of Smartness—Sentient:* is the ability of an artifact to process data derived from users, about their feelings, emotions, physical state, etc., and adapt its functioning to enhance the well-being of users.

These three smartness degrees are orthogonal to the three different degrees of connectivity used.

- *Degree 1 of Connectivity—Stand-alone:* an artifact is working on its own, without the need to be connected to anything else.
- *Degree 2 of Connectivity—Connected:* an artifact is working on its own but is connected to the Internet to get and share data with other artifacts or applications.
- *Degree 3 of Connectivity—Federated:* an artifact is working on its own but also together with other artifacts or applications for a common goal.

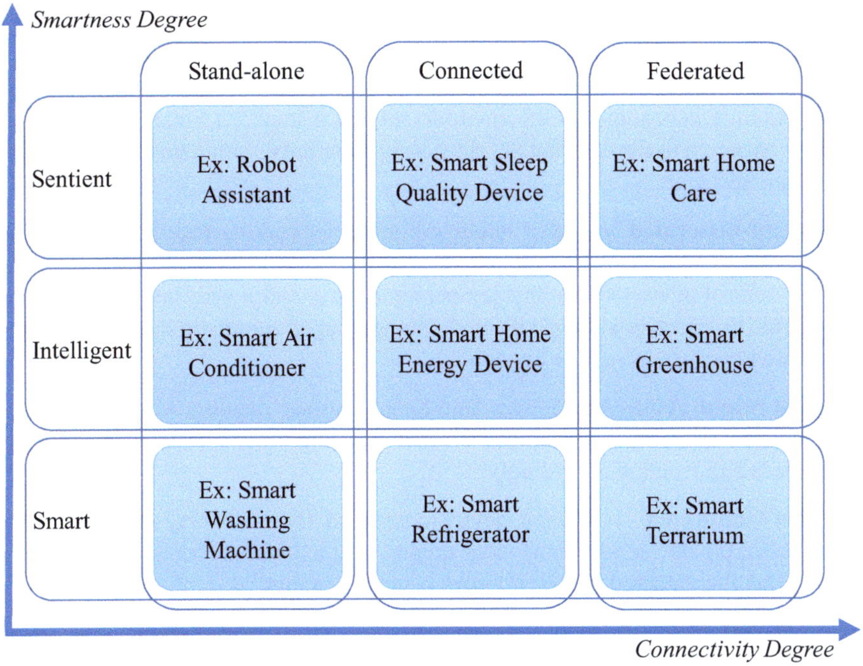

Fig. 1.1 Examples of the characterization of Smart Life

The orthogonality of smartness and connectivity implies that we can characterize $3 \times 3 = 9$ types of Smart Life. This characterization with illustrative examples is shown in Fig. 1.1.

Smart-Stand-alone An artifact that is able to adapt its behavior without external data input and/or action. For instance, a Smart washing machine selects the program depending on the laundry weight, color, etc.

Smart-Connected A connected to a network artifact that can adapt its functioning. An example is the Smart refrigerator that can order grocery foods when it detects lack of certain goods.

Smart-Federated A set of connected Smart artifacts, working together for the same goal and defining together the next action. A Smart terrarium is a good example. It is composed of several sensors (temperature, humidity, etc.), and all the collected data helps define the terrarium parameters to offer optimal conditions to animals.

Intelligent-Stand-alone A Smart artifact that uses artificial intelligence tools to modify its behavior following the context. For instance, a Smart air conditioner can adapt the temperature of the room depending on the people inside and the environment context (weather, outside temperature, etc.) using machine learning algorithms.

Intelligent-Connected An intelligent artifact connected to a network and adapting its functioning depending on the environment, for instance, a Smart home energy device connected to the distributed grid storing electricity, optimizing the consumption of the residents.

Intelligent-Federated A set of intelligent artifacts working together as a whole for a common goal. An autonomous greenhouse is a good example, as it includes a set of control devices (humidity, temperature, etc.), and it uses machine learning algorithms to interpret all the collected data to trigger automatic harvesting when plants are identified as mature enough.

Sentient-Stand-alone An independent Smart artifact dealing with well-being-oriented data of users, for example, a robot assisting elderly people, interpreting their needs and reacting accordingly.

Sentient-Connected A sentient device connected to a network, for instance, a Smart wearable device analyzing sleep quality coupled with a coaching application interpreting the gathered data to improve personal training.

Sentient-Federated A set of sentient artifacts able to work together and adapt themselves to provide well-being of users. We can cite a Smart home care application including wellness, safety, and emergency monitoring as an example.

1.4 Systemic Vision of Smart Life

We study Smart Life using the systemic approach (Nikolaev and Fortin 2020). At the heart of the Smart Life domain is a fundamental component that we call *Smart artifact*—a term deliberately chosen to avoid confusion with established terms like Smart object or Smart thing. As detailed above, Smart artifacts correspond to independent devices including the ability to capture, store, and process data to predict the next action.

Smart artifacts with comparable functional purposes within a certain scope constitute a *Smart application*. Smart applications can be identified at various levels of granularity, ranging from specific and detailed instances (e.g., a Smart lighting system incorporating multiple sensors for home and occupant monitoring) to broader applications (like a Smart home system encompassing diverse functions such as lighting, heating, and window management). Smart artifacts may be part of several Smart applications; for instance, Smart lighting systems could be present in Smart homes, Smart factories, or Smart cities. Each Smart application functions as a system composed of Smart artifacts, implying that it should have at least one emergent property. Emergent properties are features inherent to the entire

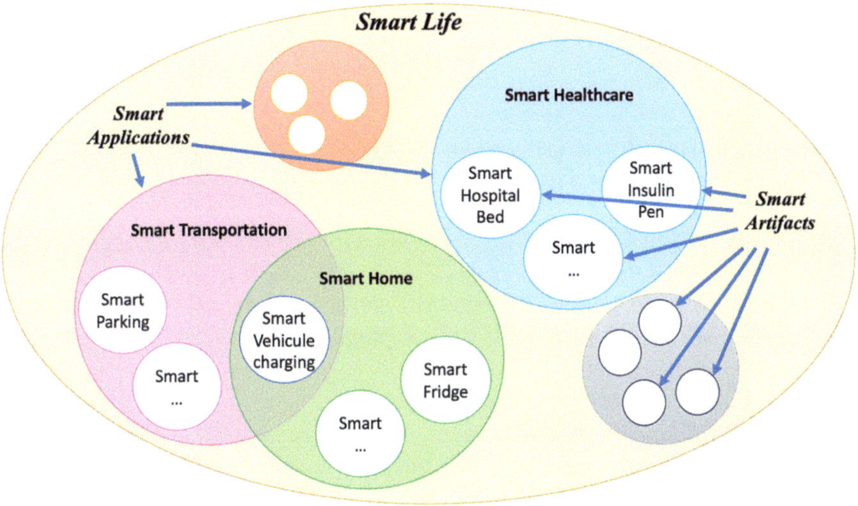

Fig. 1.2 System-oriented vision of Smart Life

system that individual elements lack. For example, all components of a car must be assembled in a specific way for the car to function.

Similarly, *Smart Life* is composed of various Smart applications, making it a system of systems. At its most basic level, Smart Life is a combination of at least two Smart applications, necessitating coordination based on the input and analysis of emergent properties. This system-oriented perspective of Smart Life is shown in Fig. 1.2. The corresponding concepts are detailed in this section, but, before that, we present a scenario to illustrate the systemic vision of Smart Life. This scenario describes the case of a citizen living in a Smart environment.

Illustrative Scenario: "A Citizen Living in a Smart Environment"

Diana, a modern urban dweller, begins her day in her Smart apartment. As she finishes the last drop of fresh milk, her Smart refrigerator detects the need for replenishment and automatically places an order at the local grocery store for a delivery within the hour.

While waiting for the delivery, Diana gets ready for the day. She checks her health app on her connected Smartphone to review her vital signs and adjust her dietary plan. The Smart thermostat automatically adjusts the temperature in her apartment according to her preferences.

Once ready, Diana heads to the parking lot of her building where she finds her electric car. Using her Smartphone, she unlocks the vehicle and starts the engine. The integrated navigation system guides her to the hospital for her medical checkup. During the journey, the car communicates with the network of Smart traffic lights to optimize her route.

At the hospital, Diana picks up her new insulin pen connected to an app on her Smartphone. This Smart device analyzes her blood composition in real time and administers the appropriate dose of insulin automatically, providing better control of her blood sugar levels.

Next, Diana heads to her Smart factory workplace. She plugs her electric car into the factory parking, ensuring optimal charging. At work, she uses various Smart devices to monitor and control production processes. Connected sensors and cameras provide real-time information on the status of machines and production lines.

At the end of the afternoon, Diana reunites with her dog Bob, equipped with a Smart collar. They set off for a bike ride using her Smart bike. During the ride, Bob's collar transmits data on his physical activity and health status to Diana's app, ensuring the well-being of her loyal companion.

As the day draws to a close, Diana returns to her Smart apartment with fresh groceries. The Smart kitchen appliances recognize the new items and suggest recipes based on the available ingredients. Diana selects a recipe using her Smart kitchen assistant, and the appliances guide her through the cooking process, ensuring a delicious and healthy dinner.

After dinner, Diana engages in some leisure time. Her Smart TV recommends personalized shows based on her preferences, and she uses voice commands to control the entertainment system. Meanwhile, the Smart lighting system adjusts the ambiance to create a relaxing atmosphere.

Before bedtime is a special time for Diana, who, as an avid bird enthusiast, installed a connected bird feeder on her balcony. She enjoys scrolling through photos taken by the feeder's camera, which automatically uploads images of visiting birds to the Internet but also to a real-time urban bird-tracking association.

Before heading to bed, Diana checks her sleep tracker app, which is synced with her Smartwatch. The app provides insights into her sleep patterns and suggests adjustments for better sleep quality. The Smart thermostat ensures the bedroom temperature is optimal for a restful night.

As Diana settles into bed, she instructs her Smart home assistant to enter "night mode," which dims the lights, locks the doors, and adjusts other settings to enhance security and conserve energy overnight. Throughout the night, various Smart devices continue to monitor and optimize her home environment, contributing to a seamless and technology-enhanced daily routine.

This illustrative day shows how Diana interacts with a multitude of Smart devices, simplifying her daily life and enhancing her management of health, mobility, and domestic affairs.

1.4.1 Smart Artifact

A *Smart artifact* is defined as any autonomous and stand-alone artifact equipped with a data processor, connected or not, that obtains, stores, processes, and utilizes data to initiate actions within its environment. Examples of Smart artifacts can be a Smart watch, Smart window, Smart toy, Smart antenna, and so on.

Referring to our ongoing example, Diana is using a lot of Smart artifacts:

- *A Smart insulin pen to regulate her blood sugar levels. This Smart device operates autonomously, without requiring any user input. Once the blood sugar level falls below the set limit, the pen delivers precisely what is needed for Diana.*
- *A Smart fridge. It features internal cameras for automated inventory management and temperature control settings that can be adjusted remotely. The refrigerator is intelligent enough to automatically place grocery orders when items are running low.*
- *A Smart TV. It is a television with integrated Internet connectivity and interactive features. It allows users to access online content, streaming services, apps, and other interactive features directly through the television, often eliminating the need for external devices like streaming boxes or game consoles.*

1.4.2 Smart Application

A *Smart application* is defined as a network of interconnected Smart artifacts, potentially including other Smart applications working together toward a shared goal. For instance, a Smart city application may consist of individual components such as a Smart parking application, a Smart energy application, and so on. Similarly, a Smart home can be composed of a Smart TV, a Smart fridge, a Smart assistant, and more. It's a requirement for a Smart application to encompass a minimum of two Smart artifacts.

Diana uses also several Smart applications.

- *Smart home. She is living in a Smart apartment. It refers to a residence equipped with various devices and systems that are connected to the Internet, allowing for remote monitoring and control. These interconnected devices enhance the automation, efficiency, and convenience of daily tasks. Examples of Smart devices within a Smart home include Smart fridges, Smart thermostats, Smart security systems, Smart home assistants, Smart TV, and so on. The goal of a Smart home is to enhance comfort, energy efficiency, and security while providing users with greater control over their living environment.*
- *Smart factory. She is working in a Smart factory. Within a Smart factory, various Smart devices and systems work together to optimize production processes. Examples of Smart applications within a Smart factory include predictive maintenance systems, Smart energy management systems, Smart parking, and so on. The aim of a Smart factory is to increase productivity, reduce costs, and improve flexibility in responding to market demands. By leveraging interconnected technologies, Smart factories transform traditional manufacturing processes into more agile, efficient, and data-driven operations.*

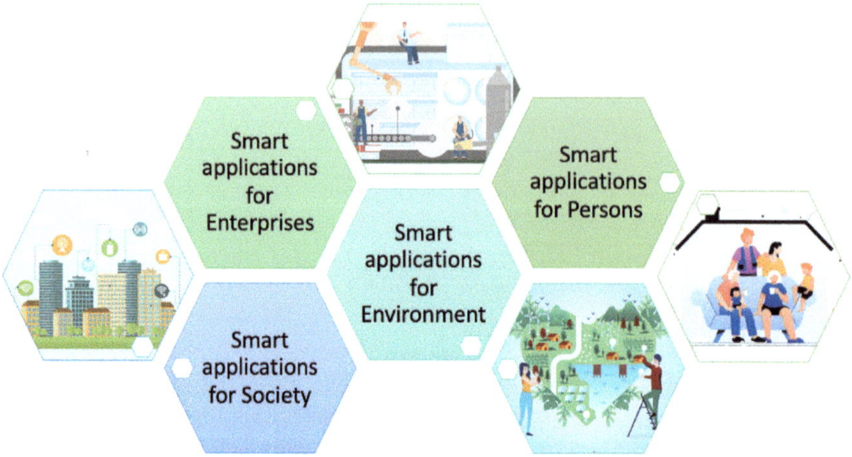

Fig. 1.3 Domains of Smart applications (Clip arts used in this figure were designed by Freepik)

– *Smart hospital. She regularly goes to a Smart hospital. It uses interconnected systems to enhance patient care. Within a Smart hospital, various Smart devices and systems work together to create a connected and intelligent healthcare environment. Examples of Smart things within a Smart hospital include Smart patient rooms, Smart medication management, Smart wearable health technologies, and so on. The goal of a Smart hospital is to improve patient outcomes, enhance the patient experience, and streamline healthcare operations through the integration of cutting-edge technologies.*

1.4.3 Smart Domain

Smart applications are grouped into four domains (cf. Fig. 1.3), which are explained in detail in Chap. 2.

Smart Applications for Persons This domain unifies various applications that concern people's personal life, such as Smart home, Smart healthcare, Smart welfare, etc.

Diana lives in a Smart home. In addition, she deals with several other applications: Diana uses a Smart home temperature management system (a Smart home application), a Smart drug delivery system (her insulin pen, from a Smart healthcare application), and a Smart training application for her dog Bob (Smart welfare of animals).

Smart Applications for Society We put in this domain all the Smart applications that are related to the society itself, like Smart city, Smart education, Smart social media, etc.

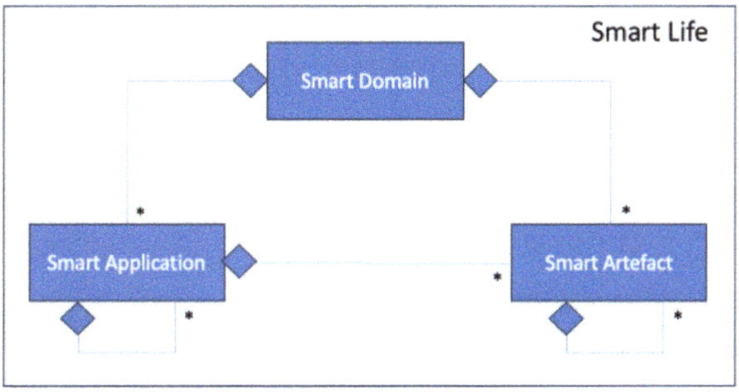

Fig. 1.4 Conceptual model of Smart Life with links between Smart concepts

Diana uses a Smart parking application in the building where she lives to charge her electric car.

Smart Applications for Environment All applications dealing with the natural environment are grouped into this domain, like Smart natural resource management, Smart disaster management systems, Smart earth, etc.

Diana uses a Smart bird feeder to help track urban birds for an ornithological association.

Smart Applications for Enterprises This domain groups all Smart applications useful for companies, like Smart industry applications, Smart transportation, Smart agriculture, etc.

Diana works in a Smart factory (a Smart industry application) and uses a Smart driving tool in her car (a Smart transportation application).

1.4.4 Smart Life

Smart Life is defined as the overall domain comprising all Smart domains, Smart applications, and Smart artifacts (as shown in the Fig. 1.4), aimed at enhancing experiences from personal, societal, environmental, and enterprise perspectives (Kornyshova et al. 2022b). It can be viewed as the societal domain that consolidates all initiatives involving the application of Smart artifacts and applications in diverse settings. Additionally, we also propose to use the term Smart Life as a comprehensive scientific research domain that encompasses all research areas exploring Smart technology, artifacts, and applications. Under this umbrella term, representatives from academia, society, and industry can convene and plan activities to promote all forms of Smart concepts.

The conceptual model of Smart Life shows a set of links between the three main elements composing Smart life: Smart domain, Smart application, and Smart artifact. We use our running example to illustrate these links.

- A Smart domain groups Smart applications and Smart artifacts within the same category.

Diana uses several Smart applications for people domain: a Smart home application, a Smart welfare application (for her dog and its training system), etc.

- Smart applications are composed of Smart artifacts.

  Diana's Smart home groups Smart artifacts, like her Smart refrigerator and her Smart assistant.
- Smart applications can be composed of other applications.

  Diana's Smart home groups other Smart applications, for instance, a Smart temperature management system.
- Smart artifacts can be composed of Smart artifacts.

  Diana's Smart bird feeder is a Smart artifact that is composed of several other artifacts: a weight sensor (to detect when a bird lands in front of the bird feeder), a camera (triggered by the weight sensor), etc.

1.4.5 Actors in Smart Life

We use the term actor for any kind of user, group, or organization that is involved in the usage and functioning of a Smart Life experience. We can observe that the actor is at the core of the Smart Life concept, itself linked to all the concepts described above, as shown in Fig. 1.5.

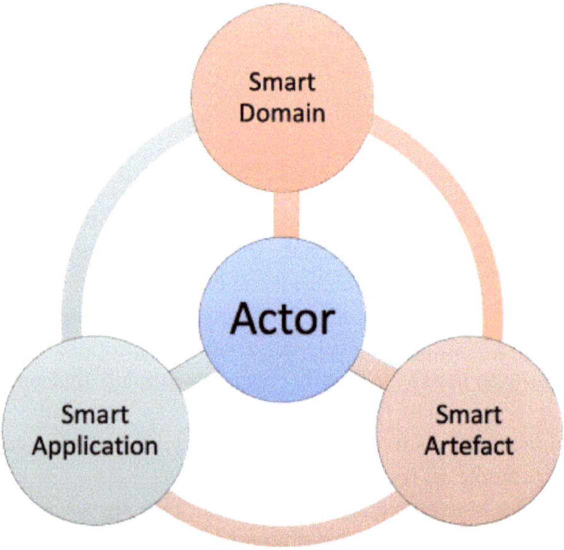

Fig. 1.5 Central role of actors

Actors can have various roles:

- *Consumer/user.* A consumer is a person who buys goods or services for their own use; in the same way, a user is someone who uses a product, machine, or service (Online Cambridge dictionary 2024b).

  Diana uses her Smart assistant to trigger some answers from her Smart home (for instance, dimming the lights at bedtime).
- *Supplier.* A supplier is a company, or a person, that provides things that people want or need (Online Cambridge Dictionary 2024a).

  All the artifacts used by Diana keep, manage, and interpret a lot of her data. To give some examples, her Smart refrigerator analyzes the presence of food to make orders to the grocery store; her driving assistant analyzes her GPS data to guide her in her way; her insulin pen manages her blood sugar level to trigger shoots of insulin; and so on. She can be considered as the supplier of all these data.
- *Designer.* A designer is a person who imagines how something could be made and draws plans for it (Online Cambridge dictionary 2024c).

  Diana had the opportunity to choose between several designs for some of her Smart artifacts. For instance, she chose the color, size, and functionalities of her Smart fridge.
- *Deployment participant.* A deployment can be defined as the movement of equipment to a place where they can be used when they are needed (Online Cambridge dictionary 2024d). A deployment participant is then a person who participates to this movement by putting a specific equipment at a certain place where it can be used effectively.

  Diana's bird feeder is deployed at her home, and the results are automatically sent to an ornithologist association for urban bird tracking.
- *Sponsor.* A sponsor can be defined as a person, or company, that supports a person, organization, or activity by giving money (Online Cambridge dictionary 2024e).

  Diana is sponsored by an urban bird-tracking association to deploy her bird feeder at her home. She paid only half of the device's price, allowing her to directly benefit from all the bird pictures and observe the birds feeding on her balcony, while the association covered the remaining cost.

1.4.6 Smart Life Engineering

Smart Life Engineering involves the application of scientific principles on the design, construction, implementation, and evolution of Smart Life applications. This is a concept that needs for a lot of elaboration on it. We highlight the importance of the progress in this field. While Smart Life Engineering shares common ground with information systems engineering, it also establishes extensive connections with research domains such as wireless network technology, artificial intelligence, urban geography, logistics, medical technology, and more.

1.5 Smart Life Governance

In the context of Smart Life, the management of artifacts is done at the level of applications (Smart home, Smart city, etc.). Smart applications, especially in the domain of Smart applications for society, imply interactions between numerous actors. In this case, it is important to define how different actors (users, designers, sponsors, etc.) participate and contribute to the whole functioning.

To understand better the various roles and interactions, we consider Smart applications as ecosystems. In this section, we introduce an organizational model, function distribution within Smart application ecosystems, and a governance matrix.

1.5.1 Organizational Model of Smart Application Ecosystem

We define a high-level organizational model for a Smart application ecosystem, detailing the different functions and requirements. The organizational model of Smart application ecosystems consists of three main components: Smart application, Smart artifacts, and actors (see Fig. 1.6).

A *Smart application* can be viewed as an ecosystem; thus, it is a network of interconnected actors and eventually other Smart applications through Smart artifacts. A Smart application can be a system of other Smart applications. For instance, Smart home application can be composed of Smart lightning application and a Smart energy heating application.

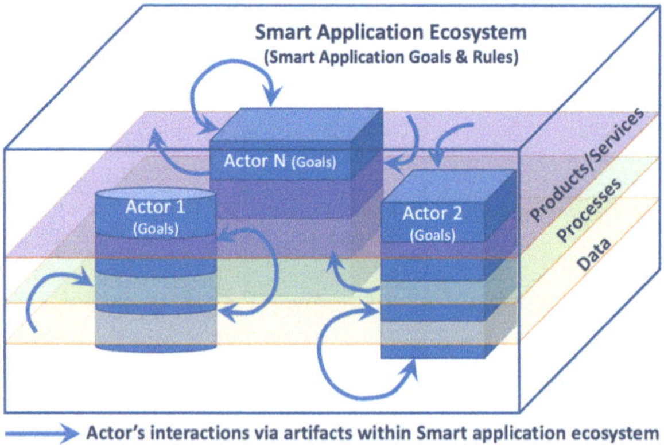

Fig. 1.6 Organization model of a Smart application ecosystem

Smart artifacts can represent various tools, such as sensors, detectors, processors, measuring tools, Smartwatches, etc. Smart artifacts, with different functions, are used by the actors to achieve their purposes. They allow applications to interact with actors. They are connected to a main Smart application that defines the collaboration rules.

Actors can have different roles including designer, developer, sponsor, or user and may assume multiple roles also simultaneously, such as consumer and supplier. Actors have goals contributing to the overall Smart application objectives. Data generation and sharing by these actors are regulated in the basis of a set of rules defined by a given actor. These actors engage in both competition and cooperation within a shared, multi-layered space encompassing products and services, processes, data, and other resources as depicted in Fig. 1.6.

1.5.2 Function Distribution in Smart Application Ecosystems

In each Smart application ecosystem, functions could be viewed at three levels: for the actors, applications, and artifacts.

Actor Functions An actor can take on several roles, and these roles give it different functions depending on its degree of involvement in the ecosystem and the level of detailed data they intend to share. Each actor occupies a portion of the multi-layered space, according to their involvement within the Smart application ecosystem. We define the following functions for actors:

- Actors define the goals of Smart applications.
- Actors have goals and contribute to the goals achievement of Smart applications.
- Actors define and set rules within the Smart application.
- Actors follow the rules established within Smart applications.
- Actors perform and prioritize their activities depending on their goals.
- Actors manage, manipulate, and share their data.
- Actors participate in both producing and consuming products and services.

Smart Application Functions In order to function correctly, within the framework of established rules, Smart applications must enable the following functions:

- Smart applications align the goals of the corresponding ecosystem to the goals of the involved actors.
- Smart applications broadcast the defined rules throughout the network.
- Smart applications check whether the actors adhere to the established rules.
- Smart applications handle the synchronization and integration of processes.
- Smart applications handle the synchronization and integration of data.
- Smart applications ensure the availability and compliance of products and services for all actors.

Smart Artifact Functions Smart artifacts are mandatory present in any Smart application. Their main contribution is that they support the whole operational functioning of Smart applications. We will not talk here about technical aspects. With regard to the functions of Smart artifacts in Smart applications, we identified the following:

- Smart artifacts support the functioning of Smart applications for the goals of the actors and are designed to satisfy this criterion.
- Smart artifacts are designed to respect various rules (security and privacy related, and so on).
- Smart artifacts participate in processes by supporting actors' activities.
- Smart artifacts collect, store, process, and report data.
- Smart artifacts constitute products and support services of Smart applications.

1.5.3 Governance Matrix

To provide additional insights for characterizing the relationships between actors, Smart applications, and Smart artifacts, we grouped the identified functions in a governance matrix (illustrated in Fig 1.7, cf. the comment below). We grouped

	Actor	Smart Application	Smart Artefact
Goals	- Actors define the goals of Smart applications. - Actors have goals and contribute to the goals achievement of Smart applications.	Smart applications align the goals of the corresponding ecosystem to the goals of the involved actors.	Smart artefacts support the functioning of Smart applications for the goals of the actors and are designed to satisfy this criterion.
Rules	- Actors define and set rules within the Smart application. - Actors follow the rules established within Smart applications.	- Smart applications broadcast the defined rules throughout the network. - Smart applications check whether the actors adhere to the established rules.	Smart artefacts are designed to respect various rules (security-, privacy-related, and so on).
Processes	Actors perform and prioritize their activities depending on their goals.	Smart applications handle the synchronization and integration of processes.	Smart artefacts participate in processes by supporting actors' activities.
Data	Actors manage, manipulate, and share their data.	Smart applications handle the synchronization and integration of data.	Smart artefacts collect, store, process, and report data.
Product and Services	Actors participate in both producing and consuming products and services.	Smart applications ensure the availability and compliance of products and services for all actors.	Smart artefacts constitute products and support services of Smart applications.

Fig. 1.7 Governance matrix for Smart application ecosystems

the functions depending on the main elements related to the organizational model: goals, rules, processes, data, and products and services.

An actor can have multiple roles and be involved in different ways in a Smart application ecosystem. Since actors interact with each other, the interactions between customer and supplier within a Smart application are recursive, with each participant potentially assuming both roles according to use case. Actors create, share, and consume resources while adhering to established rules and striving to achieve the goals of Smart applications.

Smart application ecosystems represent an intricate topic that should be studied in more detail. We tried to give some preliminary ideas to develop how its governance should be done. From these functions, there are several important requirements that a Smart application ecosystem must meet:

- Goals should be analyzed at two levels, actors and Smart applications, and both should be aligned to each other.
- All relevant actors should communicate data management rules, including compliance with the Smart application ecosystem rules.
- Each actor should focus on his/her activities depending on goals.
- Smart application ecosystems should support the integration and synchronization of processes among actors.
- Data should be managed and manipulated by their respective owners.
- Smart application ecosystems should allow the integration and synchronization of data among actors.
- Smart applications should consider the new requirements of personas representing actors.

1.6 Conclusion

In this chapter, we presented a detailed vision of the concept "Smart" and its application to various domains existing in the current landscape of digital technologies. We improved the notion of Smart Life as an umbrella concept unifying the whole spectrum of initiatives of Smart artifacts and Smart applications. We state that such a vision is important to provide more sustainable, green, human-aware, and efficient development of digital technologies.

References

Cho, Y., Lee, S., Hong, J., Pak, S., Hou, B., Lee, Y.W., Jang, J.E., Im, H., Sohn, J.I., Cha, S., Kim, J.M.: Sustainable hybrid energy harvester based on air stable quantum dot solar cells and triboelectric nanogenerator. J. Mater. Chem. (2018)

Chong, Z.J., Qin, B., Bandyopadhyay, T., Wongpiromsarn, T., Rebsamen, P., Ang Jr., M.H.: Autonomy for mobility on demand. Intell. Auton. Syst. **12**, 671–682 (2013)

Faisal, A., Kamruzzaman, M., Yigitcanlar, T., Currie, G.: Understanding autonomous vehicles: a systematic literature review on capability, impact, planning and policy. J. Transp. Land Use. **12**(1), 45–72 (2019)

Fu, J.: Intelligent hardware somatosensory design. In: 6th International Conference on Instrumentation and Measurement, Computer, Communication and Control, pp. 331–334. (2016)

González García, C., Meana Llorián, D., Pelayo García-Bustelo, B.C., Cueva Lovelle, J.V.: A review about Smart Objects, Sensors, and Actuators. Int. J. Interactive Multimedia Artif. Intell. **4**(3) (2017)

Ho, Y., Sato-Shimokawara, E., Wada, K., Yamaguchi, T., Tagawa, N.: Developing a life rhythm related human support system. In: IEEE International Symposium on Industrial Electronics, pp. 894–899. (2015)

Husain, A.: The sentient machine: the coming age of artificial intelligence. Scribner (2017)

Kornyshova, E., Gressier-Soudan, E.: Introducing sentient requirements for information systems and digital technologies. In: European, Mediterranean, and Middle Eastern Conference on Information Systems, Dubai, United Arab Emirates (2021)

Kornyshova, E., Deneckere, R., Gressier-Soudan, E., Murray, J., Brinkkemper, S.: From Smart Life to Smart Life engineering: a systematic mapping study and research agenda. In: 15th International Baltic Conference on Digital Business and Intelligent Systems. Springer, Riga, Latvia (2022a)

Kornyshova, E., Deneckere, R., Sadouki, K., Gressier-Soudan, E., Brinkkemper, S.: Smart Life: review of the contemporary smart applications. In: International Conference on Research Challenges in Information Science, pp. 302–318. (2022b)

Lee, S.H., Lee, J., Jung, J., Cho, A.R., Jeong, J.R., Dang Van, C., Nah, J., Lee, M.H.: Enhanced electrochemical performance of micro-supercapacitors via laser-scribed cobalt/reduced graphene oxide hybrids. ACS Appl. Mater. Interfaces. **13** (2021)

Liu, X., Baiocchi, O.: A comparison of the definitions for smart sensors, smart objects and Things in IoT. In: IEEE 7th Annual Information Technology, Electronics and Mobile Communication Conference, pp. 1–4. (2016)

Merriam-Webster. Intelligent. In: Merriam-Webster dictionary. https://www.merriam-webster.com/dictionary/intelligent (2024a)

Merriam-Webster. Autonomous. In: Merriam-Webster dictionary. https://www.merriam-webster.com/dictionary/autonomous (2024b)

Merriam-Webster. Stand-alone. In: Merriam-Webster dictionary. https://www.merriam-webster.com/dictionary/stand-alone (2024c)

Merriam-Webster. Sentient. In: Merriam-Webster dictionary. https://www.merriam-webster.com/dictionary/sentient (2024d)

Mizintseva, M.F.: Smart Technologies for Smart Life. "Smart Technologies" for Society, State and Economy. **155**, 653–664 (2021)

Morris, A.S., Langari, R.: Intelligent devices. Measurement Instrum., 289–314 (2016)

Nawandar, N.K., Cheggoju, N., Satpute, V.R.: Stand-alone device for IoT applications. arXiv preprint arXiv:2110.15405. (2021)

Nikolaev, M.Y., Fortin, C.: Systems thinking ontology of emergent properties for complex engineering systems. J. Phys. Conf. Ser. **1687**, 012005 (2020)

Olaverri-Monreal, C.: Autonomous vehicles and smart mobility related technologies. Infocommun. J. **8**, 17–24 (2016)

Online Cambridge dictionary. Supplier. In: Online Cambridge dictionary. https://dictionary.cambridge.org/dictionary/english-french/supplier (2024a)

Online Cambridge dictionary. Supplier. In: Online Cambridge dictionary. https://dictionary.cambridge.org/dictionary/english-french/consumer (2024b)

Online Cambridge dictionary. Designer. In: Online Cambridge dictionary. https://dictionary.cambridge.org/dictionary/english-french/designer (2024c)

Online Cambridge dictionary. Deployment. In: Online Cambridge dictionary. https://dictionary.cambridge.org/dictionary/english/deployment (2024d)

Online Cambridge dictionary. Sponsor. In: Online Cambridge dictionary. https://dictionary.cambridge.org/dictionary/english/sponsor (2024e)
Online Etymology Dictionary. Smart. In: Online Etymology Dictionary. https://www.etymonline.com/search?q=smart (2024)
Oxford Dictionary. Smart. In: Online Oxford Dictionary. https://www.oxfordlearnersdictionaries.com/definition/english/smart_1?q=smart (2024)
Schuh, G., Zeller, V., Hicking, J., Bernardy, A.: Introducing a methodology for smartification of products in manufacturing industry. Procedia CIRP. **81**, 228–233 (2019)
Sharma, K., Tayal, S.: Indian smart city ranking model using taxicab distance-based approach. Energy Syst. (2019)
Spyropoulou, I., Penttinen, M., Karlaftis, M., Vaa, T., Golias, J.: ITS solutions and accident risks: prospective and limitations. Transp. Rev. **28**, 549–572 (2008)
Thagard, P.: Computational philosophy of science. MIT Press (1993)

Chapter 2
Taxonomy of the Scientific Domain of Smart Life

Rébecca Deneckère, Elena Kornyshova, Kaoutar Sadouki, and Sjaak Brinkkemper

Abstract The field of Smart Life represents a large spectrum of various application domains coming from very established ones as Smart energy and Smart home to very recent ones as Smart environment, Smart airport, or Smart Earth. We observed a substantial growth in the scientific literature with over 126,000 papers containing "Smart" in their titles in 2021. Despite this huge number, we did not identify a detailed classification of these fields in the existing literature. There is still a notable gap in the classification and systematization of these fields. To address this, we developed a generic taxonomy for Smart applications by conducting a systematic mapping study focused on state-of-the-art and research agenda-oriented papers (2341 scientific publications in total).

Keywords Smart Life · Smart domain · Taxonomy

2.1 Introduction

There is a huge number of scientific publications in the various Smart domains. In 2021, more than 126,000 papers containing the term "Smart" in their titles were extracted from the scientific databases. In front of this quantity of scientific works, we decided to reduce our scope to state-of-the-art- and research agenda-oriented

---

R. Deneckère
Centre de Recherche en Informatique, Université Paris 1 Panthéon-Sorbonne, Paris, France
e-mail: rebecca.deneckere@univ-paris1.fr

E. Kornyshova (✉) · K. Sadouki
Centre d'Etudes et de Recherche en Informatique et Communications, Conservatoire National des Arts et Métiers, Paris, France
e-mail: elena.kornyshova@cnam.fr; kaoutar.sadouki@lecnam.net

S. Brinkkemper
Department of Information and Computing Sciences, Utrecht University, Utrecht, the Netherlands
e-mail: s.brinkkemper@uu.nl

E. Kornyshova et al. (eds.), *Smart Life and Smart Life Engineering*,
https://doi.org/10.1007/978-3-031-75887-4_2

papers. The motivation behind was to target more established sub-fields of Smart Life as the presence of this kind of publication can testify.

We discovered that the number of scientific literature reviews in Smart Life-related topics is also important and growing continuously. For instance, for the period from 1986 to the beginning of 2022, we identified 891 literature reviews on Smart industries, 384 on Smart cities, 191 on Smart homes, and 190 on Smart healthcare, to cite the most widespread ones.

Most of these state-of-the-art works deal with a particular sub-topic in the Smart domain: IoT application for energy consumption (Wang et al. 2021), security in Internet of Things (IoT) (Harbi et al. 2019), IoT usage in Smart cities with a classification of Smart technologies (Tai-hoon et al. 2017), computer technologies from the viewpoint of artificial intelligence (Yamane 2017), machine-to-machine usage (Severi et al. 2014), and so on. Despite the explosion of literature reviews in Smart domains, we noted an absence of research dedicated to the classification, organization, and systematization of these fields.

We undertook a systematic mapping study (Petersen et al. 2008) to explore and structure the scientific domain of Smart Life. Our main goals were to elaborate a taxonomy of Smart Life applications, which does not exist yet in the current literature and to understand the evolution of these applications and related concepts.

To elaborate on these goals, we established two research questions:

- *RQ 1: How can Smart applications be classified?*
- *RQ 2: How have these applications evolved through time?*

The objective of this chapter is to identify the existing Smart applications and taxonomize the scientific domain of Smart Life. We elaborated a generic taxonomy of applications around Smart Life to answer the first question. The second one is detailed in Chap. 3 of this book. Our results were partially presented in Kornyshova et al. (2022a, b).

In this chapter, we explain our research method in Sect. 2.2. We highlight the obtained results in Sect. 2.3 and each of the Smart domains in Sects. 2.4–2.7. Clusters are explained in Sect. 2.8. We conclude in Sect. 2.9.

2.2 Research Methodology

We adopted a systematic mapping design (Petersen et al. 2008) to explore the Smart Life field of research. Systematic mapping studies (SMS) share similarities with other systematic reviews (like SLR—systematic literature review—synthesizing the existing research in established fields), except in their broader inclusion criteria to select a wider range of research papers. SMS are intended to map out topics within a field classification rather than synthesize study results. Our study is focused on consolidating existing work in the Smart Life domain, following the process outlined in Petersen et al. (2008), which includes five steps: definition of research questions, finding papers, screening papers, classification scheme definition, and data extraction.

2.2.1 Step 1: Definition of the Research Questions

The objective of this chapter is to identify existing Smart applications and taxonomize the scientific domain of Smart Life. Thus, we focus on the first question (the second question is answered in Chap. 3):

- *RQ 1: How can Smart applications be classified?*

2.2.2 Step 2: Finding Papers

This step focuses on identifying a set of papers based on a relevant search string. We conducted our search and selected papers from the SCOPUS scientific database using the SCOPUS Search API in November 2021. (This database includes all "articles being published in virtually all scholarly journals of any significance in the world.")

Initially, we conducted a broad search for papers containing the term "Smart" solely in the title, yielding over 126,000 papers. Consequently, we limited our search to secondary research papers such as state of the arts and research agendas. This narrowed search resulted in obtaining 2410 sources with DOIs. The inclusion criteria related to the search string are given in Table 2.1.

2.2.3 Step 3: Screening Papers

We analyzed the titles and, when necessary, the abstracts and content of papers. We excluded 69 sources that did not represent research papers or were irrelevant to Smart Life topics. We obtained 2341 papers.[1] In Table 2.1, we summarize the exclusion criteria employed to compile the final list of papers.

[1] The complete list of these papers is available at http://cri-dist.univ-paris1.fr/rcis22/RCIS2022_Appendix%20A%20-%20references%20list.pdf

Table 2.1 Inclusion/exclusion criteria for the study on Smart topics

Selection criteria	Criteria description
Inclusion criteria (2410 sources identified)	The title includes the term "smart" and at least one of the terms "research agenda," "state of the art," "review," or "survey": Search string: TITLE(smart) AND (TITLE("research agenda") OR TITLE("State-of-the-art") OR TITLE(review) OR TITLE(survey))
Exclusion criteria (2341 sources selected)	The source is not a research paper (erratum, retracted, etc.)
	The source is related to an abbreviation SMART, for instance, SMART (stroke-like migraine attacks after radiation therapy) syndrome.
	The source mentions the term "smart," which is used in its ordinary sense, like "working smart and hard"

2.2.4 Step 4: Classification Scheme Definition

The goal of this step in the SMS is to determine the classification scheme to be applied to the acquired results. To answer the defined research questions, we grouped all relevant papers according to the Smart application category and the year of publication of the paper (the second criterion will be presented in detail in the next chapter).

2.2.5 Step 5: Data Extraction

For each paper, we identified the main topic based on the title and abstract (and content if required). Within the identified topics, we observed that they concerned either applications or artifacts. We focused only on applications. We grouped these applications in categories related to their main usage, like Smart industry, Smart healthcare, Smart agriculture, and so on. Finally, we grouped these categories into four Smart domains: persons, society, environment, and enterprises. Thus, we obtained a taxonomy composed of a hierarchy of Smart applications.

2.2.6 Validity Threats

Qualitative research relies on subjective, interpretive, and contextual data. Therefore, we analyzed the potential biases that could jeopardize the validity of our research. Thomson (2011) proposes five categories of validity. To mitigate the impact of validity threats on our study, we present them along with the corresponding mitigation actions as follows.

Descriptive validity (accuracy of the data). We standardized the concepts and criteria utilized in the study and structured the information to be collected through a data extraction form, ensuring a consistent recording of data.

Theoretical validity (ability to get the information that it is intended to capture). We used a search string and implemented it across a library encompassing the most popular digital repositories in computer sciences and software engineering. We established a set of inclusion and exclusion criteria. To mitigate the risk of overlooking available evidence, we employed two distinct search methods: an automatic search and a manual search (backward and forward snowballing). The decision to focus on English sources aimed to minimize the impact on disregarding other languages.

Generalization validity (ability to generalize the results). Our set of research questions is sufficiently broad to identify and classify the findings related to Smart applications.

Evaluative validity (conclusions reasonable given the data). Two researchers independently examined the papers, with an overlap in their studies to identify potential variations in analysis. Every conclusion was validated by at least two researchers.

Transparency validity (repeatability of the research protocol). The research process protocol is sufficiently detailed to ensure it can be thoroughly replicated.

2.3 Four Main Domains of the Smart Applications Taxonomy

Many applications have interconnections, yet a systematic structuring is necessary. To address this, we studied the subjects covered by the 2341 selected papers of the SMS (). Initially, we adopted a bottom-up approach by looking the titles of all papers. However, when titles proved insufficient in identifying the application field, we extended our examination to include abstracts. If further clarification was required, we looked into the content of the papers.

We assigned each paper a classification of 1–3 levels of applications (e.g., Smart energy → Smart grid → Smart grid communication). This classification was applied to all papers except those addressing Smart artifacts, technologies, or systems without a clear association with a concrete application field. An expert carried out the assignment of each paper to a Smart application. In cases where the alignment of a topic with a Smart domain was not straightforward, a more in-depth analysis involving two or more experts was conducted to reach a consensus.

After qualifying the papers, we structured them within a taxonomy using a top-down approach. This involved categorizing the major fields of Smart Life, such as Smart home, Smart city, Smart industry, Smart healthcare, etc. and organizing the identified application fields within these major fields. Considering the number of major application fields, we organized them into four Smart Life domains: Smart applications for persons, Smart applications for environment, Smart applications for society, and Smart applications for enterprises (Fig. 2.1).

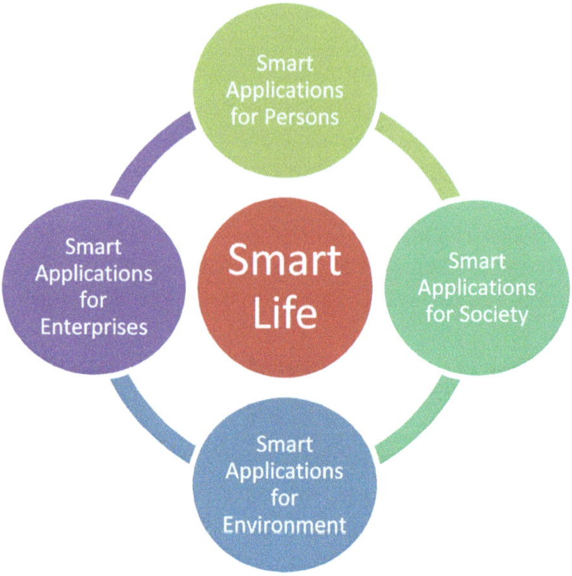

Fig. 2.1 Smart Life domains

- *Smart applications for Persons* contain applications focused on the personal Life of humans, like Smart healthcare, Smart home (Smart living), Smart welfare, etc. (see Sect. 2.4)
- *Smart applications for Environment* include various topics related to the study and preservation of the environment: Smart natural resource management, Smart earth, Smart disaster management, and Smart space exploration (see Sect. 2.5).
- *Smart applications for Society* deal with various not-for-profit aspects of human life in groups, including Smart city and Smart village. It also includes applications related to the management of people living in groups, such as Smart citizenship, Smart state, Smart policing, and so on (see Sect. 2.6).
- *Smart applications for Enterprises* concern applications in the for-profit sectors, covering three basics domains: Smart agriculture, Smart industry, and Smart service industry. This category also covers applications related to Smart transportation and Smart business management (see Sect. 2.7).

We detail the sub-categories in the following sections.

2.4 Smart Applications for Persons

In our study, we found three categories of Smart applications belonging to this domain: Smart healthcare, Smart home, and Smart welfare (Fig. 2.2).

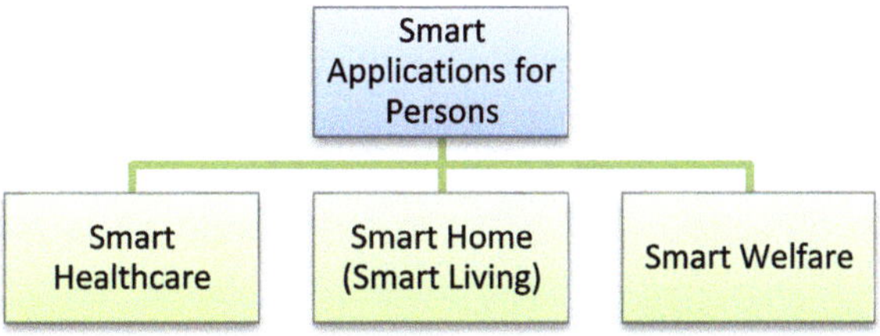

Fig. 2.2 Smart Life applications for persons

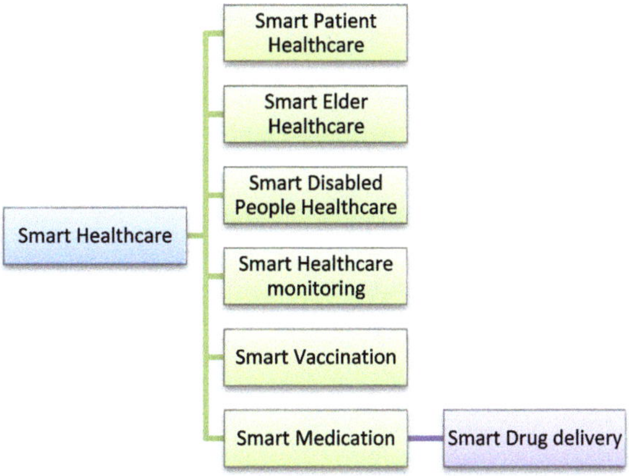

Fig. 2.3 Smart Life applications for Smart healthcare

2.4.1 Smart Healthcare

Smart healthcare does not have a unique definition. Yin et al. (2018) define Smart healthcare as that besides clinical usage; it utilizes implantable and wearable medical devices to gather, store, and process various types of physiological data during daily activities. However, our SMS allows us to identify six categories of Smart healthcare applications, as shown in Fig. 2.3.

Smart Patient Healthcare There are a lot of studies about technologies linked to the care of patients, especially for specific needs. For instance, Moraitou et al. (2017) look into the needs of vulnerable groups that need nursing for a long period of time and offer a review on the main technological, psychological, ethical, and economic challenges raised by the implementation of a Smart health caring home.

Smart Elder Healthcare Information technologies in geriatric healthcare are needed, due to rapidly ageing societies. Zhao et al. (2021) propose a review aiming to examine the extent, variety, and characteristics of existing Smart concepts and feasible healthcare technologies in nursing home settings. Demiris and Hensel (2008) look into Smart homes-needed features to consider older or disabled people.

Smart Disabled People Healthcare In the same way, there are works looking into specific technological needs for disabled people. For instance, Jamwal et al. (2020)

aim to explore the impact of Smart home and communication technology on the outcomes of people with disabilities and complex needs.

Smart Healthcare Monitoring Yusuf et al. (2020) define a health monitoring system as a system that allows patients to monitor the health-related problem to avoid further complications that could result in loss of life.

Smart Vaccination Andries et al. (2014) propose to use the current repertoire of devices used in RNA synthetic biology to propose programmable "Smart vaccines" that will revolutionize the field of RNA vaccination.

Smart Medication Medication can be identified and delivered with the help of Smart artifact. We found a subset of these Smart applications specifically addressing the delivery of drugs, essentially insulin for diabetic people.

Smart drug delivery: These artifacts are able to deliver drugs to people. For instance, Smart insulin pens, which automatically delivers insulin to people as a continuous subcutaneous infusion, were being used by 375,000 people with type 1 diabetes in 2008 (Zisser et al. 2008).

2.4.2 Smart Home (Smart Living)

The aim of the Smart home is to improve the quality of life for its residents through automating household tasks, such as energy management, security surveillance, and so on (Alaa et al. 2017). Smart home is defined in Lutolf (1992) as "the integration of different services within a home by using a common communication system. It assures an economic, secure, and comfortable operation of the home and includes a high degree of intelligent functionality and flexibility." Smart home applications can be categorized into several other type of applications, as shown in Fig. 2.4.

Smart Home Management

Smart Home Water Management. Water management is possible by real-time monitoring of water level and quality. Real-time water level monitoring can significantly reduce wastage of water due to overflow from tanks. The water management system can also help detect water leaks in a Smart home by analyzing water levels during different hours of the day (Singh and Suhaib 2020). Different Smart water frameworks, including definition and architecture, are proposed, as in (Li et al. 2020).

Smart Home Temperature Management. It groups all the applications that help regulate the temperature in a Smart home system. Malekpour et al. (2020) address these applications by studying Smart thermostats, a device which has the capability to remotely control the set points as well as to adjust set point schedules of the temperature system. In some cases, it can also monitor occupant behavior and learn from this behavior for improved operational efficiency and occupant comfort.

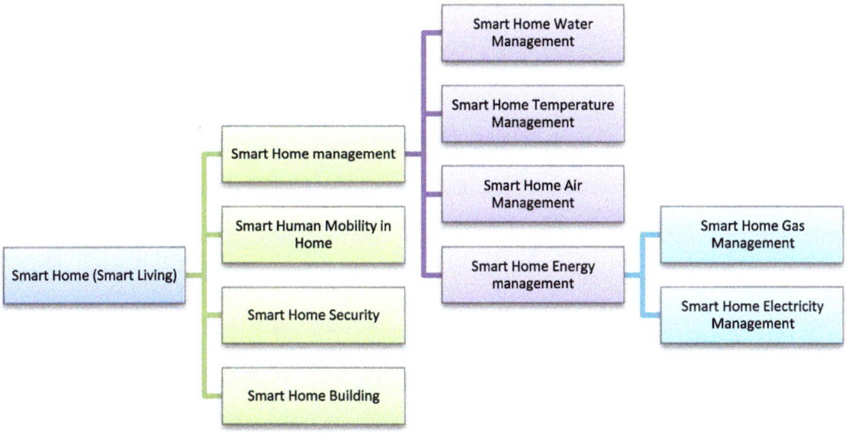

Fig. 2.4 Smart Life applications for Smart home (Smart living)

Smart Home Air Management. On the same way as water or temperature, air can be controlled by the use of sensors. Guyot et al. (2018) provide a literature review on Smart ventilation used in residential buildings, based on energy and indoor air-quality performance.

Smart Home Energy management. Various system components such as hardware elements, software algorithms, network connections, and sensors need to collaborate to offer diverse services in a Smart home environment. Energy management at the household level must consider reducing environmental impact while supporting human lifestyles (Komninos et al. 2014). We can find two different kinds of energy management specific to a Smart home system: *Smart home gas management* and *Smart home electricity management.*

Smart Human Mobility in Home Smart homes can integrate considerations for human mobility within the residence environment. For example, the use of Smart wheelchairs can lead to a seamless user experience and enable control over all household appliances (Leaman and La 2017).

Smart Home Security There is a range of security issues in a Smart home management (Lin and Bergmann 2016). Yan et al. (2021) focus on four aspects of Smart home security, Smart devices, cloud platforms, mobile applications, and communications, and summarize the attack and defense methods. Aljanah et al. (2021) specifically study the solutions offered about how to authenticate a large number of heterogeneous and possibly resource-constrained devices in a secure and efficient manner.

Smart Home Building In Smart home buildings, it is possible to manage household appliances such as lighting, air conditioning, fans, washing machines, TVs, refrigerators, security systems, and so on. Through the application of artificial

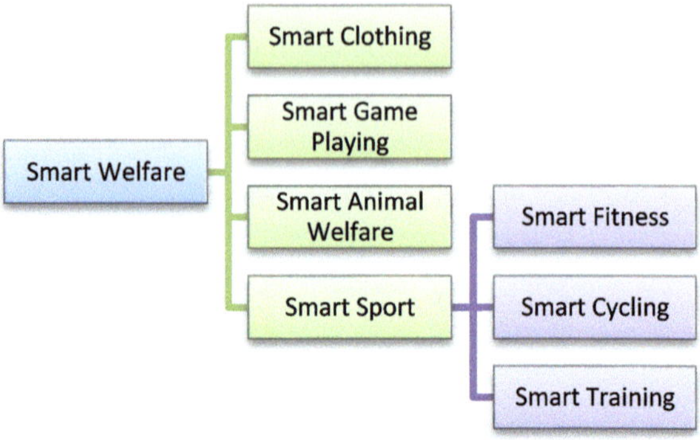

Fig. 2.5 Smart Life applications for Smart welfare

intelligence, these systems can also achieve self-control and monitoring capabilities (Shaker 2020).

Smart Welfare Smart welfare is about how Smart technologies can be applied to enhance the life quality of a person with the help of devices and sensors. Figure 2.5 shows the different types of Smart welfare applications.

Smart Clothing Smart clothes embed Smart wearables into garments. Fernandez-Carames et al. (2018) propose the paradigm of "Internet of Smart clothing," which envisions a world where Smart garments communicate with each other, with the objects on their environment, and with remote servers on the Internet in order to provide advanced services.

Smart Game Playing Costa et al. (2018) present the application of proxemics in digital games to enhance game-mediated interactions within Smart ecosystems.

Smart Animal Welfare Animal welfare refers to an assessment of whether animals are healthy, free of pain and suffering, and positively stimulated in their environment. Smart technologies can also be used for animal welfare, as studied in (Jukan et al. 2017), for instance.

Smart Sport Smart sport refers to the integration of advanced technologies and data-driven solutions in the realm of sports to enhance performance, training methodologies, and overall athlete experience. This paradigm leverages innovations such as wearables, sensors, analytics, and connectivity to collect and analyze real-time data, providing valuable insights for athletes, coaches, and sports organizations.

Smart Fitness. Smart fitness is divided into three categories: fitness trackers (including wearable and non-wearable sensors), movement analysis, and fitness applications (Farrokhi et al. 2021). The aim is to enhance training performance in a fitness environment.

Smart Cycling. These applications offer interactions between traffic participants, to help communicate the cyclist's intentions to others or to enhance playfulness and social cohesion, on and beyond the cycle path. Smart cycling technologies offer possibilities to be in touch with people who are not sharing the road with you, and a ride can be recorded, "re-lived," and shared in improvised social networks (Nikolaeva et al. 2019).

Smart Training. With the increase of participation trends in mass sporting events, as well as the involvement of people in sporting activities, there is a need for systems/applications that can guide, help, and support people in enjoying their activities. Modern technology is revolutionizing the way athletes maximize their performance and compete on a higher level than ever before (Rajsp and Fister 2020).

2.5 Smart Applications for Environment

This domain encompasses three types of applications, those dedicated to natural resource management, those focused on Smart Earth solutions, and those geared towards space exploration, as shown in Fig. 2.6.

2.5.1 Smart Natural Resource Management

The management and preservation of natural resources are paramount in today's world, driven by the pressing need for sustainability and environmental stewardship. Within this context, Smart technologies are playing an increasingly crucial role in revolutionizing how we approach resource conservation and management. This section looks into several key Smart applications focused on natural resources, highlighting innovative solutions that harness technology to address critical challenges in water management, climate engineering, forestry, and air quality, as shown in Fig. 2.7.

Smart Water Management Efficient water management has emerged as a significant concern for numerous countries and water industries. Researchers are leveraging ICT to develop self-learning systems, which possess the capability to enhance water management efficiency (Gupta et al. 2020a). We can distinguish two

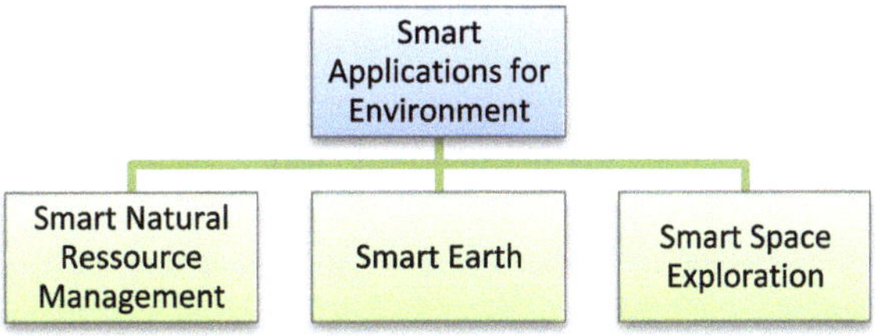

Fig. 2.6 Smart Life applications for environment

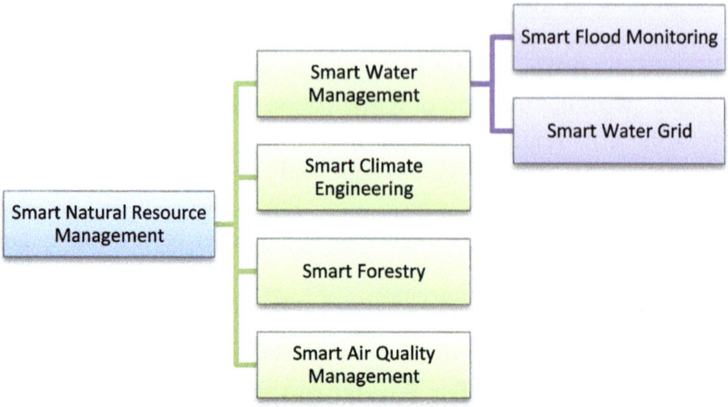

Fig. 2.7 Smart Life applications for Smart natural resource management

types of Smart water management systems: Smart flood monitoring and Smart water grids.

Smart Flood Monitoring. Smart technology is used to determine the accurate level of flooding of land, which is ordinarily dry in nature, and the connected phones are able to give the forecasting information to the affected people to prevent the unnecessary loss caused by this natural hazard (Subashini et al. 2021).

Smart Water Grid. There is a need for water management, measures to control water scarcity and a way to conserve water (Behera and Pradhan 2019).

Smart Climate Engineering Global warming represents one of the most significant challenges humanity faces. To achieve climate goals, technologies such as CO_2 capture and storage and CO_2 capture and utilization are crucial for mitigating hard-to-avoid CO_2 emissions (Wang et al. 2020).

Smart Forestry It is based on digital forestry, using cloud computing, Internet of Things, mobile Internet, big data, and other new generation information technology. It can promote the coordinated development of forestry resource management and ecosystem construction (Zou et al. 2019).

Smart Air Quality Management Air quality is a huge and pressing global issue, leading to over 7 million annual deaths according to the World Health Organization. Access to air quality information allows individuals to make informed decisions, yet analyzing this data and implementing effective solutions remains challenging. Efficient methods for analyzing big data are crucial to reveal hidden insights and address the invisible impacts of air pollution effectively (Iskandaryan et al. 2020).

2.5.2 *Smart Earth*

Smart Earth is a set of environmental applications of the Internet of Things but articulated across a much wider range of ecosystems and land use types (Bakker and Ritts 2018). Smart Earth technologies use terrestrial, aquatic, and aerial sensors, satellites, and monitoring devices.

2.5.3 *Smart Space Exploration*

Over the last century, the progress of space exploration has imposed demanding requirements on payloads and increased the spacecraft complexity, with the result of a constant rise in their average launch mass, but space industries and agencies are currently more interested in very small satellites with launch masses below 10 kg (nanosatellites, picosatellites, femtosatellites). Niccolai et al. (2019) discuss about the result of this miniaturization process with the design of integrated miniaturized components into a common substrate of silicon wafer layers. It gives the possibility of creating a single component-satellite, capable of generating and distributing power, exchanging heat with the environment, communicating, and hosting a payload, with subsystems assembled in a 20 mm × 20 mm × 3 mm monolithic integrated circuit.

2.6 Smart Applications for Society

The integration of advanced technologies into urban environments has given rise to the concept of "Smart cities," representing a significant subset of Smart applications for society. This section explores the multifaceted initiatives within the domain of Smart applications for society, as shown in Fig. 2.8.

This domain contains a wide set of Smart applications, some widely known, such as Smart city or Smart education, or a bit less studied, like Smart state or Smart citizenship.

2.6.1 *Smart City*

As defined in Washburn et al. (2009), the realization of a Smart city is about integrating software services and applications to improve regular city services and ease and facilitate the life of citizens. In Chamee (2020), Smart city is "a city that collects and utilizes data gathered from distributed sensors and video cameras that connect everything from trash bins to streetlights."

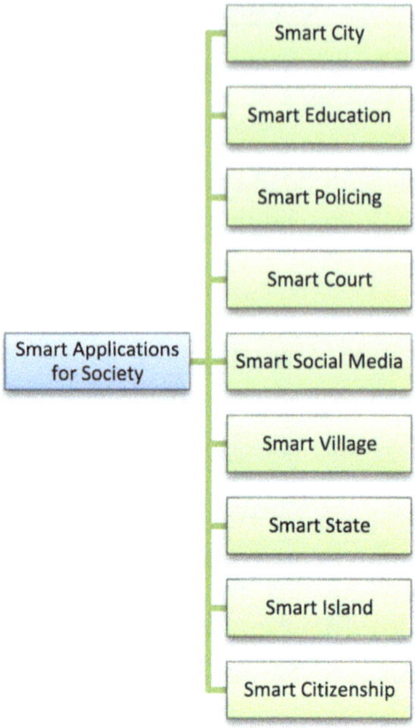

Fig. 2.8 Smart Life applications for society

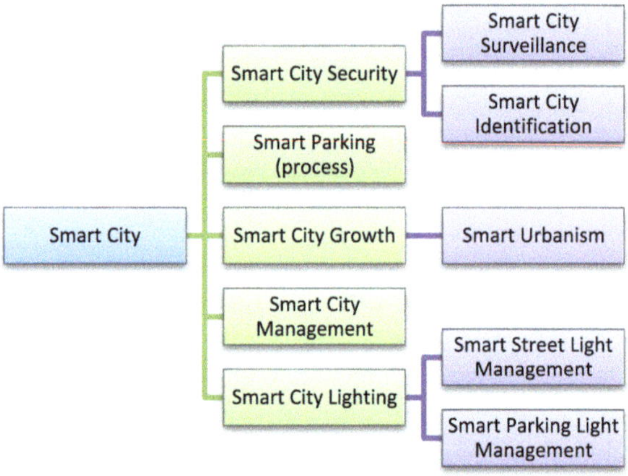

Fig. 2.9 Smart Life applications for Smart city

To provide more specific examples, the concept of Smart city concept is employed to address challenges in urban cities by providing a high-quality living environment for citizens (Al-Ani et al. 2019). Therefore, within the taxonomy, the Smart city application domain contains applications addressing issues as security, urban growth, lighting, parking, and more (see Fig. 2.9).

Smart City Security The dependence on ICT makes Smart cities prone to cyberattacks (Alibasic et al. 2017). We identify two main categories of Smart applications relative to Smart city security: Smart city surveillance and Smart city identification.

Smart City Surveillance. Smart cities enhance residents' lifestyle by offering efficient infrastructure and improved security. Continuous surveillance, often a repetitive and monotonous task, can diminish the performance of human guards over extended periods, and the use of the huge amount of data can help increase this performance (Thakur et al. 2021).

Smart City Identification. An essential component of Smart cities is their surveillance infrastructure, which necessitates intelligent techniques for analyzing video footage from surveillance cameras (Behera et al. 2020).

Smart Parking (The Parking Process) Smart parking sensors and technologies assist drivers in finding vacant parking slots while they are on the way to their destination (Zulfiqar et al. 2021).

Smart City Growth Smart growth aims to enhance housing affordability and diversity. However, one of the goals of Smart growth, compact development, restricts land development and presents challenges for affordability (Addison et al. 2013). Smart growth-related planning practices, including growth management policies and urban design tools like transit-oriented development and urban infill, can influence housing markets significantly.

Smart Urbanism. The tightening integration of urban systems, coupled with increased coordination in urban domains, enables the provision of more holistic views and synoptic city intelligence to give a better understanding of urban life (Bibri 2019).

Smart City Management The concept of Smart cities involves comprehensive city organization and management through technology. It is built and sustained by integrating technologies like sensors, electronics, and networks. The primary motivation behind investigating Smart city services is to enhance city services for citizens and improve their overall quality of life (Al-Smadi et al. 2019).

Smart City Lighting Lighting systems play an important role in the evolution process of Smart cities, thanks to their ability to affect city life at night along with people's mood and behavior (Scorpio et al. 2020).

Smart Street Light Management. Smart street light management refers to a networked system of streetlights equipped with sensors, actuators, and communication infrastructures to illuminate roads, highways, parking areas, and public spaces efficiently. Addressing environmental concerns and aiming to reduce electricity costs, utilizing these applications with real-time monitoring and energy efficiency features benefits municipalities, utility companies, and city residents alike (Mahoor et al. 2020).

Smart Parking Light Management. With the rise in population, there is a corresponding increase in the number of vehicles on roads, necessitating the development of sustainable and efficient parking solutions. However, continuous lighting in these

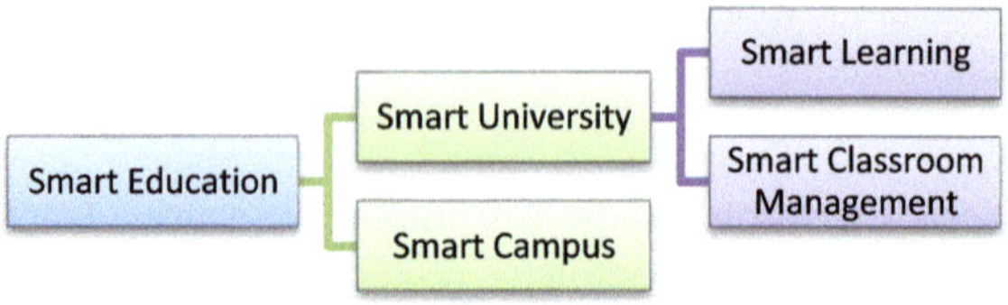

Fig. 2.10 Smart Life applications for Smart education

areas is not resource-efficient. To address this, integration of automated lighting that activates only when a vehicle is detected, thus combining Smart parking with automated lighting for a practical, sustainable, and efficient solution (Shastry et al. 2020).

2.6.2 Smart Education

Conventional teaching methods, involving classroom instruction followed by independent student exercises, are being supplanted by modern learning approaches, including distance learning, mobile learning (m-learning), personalized learning, flipped and blended learning, social collaborative learning, and game-based learning, among others (Demir 2021). Figure 2.10 shows the sub-taxonomy for Smart education.

Smart University The concept of Smart university encompasses a thorough modernization of educational processes, leading to enhanced quality across various university activities such as education, research, and commercial endeavors. This transformation includes the adoption of technologies like Smart boards, screens, and ubiquitous wireless Internet access, redefining the educational landscape with advanced tools and connectivity (Tikhomirov et al. 2015).

Smart Learning. This modern education approach is using technology integration for enhanced learning outcomes by combining Smart devices and pedagogies, to prioritize personalized and adaptive learning experiences (Wong and Li 2021).

Smart Classroom Management. Installing Smart devices and emerging trending technologies help teachers focus on student's learning process in place of wasting time in taking attendance for a large group of students, transforming traditional classrooms into Smart classrooms (Gupta et al. 2020b).

Smart Campus Similar to the goal of a Smart city, which is to make the quality of life of its population increase, the purpose of a Smart campus is also about how the quality of life of university stakeholders can be improved (Imbar et al. 2020).

2.6.3 Smart Policing

Smart policing refers to the application of data-driven approaches by police authorities. Afzal et al. (2020) present a framework to show the connections between Smart use of data and police approaches and strategies to show how Smart policing can be an area of increased interest in digital government and public management research.

2.6.4 Smart Court

A Smart court is characterized by the automation and digitization of judicial procedures, forming part of a comprehensive set of reforms aimed at establishing a more precise and consistent judiciary. In Smart courts, certain tasks may be automated using programs, potentially incorporating learning algorithms but not necessarily all. The essence of Smart courts lies in the interaction between human judges and the technology that supports them in their work during this partially automated digital judicial process (Papagianneas 2021).

2.6.5 Smart Social Media

Smart social media refers to a set of practices and approaches used to optimize the use of social media in an intelligent and effective manner. This involves leveraging advanced technologies, algorithms, and analytical tools to enhance the management, engagement, and relevance of content on social media platforms. The goal is to achieve more meaningful results in terms of visibility, interaction, and conversion through a strategic and thoughtful approach to social media (Lia et al. 2021).

2.6.6 Smart Village

The notion of a Smart village involves leveraging technology to address interconnected challenges such as financial exclusion, poverty, hygiene, and education, presenting an empowering approach to uplift underserved communities through improved access to power, education, and entrepreneurial opportunities (Kaur and Parashar 2021).

2.6.7 Smart State

There are evident trends indicating increased inter-organizational collaboration, information sharing, and integration, paving the way for what could be termed as a Smart State. Gil-Garcia (2012) delves into the promises and challenges already identified in government information sharing and integration initiatives. The case study of the Brisbane city is studied in Hortz (2016); it evaluates the Smart State strategy's effectiveness, analyzes barriers to knowledge-based urban development, explores limitations in public policy development for urban planning, and presents lessons learned to enhance frameworks for intelligent urban planning in the context of global economic development.

2.6.8 Smart Island

The European Union has clearly outlined priorities for sustainable and low-carbon energy systems, highlighting the significant role of islands. These islands are seen as ideal locations to develop and test innovative strategies and solutions, which can then be applied to accelerate the transition to sustainable energy systems on the mainland (Groppi et al. 2021). Smart island applications are then good tests for techniques that deal with such solutions in the insular contexts.

2.6.9 Smart Citizenship

To effectively develop Smart cities, it is crucial to involve citizens as integral participants. They play key roles as users, decision-makers, consumers, and sources of valuable data and information (Tadili and Fasly 2019). Smart citizenship includes Smart voting (see Fig. 2.11).

Smart Voting. In democratic countries, the voting system plays a major role during elections. Electronic voting machines can be used, but they need more manpower, are time-consuming, and also less trustworthy. For avoiding misconceptions during elections, there are lot of advanced techniques that are being proposed using various methods (Deepika et al. 2017).

Fig. 2.11 Smart Life applications for Smart citizenship

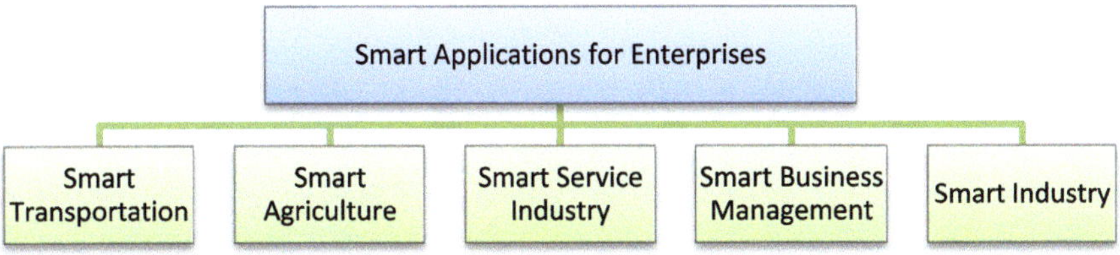

Fig. 2.12 Smart Life applications for enterprises

2.7 Smart Applications for Enterprises

This domain contains applications about transportation, agriculture, service industry, business management, and industry, as shown in Fig. 2.12.

2.7.1 Smart Transportation

Smart transportation refers to the integration of advanced technologies, data analytics, and intelligent systems to enhance the efficiency, safety, and sustainability of transportation networks. It optimizes traffic flow, improves public transit systems, enhances vehicle safety, and reduces environmental impact. Smart transportation aims to create a seamless, interconnected, and data-driven mobility ecosystem for the benefit of both commuters and the overall transportation infrastructure. The Smart transportation field includes several topics illustrated in Fig. 2.13.

Smart Driving Smart driving refers to a conscientious and environmentally friendly approach adopted by drivers in response to the growing emphasis on climate change in social and political discussions (Young et al. 2011). While traditional ergonomics research has predominantly concentrated on enhancing vehicle safety and performance efficiency, the evolving landscape demands a shift toward the development of systems that actively promote eco-conscious driving behavior. Smart driving integrates technological solutions, behavioral insights, and ergonomic considerations to contribute to sustainable and environmentally responsible transportation practices.

Smart Transportation Mobility Smart mobility, a crucial element of Smart cities, has the potential to alleviate traffic congestion, reduce commute times, lower road accidents, and offer passengers the flexibility to personalize their journeys. Planning Smart mobility solutions ranks among the foremost challenges faced by major cities globally, necessitating deliberate actions supported by advanced technologies (Biyik et al. 2021).

Smart Vehicle Relocation Traditional car-sharing systems require users to pick up and return cars at designated stations, whereas free-floating systems establish a geo-

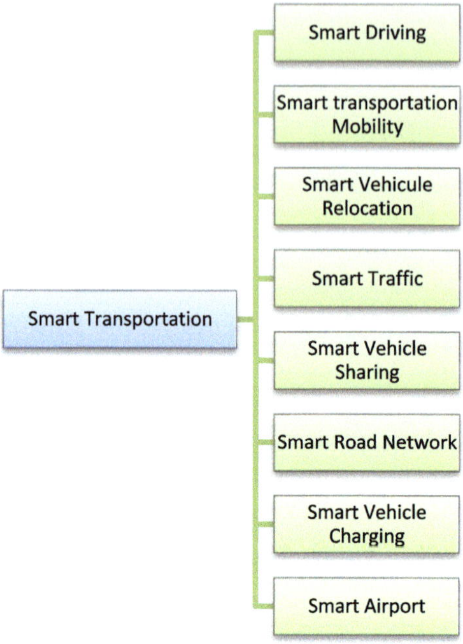

Fig. 2.13 Smart Life applications for Smart transportation

fence around the city center, allowing users to hire and drop cars directly at or near their desired locations without visiting a station (Hermann et al. 2014).

Smart Traffic The increasing number of vehicles on roads and limited capacities are making traffic networks increasingly complex and challenging, resulting in congestion and traffic jams that significantly impact the economy, environment, and human health. As a result, there is a strong motivation to develop new traffic management systems to address these issues effectively (Merrad et al. 2016).

Smart Vehicle Sharing Transport and urban planners are focused on creating policies that improve service access for transportation activities, ensuring convenient and affordable public transportation, integrating all modes effectively, ensuring safety, and developing transport infrastructure. The initial cost of fully autonomous vehicles may be prohibitive, leading to their introduction in the public market as shared-fleet services initially. On-demand mobility, incorporating both car-sharing and ride-sharing, along with automation, especially in integrated demonstrations like shared autonomous vehicles, are presented as sustainable solutions to urban mobility challenges (Golbabaei et al. 2021).

Smart Road Network The management and maintenance of road infrastructures require extensive data on their maintenance history and current condition. There is a growing need to improve the efficiency of managing and maintaining road infrastructures. In recent years, several promising technologies have emerged to address various identified challenges in this area (Carneiro et al. 2018).

Smart Vehicle Charging The transportation sector is currently grappling with challenges related to its reliance on oil-based energy models. Electric mobility represents a crucial step toward sustainability in contemporary society. The integration of plug-in electric vehicles into electrical distribution networks stands to benefit all stakeholders by enhancing system efficiency both technically and economically. Smart charging technology plays a pivotal role in achieving this ambitious objective (Garcia-Villalobos et al. 2014).

Smart Airport Smart airports enhance both passenger and airport experiences by employing technologies, sensors, and processors, to maintain an inclusive and continuous connection between passengers and various services, accessible anytime and anywhere within the airport ecosystem (Alansari et al. 2019). They establish a real-time communication framework that enables seamless responsiveness and analysis. Unlike traditional setups, passengers at these airports experience unified check-in processes, with all crucial information centralized.

2.7.2 Smart Agriculture

Smart agriculture refers to the use of advanced technologies, including the Internet of Things, sensors, data analytics, and automation, to optimize various aspects of farming processes. The goal is to enhance efficiency, productivity, and sustainability in agricultural practices by collecting and analyzing real-time data, enabling informed decision-making, and promoting resource optimization. Smart agriculture encompasses a range of applications, from precision planting and irrigation to livestock monitoring and crop management, ultimately contributing to more intelligent and resource-efficient farming practices. The sub-topics of Smart agriculture are shown in Fig. 2.14.

Smart Farming The increase of the global population and its subsequent surge in food demand pose challenges to agricultural production. Concurrently, decreasing rural workforce and rising production costs further compound the challenges faced by the agricultural sector. In response to these complexities, the concept of Smart farming, using the Internet of Things, emerges as a farm management solution. Smart farming employs IoT to address contemporary issues in food production, enhancing efficiency and sustainability (Navarro et al. 2020).

Smart Fishery Smart fishing spans various domains, as the assessment of the economic aspects of commercial fleets, electronic monitoring of catch and bycatch, identification and prediction of fishing grounds, and the simulation of fishing vessel behavior (Ebrahimi et al. 2021).

Climate-Smart Agriculture The literature contains numerous projections regarding the impact of climate change on agriculture, particularly on crop, livestock, and fishery production sectors. Understanding the scale of these impacts is crucial for

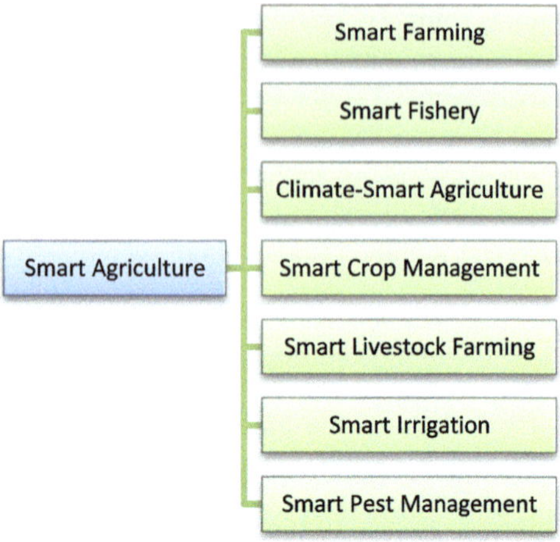

Fig. 2.14 Smart Life applications for Smart agriculture

informing adaptation strategies and developing policies that promote climate-Smart agriculture (Zougmoré et al. 2016).

Smart Crop Management In the context of Smart agriculture, contemporary farming increasingly relies on new technologies. IoT farmers can remotely monitor their crops and equipment using smartphones and computers (Mekala and Viswanathan 2017). Crop production in agriculture is influenced by numerous factors including climate, geography, biology, economics, history, politics, socioeconomic conditions, and agro-ecological zoning. Intelligent agro-ecological zoning plays a crucial role in this context, aiming to accurately suggest and predict crops that optimize production yields (Chetan et al. 2021).

Smart Livestock Farming The future of livestock farming is marked by precision, sustainability, and intelligence. By harnessing modern information technology, precision livestock farming addresses traditional farming challenges, paving the way for modernization and stimulating sustainable growth within the livestock sector (Zhang et al. 2021).

Smart Irrigation In most parts of the world, the lack of efficient irrigation methods leads to wastage or excessive use of irrigation water. Installation of Smart water irrigation systems can prove useful for saving water, time, and cost (Issaka et al. 2018).

Smart Pest Management Insect pests pose a significant threat to global agricultural crop yield and quality. Efficient and accurate monitoring of insect pest populations is vital for prediction and control measures. The emergence of Smart pest monitoring, driven by advancements in artificial intelligence theories and technologies, aims to enhance the automatic and intelligent collection of crucial crop insect pest data (Li et al. 2021).

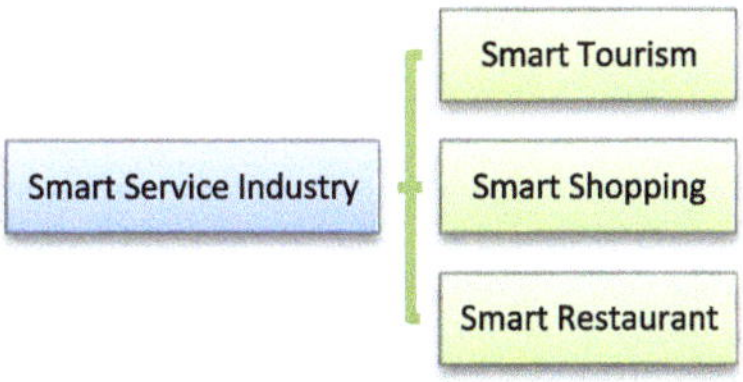

Fig. 2.15 Smart Life applications for Smart service industry

2.7.3 Smart Service Industry

The concept of a "Smart service industry" encapsulates a diverse array of applications that include cutting-edge technologies to enhance customer experiences, improve operational efficiency, and drive sustainable practices across various sectors, from data-driven insights in tourism to streamlined shopping experiences and optimized restaurant operations, as shown in Fig. 2.15.

Smart Tourism Smart tourism denotes the growing reliance of tourism stakeholders on emerging information and communication technologies for substantial data transformation, leading to enhanced tourist experiences, heightened destination competitiveness, and improved sustainability. The application of software and analytics to analyze and predict tourist behaviors represents a notable trend among practitioners, ultimately benefiting tourists, industry players, and destinations alike (Ye et al. 2020).

Smart Shopping Smart shopping includes consumers' efforts to minimize the expenditure of time, money, or energy while maximizing the hedonic and utilitarian value derived from the shopping experience (Green Atkins and Youn-Kyung 2012).

Smart Restaurant Accurate demand forecasting plays a pivotal role in the effectiveness of a restaurant's yield and revenue management system, a critical aspect for both independent restaurants and larger restaurant chains (Lasek et al. 2016).

2.7.4 Smart Business Management

To ensure the sustainability of their businesses, various companies, especially for small and medium-sized enterprises (SMEs), must embrace the Internet as a crucial element in designing new business model values, enhancing customer experiences, and bolstering internal capabilities that support key operations. Companies need to leverage information and communication technology in their business operations to remain competitive and meet evolving market demands (Rozmi et al. 2021).

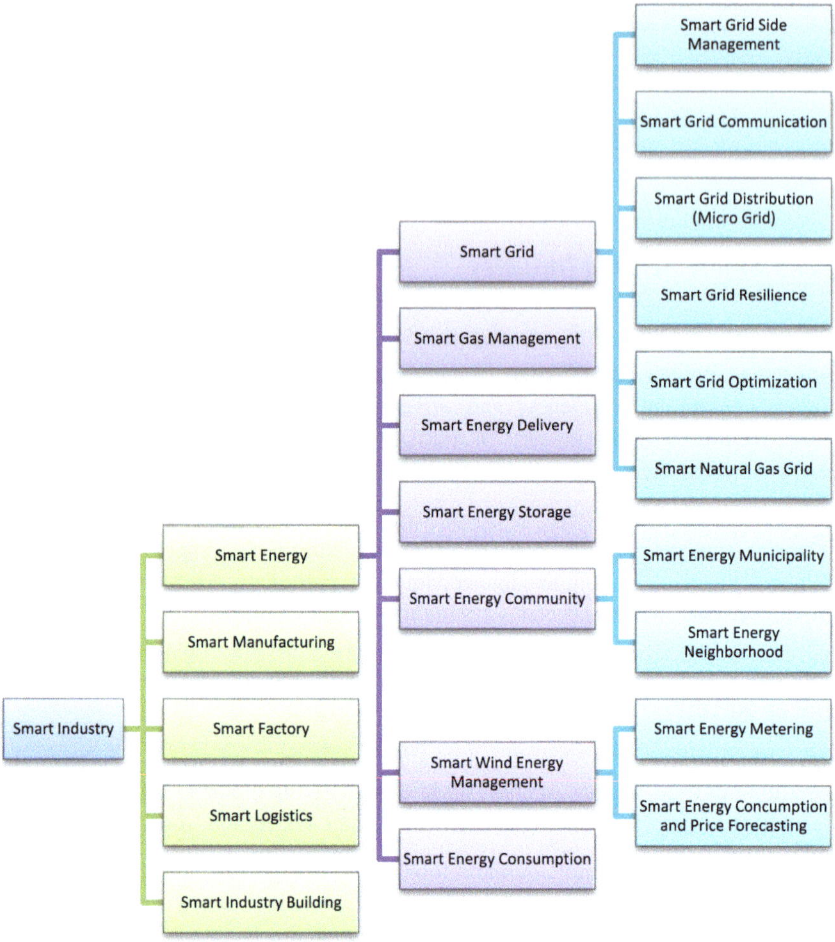

Fig. 2.16 Smart Life applications for Smart industry

2.7.5 *Smart Industry*

A "Smart industry" application refers to an application to manufacturing and production that integrates IoT advanced technologies to optimize processes, improve efficiency, and enhance decision-making. We can find several kinds of applications related to Smart industry, especially Smart energy ones, as shown in Fig. 2.16.

Smart Energy Being the most widespread in the manufacturing sector, Smart energy applications have a significant impact on sustainability and the environment. These include renewable energies such as solar, wind, hydropower, and biomass, as well as Smart grids, catalysis industry advancements, and innovations in power storage and distribution (Rangel-Martinez et al. 2021).

Smart Grid. The term "Smart grid" typically refers to a technology class enabled by two-way communication techniques. These techniques facilitate real-time data transfer, essential for control systems to enhance efficiency, reliability, and flexibility (Abdelwahab et al. 2019). We can distinguish six different types of Smart grid applications: for side management, for communication, for distribution (micro-grid), for resilience, for optimization, and for natural gas.

Smart Gas Management. Smart gas management includes various applications related to the handling of gas resources. For example, Smart gas sensing integrates physical and chemical material sciences, electronic circuits, statistics, chemometrics, communication networks, and machine learning methods. The general process of Smart gas sensing technology includes sensing materials and sensor arrays, signal processing for drift compensation and feature extraction, and gas pattern recognition technology based on machine learning, as outlined by Feng et al. (2019).

Smart Energy Delivery. In energy-related sectors, direct interaction between utility providers and consumers from residential, industrial, and commercial sectors is crucial. The integration of digital computation and communication technologies ensures secure, efficient, and reliable electricity delivery and information exchange among power generators, utility companies, and electric power consumers (Reka and Dragicevic 2018).

Smart Energy Storage. Energy storage technologies are central in today's context, spanning from low-capacity mobile storage batteries to high-capacity batteries linked with intermittent renewable energy sources (Sufyan et al. 2019).

Smart Energy Community. Community energy storage represents a new generation of energy storage important to Smart grids. Its placement at the grid's edge and proximity to customers provide significant advantages over storage located at substations (Sardi and Mithulananthan 2014). We can identify two types of Smart energy community applications, those aiming to help municipality and those addressed to the neighborhood.

Smart Wind Energy Management. Given that renewable energy sources depend on weather conditions beyond human control, there is a growing need for new functionalities within electricity networks (Xing et al. 2013). The study and integration of wind power are crucial aspects of Smart wind energy management applications. Two different kinds of Smart applications related to Smart wind energy management can be identified: for energy metering and for energy consumption and price forecasting.

Smart Energy Consumption. There is a gradual increase in electricity demand, but establishing new power plants for electricity generation is challenging due to stringent pollution control policies and increased government awareness of environmental preservation. To address this challenge, sufficient profiling of electricity consumption can be used to explore alternative methods for managing electricity loads in the future while utilizing existing generation capacity (Ahmad et al. 2018).

Smart Manufacturing In response to the growing demand for highly customized products and smaller lot sizes, companies must rapidly adapt to new market opportunities to thrive in a competitive environment, underscoring the importance for manufacturers to cultivate approaches fostering dynamism, flexibility, and reconfigurability at the factory level (Alemao et al. 2021).

Smart Factory Quite close to Smart manufacturing, Smart factories focus on the transformation of factories into smarter, more efficient, safer, and environmentally sustainable environments results from the amalgamation and integration of production technologies, devices, information and communication systems, and data in network infrastructures. Illustratively, in a Smart factory, the capabilities of flexibility and re-configurability in production, coupled with enhanced customer interaction for understanding their needs, enable the customization of goods and services with cost efficiency comparable to mass production (Strozzi et al. 2017).

Smart Logistics Smart logistics enables the intelligent implementation of an integrated logistics system through real-time processing and comprehensive analysis of logistical information. It enhances end-to-end visibility; optimizes logistics processes including transportation, warehousing, and distribution; and provides efficient information services. Smart logistics not only contributes to significant time and cost savings but also holds the potential to mitigate environmental pollution associated with logistical activities (Song et al. 2021).

Smart Industry Building Buildings are evolving toward interactive features that can dynamically adjust to users' needs and changing conditions, be it external factors like climate and grid prices or internal factors such as occupants' requirements. This transition reflects a shift from unresponsive buildings to highly efficient ones capable of energy consumption, production, storage, and distribution (Al Dakheel et al. 2020).

2.8 Clusters

In addition to this main taxonomy, we've discovered the existence of generic clusters that have relevance across multiple areas; thus, they are applied across various Smart applications. We can cite Smart energy and Smart transportation clusters.

Smart energy can be seen as an independent application domain within the Smart industry. However, its presence extends beyond this application, making appearances in other fields such as Smart city, Smart home, etc. In case of Smart cities, energy applications are vital, as energy management systems enhance energy economics, consumption efficiency, grid stability, and reliability. The residential sector significantly impacts global energy consumption and offers flexibility in adjusting consumption patterns, helping address major global challenges (Mahmood et al. 2021). For Smart homes, energy applications allow to reduce environmental impact and supports lifestyles. They push residents to participate in the energy market and addresses technical aspects like peak shaving, load shifting, and strategic conservation while also having significant socioeconomic impacts (Amer et al. 2014).

Another identified cluster is Smart transportation, which designates applications specifically associated with the transportation and mobility field. For instance, Smart transportation applications in Smart cities include Smart electric vehicles. Smart vehicle charging could be applied in Smart cities to monitor the flow of electric vehicles. They involve a wide range of technologies from road and rail vehicles to surface and underwater vessels and even electric aircraft (Shuai et al. 2016). It allows to contribute to the overall efficiency and resilience of Smart cities.

Smart transportation also contributes to the energy distribution in the grid, for instance, through the charging of electric vehicles. To ensure the sustainability, reliability, and efficiency of the electric-power distribution grid, it is essential to develop and implement Smart charging techniques. By integrating Smart transportation with Smart energy solutions, it is possible to promote sustainable mobility while optimizing energy distribution and usage (Igbinovia et al. 2016).

2.9 Conclusion

In this chapter, we presented a classification of Smart Life applications by means of a unique taxonomy. We conducted a systematic mapping study based on 2341 publications to define this Smart application taxonomy.

We observed the introduction of some more special concepts in the literature, even if they are not fully implemented yet.

- *Smart Earth* is defined as an innovative approach to environmental monitoring in (Bakker and Ritts 2018).
- *Smart island* aims to classify current Smart-related methodologies in the urban context and assess their potential applicability to islands (Desogus et al. 2019).
- The concept of *Smart State* (Gil-Garcia 2012) aligns with the notion of "knowledge-based urban development."
- Kaur and Parashar (2021) provide a literature review on the use of blockchain technology in *Smart villages*.

Finally, the term Smart world appeared in the literature (Kumari et al. 2020) (Liu et al. 2019) as a unifying term encompassing various Smart applications. For instance, Liu et al. (2019) define a Smart world as "an attractive prospect with comprehensive development of ubiquitous computing involving penetrative intelligence into ubiquitous things." In our perspective, this term corresponds with our vision of Smart Life.

In developing the taxonomy for Smart Life applications, we deliberately excluded 328 sources only focused on Smart artifacts, Smart technologies, and

Smart systems without clear associations with specific application domains. Additionally, the taxonomy omits Smart infrastructure-related applications as we consider them as transversal issues (infrastructure can be found in almost all major Smart applications fields).

This taxonomy will not be a static structure; it will evolve just like taxonomies in other domains. We plan to develop our taxonomy by extracting a classification of the Smart artifacts and link them to the Smart applications and Smart domains identified in this taxonomy. We also plan to carry out a bibliometric study to explore the relationships between the Smart applications. Finally, we also intend to pursue investigations into the variety research challenges in the field of Smart Life and Smart Life Engineering. Our main goal is to discover whether a common methodological basis could be identified in the field of Smart Life and its engineering approaches.

References

Abdelwahab, R.H., El-Habrouk, M., Abdelhamid, T.H.: Survey of communication techniques in smart grids. In: 21st International Middle East Power Systems Conference. (2019)

Addison, C., Zhang, S., Coomes, B.: Smart growth and housing affordability: a review of regulatory mechanisms and planning practices. J. Plan. Lit. (2013)

Afzal, M., Panagiotopoulos, P.: Smart policing: a critical review of the literature. Int. Conf. Electron. Gov. **12219**, 59–70 (2020)

Ahmad, T., Chen, H., Wang, J., Guo, Y.: Review of various modeling techniques for the detection of electricity theft in smart grid environment. Renew. Sust. Energ. Rev. (2018)

Alaa, M., Zaidan, A.A., Zaidan, B.B., Talal, M., Kiah, M.L.M.: A review of smart home applications based on Internet of Things. J. Netw. Comput. Appl. **97**, 48–65 (2017)

Al-Ani, K.W., Abdalkafor, A.S., Nassar, A.M.: Smart city applications: a survey. In: 9th International Conference on Information Systems and Technologies. (2019)

Alansari, Z., Soomro, S., Belgaum, M.R.: Smart airports: review and open research issues. In: Emerging Technologies in Computing, pp. 136–148. (2019)

Al Dakheel, J., Del Pero, C., Aste, N., Leonforte, F.: Smart buildings features and key performance indicators: a review. In: Sustainable Cities and Society. (2020)

Alemão, D., Rocha, A.D., Barata, J.: Smart manufacturing scheduling approaches—systematic review and future directions. Appl. Sci. (Switzerland) (2021)

Alibasic, A., Al Junaibi, R., Aung, Z., Woon, W.L., Omar, M.A.: Cybersecurity for smart cities: a brief review. In: International Workshop on Data Analytics for Renewable Energy Integration. (2017)

Aljanah, S., Zhang, N., Tay, S.W.: A survey on smart home authentication: toward secure, multilevel and interaction-based identification. IEEE Access. (2021)

Al-Smadi, A.M., Alsmadi, M.K., Baareh, A.K., Almarashdeh, I., Abouelmagd, H., Ahmed, O.S.S.: Emergent situations for smart cities: a survey. Int. J. Electric. Comput. Eng. (2019)

Amer, M., Naaman, A., M'Sirdi, N.K., El-Zonkoly, A.M.: Smart home energy management systems survey. In: International Conference on Renewable Energies for Developing Countries (2014)

Andries, O., Kitada, T., Bodner, K., Sanders, N.N., Weiss, R.: Synthetic biology devices and circuits for RNA-based 'smart vaccines': a propositional review. In: Expert Review of Vaccines. (2014)

Bakker, K., Ritts, M.: Smart Earth: a meta-review and implications for environmental governance. In: Global Environmental Change (2018)
Behera, S.K., Pradhan, B.B.: Review on implementing smart water grid for smart cities in India. Int. J. Psychosoc. Rehab. (2019)
Behera, N.K.S., Sa, P.K., Bakshi, S.: Person re-identification for smart cities: state-of-the-art and the path ahead. Pattern Recogn. Lett. (2020)
Bibri, S.E.: The leading smart sustainable paradigm of urbanism and big data computing: a topical literature review. Adv. Sci. Technol. Innov. (2019)
Bıyık, C., Abareshi, A., Paz, A., Ruiz, R.A., Battarra, R., Rogers, C.D.F., Lizarraga, C.: Smart mobility adoption: a review of the literature. J. Open Innov. Technol. Mark. Complex. (2021)
Carneiro, J., Rossetti, R.J.F., Silva, D.C., Oliveira, E.C.: BIM, GIS, IoT, and AR/VR integration for smart maintenance and management of road networks: a review. In: IEEE International Smart Cities Conference. (2018)
Chamee, Y.: Historicizing the smart cities: genealogy as a method of critique for smart urbanism. Telematics Inform. **55** (2020)
Chetan, R., Ashoka, D.V., Ajay Prakash, B.V.: Smart agro-ecological zoning for crop suggestion and prediction using machine learning: an comprehensive review. In: Advances in Intelligent Systems and Computing (2021)
Costa, L.V., Veloso, A.I., Mealha, Ó.: A review of proxemics in 'smart game-playing'. In: Smart Innovation, Systems and Technologies (2018)
Deepika, J., Kalaiselvi, S., Mahalakshmi, S., Agnes Shifani, S.: Smart electronic voting system based on biometrie identification-survey. In: 3rd IEEE International Conference on Science Technology, Engineering and Management (2017)
Demir, K.A.: Smart education framework. Smart Learn. Environ. **8**, 29 (2021)
Demiris, G., Hensel, B.K.: Technologies for an aging society: a systematic review of "smart home" applications. In: Yearbook of Medical Informatics (2008)
Desogus, G., Mistretta, P., Garau, C.: Smart islands: a systematic review on urban policies and smart governance. In: International Conference on Computational Science and Its Applications (2019)
Ebrahimi, S.H., Ossewaarde, M., Need, A.: Smart fishery: a systematic review and research agenda for sustainable fisheries in the age of AI. Sustainability (Switzerland). (2021)
Farrokhi, A., Farahbakhsh, R., Rezazadeh, J., Minerva, R.: Application of Internet of Things and artificial intelligence for smart fitness: a survey. Computer Networks (2021)
Feng, S., Farha, F., Li, Q., Wan, Y., Xu, Y., Zhang, T., Ning, H.: Review on smart gas sensing technology. Sensors (Switzerland). (2019)
Fernández-Caramés, T.M., Fraga-Lamas, P.: Towards the internet-of-smart-clothing: a review on IoT wearables and garments for creating intelligent connected E-textiles. Electronics (Switzerland). (2018)
García-Villalobos, J., Zamora, I., San Martín, J.I., Asensio, F.J., Aperribay, V.: Plug-in electric vehicles in electric distribution networks: a review of smart charging approaches. Renew. Sustain. Energy Rev. (2014)
Gil-Garcia, J.R.: Towards a smart State? Inter-agency collaboration, information integration, and beyond. Inf. Polity. **17**(3–4), 269–280 (2012)
Golbabaei, F., Yigitcanlar, T., Bunker, J.: The role of shared autonomous vehicle systems in delivering smart urban mobility: a systematic review of the literature. Int. J. Sustain. Transp. (2021)
Green Atkins, K., Youn-Kyung, K.: Smart shopping: conceptualization and measurement. Int. J. Retail Distrib. Manag. **40**(5), 360–375 (2012)
Groppi, D., Pfeifer, A., Garcia, D.A., Krajačić, G., Duić, N.: A review on energy storage and demand side management solutions in smart energy islands. Renew. Sust. Energ. Rev. (2021)
Gupta, A.D., Pandey, P., Feijóo, A., Yaseen, Z.M., Bokde, N.D.: Smart water technology for efficient water resource management: a review. Energies. (2020a)
Gupta, D., Nayak, P.K., Parashar, Y., Goel, V., Nath, V.: Internet of things for smart class rooms: a review. In: Lecture Notes in Electrical Engineering (2020b)

Guyot, G., Sherman, M.H., Walker, I.S.: Smart ventilation energy and indoor air quality performance in residential buildings: a review. Energy Build. (2018)
Harbi, Y., Aliouat, Z., Harous, S., Bentaleb, A., Refoufi, A.: A review of security in internet of things. Wirel. Pers. Commun. **108**, 325–344 (2019)
Herrmann, S., Schulte, F., Voß, S.: Increasing acceptance of free-floating car sharing systems using smart relocation strategies: a survey based study of car2go Hamburg. In: International Conference on Computational Logistics (2014)
Hortz, T.: The Smart State test: a critical review of the Smart State Strategy 2005-2015's Knowledge-Based Urban Development. Int. J. Knowl. Based Dev. (2016)
Igbinovia, F.O., Fandi, G., Mahmoud, R., Tlustý, J.: A review of electric vehicles emissions and its smart charging techniques influence on power distribution grid. J. Eng. Sci. Technol. Rev. (2016)
Imbar, R.V., Supangkat, S.H., Langi, A.Z.R.: Smart campus model: a literature review. In: 7th International Conference on ICT for Smart Society (2020)
Iskandaryan, D., Ramos, F., Trilles, S.: Air quality prediction in smart cities using machine learning technologies based on sensor data: a review. Appl. Sci. (Switzerland). (2020)
Issaka, Z., Li, H., Yue, J., Tang, P., Darko, R.O.: Water-smart sprinkler irrigation, prerequisite to climate change adaptation: a review. J. Water Clim. Change. (2018)
Jamwal, R., Jarman, H.K., Roseingrave, E., Douglas, J., Winkler, D.: Smart home and communication technology for people with disability: a scoping review. In: Disability and Rehabilitation: Assistive Technology (2020)
Jukan, A., Masip-Bruin, X., Amla, N.: Smart computing and sensing technologies for animal welfare: a systematic review. ACM Comput. Surv. (2017)
Kaur, P., Parashar, A.: A systematic literature review of blockchain technology for smart villages. In: Archives of Computational Methods in Engineering (2021)
Komninos, N., Philippou, E., Pitsillides, A.: Survey in smart grid and smart home security: issues, challenges and countermeasures. IEEE Commun. Surv. Tutor. (2014)
Kornyshova, E., Deneckere, R., Gressier-Soudan, E., Murray, J., Brinkkemper, S.: From smart life to smart life engineering: a systematic mapping study and research agenda. In: 15th International Baltic Conference on Digital Business and Intelligent Systems. Springer, Riga, Latvia (2022a)
Kornyshova, E., Deneckere, R., Sadouki, K., Gressier-Soudan, E., Brinkkemper, S.: Smart Life: review of the contemporary smart applications. In: International Conference on Research Challenges in Information Science, pp. 302–318 (2022b)
Kumari, M., Sharma, R., Sheetal, A.: A review on hybrid WSN-NGPON2 network for smart world. In: Advances in Intelligent Systems and Computing (2020)
Leaman, J., La, H.M.: A comprehensive review of smart wheelchairs: past, present, and future. In: IEEE Transactions on Human-Machine Systems (2017)
Lasek, A., Cercone, N., Saunders, J.: Smart restaurants: survey on customer demand and sales forecasting. In: Smart Cities and Homes, Key Enabling Technologies (2016)
Li, J., Yang, X., Sitzenfrei, R.: Rethinking the framework of smart water system: a review. Water (Switzerland). (2020)
Li, W., Zheng, T., Yang, Z., Li, M., Sun, C., Yang, X.: Classification and detection of insects from field images using deep learning for smart pest management: systematic review. Ecol. Inf. (2021)
Liao, H.T., Zhou, Z., Zhou, Y.: A systematic review of social media for intelligent human-computer interaction research: why smart social media is not enough. In: International Conference on Intelligent Human Computer Interaction (2021)
Lin, H., Bergmann, N.W.: IoT privacy and security challenges for smart home environments. Information. **7**(3), 44 (2016)
Liu, H., Ning, H., Mu, Q., Zheng, Y., Zeng, J., Yang, L.T., Huang, R., Ma, J.: A review of the smart world. In: Future Generation Computer Systems (2019)

Lutolf, R.: Smart home concept and the integration of energy meters into a home based system. In: 7th international conference metering apparatus and tariffs for electricity supply, pp. 277–278. (1992)
Mahmood, D., Latif, S., Anwar, A., Hussain, S.J., Jhanjhi, N.Z., Sama, N.U., Humayun, M.: Utilization of ICT and AI techniques in harnessing residential energy consumption for an energy-aware smart city: a review. Int. J. Adv. Appl. Sci. (2021)
Mahoor, M., Hosseini, Z.S., Khodaei, A., Paaso, A., Kushner, D.: State-of-the-art in smart streetlight systems: a review. In: IET Smart Cities. (2020)
Malekpour Koupaei, D., Song, T., Cetin, K.S., Im, J.: An assessment of opinions and perceptions of smart thermostats using aspect-based sentiment analysis of online reviews. Build. Environ. (2020)
Mekala, M.S., Viswanathan, P.: A survey: smart agriculture IoT with cloud computing. In: International Conference on Microelectronic Devices, Circuits and Systems (2017)
Merrad, W., Rachedi, A., Busawon, K., Binns, R.: A survey on smart traffic network control and optimization. In: 1st International Conference on Multidisciplinary Engineering Design Optimization. (2016)
Moraitou, M., Pateli, A., Fotiou, S.: Smart health caring home: a systematic review of smart home care for elders and chronic disease patients. Adv. Exp. Med. Biol. (2017)
Navarro, E., Costa, N., Pereira, A.: A systematic review of IoT solutions for smart farming. Sensors (Switzerland). (2020)
Niccolai, L., Bassetto, M., Quarta, A.A., Mengali, G.: A review of Smart Dust architecture, dynamics, and mission applications. In: Progress in Aerospace Sciences (2019)
Nikolaeva, A., te Brömmelstroet, M., Raven, R., Ranson, J.: Smart cycling futures: charting a new terrain and moving towards a research agenda. J. Transp. Geogr. (2019)
Papagianneas, S.: Towards smarter and fairer justice? A review of the Chinese scholarship on building smart courts and automating justice. J. Curr. Chin. Aff. (2021)
Petersen, K., Feldt, R., Mujtaba, S., Mattsson, M.: Systematic mapping studies in software engineering. In: 12th International Conference on Evaluation and Assessment in Software Engineering, vol. 17. (2008)
Rajšp, A., Fister, I.: A systematic literature review of intelligent data analysis methods for smart sport training. Appl. Sci. (Switzerland). (2020)
Rangel-Martinez, D., Nigam, K.D.P., Ricardez-Sandoval, L.A.: Machine learning on sustainable energy: a review and outlook on renewable energy systems, catalysis, smart grid and energy storage. Chem. Eng. Res. Des. (2021)
Reka, S.S., Dragicevic, T.: Future effectual role of energy delivery: a comprehensive review of Internet of Things and smart grid. Renew. Sust. Energ. Rev. (2018)
Rozmi, A.N.A., Nohuddin, P.P.N.E., Hadi, A.R.A., Bakar, M.I.A.: Identifying Small and medium enterprise smart entrepreneurship training framework components using thematic analysis and expert review. Int. J. Adv. Comput. Sci. Appl. (2021)
Sardi, J., Mithulananthan, N.: Community energy storage, a critical element in smart grid: a review of technology, prospect, challenges and opportunity. In: 4th International Conference on Engineering Technology and Technopreneuship. (2014)
Scorpio, M., Laffi, R., Masullo, M., Ciampi, G., Rosato, A., Maffei, L., Sibilio, S.: Virtual reality for smart urban lighting design: Review, applications and opportunities. Energies. (2020)
Severi, S., Sottile, F., Abreu, G., Pastrone, C., Spirito, M., Berens, F.: M2M technologies: enablers for a pervasive internet of things. In: European Conference on Networks and Communications. (2014).
Shaker, A.S.: A survey of smart buildings and homes using low-power wide-area network (LoRa WAN). In: 4th International Symposium on Multidisciplinary Studies and Innovative Technologies. (2020)
Shastry, R., Ramana Murthy, B.V., Kishor Kumar Reddy, C., Anisha, P.R.: Automated lighting smart parking using internet of things. In: Intelligent Computing, Information and Control Systems, vol. 1039. Springer, Cham (2020)

Shuai, W., Maille, P., Pelov, A.: Charging electric vehicles in the smart city: a survey of economy-driven approaches. In: IEEE Transactions on Intelligent Transportation Systems (2016)
Singh, M., Ahmed, S.: IoT based smart water management systems: a systematic review. In: Materials Today: Proceedings. (2020)
Song, Y., Yu, F.R., Zhou, L., Yang, X., He, Z.: Applications of the internet of things (IoT) in smart logistics: a comprehensive survey. IEEE Internet Things J. (2021)
Strozzi, F., Colicchia, C., Creazza, A., Noè, C.: Literature review on the 'smart factory' concept using bibliometric tools. Int. J. Prod. Res. (2017)
Subashini, M.J., Sudarmani, R., Gobika, S., Varshini, R.: Development of smart flood monitoring and early warning system using weather forecasting data and wireless sensor networks – a review. In: 3rd International Conference on Intelligent Communication Technologies and Virtual Mobile Networks (2021)
Sufyan, M., Rahim, N.A., Aman, M.M., Tan, C.K., Raihan, S.R.S.: Sizing and applications of battery energy storage technologies in smart grid system: a review. J. Renew. Sustain. Energy. (2019)
Tadili, J., Fasly, H.: Citizen participation in smart cities: a survey, pervasive health. In: Pervasive Computing Technologies for Healthcare (2019)
Tai-hoon, Kim, T., Ramos, C., Mohammed, S.: Smart city and IoT. Futur. Gener. Comput. Syst. **76**, 159–162 (2017)
Thakur, N., Nagrath, P., Jain, R., Saini, D., Sharma, N., Hemanth, D.J.: Artificial intelligence techniques in smart cities surveillance using UAVs: a survey. In: Studies in Computational Intelligence (2021)
Thomson, S.B.: Qualitative research: validity. J. Adm. Gov. **6**(1) (2011)
Tikhomirov, V., Dneprovskaya, N.: Development of strategy for smart University. In: Open Education Global International Conference, Banff, Canada, pp. 22–24 (2015)
Wang, D., Zhong, D., Souri, A.: Energy management solutions in the Internet of Things applications: technical analysis and new research directions. Cogn. Syst. Res. **67**, 33–49 (2021)
Wang, H., Liu, Y., Laaksonen, A., Krook-Riekkola, A., Yang, Z., Lu, X., Ji, X.: Carbon recycling – An immense resource and key to a smart climate engineering: a survey of technologies, cost and impurity impact. Renew. Sust. Energ. Rev. (2020)
Washburn, D., Sindhu, U., Balaouras, S., Dines, R.A., Hayes, N.M., Nelson, L.E.: Helping CIOs understand smart city initiatives. Forres Res Growth. **17** (2009)
Wong, B.T.M., Li, K.C.: The benefits and challenges of smart learning: a literature review. In: International Symposium on Educational Technology (2021)
Xing, T.W., Hong, S., Jian, D., Lei, D., Han, J.H., Song, Y.T.: Survey of wind power and integration smart grid technologies. Adv. Mater. Res. (2013)
Yamane, S.: Deductively verifying embedded software in the era of artificial intelligence = machine learning + software science. In: 6th IEEE Global Conference on Consumer Electronics (2017)
Yan, H., Peng, G., Luo, Y., Liu, S.: Survey on smart home attack and defense methods. J. Cyber Secur. (2021)
Ye, B.H., Ye, H., Law, R.: Systematic review of smart tourism research. Sustainability (Switzerland). (2020)
Yin, H., Akmandor, A.O., Mosenia, A., Jha, N.K.: Smart healthcare. Foundations and Trends®. Electron. Des. Autom. **12**(4), 401–466 (2018)
Young, M.S., Birrell, S.A., Stanton, N.A.: Safe driving in a green world: a review of driver performance benchmarks and technologies to support 'smart' driving. Appl. Ergon. (2011)
Yusuf, N., Hamza, A., Muhammad, R.S., Suleiman, M.A., Abubakar, Z.A.: Smart health internet of thing for continuous glucose monitoring: a survey. Int. J. Integr. Eng. (2020)
Zhang, M., Wang, X., Feng, H., Huang, Q., Xiao, X., Zhang, X.: Wearable Internet of Things enabled precision livestock farming in smart farms: a review of technical solutions for precise perception, biocompatibility, and sustainability monitoring. J. Clean. Prod. (2021)

Zhao, Y., Rokhani, F.Z., Shariff Ghazali, S., Chew, B.H.: Defining the concepts of a smart nursing home and its potential technology utilities that integrate medical services and are acceptable to stakeholders: a scoping review protocol. BMJ Open. (2021)
Zisser, H., Robinson, L., Bevier, W., Dassau, E., Ellingsen, C., Doyle, F.J., Jovanovic, L.: Bolus calculator: a review of four "smart" insulin pumps. In: Diabetes Technology and Therapeutics (2008)
Zou, W., Jing, W., Chen, G., Lu, Y., Song, H.: A survey of big data analytics for smart forestry. In: IEEE Access (2019)
Zougmoré, R., Partey, S., Ouédraogo, M., Omitoyin, B., Thomas, T., Ayantunde, A., Ericksen, P., Said, M., Jalloh, A.: Toward climate-smart agriculture in West Africa: a review of climate change impacts, adaptation strategies and policy developments for the livestock, fishery and crop production sectors. In: Agriculture and Food Security (2016)
Zulfiqar, H., Haque, U., Mahfooz, H., Tariq, F., Khan, R.M.: A survey on smart parking systems in urban cities. In: Concurrency and Computation: Practice and Experience (2021)

Chapter 3
Evolution of the Scientific Domain of Smart Life

Rébecca Deneckère, Elena Kornyshova, and Sjaak Brinkkemper

Abstract Research in "Smart" domains has proliferated over recent decades, branching into various subfields including Smart energy, Smart cities, and Smart homes and, more recently, Smart farming, Smart universities, and Smart tourism. Building on a bibliographic study of 2341 literature reviews and state-of-the-art papers, this chapter addresses the research question: *How have Smart applications evolved through time?* We show the growth of the Smart Life scientific domain reflecting a rising interest among researchers and society and provide an analysis of the increasing diversity of the research concepts in Smart Life. Finally, we present the evolution of four key Smart domains: Smart applications for enterprises, persons, environment, and society. Therefore, this chapter illustrates the surge in publications over the past decade underscoring the expanding relevance and impact of Smart Life in contemporary technological and societal contexts.

Keywords Smart Life · Evolution · Bibliographic study

3.1 Introduction

Research in the "Smart" domains expands continuously, with various subfields emerging over the past decades. We developed in the previous chapter the taxonomy of various Smart Life applications. We studied 2341 state-of-the-art and research

---

R. Deneckère
Centre de Recherche en Informatique, Université Paris 1 Panthéon-Sorbonne, Paris, France
e-mail: rebecca.deneckere@univ-paris1.fr

E. Kornyshova (✉)
Centre d'Etudes et de Recherche en Informatique et Communications, Conservatoire National des Arts et Métiers, Paris, France
e-mail: elena.kornyshova@cnam.fr

S. Brinkkemper
Department of Information and Computing Sciences, Utrecht University, Utrecht, the Netherlands
e-mail: s.brinkkemper@uu.nl

E. Kornyshova et al. (eds.), *Smart Life and Smart Life Engineering*,
https://doi.org/10.1007/978-3-031-75887-4_3

agenda papers on Smart Life.[1] We detailed different Smart applications, such as Smart energy (Loganathan et al. 2018), Smart cities (Chamee 2020), Smart homes (Lutolf 1992), Smart farming or Smart agriculture (Hidayat et al. 2020), Smart university (Al-Shoqran and Shorman 2021), Smart tourism (Mehraliyev et al. 2020), and so on.

This work led to the specification of a taxonomy on Smart applications. In this chapter, we investigate their evolution and distribution over time. Thus, we aim at answering the second research question elaborated in the research methodology section of the previous chapter *RQ2: How have Smart applications evolved through time?*

The growth of the scientific domain of Smart Life with a detailed analysis of the related research concepts is studied in Sect. 3.2. Section 3.3 proposes a deeper look on the evolution of the four domains of Smart Life: Smart applications for enterprises, for persons, for environment, and for society. Section 3.4 explains the segmentation of the Smart applications type into each of these four domains. We conclude in Sect. 3.5.

3.2 Growth of the Scientific Domain of Smart Life

During a preliminary examination of research papers containing the strict term of "Smart Life," we observed an increasing number of research articles interested on this domain (Kornyshova et al. 2022a). As shown in Fig. 3.1, the number of papers on Smart Life just has increased in the last decade. A nearly consistent rise has been detected since 2011, with a stable progression in the number of papers on Smart Life, particularly since 2016.

However, the number of papers on Smart Life was restricted; thus, we undertook a larger study to better understand the evolution of this field (the study of 2431 research articles). In the following, we present the evolution of Smart Life-related concepts since the appearance of the first states of the art in 1986 issue from this study. We start by the concepts for the whole period, and then we present them by sub-periods.

Main concepts used in Smart Life The main concepts discussed in the Smart Life paper corpus during the whole period are shown in Fig. 3.2. To construct and visualize the network, we used the VOSviewer tool (https://www.vosviewer.com/) with all the meta-data of the 2341 papers, ranging from 1986 to 2022. The obtained network highlights several important clusters, like *technology-oriented* (Internet of things, big data, sensors, cloud computing, and blockchain), *goal-oriented*

[1] The complete list of these papers is available at http://cri-dist.univ-paris1.fr/rcis22/RCIS2022_Appendix%20A%20-%20references%20list.pdf

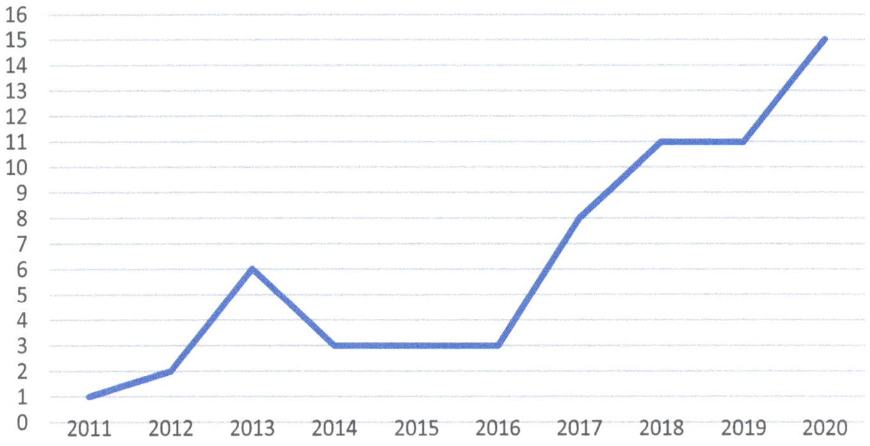

Fig. 3.1 Growth of the number of papers on Smart Life from 2011 to 2020

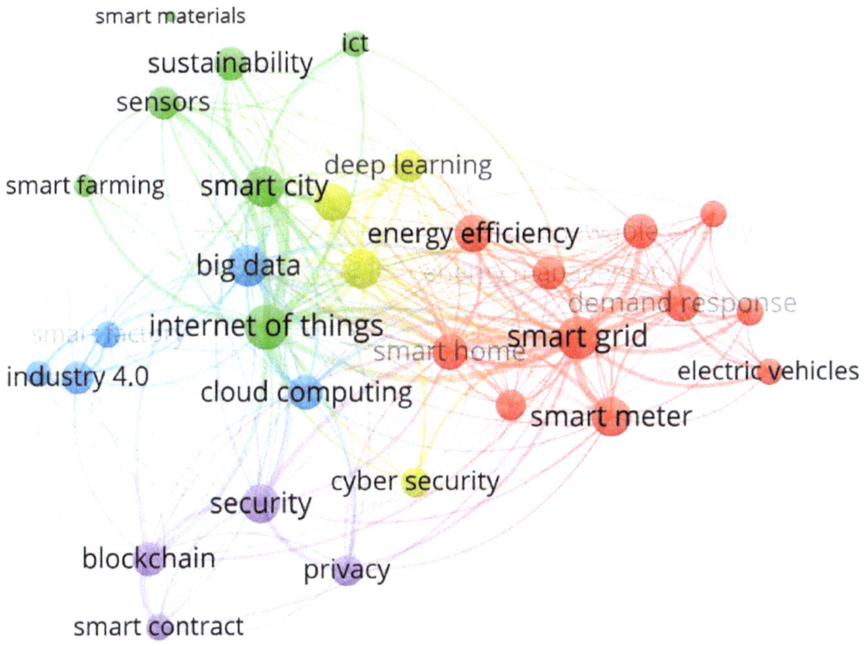

Fig. 3.2 Concepts used in the meta-data of the studied papers for the entire period

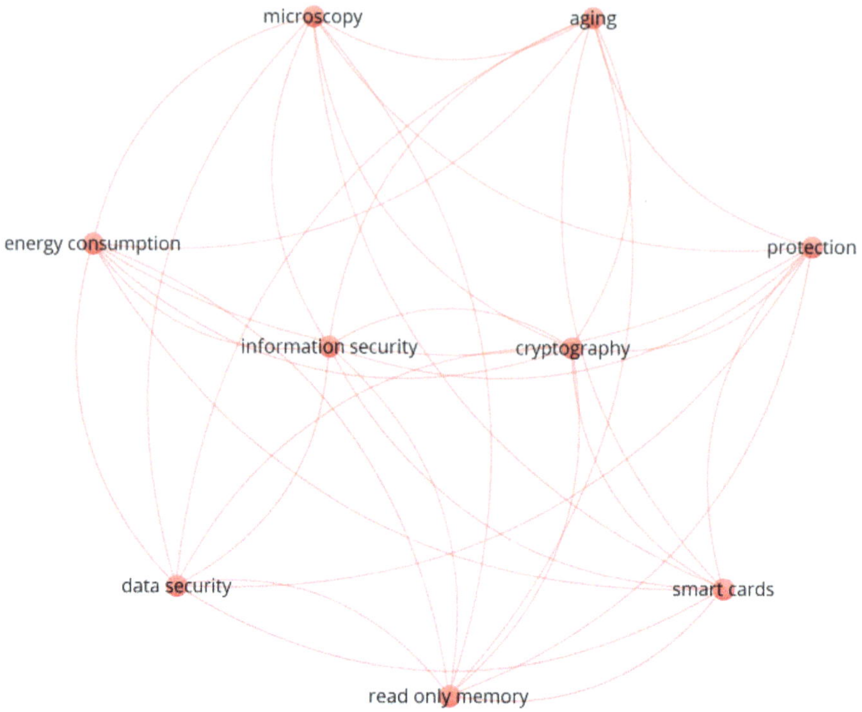

Fig. 3.3 Concepts in the meta-data of the studied papers from 1986 to 2005

(security, energy-efficiency, privacy, and sustainability), and *application-oriented* (Smart grids/meter, Smart home, and Smart city).

To understand better the evolution of Smart Life concepts, we decomposed the paper corpus into three time periods: 1986–2005 (20 years), 2006–2014 (9 years), and 2015–2022 (8 years).

The Main Concepts Used in Smart Life from 1986 to 2005 (34 Papers)

Smart Life was at its very beginning in those days and applied in some domains, which will become more and more important later on (Fig. 3.3). For instance, "energy consumption" problematics were at the root of the appearance of Smart energy applications. Similarly, Smart healthcare applications began with "aging" people care. The concepts of "data security," "information security," "protection," and "cryptography" were already the core of the area related to data collected by the sensors and the complexity to manage them correctly and confidentially. Technology-oriented concepts are also present, with "microscopy," "Smart cards," and "read on memory."

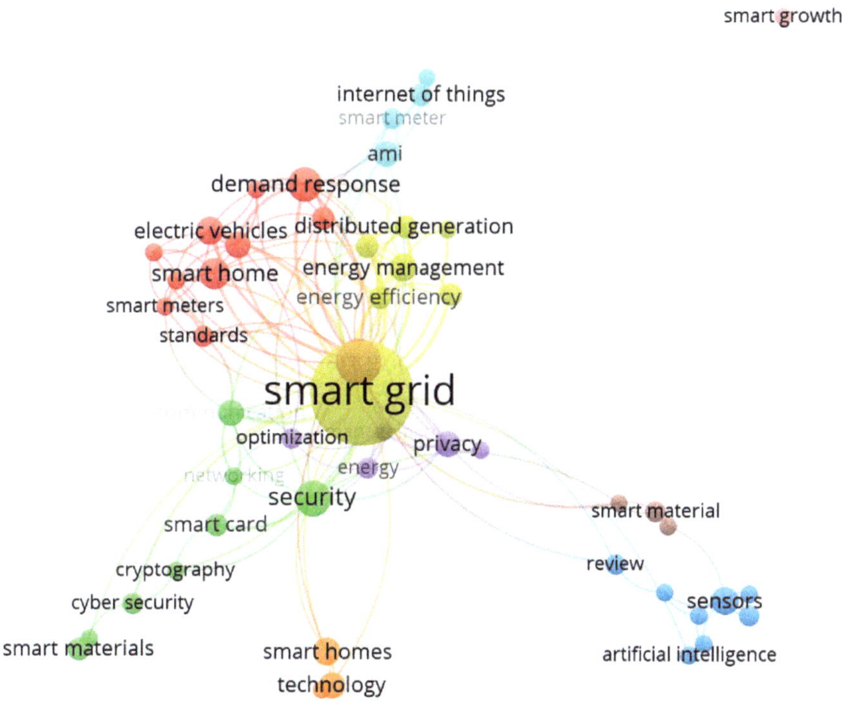

Fig. 3.4 Concepts in the meta-data of the studied papers from 2006 to 2014

The Main Concepts Used in Smart Life from 2006 to 2014 (310 Papers)
As shown in Fig. 3.4, this period of time highlights the explosion of the Smart energy applications, essentially dedicated to the "Smart grid" ones but also to other kind of applications, like "energy management," "energy efficiency," and so on. "Sensors" or "Smart materials" are also representing a good set of concepts in the figure. "Artificial intelligence" makes its appearance. "Smart home" emerges in this period. "Security," "privacy," and "optimization" are representing all the goal-oriented concepts. It is remarkable that some concepts about sustainability appear, like "Smart growth." However, this is not related to the other Smart Life concepts yet.

The Main Concepts Used in Smart Life from 2015 to 2022 (1997 Papers)
Figure 3.5 illustrates the network of papers for this period. Eighty-five percent of our paper corpus were published in this last period of time, which shows the incredible expansion of the Smart Life domain on the last decade. A lot of new Smart applications appear, like "Smart agriculture," "Smart governance," and "Smart building." However, even if we find a lot of these new concepts, the main ones appearing in this network are "Smart grid" (same as in the preceding period) and "Internet of Things," which shows the importance of technology in this area. Related to IoT, we find all the "Smart devices" concepts, like "actuator," "arduino,"

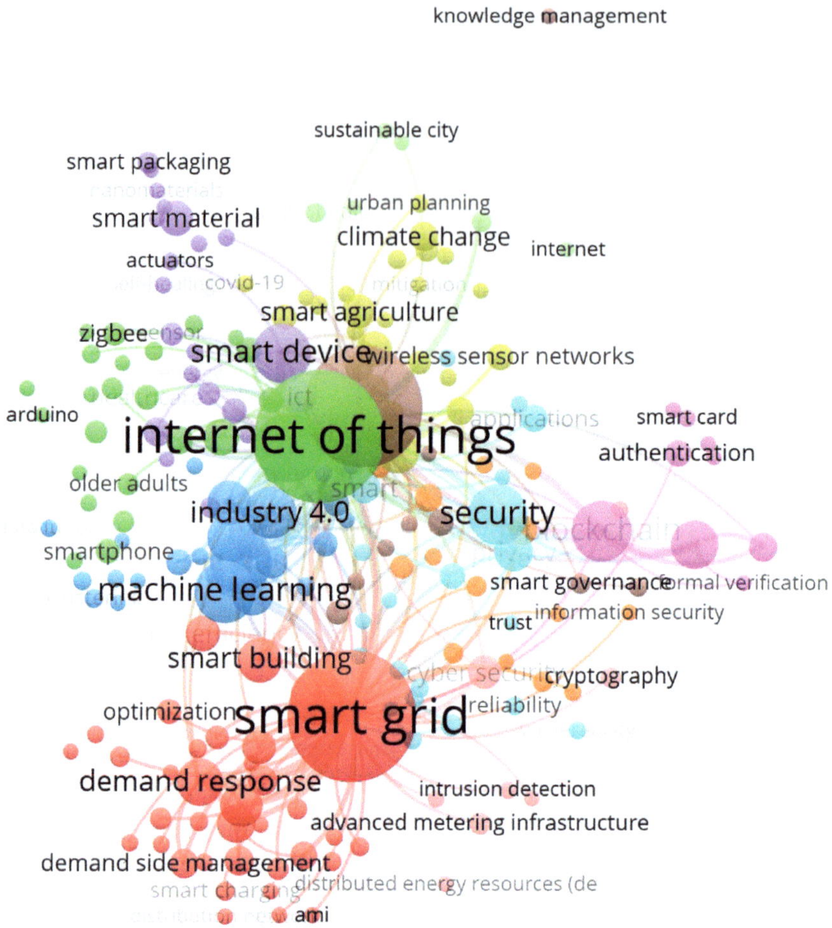

Fig. 3.5 Concepts in the meta-data of the studied papers from 2015 to 2022

or "zigbee." We also find other concepts like "Industry 4.0," "machine learning," and "Internet," which contribute to the number of technology-oriented concepts. Next to that, novel considerations about sustainability appear, like "sustainable city" and "climate change," which are now completely related to the other concepts of the Smart Life domain.

3.3 Evolution of Smart Domains

The evolution of four Smart domains is illustrated in Table 3.1 covering the period from 1986 to 2022 (we should mention that the year 2022 is not complete as the study was done during 2022). The initial 21 years are aggregated into a single

Table 3.1 Smart domains evolution (from Kornyshova et al. 2022b)

Smart Life domains	1986–2006	2007	2008	2009	2010	2011	2012	2013	2014	2015	2016	2017	2018	2019	2020	2021	2022	Total
Persons	3	4	6	9	3	6	9	13	9	10	25	21	45	64	93	84	4	408
Smart healthcare	3	3	5	4	2	3	4	5	6	5	7	11	13	31	39	47	2	190
Smart home (Smart living)		1	1	4	1	2	5	8	3	4	18	9	27	29	45	33	1	191
Smart welfare				1		1				1		1	5	4	9	4	1	27
Society	1	1		1		1	2	4	6	13	23	37	50	107	89	100	5	440
Smart city	1	1		1		1	1	3	6	12	16	32	42	96	80	87	5	384
Smart											1	1		1				3
Smart court							1											1
Smart education										1	5	4	6	9	7	11		43
Smart island														1				1
Smart policing															1			1
Smart social media								1							1	1		3
Smart state											1							1
Smart village													2			1		3
Environment				1					1	3			1	2	2	6		16
Smart disaster management									1						1	3		5
Smart earth													1					1
Smart natural resource management				1						3				1	1	3		9
Smart space exploration														1				1
Enterprises		1		2	11	15	40	39	43	56	98	89	130	179	199	231	9	1142
Smart agriculture								1	2	1	2	9	8	12	26	41	2	104
Smart business management								1				2	5	10	15	24	3	60
Smart industry	7	1		2	11	14	38	37	37	50	91	72	108	137	137	145	4	891
Smart service industry									1		1	1		5	5	3		16
Smart transportation						1	2		3	5	4	5	9	15	16	18		78
Total by year	1	6	6	13	14	22	51	56	59	82	146	147	226	352	383	421	18	2013

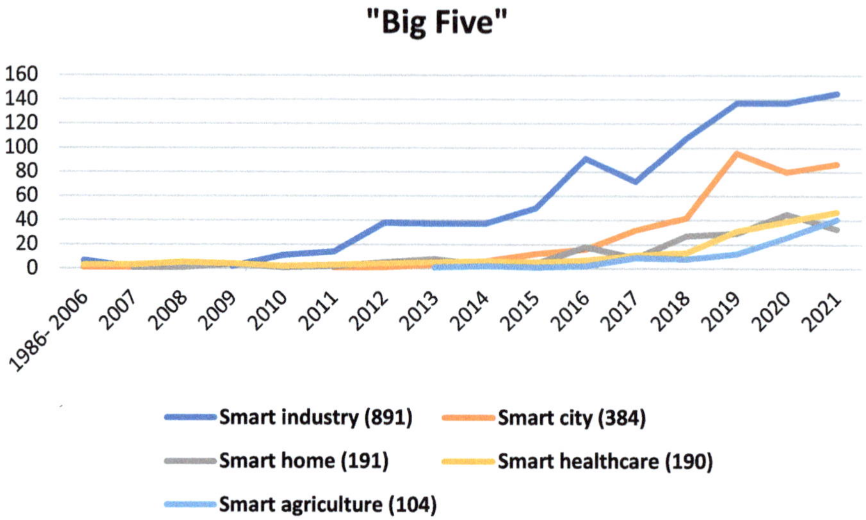

Fig. 3.6 Evolution over time of the five largest Smart applications

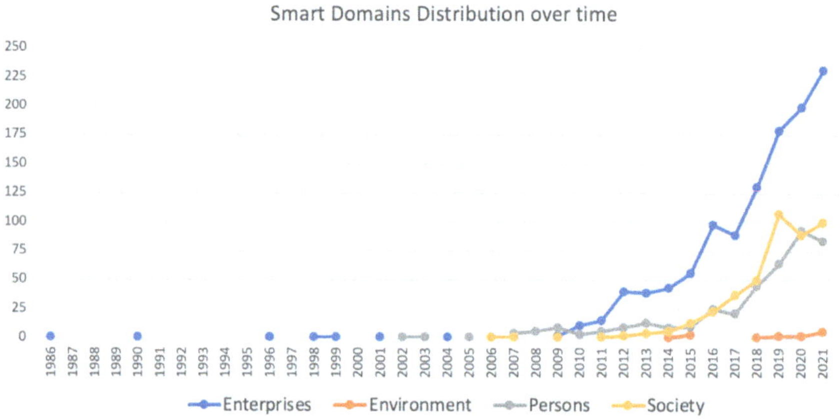

Fig. 3.7 Smart domains distribution over time

column due to the considerably low number of publications during this period. We complete this chronological perspective with two graphical representations, the first one highlighting the evolution of the five largest Smart applications (see Fig. 3.6) and the second one illustrating the distribution of Smart domains (see Fig. 3.7).

We can note that the earliest reviews in the literature focus on Smart applications for enterprises dating back before 2006. Subsequently, the literature shows an increasing interest in two other domains, Smart applications for persons and for society, particularly during the 2000s. More recently, Smart applications for environment came out more prominently.

We can identify the growth of the five most studied Smart applications as shown in Fig. 3.6. For instance, Smart industry and Smart city are the most popular and represented in 891 and 384 state-of-the-art or research agenda papers, respectively, in this 36-year period of time.

The evolution of the four Smart domains is shown in Fig. 3.7 (excluding papers of 2022 as the year was not complete for the study). Within the domain of Smart applications for enterprises (1142 papers), Smart industry dominates (891 papers), with a substantial focus on Smart energy-related topics, followed by Smart agriculture (104 papers), Smart transportation (78 papers), and Smart business management (60 papers).

Smart home and Smart healthcare are equally represented in Smart applications for persons (191 and 190 papers, respectively, over 408), with a smaller portion dedicated to Smart welfare.

Smart applications for environment are relatively limited, with only 16 papers; half of them focused on Smart natural resource management (nine papers).

Smart city dominates the Smart applications for society (384 papers out of 440), followed by Smart education (43 papers).

On the whole, the first works to appear on Smart applications were of the enterprises domain and still correspond to more than half the works published in the Smart Life field. Then we find the Smart applications for persons and society. The last domain, Smart applications for environment, began to appear in 2014.

3.4 Segmentation of the Smart Domains

Besides the evolution of the four domains over time, it is interesting to know the segmentation of the papers in each of the domains. Figure 3.8 shows this segmentation for each domain.

Smart applications for Enterprises are divided into five main types, as shown in Fig. 3.8a. The most dominant one is Smart industry (78% of the corpus), one of the Big Five (See Fig. 3.6) that comprises the Smart energy and Smart grid fields, which we already identified as really common Smart applications. We find then Smart agriculture, Smart transportation, and Smart business management. Finally, Smart service industry appear with only 1% of the corpus papers.

Smart applications for Persons are separated into three main types (Fig. 3.8b). Smart home and Smart healthcare applications take the best part of the share with 47% and 46% each. Smart welfare applications area come as a challenger in this domain with new Smart applications like Smart clothing or Smart sports.

Smart applications for Environment can be considered as belonging to four main types, as shown in Fig. 3.8c. Smart natural resource management applications are represented in more than half of the paper corpus (56%), with the increase of the environment problematics awareness. Smart disaster management applications share (32%) also shows a growing interest with increasingly frequent environmental disasters, such as repeated floods or fires.

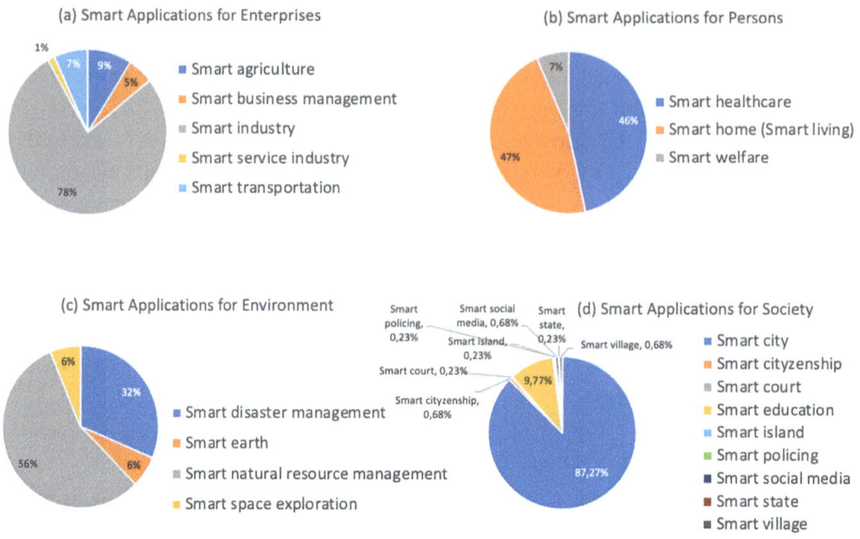

Fig. 3.8 Distribution of Smart applications (**a**) for enterprises, (**b**) for persons, (**c**) for environment, and (**d**) for society

Smart applications for Society (see Fig. 3.8d) is mainly concerned with Smart home applications, as it was one of the first Smart application to appear in the domain (87.27%). 9.77% of our paper corpus represent Smart healthcare applications. There are also a set of seven other Smart application types which appear on a marginal way (compared to these two first types).

3.5 Conclusion

In this chapter, we have looked at the evolution of the Smart Life area over time, both by closely examining the terms and concepts used in the corpus articles and through the lens of the four domains identified in the previous chapter: Smart applications for enterprises, for persons, for environment, and for society. This bibliographic study demonstrates that the research domain concerning Smart Life involves an increasingly diverse yet strongly interconnected range of fields. The huge expansion in the number of publications in the last decade indicates a growing interest among researchers in these issues, which also reflects a growing interest of our society in Smart Life.

References

Al-Shoqran, M., Shorman, S.: A review on smart universities and artificial intelligence. In: Studies in Computational Intelligence. (2021)

Chamee, Y.: Historicizing the smart cities: genealogy as a method of critique for smart urbanism. In: Telematics and Informatics, vol. 55. (2020)

Hidayat, T., Mahardiko, R., Franky, S., Tigor, D.: Method of systematic literature review for internet of things in ZigBee smart agriculture. In: 8th International Conference on Information and Communication Technology. (2020)

Kornyshova, E., Deneckere, R., Gressier-Soudan, E., Murray, J., Brinkkemper, S.: From smart life to smart life engineering: a systematic mapping study and research agenda. In: In: 15th International Baltic Conference on Digital Business and Intelligent Systems. Springer, Riga, Latvia (2022a)

Kornyshova, E., Deneckere, R., Sadouki, K., Gressier-Soudan, E., Brinkkemper, S.: Smart life: review of the contemporary smart applications. In: International Conference on Research Challenges in Information Science, pp. 302–318. (2022b)

Loganathan, N., Mayurappriyan, P.S., Lakshmi, K.: Smart energy management systems: a literature review. In: MATEC Web of Conferences. (2018)

Lutolf, R.: Smart home concept and the integration of energy meters into a home based system. In: 7th International Conference Metering Apparatus and Tariffs for Electricity Supply, pp. 277–278. (1992)

Mehraliyev, F., Chan, I., Cheng, C., Choi, Y., Koseoglu, M.A., Law, R.: A state-of-the-art review of smart tourism research. J. Travel Tour. Mark. (2020)

Chapter 4
A Review of Social, Behavioral, and Ethical Considerations for Smart Life Engineering

John Murray

Abstract Smart Life (SL) systems do not exist in a technological vacuum; they are embedded in a social ecosystem and have rich and complex interactions with their surroundings. It is important to recognize that their design and implementation will have an impact on the individuals and communities around them. This chapter examines the social, behavioral, and ethical issues to be considered in a holistic systems approach to SL engineering, to help practitioners and stakeholders to design the strategies needed for successful SL deployments. It addresses these topics from several disciplinary viewpoints and provides a comprehensive set of references for those requiring further detailed information.

Keywords Socio-technical systems · Engineering ethics · Human-centric design

4.1 Introduction

In the process of examining the key tenets of Smart Life (SL) engineering—or indeed any comprehensive technological infrastructure—it is important to recognize that these technologies do not exist in a vacuum but are embedded in the host environment or social ecosystem. They influence, and are influenced by, contextual settings that involve autonomous elements and independent actors whose behaviors and interactions with the infrastructure are often unpredictable and difficult to model. At the center of these so-called externalities are of course humans, both as individuals and as groups or communities.

The purpose of this chapter is to explore the various forms of human and societal interactions within and among the major elements of this ecosystem, to identify some of the core requirements for designing and deploying SL systems in this context, and to help structure the plans and policies for administering and guiding them successfully.

J. Murray (✉)
San José State University, California, USA
e-mail: jxm@acm.org

E. Kornyshova et al. (eds.), *Smart Life and Smart Life Engineering*,
https://doi.org/10.1007/978-3-031-75887-4_4

The next section describes a *system-level approach to SL Engineering*, which emerges from a heritage that includes cyber-physical systems, ubiquitous computing, and socio-technical systems, among others. That is followed by a discussion of the *ethical design requirements* and the techniques and principles that have been successfully implemented by various practitioners.

The succeeding section examines several key issues related to *system control, safety, and security* of SL systems. These concerns include the vulnerability of systems to cyberattacks and tampering, the importance of strong leadership at the policy-making level, as well as the typically inadequate sensitivity to data quality and provenance.

The next area to consider is the topic of *accessibility to Smart Life applications*. While civil rights policies and legislation are in place to mitigate discrimination against those with disabilities in the physical environment, there is still considerable work to be done to provide equivalent accessibility in the digital domain.

This is followed by a discussion of the *ethical concerns with Smart military systems*, which includes some notes on the relevant parallels and technical applicability of particular features to the safety and security of SL systems in a civilian environment.

The topic of *engineering education and ethics awareness* is then addressed, with some suggestions and proposals for pedagogical strategy, curriculum content, and professional certifications.

The final area to be covered is a brief summary of the regulatory landscape for *oversight of SL human research ethics*. This section outlines the context and challenges for ethics oversight committees when social studies research is part of their purview.

The chapter is rounded out with some overall conclusions, followed by author acknowledgments and references.

4.2 System-Level Approach to Smart Life Engineering

An important consideration in the exploration of Smart Life engineering is the development of a comprehensive systems approach to technologies being deployed. Such technologies do not exist in a vacuum but are embedded in the host environment or social ecosystem. They influence, and are influenced by, a contextual setting that may be more or less controlled, more or less chaotic, and more or less hostile or benign.

In this respect, SL engineering draws upon an extensive heritage of several longstanding fields of engineering research and practice, as well as human behavioral studies. These include early work on cybernetics and society (Wiener 1954), human augmentation (Engelbart 1962), and socio-technical systems (Emery & Trist 1960), together with ubiquitous computing or ubicomp (Weiser 1993), cyber-physical systems (Talcott 2008), and cyber-physical-social systems (Reine et al. 2021). Not to mention the many recent deployments of AI-based technologies across numerous sectors, especially those involving extensive edge computing capabilities.

In order to characterize the domain of SL engineering, we can use the extensive work in these disciplines to inspire the strategies needed to interpret and understand these systems. But what are the core differences between these various heritage fields and the smart life of today? In pursuit of these answers, we can identify several key connected features of interest.

Digital vs Physical One important element relates to the direct physical manifestations of "smartness." For example, the development of tangible computing enables hybrid interfaces to be designed, which take advantage of the fact that digital and physical resources have different and complementary properties (Fraser et al. 2018).

Ubicomp, often referred to as pervasive computing (Satyanarayanan 2001), traditionally centered upon the conceptual separation of digital and physical materials, but innovative manufacturing techniques have enabled the deployment of information processing capabilities in new embodiments.

Form vs. Function As new types of functional materials gain prominence, the differences in the *form* of a product, which is traditionally physical, and its *function*, which is traditionally digital, become increasingly difficult to separate across the physical-digital divide. This change has important effects on users' interactions with such technologies, since the system outputs to users, and its sensing of their inputs, are predominantly in the physical domain.

As an example, the production of nano-fabrics using stimuli-responsive polymers enabled the development of smart clothing and sensing systems, which has implications for entirely new design principles that emphasize combining physical manifestations of form and function (Dang and Zhao 2021, Haque 2019).

This work derives from an extensive research background in the use of electroactive polymers for human performance augmentation, in particular in support of prosthetic devices such as artificial muscles (Chiba et al. 2006). As with 3-D printing, the traditional consumer product design themes of economy, agency, creativity, and sustainability become significantly disrupted by innovative fabrication techniques.

Participatory Design For a long time, numerous public programs involving socio-technical systems have emphasized the need for stakeholder participation from the early stages of the proposed system design (Schuler & Namioka 1993). This approach has its origins in 1970s Scandinavia, where user involvement and cooperative design became particularly prevalent. This was especially the case in situations where automation and computer technologies were being introduced in many workplaces (Ehn & Kyng 1987).

The expansion of this type of collaborative design to broader communities offers some useful insights for SL engineering. For example, the Array of Things (AoT) project in Chicago, Illinois, incorporates several key features concerning community involvement (Catlett et al. 2020). At the core of the AoT project was the deployment of an urban-scale intelligent measurement system, which centered upon the application of software-defined sensors to understand urban activity patterns and support social and behavioral science investigations. The advantage of software-defined sensors is that it's not necessary to define all possible measurements prior to building and installing devices.

Environmental Observations While common sensor networks are relatively straightforward to build and scale, closely involving the community draws attention to the need for both traditional sensor data acquisition and new types of measurements—*observations*—that require extensive edge computing capabilities. Processing images within the devices enhances the opportunities to maintain stricter privacy norms, since data can be interpreted and acted upon without the need to rely on telemetry streaming to central servers for remote analysis. As was the case in with the AoT project, much attention needs to be paid to privacy and ethics considerations.

In essence, these types of projects can deploy general-purpose sensing platforms that may be tuned to the needs of individual communities. This provided considerable flexibility to the project organizers, enabling them to dynamically address and accommodate the particular issues and interests of specific districts. For example, residents of some AoT neighborhoods expressed concerns about air quality and/or noise, whereas other communities were in need of better data about traffic-related activities.

The Urban Wellbeing Project is another innovative use of sensing network data to gain insights into the relationships between environmental conditions and human health (Johnson & Kanjo 2023). In this case, a smartphone app accessed local air quality and noise sensor data in Nottingham, UK, and combined it with dynamic surveys of the user's momentary mental well-being. The research demonstrated the community health effects of busy, polluted, and green spaces, as well as impacts of poor air quality and loud ambient noise on perceptions of negative well-being.

4.3 Ethical Design Requirements

The proliferation of open-source software and auto-generated programming has introduced broad opportunities for non-proprietary, non-classically engineered software development. The result is a critical need for research to support rigorous assessment of such software to minimize vulnerabilities and protect against malicious alteration upon its deployment. As the ACM technical policy advisors have noted:

> Innovations in the tools and techniques for rigorously defining design requirements for software, hardware, and data – and for assuring that those requirements are correctly implemented – have significant potential for enhancing the security and trustworthiness of critical components of the digital ecosystem. (ACM 2023)

This assertion raises the question of whether we're really talking just about *engineering* anymore. The salient answer is no, it's more about *design*. Clearly, among the design requirements is the need to develop more awareness of ethical implications during the design phase of SL systems, rather than trying to incorporate those concerns later as an afterthought.

In the context of SL environments, we are concerned with dynamic networks of technology agents, some of which may have some form of autonomy, possibly because there are active software socio-cognitive agents purposely participating within the SL system. Alternatively, it is possible that the underlying infrastructure incorporates some type of agency, perhaps by actively producing unexpected user outcomes, or because third parties may deliberately or unintentionally interact with the system.

It is therefore desirable to find a design strategy that can be used to attend to such ethical issues when designing these types of environments. A potential candidate is value-sensitive design (VSD) (Friedman et al. 2017), which provides a theoretically grounded approach to the design of technology that accounts for human values in a principled and systematic manner throughout the process. VSD incorporates a suite of design methods focused upon identifying particular values in technology, which serve such purposes as stakeholder identification and legitimation, value representation and elicitation, and values analysis.

However, a salient shortcoming of VSD is that unintended principles can often be immersed, typically unconsciously, in technological artifacts during a system design and development phases. The process lacks a specific critical reflection activity to help expose such unconscious inscription of values. To overcome this limitation, principles of *Conscientious Design* (*CD*) (Noriega et al. 2021) have been proposed; they are underpinned by ethical and social values and extend the approach used by the VSD research framework.

In particular, CD responds to three key properties of conscientiousness; *thoroughness*, *mindfulness*, and *responsibility*. These are summarized in Table 4.1.

CD also draws inspiration from other well-established human-centric design practices, including Alexander's "habitable spaces" in physical architecture (Alexander 1979) and Deming's evolutionary approach to total quality management (TQM), with the goal of achieving product excellence over time (Deming 1982).

In support of this integration of physical and social elements, CD describes IT-enabled systems that (1) afford collective activities involving individuals, both human or artificial, (2) reason about the ethical aspects of social interaction, and (3) can act within a stable shared social space. This is essentially equivalent to socio-technical systems and is also an appropriate characterization of Smart Life systems. Conscientious design provides a useful means for mapping ethical design principles for building trustworthy autonomous and intelligent systems that conform to broader international initiatives for ethical alignment, such as those from the European Union and the IEEE (EU HLEG 2019, IEEE 2019).

Table 4.1 The key principles of *conscientious design*

Property	Definition	Techniques entailed
Thoroughness	The system is provably technically correct; all the requirements have been properly identified and faithfully implemented	Appropriate formal methods, tools, accurate system modelling, simulations, digital twins, and proper use of verification tools
Mindfulness	Supra-functional features provide users with awareness of the characteristics of the system and the possibility of selecting a satisfactory tailoring to individual needs or preferences	Incorporated techniques should include ergonomics, governance, coherence of purpose and means, identification of side effects, no hidden agency, and the avoidance of unnecessary affordances
Responsibility	Leadership is empowered to honor commitments, and responsiveness to stake-holders' legitimate interests is required. This responsibility applies both to individual users and participants, as well as the obligations involving society in general	Required features include scrutability, transparency, and accountability, alongside a proper support of privacy, a "right to forget"; proper handling of identity and ownership, liabilities, and proper risk allocation; and support of values like justice, fairness, and trustworthiness

4.4 System Control, Safety, and Cybersecurity

All Smart Life systems interact in some manner with the world and its human occupants, and any autonomous SL system would need to be able to reason using some sort of underlying world model, in order to make coherent and sensible decisions. Undertaking this type of analysis involves sophisticated logical processes, such as causality and counterfactuals, which form the groundwork for ethical reasoning and explainability (Pearl & Mackenzie 2018). Such capabilities would typically be extensions beyond what is needed to support the primary functions of the SL system.

For example, a fully autonomous road vehicle needs coherent decision-making guidelines to arbitrate among conflicting collision warnings. The uncoordinated approach to regulating autonomous vehicles, along with the legal wrangling after injury accidents, demonstrates the significant shortcomings in this area (Thadani 2023). The process for "optimizing" the outcomes of an impending serious accident may involve moral and ethical dilemmas that SL systems are ill-equipped to handle (Kulicki et al. 2018).

Here are some key safety and risk issues of concern for Smart Life systems:

Ad Hoc Loosely Coupled Networks: The ecosystem of most SL systems spans multiple organizations and diverse stakeholder entities and groups. As a result, a common outcome of SL technical integration projects is a predominantly ad hoc, loosely coupled network of many autonomous subsystems of varying quality and provenance. In this context, little attention is often paid to issues of system-wide maintenance, reliability, and safety.

For a long time, *failure modes and effects analysis* (FMEA) strategies provide approaches to addressing these issues (Stamatis 2019, Paté-Cornell, 2002). FMEA is a common method of interpreting the behavior of a complex, centrally managed system and often places particular emphasis on stakeholder consultation and impacts. However, it is less used with highly distributed, locally managed federated systems, like those envisioned in Smart Life engineering.

Humans-in-the-Loop: Consumer electronics product developers largely ignore the human users and operators in the loop, when framing safety and cybersecurity solutions in real-world situations. For example, Kukkala et al. (2022) provide a comprehensive technical roadmap for strengthening cybersecurity in autonomous transportation systems, yet the work makes no meaningful reference to "users" or "humans" at all.

This type of omission motivates the need for a human-centric approach to cybersecurity, in particular by shifting focus from "humans as a problem" to "humans as a solution." An example of such a strategy is the *security and privacy preserving* model, as proposed by Rohan et al. (2022), which illustrates how a human-centric approach is initiated, explains its important components, and demonstrates how security and privacy can be preserved with a human focus. Essentially, user interactions with IoT systems are examined using a four-layer framework that addresses discovery, inference, choice, and communication. See Table 4.2.

Cyberattack Portals: The potential for Internet of Things (IoT) devices and other SL network elements being used as portals for cyberattacks is significant. There is a clear need for better resilience under adversarial conditions, yet the topic often receives little or no attention in the IoT engineering community. Given the extent to which modern civil and military infrastructures and economies rely on digital technologies and embedded systems, it is likely that any future great-power war will probably start with a comprehensive and coordinated set of cyberstrikes. The pervasive use of generic, ill-secured IoT devices in many cyber-physical systems

Table 4.2 Security and privacy preserving framework, structuring the relationship that humans have with IoT devices and services

Layer	Factors of concern
Discovery	How does a person discover the presence of IoT devices and services in their surroundings? What data is being collected about them, and what privacy properties are applicable in the vicinity?
Inference	What inferences can a person make from the information provided in the discovery layer? How do they interpret the effects of this data collection on their personal security and privacy?
Choice	How can the person be helped with regard to making decisions about their preferences? What is the process for expressing these preferences?
Communication	What is the nature of the communication between the IoT device or service? What notifications or alerts are appropriate, and how are they expressed?

render them vulnerable to attacks and has led to numerous calls for mandating better resilience and improved security measures.

Data Provenance: Cybersecurity professionals have pointed out that most regulatory strategy to date, in the domain of embedded systems, has focused on the safety and security of critical physical infrastructure, with little or no attention paid to the reliability and provenance of the incoming data being used to support that those systems (ACM 2023).

For example, conventional digital signatures are not routinely used for data authentication or provenance. It is important to ensure that decision support systems are sensitive to the characteristics of the data they process, for example, to check whether input data was compromised or of low quality. In addition, for most systems, it's not clear how to provide resiliency when a data source has been found to be compromised.

Cultural and Legal Issues: There are extensive cultural and legal issues related to the control and access to SL data products and related surveillance information (Zuboff 2019). It is clear that perceptions of personal data ownership and rights differ substantially between the United States, the European Union, and the People's Republic of China. On the other hand, SL systems can empower communities that are underserved or ignored by governing authorities, enabling them to take grassroots action to improve their living conditions. For example, the Ushahidi (2023) open-source platform provides crowdsourcing and mapping resources to communities seeking gather and report real-time information about safety problems and hazards in their neighborhoods.

Chief Information Security Officer (CISO): The leadership role of the CSIO or equivalent is pivotal in overseeing cybersecurity policies across an entire municipal administration or network of agencies. The task of coordinating such strategies must be managed at the highest echelons of the organization, yet the CISO typically lacks the authority and resources to mandate cybersecurity requirements within and among the various departments and agencies (SIW 2023). Even in commercial businesses where the ultimate responsibility lies with the corporate board of directors, the CISO's ability to influence decisions is usually quite modest, in comparison to the clout of the chief financial officer or the vice presidents of the individual operational units. The development and maintenance of loosely coupled networks of departmental champions across the organization is often the best approach to addressing this challenge (Metcalf et al. 2019).

In summary, the key role of ethical sensitivity in treating the human element when defining and managing safety and security for SL engineering cannot be overstated.

4.5 Accessibility of Smart Life Applications

In the area of accessibility, it is important to ensure that Smart Life design and engineering professionals are provided with adequate resources to implement accessible systems. The domain offers particularly valuable opportunities for innovative accessibility design, because of its close integration with the built environment.

There are already social and legislative responsibilities in place for preventing discrimination and exclusion in the physical world on the basis of impairment or disability. For example, discrimination occurs when a person with limited mobility cannot access transportation systems, government offices, or business premises.

Numerous regulations are already in place to mitigate the "socially created disadvantage and marginalization" experienced when someone with accessibility challenges is treated differently and less favorably due to their impairment (Lawson & Beckett 2021). Civil rights and equality laws and policies, including the US Americans with Disabilities Act, prohibit discrimination on the basis of disability (ADA 2010).

Taking this situation in the built environment as a starting point, it is important to examine the gaps in designing the digital world that lead to inaccessible technology and disability discrimination (Horton 2022).

The four key capability areas for attention are the visual, hearing, cognitive, and motor domains. Although there are still no formal regulatory frameworks in place yet, a well-established suite of solid building blocks is already available to support accessibility professionalism across all four of these areas in the digital environment.

For example, in 2012, the International Organization for Standardization published ISO/IEC 40500 that identifies the specifications and requirements for supporting accessibility in digital resources. This standard, which is based upon Web Content Accessibility Guidelines (Kirkpatrick et al. 2018), provides the measures used to assess compliance with nondiscrimination laws and policies. Unfortunately, these standards are not yet widely recognized among technology professionals.

In the healthcare arena, a useful taxonomy and architecture for accessibility to IoT devices has been developed (Lopes 2020). The architecture encompasses the perspectives of healthcare stakeholders and other generic requirements. There is good scope for extending these types of resources for applicability to broader areas of SL engineering.

There are a number of outreach initiatives focused on advancing accessibility awareness in education and professional development. These include curriculum development, mentoring, and advocacy, to address industry demands for accessibility skills. For example, TeachAccess has developed a strategic plan that addresses the digital accessibility skills gap (TeachAccess 2021). Similarly, Teaching Accessibility in the Digital Skillset (TeachingAccessibility 2022) is undertaking research on developing effective accessibility teaching pedagogy and related curriculum resources that will be applicable across multiple technology disciplines.

In addition, several influential organizations provide professional certification programs on accessibility topics in digital and built environments. These include the International Association of Accessibility Professionals (2023) and the US Department of Homeland Security (2023). However, these types of specialist certification do not address the need for core competency in accessibility across technology design and engineering professions.

4.6 Ethical Concerns with Smart Military Systems

Descriptions of technical equipment and systems that are designed for law enforcement and military applications introduce additional nuances of the term *smart*. In some cases, the term is used primarily for marketing and promotional purposes, rather than any inherent sophisticated quality of smartness. For example, a *Smart bullet* is essentially a miniaturized version of a precision-guided missile that relies on a laser or other directing system to identify its target (Barrett 1997). Similarly, the term *Smart gun* may be used to describe a weapon equipped with user sensing technology, such as fingerprint recognition or RFID tagging, to ensure that only an authorized individual can activate it.

On the other hand, equipment intended for the projection of disabling or lethal force may also be described as smart, for example, when they include functionality to reduce or eliminate accidental fratricide or "friendly fire." Similarly, remotely guided weapon systems or robotic drones often incorporate capabilities, such as target recognition features, so that they can operate autonomously in particular combat situations.

Smart military assets typically operate as networked clusters or linked devices that communicate their status and coordinate their actions. For example, the ability of smart surveillance systems to disambiguate multiple sightings of the same enemy resource helps reduce battlefield confusion, and the use of sensor fusion improves the accuracy of identifying intended targets. In this regard, the concept of "smartness" may therefore be thought of as existing across the network, as in other cyber-physical systems, rather than residing in individual self-managing units (Zhang 2014).

In the case of fully autonomous weapon systems (AWS), some key ethical considerations center upon aspirations to apply situation awareness judgement principles in the absence of timely human-in-the-loop capabilities. There has been widespread discussion concerning the extent to which AI-based systems could ever reach a level of sophistication that made them better than humans at making moral judgments (Purves et al. 2015, Lorca Albareda 2024). On the other hand, it is possible that an AWS could be trained to avoid engaging putative noncombatants, only to use proportional, less-than-lethal force, and never to attack retreating or defenseless combatants. From an ethical standpoint, the core question is what data sources would be used to train such systems and, more to the point, who gets to decide which datasets would be used (Cogley 2017). The same ethical reasoning applies equally to non-military SL systems, where autonomous decision-making may impact the well-being of any stakeholders and bystanders alike.

The potential for cyberstrikes on military systems is as significant, or perhaps greater, than other civilian SL systems. But beyond these issues, there are also particular concerns about ensuring that smart military equipment can be neutralized or disabled if it is in danger of falling into enemy hands. A further refinement of this requirement is the ability to reconfigure autonomous networked equipment and modify functionality to reflect changing political priorities and accommodate adjusting alliances among partner forces.

On a broader front, there is also a requirement to reconfigure or repurpose technical systems when military command structures need to be rearranged. Dynamic changes to the *unit task organization* become necessary when individual elements or subgroups become incapacitated or have to be reassigned or merged for operational reasons (Donnelly 2011). The ability to easily modify the relationships among semi-autonomous devices, and to adjust corresponding roles and responsibilities among them, has clear advantages for managing many Smart Life systems, well beyond the strictly military command and control networks.

Finally, there are significant impediments to introduce innovative new technologies into military systems, because of the burdensome and bureaucratic procurement processes involved (Clifton & Copeland 2008). This has led to calls for adopting a broader, stakeholder-centric *design studio* approach to seek out novel concepts and to develop and simulate smart systems using processes that are ten times faster than the current acquisition procedures (Schmidt 2023).

In conclusion, although some unique requirements are associated with designing and deploying smart military systems, there are many operational features and challenges that have parallels in civilian SL systems. We would do well to understand the techniques and solutions used, to learn from them, and to improve the safety and security of all smart systems.

4.7 Engineering Education and Ethics Awareness

Topics in professional ethics have long been an educational staple in fields involving proficiency certification or licensing, including medicine, law, and business. In addition, as noted earlier, there are research ethics awareness and oversight requirements for many studies involving human subjects, especially those relating to the approval of medical devices or clinical trials.

In the broader technology domain, it is almost 70 years since Jacques Ellul (1954) presented a penetrating analysis of how *la technique* transitions from a support system for humankind into an ongoing deployment of dominating systems that are solely intended to meet their own ends. Likewise, the technology ethics community has been actively promoting the moral aspects of automation for quite some time (Sullins 2011).

Yet until recently, the general topic of professional ethics was marginalized or ignored completely in most standard engineering and computer science curriculums. Although model syllabuses and quality course materials are widely available (De Witte 2022), they have rarely been mandated as part of the core requirements for completion of degree programs in engineering and computer science.

In discussing the lecture series *Ethics for Nerds* at Saarland University, Baum and Stern (2022) observe that students of computer science and related subjects should receive at least a basic ethical education to be able to do justice to their ever-growing responsibilities and duties. They describe experiences with and best practices of their teaching approach and offer advice on how to design a successful ethics course as part of a computer science study program.

There is a need for increased attention by product developers of the human context in complex systems. A key design strategy is to emphasize *human-machine teaming* rather than basic user interaction modeling (Ozkaya 2020). Using effective teaming models implies having a shared awareness of the task, team, and operational situation, as well as a common interpretation of the intended end goals to be achieved.

It is important to recognize the behavioral science of software engineering from a professional education point of view. An important feature of this strategy is to ensure that expectations of trust, ethics, and privacy should be prioritized from the start of any system design process. This should not be difficult since once the human context is introduced into the curriculum, topics like ethics and trust almost "slip in" through the backdoor, as it were.

A useful ethically oriented technique for characterizing the level of community involvement in technology projects is provided by a research team from INRIA in France (Anderson and Fort, 2022). Specifically, the approach focuses upon three dimensions of human participation in such projects—inclusion, guidance, and persistence (IGP). This strategy seeks to replace the much-overused term *human-in-the-loop*, originally coined more than 65 years ago (Bennett 1957), which has been continuously redefined to suit whatever fashionable command-and-control decision-making policies and regulations need to be promoted.

The INRIA authors note that there is a logical contradiction inherent in the original intent behind the terminology that hinders an appropriate ethics-centric framework. Inspired by the work of Bruno Latour (2008), they observe that just as the provenance of the technological object can be forgotten, the incorporation of a human as a simple component of the loop also trivializes the role that the individual plays within the community that is creating and operating the technology.

The IGP approach seeks to move away from an attitude that assume human oversight from *outside* of the technology toward direct participation *in* the creation of the technology. It lays the foundation for a more meaningful ethical engagement in the project, where community members are dynamically engaged in the technology producing process. Mere oversight by humans is thus transformed into active *guidance* as an involved community, which transforms the negative perspective of seeking to removes humans when possible.

Table 4.3 IGP template for accessing levels of community involvement in technology projects

IGP term	Level	Definition
Inclusion	Replaceable	Technology community views a human as replaceable by any other human
	Experienced	Technology community views human as experienced in multiple activities
	Unique	Technology community develops technology around a human's unique skills and life context
Guidance	Tester	Human's use of system is merely "registered" (passive)
	Trainer	Human's suggestions regarding system are implemented
	Designer	Human designs complex parts of the system with others
Persistence	Brief	Human initiates or contributes to an abstracted phase of a technology community
	Sustained	Human contributes to the actions of a technology community up to the completion of the technology community's goals
	Evolving	Human contributes to the process of a technology community as it overlaps and weaves into different technology communities beyond itself

Table 4.3 summarizes a candidate set of IGP ranges that could be used for this purpose.

Steen (2023) provides a useful model curriculum for participatory and iterative reflection, inquiry, and deliberation on ethical issues in product development, both to better understand the problem and to envision and create solutions. The model promotes design process elements drawn from responsible innovation (Stilgoe et al. 2013) that involves people with diverse backgrounds and types of expertise, as well as individuals representing groups of citizens or societal organizations.

Another practical framework for discussing ethical concerns with smart systems is provided by Singh et al. (2023). Specifically, they represent smart cities as sociotechnical systems and model stakeholder values along multiple ethical dimensions using moral foundations theory (Graham et al. 2013).

Finally, in terms of resources for raising general public awareness of the ethical considerations for Smart Life systems, the European Union has published a set of educator guidelines on the use of AI and data in teaching (European Commission 2022). These include issues related to human agency, fairness, human dignity, and justified choice.

4.8 Oversight of Smart Life Research Ethics

The importance of ethical oversight and reviews is well understood in many areas of human participant research, particularly in fields like pharmaceutical studies or medical device design. In 1979, following a series of high-profile research studies in the United States that involved unethical treatment of individual participants, the

Belmont Report established the ethical principles and guidelines for human subject research (US DEHEW 1979). That became the foundation for a comprehensive set of guidelines and standards, which include special provisions to protect vulnerable populations like institutionalized individuals, children, prisoners, etc. Corresponding regulations have been implemented internationally and enable life sciences research to be undertaken ethically and efficiently across multiple jurisdictions. As an example, the process for undertaking international clinical trials for products like vaccines are well-known and widely understood.

However, in social science research, processes for ethical oversight and guidance are much less well coordinated. In the United States, institutional review board (IRB) approval is needed for human research supported by governments or private foundations. Nevertheless, when it comes to collaboration between academic research institutions and for-profit corporations, IRBs may simply step away from their oversight responsibilities for individual sensitivity and vigilance regarding personal privacy issues.

For example, in 2012, the Cornell University IRB considered Facebook's Emotional Contagion Study to be beyond its purview, although the feelings of over 600,000 users were deliberately manipulated without their consent by the social network company (Kramer et al. 2014).

Furthermore, the extent to which ethics oversight committees in non-US jurisdictions consider social studies research as part of their purview is very inconsistent (Murray et al. 2012, Murray & Fairfield 2014), and in any case, there is a persisting need for ethics committees to have better understanding of the technical risks, especially when it comes to managing data privacy and security (Huh-Yoo et al. 2021). The Menlo Report, which was published in 2012, was intended to address these shortcomings, but progress on implementation has been slow (Bailey et al. 2012). More recently, the Ada Lovelace Institute has published materials for promoting technical expertise and support for research ethics committees (Strait 2023).

There have also been ongoing concerns in the computer science community about who should be responsible for ensuring proper ethical oversight of human-related research. Conference program committees have frequently mandated that any ethics issues are properly documented and addressed as an acceptance condition for presentation and publication of papers (Allman 2008). However, by the time the study is complete and the findings are ready for publication, it is typically much too late to address any individual or group harms that were caused.

Numerous professional associations and consulting organizations in the technology field have voluntary codes of ethical conduct that apply to their members, but they frequently lack adequate powers of for meaningful enforcement. Likewise, when it comes to social studies research undertaken by commercial enterprises and private corporations, there are no regulatory requirements that correspond to those for IRBs. In the case of technology product-related research undertaken by business ventures, some firms have voluntarily implemented ethics oversight procedures (see, e.g., Jackman & Kanerva 2016). The underlying problem for the private sector is that such research ethics regulations and guidelines are not well structured to simply port them over to a product development environment. In particular, they are not designed to track downstream consequences over impacted populations and do not support the iterative product development and deployment cycles used by technology enterprises (Moss & Metcalf 2020).

In general, corporate approaches to research ethics oversight have been quite ad hoc and, in the case of social media companies, have sometimes been implemented primarily as a result of adverse publicity. As a result, an agreed-upon consistent strategy or set of guidelines for reviewing this type of research has yet to emerge, although the Future of Privacy Forum has developed a promising candidate (Tene & Polonetsky 2016). The multi-part framework identifies the data or other material to be reviewed, when would a review be conducted and by whom, and what principles should apply. It also discusses the extent to which research using non-personally identifiable information should also be subject to oversight.

More recently, some initial work has been undertaken to measure the level of ethical awareness among corporate data scientists (Weaver 2022). However, further research is required to solidly validate the instruments used in that study.

The message here for Smart Life research is that significant attention needs to be paid to the personal and societal effects of studies that are intended to assess the effects and impacts of SL technologies, in particular upon individuals and groups who are unaware of the experimental nature of their exposure to the systems.

4.9 Conclusions

The material in this chapter has provided an introductory view of some key Smart Life engineering issues from different social and behavioral standpoints. As Steen (2023) has pointed out, the process of *doing ethics* is a participatory and iterative activity, involving thoughtful reflection, inquiry, and deliberation. A system-level approach to SL engineering helps situate this activity, by empowering practitioners to explore diverse perspectives, question implicit design assumptions, and explore the relationships between overall stakeholder experiences and underlying technical decisions and trade-offs.

The so-called *soft-science* topics of human-centric values and ethics can sometimes be challenging for highly technical experts and specialists to grapple with. The need to contend with design questions that have no provably correct answers, and value trade-offs that have no demonstrably optimal solutions, often does not come naturally to skilled practitioners in the hard sciences. Unlike our colleagues in medicine and law, the engineering profession lacks a historically strong tradition of formally incorporating studies of human-centric values and ethics in the process of formative education and career progression. Yet the awareness of such issues is crucial for the successful deployment of complex socio-technical Smart Life systems that are embedded in the real world.

It is anticipated that this chapter's material and the comprehensive reference list will be helpful to those needing further insights and guidance.

Acknowledgments The helpful assistance and feedback from reviewers of earlier drafts of this chapter are gratefully recognized. The author acknowledges the funding support for this work that has been provided by Linqto Inc. (www.linqto.com) and Incióna LLC (www.inciona.com).

References

ACM: USTPC response to the USG request for information on the 2023 Federal Cybersecurity Research and Development Strategic Plan (2023). https://www.acm.org/binaries/content/assets/public-policy/ustpc-cybersec-comments.pdf

ADA: Americans with Disabilities Act Title III Regulations, [Online] (2010). Available: https://www.ada.gov/regs2010/titleIII_2010/titleIII_2010_regulations.htm

Alexander, C.: The Timeless Way of Building, vol. 1. Oxford University Press (1979)

Allman, M.: What ought a program committee to do? In: Proceedings of Conference on Organizing Workshops, Conferences, and Symposia for Computer Systems, pp. 1–5. USENIX Association, Berkeley (2008)

Anderson, M., Fort, K.: Human where? A new scale defining human involvement in technology communities from an ethical standpoint: ethics in the age of smart systems. International Review of Information Ethics. **31**(1) (2022)

Bailey, M., Dittrich, D., Kenneally, E., Maughan, D.: The Menlo report. IEEE Security & Privacy. **10**(2), 71–75 (2012). https://doi.org/10.1109/MSP.2012.52

Barrett, R.: Guided Bullet. US Patent 5788178-A (1997). https://patents.google.com/patent/US5788178A/

Baum, K., Stern, S.: Ethics for nerds. Int. Rev. Inf. Ethics. **31**(08) (2022)

Bennet, C.: Some experimentation on the tie-in of the human operator to the control loop of an airborne navigational digital computer system. In: IRE-ACM-AIEE '57 (Eastern), 1957, pp. 68–71 (1957). https://doi.org/10.1145/1457720.1457732

Catlett, C., et al.: Measuring cities with software-defined sensors. Journal of Social Computing. **1**(1), 14–27 (2020) ISSN 2688-5255ll02/06ll. https://arrayofthings.github.io/

Chiba, S., et al.: Electroactive polymer artificial muscle. JRSJ. **24**(4), 38–42 (2006)

Clifton, N., Copeland, D.: The Land Warrior Soldier System: a Case Study for the Acquisition of Soldier Systems, MBA Professional Report. Naval Postgraduate School (2008)

Cogley, Z.: Future autonomous weapons will make moral judgments. In: Leben, D., et al. (eds.) Proc. of Intl Assn for Computing and Philosophy Annual Meeting, June 26–28, Stanford CA (2017)

Dang, T., Zhao, M.: The application of smart fibers and smart textiles. J. Phys. Conf. Ser. **1790**, 012084 (2021). https://doi.org/10.1088/1742-6596/1790/1/012084

De Witte, M.: A New Program at Stanford Is Embedding Ethics into Computer Science. Stanford Engineering (2022) https://engineering.stanford.edu/magazine/new-program-stanford-embedding-ethics-computer-science

Deming, W.: Quality, Productivity, and Competitive Position. MIT Press (1982)

Donnelly, R.: Impact of the network on a common operating environment. In: MILCOM Military Comms Conf, Baltimore MD (2011). https://doi.org/10.1109/MILCOM.2011.6127521

Ehn, P., Kyng, M.: The collective resource approach to systems design. In: Computers and Democracy - A Scandinavian Challenge, pp. 17–58. Avebury, Aldershot (1987)

Ellul, J.: The Technological Society. Vintage, New York (1954)

Emery, F., Trist, L.: Socio-technical systems. In: Churchman, C.W., Verhulst, M. (eds.) Management science: models and techniques. Pergamon, London (1960)

Engelbart, D.: Augmenting Human Intellect: A Conceptual Framework. SRI Summary Report AFOSR-3223. Director of Information Sciences, US Air Force Office of Scientific Research (1962)

EU HLEG: Ethics Guidelines for Trustworthy AI. High-Level Expert Group on AI (2019)

European Commission: Ethical Guidelines on the Use of Artificial Intelligence (AI) and Data in Teaching and Learning for Educators. Directorate-General for Education, Youth, Sport and Culture. Pubs Office of the EU. Pubs Office of the EU (2022) https://data.europa.eu/doi/10.2766/153756

Fraser, M., et al.: Digital-Is-Physical: How Functional Fabrication Disrupts Ubicomp Design Principles, Woodstock '18, June 03–05. Woodstock, New York (2018)

Friedman, B., et al.: A survey of value sensitive design methods. Foundations and Trends in Human-Computer Interaction. **11**(23), 63–125 (2017)

Graham, J., et al.: Moral foundations theory: the pragmatic validity of moral pluralism. In: Advances in Experimental Social Psychology, vol. 47, pp. 55–130. Academic Press (2013)

Haque, M.: Nano fabrics in the 21st century: a review. Asian J. Nanosci. Mater. **2**(2), 131–148 (2019)

Horton, S.: Building an accessible digital world. IEEE Comput. **55**(1), 98–102 (2022)

Huh-Yoo, J., Kadri, R., Buis, L.: Pervasive healthcare IRBs and ethics reviews in research: going beyond the paperwork. IEEE Pervasive Comput. **20**(1), 40–44 (2021)

IEEE: Ethically aligned design: a vision for prioritizing human well-being with autonomous and intelligent systems, first edition. In: IEEE Global Initiative on Ethics of Autonomous and Intelligent Systems (2019)

International Association of Accessibility Professionals: (2023). https://www.accessibilityassociation.org/s/

Jackman, M., Kanerva, L.: Evolving the IRB: building robust review for industry research. Wash. Lee Law Rev. Online. **72**, 3 (2016) https://scholarlycommons.Law.wlu.edu/cgi/viewcontent.cgi?article=1042&context=wlulr-online

Johnson, T., Kanjo, E.: Urban wellbeing: a portable sensing approach to unravel the link between environment and mental wellbeing. IEEE Sens. Lett. **7**, 1–4 (2023)

Kirkpatrick, A., et al.: Web Content Accessibility Guidelines (WCAG) 2.1. W3C Recommendation (2018) https://www.w3.org/TR/WCAG21/

Kramer, A., et al.: Experimental evidence of massive-scale emotional contagion through social networks. Proc. Natl. Acad. Sci. USA. **111**(24), 8788–8790 (2014). https://doi.org/10.1073/pnas.1320040111

Kukkala, V., Thiruloga, S., Pasricha, S.: Roadmap for cybersecurity in autonomous vehicles. IEEE Consum Electron Mag. **11**(6), 13–23 (2022). https://doi.org/10.1109/MCE.2022.3154346

Kulicki, P., Trypuz, R., Musielewicz, M.: Towards a formal ethics for autonomous cars. In: 14th International Conference on Deontic Logic and Normative Systems (DEON), Utrecht, The Netherlands (2018)

Latour, B.: What Is the Style in Matters of Concern? Van Gorcum, Assen (2008)

Lawson, A., Beckett, A.: The social and human rights models of disability: towards a complementarity thesis. Int. J. Human Rights. **25**(2), 348–379 (2021). https://doi.org/10.1080/13642987.2020.1783533

Llorca Albareda, J., García, P., Lara, F.: The moral status of AI entities. In: Ethics of Artificial Intelligence, pp. 59–83. Cham, Springer (2024)

Lopes, N.: Internet of Things feasibility for disabled people. Trans. Emerg. Telecommun. Technol. **31**, e3906 (2020). https://doi.org/10.1002/ett.3906/

Metcalf, L., Askay, D., Rosenberg, L.: Keeping humans in the loop: pooling knowledge through artificial swarm intelligence to improve business decision making. Calif. Manag. Rev. **61**(4), 84–109 (2019)

Moss, E., Metcalf, J.: Ethics Owners: a New Model of Organizational Responsibility in Data-Driven Technology Companies. Analysis & Policy Observatory, Data & Society Research Institute, Hawthorn (2020) https://apo.org.au/sites/default/files/resource-files/2020-09/apo-nid308440.pdf

Murray, J., Fairfield, J.: Global ethics and virtual worlds: ensuring functional integrity in transnational research studies. In: IEEE Intl Symposium on Ethics in Science, Technology and Engineering, Chicago IL (2014)

Murray, J., et al.: Reynard Verus Final Report. SRI International (2012) AFRL-RY-WP-TR-2012-0286
Noriega, P., et al.: Manifesto for conscientious design of hybrid online social systems. IEEE Internet Comput. **25**(6), 58–64 (2021)
Ozkaya, I.: The behavioral science of software engineering and human–machine teaming. IEEE Softw. **37**(6), 3–6 (2020)
Paté-Cornell, E.: Finding and fixing systems weaknesses: probabilistic methods and applications of engineering risk analysis. Risk Anal. **22**(2), 319–334 (2002)
Pearl, J., Mackenzie, D.: The Book of Why: the New Science of Cause and Effect. Basic Books, New York (2018)
Purves, D., et al.: Autonomous machines, moral judgment, and acting for the right reasons. Ethical Theory Moral Pract. **18**(4), 851–872 (2015). https://doi.org/10.1007/s10677-015-9563-y
Reine, R., et al.: Cyber-physical-social systems: an overview. In: Smart Connected World: Technologies and Applications Shaping the Future, pp. 25–45 (2021)
Rohan, R., Funilkul, S., Pal, D., Thapliyal, H.: Humans in the loop: cybersecurity aspects in the consumer IoT context. IEEE Consum Electron Mag. **11**(4), 78–84 (2022). https://doi.org/10.1109/MCE.2021.3095385
Satyanarayanan, M.: Pervasive computing: vision and challenges. IEEE Pers. Commun. **8**(4), 10–17 (2001). https://doi.org/10.1109/98.943998
Schmidt, E.: Innovation power: why technology will define the future of geopolitics. Foreign Aff. **102**(2), 38 (2023)
Schuler, D., Namioka, A. (eds.): Participatory Design: Principles and Practices. CRC Press (1993)
Singh, M., Murukannaiah, P.K.: Toward an ethical framework for smart cities and the Internet of Things. IEEE Internet Comput. **27**(2), 51–56 (2023)
SIW: Security Information Watch: Q&A Maria Sumnicht. GSO (2023) https://www.securityinfowatch.com/security-executives/article/53065145/gso-2025-qa-maria-sumnicht
Stamatis, D.: Risk Management Using Failure Mode and Effect Analysis (FMEA). Quality Press (2019)
Steen, M.: Ethics as a participatory and iterative process. Commun. ACM. **66**(5), 27 (2023). https://doi.org/10.1145/3550069
Stilgoe, J., Owen, R., Macnaghten, P.: Developing a framework for responsible innovation. Res. Policy. **42**(9), 1568–1580 (2013)
Strait, A.: Supporting AI Research Ethics Committees. Ada Lovelace Institute (2023) https://www.adalovelaceinstitute.org/project/supporting-ai-research-ethics-committees/
Sullins, J.: When is a robot a moral agent. Machine Ethics. **6**(2001), 151–161 (2011)
Talcott, C.: Cyber-physical systems and events. In: Software-Intensive Systems and New Computing Paradigms: Challenges and Visions. Springer, Berlin, Heidelberg (2008)
TeachAccess: TeachAccess strategic plan. (2021). https://teachaccess.org/about/mission-vision/
TeachingAccessibility: How is digital accessibility taught and learned? (2022). https://teachingaccessibility.ac.uk/
Tene, O., Polonetsky, J.: Beyond IRBs: ethical guidelines for data research. Wash Lee Law Rev. **72**, 458 (2016) https://scholarlycommons.law.wlu.edu/wlulr-online/vol72/iss3/7
Thadani, T.: How a robotaxi crash got Cruise's self-driving cars pulled from Californian roads. The Washington Post, Oct 23. (2023) https://www.washingtonpost.com/technology/2023/10/28/robotaxi-cruise-crash-driverless-car-san-francisco/
US DHEW: Belmont report: ethical principles and guidelines for the protection of human subjects of research. US Department of Health, Education and Welfare Federal Register. **44**(76), 23191–23197 (1979)
US DHS: Department of Homeland Security Trusted Tester program. (2023). https://dhs.gov/508-training
Ushahidi: (2023). https://www.ushahidi.com/about/our-story/

Weaver, J.: Measuring the Ethical Awareness of Corporate Data Scientists. The Chicago School of Professional Psychology (2022) https://www.researchgate.net/profile/Jessica-Weaver-16/publication/366408998

Weiser, M.: Some computer science issues in ubiquitous computing. Commun. ACM. **36**(7), 75–84 (1993). https://doi.org/10.1145/159544.159617

Wiener, N.: The Human Use of Human Beings: Cybernetics and Society. Houghton Mifflin (1954)

Zhang, L.: Designing big data driven cyber physical systems based on AADL. In: IEEE International Conference on Systems, Man, and Cybernetics (SMC), San Diego, CA, USA, pp. 3072–3077 (2014). https://doi.org/10.1109/SMC.2014.6974399

Zuboff, S.: The Age of Surveillance Capitalism. Profile Books (2019) ISBN 9781781256855

Part II
Conceptual Contributions to Smart Life

Chapter 5
Smart Environments: Implications for Environmental Governance

Karen Bakker and Max Ritts

Abstract Environmental governance has the potential to be significantly transformed by Smart Environments technologies, e.g., technologies that enabled enhanced environmental monitoring and analytic procedures via combinations of information and communication technologies (ICT), conventional monitoring approaches (e.g., remote sensing), and Internet of Things (IoT) applications (e.g., Environmental Sensor Networks (ESNs)). This chapter offers an update of a 2018 paper that assessed these developments through the term "Smart Earth," and which likewise engaged the potential implications and pitfalls of new digital technologies for environmental governance. Here, we offer a meta-review of research on what we now call "Smart Environments," ranging from ecological informatics to the digital humanities. We pair this with a critical perspective on pathways for evolution in environmental governance frameworks, exploring five key Smart Environments issues relevant to environmental governance: data, real-time regulation, predictive management, open source, and citizen sensing. We conclude with suggestions for future research directions and transdisciplinary conversations about environmental governance in a Smart Environments world.

Keywords Environmental governance · Data · Smart technology · Nature

The completion of this chapter was tragically complicated by the passing of its lead author, Karen Bakker, in August 2023. The second author and the editors of this book wish to dedicate the chapter to Karen's memory. Together, we celebrate the considerable impact Karen had in shaping the fields of environmental geography, water governance, and digital environmental technologies.

K. Bakker
Department of Geography and Institute for Resources, Environment, and Sustainability, University of British Columbia, Vancouver, BC, Canada

M. Ritts (✉)
Department of Geography, Clark University, Worcester, MA, USA
e-mail: mritts@clarku.edu

E. Kornyshova et al. (eds.), *Smart Life and Smart Life Engineering*,
https://doi.org/10.1007/978-3-031-75887-4_5

5.1 Introduction

The application of digital technologies to environmental monitoring is radically redefining the prospects for environmental governance in the twenty-first century. Collectively, the proliferating examples featuring in this space are establishing new rationalities and practices for governing environments—with implications for governance at a range of scales. As explored below, digital technologies are now being applied in many sectors and for a broad range of purposes: to monitor and manage ecosystems; to detect and minimize pollution; to surveil and respond to environmental crimes; to measure, profile, and gain access to resources; and to mitigate environmental threats such as floods, fires, climate change, and biodiversity loss. Smart Environments are analogous to Smart Cities, and as an intellectual and governance framework share many of their enabling discourses, including cybernetics, systems theory, and military rationality. As with Smart Cities, the Smart Environments agenda also raises serious concerns about new forms of privacy and surveillance, the deepening involvement of corporate actors in governance, and new modalities of social exclusion and structural inequality.[1] This chapter overviews these issues through the lens of environmental governance. We draw on the conceptualization developed by Bridge and Perrault to identify a particular trajectory of interest to us: environmental governance as "designing responsive and flexible social mechanisms that allow adaptation as new information becomes available."[2] The merit of Bridge and Perrault's approach is its emphasis on the significance of "information," which manifests in the present case as aggregations of data. Expressions of smart governance share an overarching interest in measuring—and datafying—ecosystem processes in new and sometimes intimate ways. They are consciously attuned to prospect of novel environmental shocks and stochastic changes. But above all, they are utopian in the possibilities governance can claim to draw from data as a constantly issuing stream of diverse environmental processes.

Our central claim is that the data provided by Smart Environments technologies—our central focus in this chapter—are creating conditions for significant change across the global assemblage of actors and institutions, laws, and norms that structure environmental decision-making regarding across spheres of environmental management and conservation (e.g., "environmental governance"). Smart Environments technologies dramatically increase the availability of data and seek to decrease or even eliminate the time lag between data collection and analysis all while expanding the types of variables that can be assessed. The resulting hyper-abundance of data (rather than scarce data) is repeatedly touted by decision-makers for enabling new optimizable and real-time (rather than post hoc) regulatory responses. But this promise is not without its intellectual critics, nor a slate of evident real-world problems. Below, we explore the significance of these

---

[1] See Bakker and Ritts (2018); Marvin et al. (2015); Luque-Alaya and Marvin (2020); Halpern and Mitchell (2023).

[2] Bridge and Perrault (2009), p. 480.

developments. We begin by looking at some of the intellectual converges shaping this discussion space. Then we look at applications of Smart Environments before turning to the risks and harms of their further expansions and imbrications with governance.[3]

5.2 Digitization at a Planetary Scale? Intellectual Convergences in Smart Environments Technologies

Twenty years ago, many of the technologies that now aggregated under Smart Environments were nascent or nonexistent. A range of intellectual traditions existed concerning the possibilities of computationally enhanced forms of spatial governance (for a good history, see Halpern and Mitchell 2023). But conversations had yet to form—or at least become formalized—across many of the scientific disciplines that deploy and debate these technologies today. But in the ensuing two decades, new interdisciplinary journals emerged, including *Ecological Informatics* (founded in 2006) and the *International Journal of Digital Earth* (2008), that sought to convene growing cross-disciplinary interests. Entirely new sub-disciplines—such as the environmental humanities, a field designed to explore interconnections across environmental history, philosophy, human geography, and political ecology—also evolved and would be regularly engaged with the environmental data politics questions that subtend expansion of Smart Environments.[4] Meanwhile, journals concerned with the technical and applied aspects of Smart Environments—such as those involving computer engineering, remote sensing, and biological sciences communities—display a growing interest in their environmental governance implications.[5] These intellectual convergences are being spurred on by the entrance of an additional actor: private corporations. Since the mid-2010s, companies like Microsoft and Google have been investing significant amounts of capital into the development of AI-supported "Earth algorithms" that would guide smart environmental practices.[6] Other notable initiatives include Nokia's "Sensor Planet," IBM's "A Smarter Planet," HP Labs' "Central Nervous System for the Earth" (CeNSE), NASA's Earth Observing System Data and Information System (EOSDIS), and Cisco/NASA's collaborative "Planetary Skin Institute," together with a rapidly proliferating ecosystem of apps.[7]

Many of these initiatives focus on the interface between proliferating digital environmental sensors (e.g., motion detectors, hydrophones, cameras) and Internet-based communications technologies, which, combined with cloud-based

[3] This chapter has been adapted and updated from Bakker and Ritts (2018).

[4] See Gabrys et al. (2016).

[5] For examples, see Jackson and Borbow (2015); Galaz et al. (2017).

[6] Joppa (2017).

[7] Jepson and Ladle (2015).

data storage, enable unprecedented real-time tracking and visualization.[8] Sensors, we should note, are significant to Smart Environments in large part because of their ability to "fragment" environmental spaces and processes into "small spatiotemporal units of data," effectively making them amenable to new governance directives.[9] Smart Environments initiatives also frequently combine well-established approaches—such as remote sensing and long-term ecological monitoring—with newer technologies (animal biotelemetry, bacteria-based biosensors) and modalities of data collection (such as drones, Google Earth, and citizen sensing).[10] The most frequent targets of these applications are natural resources (such as forests), species prioritized for conservation (such as marine mammals), earth "boundary conditions" and "ecosystem services" (such as freshwater, atmospheric carbon), and environmental security (natural disasters such as floods and fires).

A quick survey into the case of acoustics can bring further clarification into the resultant changes. Scientists have long recognized sound as "a medium for intra- and interspecific communication among . . . animals." Their socio-technical ability to glean biological and ecological insight was limited to site-specific recording engagements (Krause and Farina 2016, p. 245). For a long time, they had difficulties ascertaining the biological and ecological value of sound, owing to the perceived absence of measurable variables to compare across spaces. The rise of a digitally enabled "conservation acoustics," premised on the novel availability of cheap recording technologies, algorithms, and novel forms of expertise, has completely transformed this situation. Today, a range of Smart Environments technologies—hydrophones, acoustical observatories, audio moths—are being used across a range of conservation projects and governance projects, fixated on everything from elephant calls to poacher gunfire.[11] New research is asserting that carbon-sharing trees exchange acoustic signals and that kelp forests exhibit distinct lunar and seasonal trends in sound production.[12] Globally, the bioacoustics sensor market is expected to reach 8.7 billion (USD) by 2024, up from 5.6 billion in 2017.[13]

New technologies are at the forefront of the interest in digital sound for terrestrial environmental governance. But equally paradigmatic examples of Smart Environments technologies redefining governance can be found in marine space.[14] EarthNC's (2016) SharkNet, which displays the near-real-time locations of great white sharks and marine mammals, gathering data from a network of mobile robots and moored listening stations connected to sensors carried by marine wildlife.[15]

[8] See Gale et al. (2017).

[9] Luque-Alaya and Marvin (2020), p. 6.

[10] Bakker and Ritts (2018).

[11] See Ritts et al. (2016); Roe et al. (2021a); Ritts and Bakker (2021); Ritts et al. (2024).

[12] Klein et al. (2016); Butler et al. (2021); see also Bakker (2022b).

[13] As discussed in Ritts and Bakker (2021).

[14] The literature here is extensive. For a few examples from the geography discipline, see Lehman (2020); Havice et al. (2022); Bakker (2022a).

[15] www.sharknet.com.

Like many marine animal tracking efforts, SharkNet emerged from long-standing collaboration among scientists interested in monitoring animals across large spatial ranges. Related "citizen sensing" projects have geotagged fish, such as important commercial species like Pacific salmon, whose movements can likewise be detected by networks of underwater cameras.[16] Although the focus of Smart Environments has tended to be on terrestrial processes, ocean environments have also been the focus of various kinds of technical, logistical, and institutional innovation.[17]

As Lehman emphasizes, "new sensing technologies do not simply produce more data at more ambitious spatial and temporal scales. They have the potential to produce new environmental sensibilities as well as new relationships between scientists, technologies, and environments."[18] Across a range of ecosystems and disciplines, scientists and engineers have created new devices to assess changing oceanographic conditions, including an automated network christened "FitBit for the Oceans."[19] The network incorporates cable and sensor technologies to measure geological, physical, chemical, and biological variables in the ocean and seafloor, producing over 200 different kinds of data. These marine developments are emblematic of the ways in which Smart Environments technologies enable comprehensive data acquisition infrastructures to monitor environmental conditions, emergent risks, and geo-hazards.[20]

Another salient finding from the review of Smart Environments technologies is the variability of scales at which they are being conceived, defined, and operated. Scale is critical in assessing Smart Environments because of the spatial variability of the ecological processes involved in global environmental governance. For instance, the designers of BeachObserver propose that coastal communities "self-monitor" locally occurring marine debris, whereas projects like Argos aim for systemic reviews of marine-ecological change occurring at the planetary scale.[21] Meanwhile, continent-wide scale networks of digital acoustic monitoring are now being conceived, as is exemplified in the case of Australian Acoustic Observatory.[22] A single review is unable to capture all the scalar variability in Smart Environments, and certain projects (BirdTracker) should also be recognizing for straddling multiple scales concurrently. However, it is important for assessing the political risks of Smart Environments technologies that the challenges of integrating technologies operating at multiple and distinct scales be at least considered, which we seek to do below.

[16] Matabos et al. (2017); see also Bakker (2022a).

[17] For examples, Favali et al. (2015).

[18] Lehman (2020), p. 172.

[19] Quoted in Ocean Observatories (2023). Unpaginated.

[20] See Bakker and Ritts (2018); Lehman (2016, 2020); Lindenmayer et al. (2017).

[21] See Benson (2015). For BeachObserver, see https://scistarter.org/beachobserver.

[22] Roe et al. (2021b).

5.3 Environmental Governance in a Smart Environments World: Issues and Critiques

This section of the chapter overviews some of prevailing critiques of Smart Environments for environmental governance. Interest in this area has grown rapidly in recent years; due to space restrictions, we confined our analysis to five themes: data, "real-time" analysis and regulation, the changing nature of prediction, the meaning and extent of "open data," and the role of non-scientists, notably "citizen sensors."

5.3.1 *Data*

Data, Kitchin suggests, refer to any element that can be abstracted from phenomena.[23] What is helpful about this definition is how it captures a key aspect of Smart Environmental technologies: a capacious, seemingly indiscriminate, and hence socially problematic interest in sourcing of environmental data. Exemplifying this tendency, between 2018 and 2023, the volume of data from NASA's Earth Observing System Data and Information System grew from 26.8 petabytes to 151.1 petabytes.[24] The trend is indexical of a larger insight, e.g., that a world of Smart Environments is a world in which planetary data is becoming more abundant than existing supercomputers—and, perhaps, ecologies—can handle. After years of little coverage, massive server farms, with energy-demands constituent of a "data center industrial complex," have become the recognized underbelly of seemingly frictionless Smart Environmental space.[25] Numerous actors are asking how can the petabytes—or even exabytes—of data systems be stored, sorted, summoned, and processed in such a manner that efficiencies are not lost in the cost of hosting the data? Another issue is the dependency on massive amounts energy and electricity, an issue made plain in the case of neural networks.[26] Cubitt's claim that insufficient electricity, not oil, is the leading threat to co-ordinations of global governance takes on added salience here.[27] Costly to train and develop from an energy standpoint (e.g., hardware costs, cloud compute) and resulting in massive carbon footprints (e.g., to fuel modern tensor processing hardware), "data deluge" has spurred a kind of new self-reflexive green energy focus: the sustainable data center management strategy.[28]

[23] Kitchin (2014), p. 2.

[24] NASA (2023).

[25] "Data center industrial complex" is the title of Hogan (2021).

[26] Strubell et al. (2019).

[27] See Cubitt (2017).

[28] For an example, see Crouse (2023).

As scientists and innovators continue to focus on automated decision-making systems, issues of resource use will only intensify. One sector in which the growing embrace of automated management techniques deserves special mention is "precision agriculture," an agenda that promises that digitizing agricultural processes can, on average, yield greater volumes more food, on less land, and with fewer inputs, through the intercession of Internet of Things technologies.[29] However, multiple real-time data streams and interoperable technologies have not necessarily engendered more efficient or transparent agricultural systems—in part because proprietary relations over the data collected mitigates against the pooling of knowledge and even the repair of farming machinery.[30] Digitalization can exacerbate already-existing power inequities in the food system and increase corporate control over an already centralized economy.[31]

Galaz and Mouazen highlight a revealing paradox: many of the most powerful algorithms underlying automated decision-making systems featured in Smart Environments are likely to be of limited accessibility or transparency—raising the risk of replication of biases in decision-making.[32] As many scholars have pointed out, AI and machine-learning-driven approaches often contain implicit bias; incomplete datasets and flawed algorithms can prove counterproductive and ecologically damaging.[33] Moreover, algorithms do not reconcile value-laden tensions between competing uses and ecosystem services (e.g., economic versus spiritual values), leaving the question of arbitration incomplete. Perhaps counterintuitively, algorithmic modes of environmental governance can be expected to create the need for new forms of human supervision as the automation of decision-making becomes more commonplace.[34]

A related issue that threatens the success (if not the rollout) of Smart Environments is the lack of data standards. Our meta-review revealed persistent appeals for cross-disciplinary collaboration on data standards and data sharing.[35] It is thus surprising to note that "silo-ing" persists across academic uptakes of Smart Environments. This can be partially attributed to the long-standing challenges of combining ecological datasets. Pre-ICT approaches were characterized by a diversity of standards, for example, one set of standards applied to the longer-term data gathered by professional scientists (often for the purposes of testing single hypotheses) while another set of standards often applied to shorter-term data collected by professional environmental consultants in response to specific

[29] Clapp and Ruder (2020).

[30] For the now-infamous example involving John Deere tractors, see Wiens and Chamberlain (2018).

[31] Rotz et al. (2019).

[32] Galaz and Mouazen (2017).

[33] See Caliskan et al. (2017); Galaz and Mouazen (2017); Machen and Nost (2021).

[34] Galaz and Mouazen (2017), p. 629.

[35] The issue has long been recognized as salient to environmental governance. See Frew and Dozier (2012); Hampton et al. (2013); Michener and Jones (2012); Michener (2015).

ecological threats (such as pollution incidents) and distinct (or no) standards were applied to data collected by citizen scientists (such as fish and wildlife harvest data), which was housed separately, and rarely accessed or used by scientists or governments.[36] The challenge of combining and communicating data gathered through disparate data collection efforts remains unresolved, although significant efforts have been made to address this issue by a variety of organizations, including NASA's Socioeconomic Data and Applications Center (SEDAC, a Data Center in NASA's Earth Observing System Data and Information System (EOSDIS)), The Amazon Tall Tower Observatory (ATTO), and the National Ecological Observatory Network.

This data-sharing challenge may nevertheless be largely resolved in the near-term future. "Big ecology" policies, combined with diminished costs for information technologies and new cloud-based data-archiving tools and repositories, have proliferated in recent years, supported by an increasing number of eco-informatics scientists and also by organizations such as the Ecological Society of America's Committee on the Future of Long-term Ecological Data (FLED).[37] Scholars working in ecological informatics have longed predicted that new generations of data-sharing networks will grow exponentially faster than its predecessors.[38] Attesting to these claims is the case of the US Long Term Ecological Research Network (LTER), which, after several decades of operation, had 6000 shared datasets.[39] In contrast, by mid-2022, after less than a decade and a half of operation, DataONE easily exceeded one million data objects.[40] This growth has been facilitated by the expansion of networking capacities among researchers, along with corresponding changes in the cyberinfrastructure landscape. Important data science innovations—including data and metadata standards, persistent identifiers, and search/discovery tools—have enabled more widespread data sharing than in the past.[41]

In summary, much of the Smart Environments literature focuses on addressing data gaps, the need for more collaborative data sharing, and issues relating to data quality. The underlying assumption is that more comprehensive and higher-quality data will lead to more effective environmental governance. As a wealth of literature in science and technology studies shows, however, this assumption is problematic.[42] For one thing, it largely proceeds according to a technocratic worldview, which holds that solutions exist for problems that may in fact be irresolvable under present institutional, political, and technological configurations.[43] The political commitments associated with measurement-related decisions—in particular, the

[36] The foundational piece here remains Goodchild (2007).

[37] See Porter (2010); Michener (2015).

[38] Michener (2015); Porter (2010); Reichman et al. (2011).

[39] Porter (2010).

[40] https://www.dataone.org.

[41] Michener (2015).

[42] Gabrys (2016).

[43] Morozov (2013).

question of who selects variables to measure and for whom they are selected—are rarely discussed in the large institutional settings overseeing the use of Smart Environments technologies, like the World Economic Forum.[44] Because data gaps are likely to result from the uneven political economies that preside over governance in a Smart Environments world, questions of "what is measured, matters" or "what is counted, counts" (and, by extension, what is not counted, doesn't) are likely to intensify.

5.3.2 *Real-Time Regulation*

The concept of "real" or "near real" time–e.g., the increasingly instantaneous "actual" time elapsed in the performance of a computation—is central to Smart Environmental governance.[45] Interest in this area can be traced to the techno-managerial discourses of late 1990s urban policy.[46] Initial focus includes real-time pricing in "Smart Grids" and "Smart" water distribution systems.[47] In the last decade, a rapid decline in the cost of monitoring technologies (driven by innovation in computing and communications) has increased the capacity to conduct real-time assessment of environmental changes.[48] Managers are evaluating the success of real-time location information via software applications on location-aware devices, such as cellphones, laptops, acoustic sensors, and apps.[49] The implementation of updatable navigational hazards and "real-time speed advisory signs" in transportation systems is now common in larger environmental governance contexts.[50] Prominent applications include marine governance, where ship rerouting efforts proceed in connection in response to wildlife detections in a number of contexts, and pipeline logistics, wherein materials flows are routinely rerouted into different distribution terminals across vast interregional logistics networks.[51]

A paradigmatic example is the work of Conserve.IO, an organization that assists conservation groups with leveraging mobile, cloud-based, and big data technologies through data collection at scale (involving crowdsourced data from humans and from passive environmental sensors). The mobile applications ("apps") produced by Conserve.IO—such as its award-winning "Sharktivity" (2020)—employ visual analytics to enhance situational awareness and real-time responses to environmental

[44] For example, see World Economic Forum (2021).
[45] De Longueville et al. (2010).
[46] See Komninos (2002); Luque-Alaya and Marvin (2020).
[47] See Kratz et al. (2006); Arts et al. (2015).
[48] Koomey et al. (2013).
[49] Goodchild and Glennon (2010); Jepson and Ladle (2015).
[50] Haque et al. (2013), p. 25.
[51] See Bakker (2023); Ritts and Simpson (2023).

changes.[52] In what has become a common tactic in an age of ubiquitous computing, "Whale Trail" aggregates different smartphone-user submissions of a single species encounter to calculate a highly accurate track using intersection points.[53]

Whereas management and critical policy literatures focus on real-time resource distribution concerns—e.g., coordinating flows of energy, bodies, and commodities—ecologists and biologists are engaging novel possibilities for species "tracking" (Ritts and Bakker 2021). Thanks to advances in predictive analytics, tracking technologies can be used to pursue, distill, and anticipate real-time ecological events. Sensing technologies, such as conservation drones, camera traps, and acoustic recorders, are being presented as adaptive solutions for a host of "monitoring-adjacent" activities, such as anti-poaching and law enforcement.[54] Rather than static sensing regimes, large-scale observatories—such as the Australian Acoustic Observatory—typically host shifting regimes of sensor arrays that appeal to multiple research communities (Roe et al. 2021a).

The challenge (and opportunity) posed by real-time data streams is one of the most salient issues for environmental governance under Smart Environments. Real-time data streams and real-time analysis make the idea of "real-time" regulation possible: e.g., the capacity to rapidly shift resources and monitoring capacities in response to unforeseen developments. For example, Little et al. (2015) survey real-time spatial management approaches to reduce fisheries bycatch and discards. Kumar et al. (2015) explore the rise of low-cost sensing for managing urban air pollution. The developments they capture likewise sound a note of caution. Real-time regulation poses significant administrative challenges, insofar as organizing simultaneous temporal attributes (or tracking efforts), including time of acquisition, integration/dwell time, sampling interval, and aggregation time span, can easily overwhelm computing power or lead to insufficient data.[55] It is likewise impossible to guarantee that ecological wellbeing will form the basis of real-time responses, which may in fact embolden more tactical political decision-making favoring certain actors.

5.3.3 *Prediction*

Many papers discussing Smart Environments highlight the benefits of predicting conditions for sustainable development and resource use. In distinction from previous approaches to predictability, ecological changes are increasingly conceived as predictable and "programmable."[56] This innovative emphasis on programma-

[52] https://www.atlanticwhiteshark.org/sharktivity-app

[53] Meynecke and Liebish (2021).

[54] See Kang and Hudson (2022); Ritts and Bakker (2021); Sandbrook (2015); Ritts et al. (2024).

[55] Frew and Dozier (2012); Benson (2015).

[56] Frew and Dozier (2012); Gabrys (2016); Murai (2010).

bility as an inherent—and in some formulations, paramount—characteristic of predictability builds on developments in "adaptive monitoring" and "adaptive management."[57] For example, many publications provide examples of enhancements to predictive capacities enabled by new Web platforms, such as OakMapper, Whale Alert, and Global Forest Watch.[58] Managers and scientists alike can source data inputs for environmental niche models, which are able to predict risks, disturbances, and terrestrial transformations.[59]

Smart Environments also create innovative possibilities for predictability for an expanded set of environmental variables. For example, the literature has many examples of novel prediction capabilities across environmental phenomena, which were previously characterized by limited predictability—with seasonal whale migrations and the sonification of advancing "P-Waves" being two prominent examples.[60] Prediction has also garnered considerable attention in remote sensing where new measurement techniques and modeling and visualization capacities are being used to describe and predict local weather patterns in the context of climate change, species diversity estimates, lake monitoring, and management priorities.[61] There are a range of studies centered on the prediction, with increasingly high degrees of accuracy, of changing forest structure and aboveground biomass, food web structure, and animal migration.[62] Yet despite their potential, the actual success rate of predictive efforts has been questioned. Such determinations will have to contend with unexpected developments in price structures and consumption patterns, among other variables. Predictive capacities are necessarily limited by the present-day assumptions of their programmers, and they are often unable to internalize challenges that arise outside their framing contexts.[63] The challenge of flexibility alongside predictive capacity can be expected to loom as a major tension in Smart Environments governance moving forward.

In short, Smart Environments enable new modes of prediction, which create new possibilities for environmental governance. Adaptation and anticipation have become more central to environmental governance in the increasingly predicted (if not necessarily more predictable) "time-space" of a Smart Environments world. These developments align with current debates over the implications of what Mahony calls the "predictive state" and associated forms of geographical intelligence.[64] Carruth and Marzec join others in focusing concern on ethical issues

[57] Carruth and Marzec (2014); Lindenmayer et al. (2017).

[58] See https://oakmapper.org, https://whale-alert.io, https://pro.globalforestwatch.org.

[59] Kluza et al. (2007); Clark et al. (2009).

[60] For discussion, see Pötzsch (2015); Gale et al. (2017).

[61] Mairota et al. (2015); Rocchini et al. (2015); Dörnhöfer and Oppelt (2016); Pettorelli et al. (2014).

[62] Woodward et al. (2013).

[63] Amoore (2021).

[64] See Mahony (2014). For more discussion, see Crampton et al. (2013); Wood (2013); Thatcher (2014).

of privacy, freedom, and security.[65] Cubitt's remark that "databases predict the predictable" is a reminder that certain ecological forms and processes may be excluded under automated tracking systems.[66]

5.3.4 Open Source

A Smart Environments world abounds in rapidly circulating, often insufficiently labelled, "open-source" data.[67] In the ecological sciences, there is now a pervasive conviction that biodiversity conservation will be augmented by the provision of open-access data.[68] Projects like eBird tout the value of sharing small, localized citizen-science-based observations, which, when aggregated, propose broader understandings of ecological phenomena. The "Air Quality Egg" project, an EU-supported effort to collaboratively devise a "smart" air quality sensor network, is being proclaimed as a best-practice example of bottom-up environmental governance.[69] In contrast, "Open source" is defined by other scholars to facilitate customization in environmental governance ensuring the local determination of environmental decision-making at a time of planetary-scale organization.[70] At its most utopian, open source proposes that "ubiquitously available" data can serve as both a key feature of environmental governance and an "essential component of democracy."[71]

Efforts to survey the dizzying array of open-source archives currently engaged within governments, research projects, and NGOs have resulted in several detailed reviews.[72] Michener examines how "Big Data" informational policies have historically encouraged the present deluge of open-source data—noting in particular the foundational significance of Long-Term Research Networks (LTRNs), Ecological Observatory Networks (EONs), and Coordinated Distributed Experiments and Observations Networks (CDEOs).[73] Despite the fact that scientists have long used decentralized groups of non-professionals to gather ecological information, many observers note that recent "success stories" remain without truly democratic cultures of "collaboration" and "sharing."[74] Collaboration and data sharing as such remain considerably removed from the actual opportunities enabled by Smart

[65] Carruth and Marzec (2014). See also Wood (2013); DeLoughrey (2014).

[66] Cubitt (2017), p. 159.

[67] See Gunningham and Holley (2016); Mairota et al. (2015); Rocchini et al. (2017).

[68] Morris and White (2013); Turner et al. (2015).

[69] As discussed in Zandbergen (2017).

[70] Gale et al. (2017).

[71] Mooney and Corcoran (2014), p. 534.

[72] Roche et al. (2015); Gale et al. (2017).

[73] Michener (2015).

[74] Connors et al. (2012); Faniel and Zimmerman (2011).

Environments.[75] Reviews of marine-based sciences have made similar observations as have conversations within environmental and digital humanities.[76] A commonly raised concern is the absence of proper institutional support for collaborative data sharing, which in certain cases might translate into prescriptions for greater incentives to share, as well as the embrace of novel administrative frameworks.[77] Humanities scholars have been particularly keen to critique "crowdsourcing" as a source of ecological knowledge that tends to reinforce the expert hierarchies it proposes to disable.[78]

For many observers, open-source data leads inexorably to the problem of data standards, an issue with far-reaching consequence to Smart Environments environmental governance. Roche et al. surveyed 100 datasets associated with studies in journals that commonly publish ecological and evolutionary research, finding that 56% of the articles were linked to incompletely archived datasets.[79] Calls for improved metadata have become increasingly common in ecology and biodiversity science.[80] "Good news narratives," showcasing the purported benefits of Smart Environments technologies, often obscure questions of quality controls and who will set them.[81] The question of just what constitutes "good enough data" prefigures a growing politics of "open-source" legitimacy in Smart Environments environmental governance.[82] At a time when increasing amounts of data freely circulate, and many scientists advocate for the continued diversification of research models, the integration of data from multiple sensors poses institutional challenges and social tensions. Moreover, what role do different data sources play in the actual conduct of environmental governance? And what about the related issue of expanding risks occurring from institutional propensities to exploit datasets in ways original architects had not intended? Sun-ha Hong has coined the term "control creep" to describe how "data-driven technologies tend to be pitched for a particular context and purpose, but quickly expand into new forms of control."[83] As incentives to monetize environmental data in new ways become knowable, the ability to not only ensure privacy and personal freedoms, but the provenance of data for broader environmental applications (such as large-scale worker-monitoring), is impacted. The actual provision of open-source data articulates a fundamental ambiguity of the Smart Environments governance regime: are data flows simply feeding into the

[75] Reichman et al. (2011); Hampton et al. (2013); Volk et al. (2014).

[76] Cubitt (2017).

[77] Michener and Jones (2012); Roche et al. (2015); Specht et al. (2015); Hampton et al. (2013); Verburg et al. (2016).

[78] Gabrys (2016); Swanstrom (2016); Pearson et al. (2016).

[79] Roche et al. (2015).

[80] Frew and Dozier (2012); Specht et al. (2015); O'Brien et al. (2016).

[81] Quoted in Arts et al. (2015), p. 661.

[82] Gabrys et al. (2016).

[83] Hong (2018), p. 1.

predetermined interests of large multinationals, or are they truly a site of continual "bottom-up" modifications and "hacker-led" transformations?[84]

5.3.5 *Citizen Science/Sensing*

Smart Environments engage a broad set of agencies, species, and even biophysical materials. Researchers in disciplines as diverse as computer engineering, oceanography, political science, and architecture utilize its associate discourses and concepts. "Crowdsourcing" is the operative term of bundling these entities together, increasingly in contexts that would otherwise have involved the state (e.g., traffic monitoring).[85] Scholars are increasingly exploring the contributions of artificial intelligence (AI) in this regard, invoking parallels with related transitions from "Web 2.0" to "Web 3.0," in which environmental governance is enabled by a connective intelligence across sensors, humans, non-humans, data, and decision-making apps.[86]

This transition will be intensified by Smart Environment's multiplication of sensing practices across different spaces and scales of governance. Recent innovations create the potential for universal biotic sensors, in which every organism potentially performs as a sensor to be integrated into an array of data hubs and initiatives (such as the Sensor Web, Participatory Geoweb initiatives, and Google Earth).[87] Smart Environments research agendas deploy many technologies that make use of the filtering and transducing capacities of biosensors (eyes, ears, skin, etc.), as well as providing actionable data to users (via geospatial visualizations and geo-visual analytics).[88] In short, Smart Environments expand sensing modalities—tactile, auditory, and even olfactory—by both humans and non-humans.

The most widespread application of this technology to date involves projects of "citizen sensing," e.g., the intimate, experiential monitoring of environments by human and non-human users. Interest in this area has only intensified in the wake of the Covid-19 pandemic, which has deposited an array of extensive experiments in user-produced location health data across national territories and jurisdictions. Often, citizen sensing builds on existing citizen science initiatives, including those administered by non-governmental groups like the Citizen Science Center and government agencies like the Environmental Protection Agency.[89] For Gabrys, "citizen sensing" is a subset of the broader phenomenon of citizen science:

[84] This is part of a much larger debate on big data and society. See Crampton et al. (2013); Crampton et al. (2014); Wood (2013); Hemmi and Graham (2014).

[85] Liu (2021).

[86] Dauvergne (2021).

[87] Goodchild (2007); Huang and Liang (2014).

[88] Helbig et al. (2017); Khan et al. (2013).

[89] Citizen Science Center (2017).

"research projects in which the public is enlisted in scientific endeavors."[90] In Smart Environments, citizen sensing has become a privileged means by which IT-enhanced data collection, learning, decision-making, and participation scale up from discrete local encounters to governance initiatives. To improve the quality and usefulness of citizen-sensed data, and to validate it against third-party critiques, scientists are now devoting vast resources to automation, which has evolved out of efforts to compare the data outputs of practitioners, algorithms, and non-experts.[91]

The impress of Smart Environments technologies is revealing for the way such "citizen sensing" activities are oftentimes solicited by and dependent on the coordinating force of state-institutions. Coastline areas are undergoing rapid change and are increasingly populated by new environmental "risks" (e.g., marine debris, oil spills, whale-vessel strikes). In North America's Pacific Northwest, coastal residents have become central in efforts to construct the "Smartest Coast in the World."[92] Likewise, the Chinese context reveals growing efforts to utilize citizen capacities to improve "overall marine operational situational awareness" (Heesemann et al. 2014, p. 153; See: Guo et al. 2010, 2017). Through sensing, key questions of citizenship become articulated to discrete capacities to generate environmental knowledge from different ecological processes (see Gabrys 2016). For citizens, the opportunity to "sense" and not merely "collects" data is a highly relevant enticement within these schemes. Sensing becomes a privileged means to attract and intrigue non-expert researchers about changing littoral regions. For example, the Ocean Observatories Initiative (OOI) entrains viewers to their Web sites to listen to underwater sounds captured by hydrophones in real time: both a means to fundraise and an opportunity to build network effects.

The worldwide growth of Smart Environment technologies potentially converts every citizen into an environmental sensing device (Elwood and Leszczynski 2013; Georgiadou et al. 2014; Amoore 2020). This raises questions that cut to the heart of widespread societal concerns over data privacy and individual liberties. What does it mean to subject racialized bodies to predetermined repertoires of "smart" practices? How are such determinations inflected by the ongoing histories of profiling, devaluation, and police violence (Jefferson 2020)? Insofar as citizen sensing efforts presuppose liberal conceptions of citizenship, they double as a new means for digitalized exclusion and worse. How might the resulting conflictual forms of citizen science be managed via Smart Environments environmental governance?

Privacy issues are also significant. Smart Environments are defined by "extra-political" protocol and models of citizen-activated management—algorithmic systems that bypass standard forms of representation and even legibility.[93] For example, in projects like IBM's "A Smarter Planet" and Hewlett-Packard's CeNSE,

[90] Gabrys (2016), p. 212.

[91] For a "hopeful" application of these tools, see Matabos et al. (2017). For a general critique, see Andrejevic (2019).

[92] Ritts and Simpson (2023).

[93] Amoore (2020).

individual citizens increasingly operate as essential operational and functional elements of environmental regulation. In transforming citizenship into citizen sensing, the public becomes a constitutive element of an emerging "computational apparatus."[94] Citizens interacting with Smart Environment technologies will voluntarily submit to surveillance, providing data while having their online actions thoroughly indexed. Such "non-voluntary" systems of locational disclosure are built into many applications that individuals implicitly endorse to when participating in Smart Environments—something the Pegasus "spyware" scandal made abundantly clear.[95] Because such disclosures cannot easily be controlled by individuals through settings adjustments to any one device, volunteered geo-data about Earth Processes can become an unintended byproduct, resulting in new forms of "geosurveillance," including by state security organizations and private contractors.[96] There is thus potential for exploitative modes of recruitment and usage if proper checks are not established.

5.4 Conclusion

As summarized here, Smart Environments technologies not only create conditions for significant shifts in environmental governance but appear to be having this effect across a range of environmental spaces today. This review has provided insight into some of the ensuing challenges, debates, and critiques. In focusing on relations of environmental governance and data, our analysis has emphasized the point that better data does not necessarily lead to better governance. Indeed, we have suggested that algorithms might selectively reduce the sphere of possible intervention and analysis within a particular landscape. Mitigating against this tendency for the purposes of robust citizenship as well as sustainable ecosystem management requires democratizing access to environmental information, as mediated by constantly evolving socio-technical relations. In parallel, new analysis of regulatory gaps is required, aligned with an analysis of the growth in integrative architectures currently being positioned as global frameworks for storing, analyzing, and disseminating Smart Environments data. In this context, a more comprehensive understanding of Smart Environments requires appreciating the changing nature of multi-actor and multilevel environmental governance—a key theme but one beyond the scope of this meta-review.

Another key gap in the literature is a critical analysis of the role of the state, historically a key player in facilitating multi-scalar processes of environmental change.[97] While many states today are key promoters of Smart Environments tech-

[94] The phrase is used in Gabrys (2016). For CeNSE, see http://www.hp.com/united-states/do-amazing/cense_innovation.html. For "A Smarter Planet," see https://public.dhe.ibm.com/partnerworld/pub/pdf/pw_program_overview_brochure.pdf

[95] Timberg and Harwell (2021).

[96] Kitchin (2014).

[97] Robertson and Wainwright (2013).

nologies, the question of how these trajectories emerge in the ways they do demands further scrutiny. In Canada, for instance, it is notable that the Smart Oceans™ initiative enjoys considerable state support and harmonizes both with regulatory goals in sustainable marine development and state-led efforts to commercialize Canada's marine technology sector.[98] The government of China has also been very active in Digital Earth and related marine initiatives, but with combinations of regulatory goals and economic interests.[99] Future work needs to critically evaluate how different state forms and political cultures enable, direct, and/or delimit Smart Environments processes across different geographical and cultural contexts. As such, much research is required into the emerging geopolitical dimensions of Smart Environments governance.

Questions of ethics also merit more scrutiny. Smart Environments governance implies a shift not only from "government to governance" but also from "manual to automated" eco-governance. Emergent regimes of state-sponsored surveillance consolidated around environmental big data—such as the Smart Oceans™ project noted above—are mobilizing in support of security objectives rather than equitable access or efficiency.[100] Smart Environments raise other fundamental issues. Elderly residents and those unable to own a smartphone face diminished opportunities to participate in Smart Environments governance (Crawford 2021). These social inequalities could be exacerbated by expanding uptakes of Smart Environments governance. As Leszczynski explains: "Algorithmic governmentality cannot divest itself of actual realities of socio-spatial stratification to which the derivative is theoretically indifferent."[101] Finally, we must note the fundamental questions of energy and ecological wellbeing raised by Smart Environmental technologies. It is now well established that sensors, cables, and various other forms of hardware generate huge amounts of e-waste, an issue that will only intensify in the coming years.[102] Critical case studies of these issues (and their possible solutions) are increasingly appearing in the literature.[103] Many more will be needed.

Given these concerns, Galaz and Mouazen are well justified to call for a code of conduct (which they term a "bio-code") that allows citizens and institutions an opportunity to take stock of the proliferation of new social relationships and ethical challenges created by Smart Environments' forms of governance.[104] Data-sharing policies and ecological measurements standards, key mechanisms by which Smart infrastructure attains the obscurity its planners routinely "seek," require new forms of visibility in public education and debate.[105] In this framing, ethics is not an

---

[98] Oceans Protection Plan (2016). For a critical overview, see: Ritts and Simpson (2023).

[99] Guo (2012); Guo et al. (2017).

[100] Zandbergen (2017); Amoore (2020); Jefferson (2020).

[101] Leszczynski (2015), p. 1693.

[102] Cubitt (2017); Hogan (2021).

[103] See Reddy (2016).

[104] Galaz and Mouazen (2017).

[105] Jackson and Bobrow (2015), p. 1770.

"afterthought" or addition to design but a crucial input across the life cycle of a given system—particularly one as ambitious and far-reaching as the Smart Environments agenda.

References

Amoore, L.: Cloud Ethics. Duke University Press (2020)
Amoore, L.: Cloud Ethics. Durham: Duke University Press (2021)
Andrejevic, M.: Automated Media. Routledge, London (2019)
Arts, K.A.J., van der Wal, R., Adams, W.M.: Digital technology and the conservation of nature. Ambio. **44**(4), 661–673 (2015)
Bakker, K.: Smart oceans: artificial intelligence and marine protected area governance. Earth. Syst. Gov. **13**, 100141 (2022a)
Bakker, K.: The Sounds of Life: How Digital Technology Is Bringing Us Closer to the Worlds of Animals and Plants. Princeton University Press (2022b)
Bakker, K.: The Sounds of Life. Princeton: Princeton University Press (2023)
Bakker, K., Ritts, M.: Smart earth: a meta-review and implications for environmental governance. Glob. Environ. Chang. **52**, 201–211 (2018)
Benson, E.: Generating infrastructural invisibility: insulation, interconnection, and avian excrement in the Southern California power grid. Environ. Humanit. **6**(1), 103–130 (2015)
Bridge, G., Perreault, T.: Environmental governance. In: Castree, N., Demeritt, D., Liverman, D., Rhoads, B. (eds.) A companion to environmental geography, pp. 475–497. John Wiley, Hoboken, NJ (2009)
Butler, J., Pagniello, C.M.L.S., Jaffe, J.S., Parnell, P.E., Širovic, A.: Diel and seasonal variability in kelp forest soundscapes off the Southern California Coast. Front. Mar. Sci. **8**, 629643 (2021)
Caliskan, A., Bryson, J.J., Narayanan, A.: Semantics derived automatically from language corpora contain human-like biases. Science. **356**(6334), 183–186 (2017)
Carruth, A., Marzec, R.P.: Environmental visualization in the Anthropocene: technologies, aesthetics, ethics. Public Cult. **26**(2–73), 205–211 (2014)
Citizen Science Center (CitizenScience.gov). Air Sensor Toolbox. https://www.citizenscience.gov/catalog/489/# (2017)
Clapp, J., Ruder, S.: Precision technologies for agriculture: digital farming, gene-edited crops, and the politics of sustainability. Glob. Environ. Polit. **20**(3), 49–69 (2020)
Clark, C.W., Ellison, W.T., Southall, B.L., et al.: Acoustic masking in marine ecosystems: intuitions, analysis, and implication. Mar. Ecol. Prog. Ser. **395**, 201–222 (2009)
Connors, J.P., Lei, S., Kelly, M.: Citizen science in the age of neogeography: utilizing volunteered geographic information for environmental monitoring. Ann. Assoc. Am. Geogr. **102**(6), 1267–1289 (2012)
Crampton, J.W., Graham, M., Poorthuis, A., et al.: Beyond the geotag: situating 'big data' and leveraging the potential of the geoweb. Cartogr. Geogr. Inf. Sci. **40**(2), 130–139 (2013)
Crampton, J.W., Roberts, S.M., Poorthuis, A.: The new political economy of geographical intelligence. Ann. Assoc. Am. Geogr. **104**(1), 196–214 (2014)
Crawford, K.: The Atlas of AI: Power, Politics, and the Planetary Costs of Artificial Intelligence. Yale University Press (2021)
Crouse, A.: Dell's Sustainable Data Center Management Strategy: Interview with Expert Alyson Freeman. Tech Republic (2023) Online: https://www.techrepublic.com/article/dells-sustainable-data-center-management-strategy/
Cubitt, S.: Finite Media: Environmental Implications of Digital Technologies. Duke University Press, Durham (2017)

Dauvergne, P.: AI in the Wild: Sustainability in the Age of Artificial Intelligence. The MIT Press, Cambridge (2021)
De Longueville, B., Annoni, A., Schade, S., et al.: Digital Earth's nervous system for crisis events: real-time sensor web enablement of volunteered geographic information. Int. J. Digit. Earth. **3**(3), 242–259 (2010)
DeLoughrey, E.: Satellite planetarity and the ends of the earth. Public Cult. **26**(2–73), 257–280 (2014)
Dörnhöfer, K., Oppelt, N.: Remote sensing for lake research and monitoring—recent advances. Ecol. Indic. **64**, 105–122 (2016)
Elwood, S., Leszczynski, A.: New spatial media, new knowledge politics. Trans. Inst. Br. Geogr. **38**(4), 544–559 (2013)
Faniel, I.M., Zimmerman, A.: Beyond the data deluge: a research agenda for large-scale data sharing and reuse. Int. J. Digit. Curation. **6**(1), 58–69 (2011)
Favali, P., Beranzoli, L., De Santis, A.: Seafloor Observatories: a New Vision of the Earth from the Abyss. Springer, Berlin, Heidelberg (2015)
Frew, J.E., Dozier, J.: Environmental informatics. Ann. Rev. Environ. Resour. **37**(1), 449–472 (2012)
Gabrys, J.: Program Earth: Environmental Sensing Technology and the Making of a Computational Planet. University of Minnesota Press, Minneapolis (2016)
Gabrys, J., Pritchard, H., Barratt, B.: Just good enough data: figuring data citizenships through air pollution sensing and data stories. Big Data Soc. **3**(2), 1–14 (2016)
Galaz, V., Mouazen, A.M.: 'New wilderness' requires algorithmic transparency: a response to Cantrell et al. Trends Ecol. Evol. **32**(9), 628–629 (2017)
Gale, F., Ascui, F., Lovell, H.: Sensing reality? New monitoring technologies for global sustainability standards. Glob. Environ. Polit. **17**(2), 65–83 (2017)
Georgiadou, Y., Lungo, J.H., Richter, C.: Citizen sensors or extreme publics? Transparency and accountability interventions on the mobile geoweb. Int. J. Digit. Earth. **7**(7), 516–533 (2014)
Goodchild, M.F.: Citizens as sensors: the world of volunteered geography. GeoJournal. **69**(4), 211–221 (2007)
Goodchild, M.F., Glennon, J.A.: Crowdsourcing geographic information for disaster response: a research frontier. Int. J. Digit. Earth. **3**(3), 231–241 (2010)
Gunningham, N., Holley, C.: Next-generation environmental regulation: law, regulation, and governance. Ann. Rev. Law Soc. Sci. **12**(1), 273–293 (2016)
Guo, H.: China's earth observing satellites for building a digital earth. Int. J. Digit. Earth. **5**(3), 185–188 (2012)
Guo, H.D., Liu, Z., Zhu, L.W.: Digital earth: decadal experiences and some thoughts. Int. J. Digit. Earth. **3**(1), 31–46 (2010)
Guo, H., Liu, Z., Jiang, H., Wang, C., et al.: Big earth data: a new challenge and opportunity for digital Earth's development. Int. J. Digit. Earth. **10**(1), 1–12 (2017)
Halpern, O., Mitchell, R.: The Smartness Mandate. MIT Press, Boston (2023)
Hampton, S.E., Strasser, C.A., Tewksbury, J.J., et al.: Big data and the future of ecology. Front. Ecol. Environ. **11**(3), 156–162 (2013)
Haque, M.M., Chin, H.C., Debnath, A.K.: Sustainable, safe, smart—three key elements of Singapore's evolving transport policies. Transp. Policy. **27**(20), 20–31 (2013)
Havice, E., Campbell, L., Boustany, A.: New data technologies and the politics of scale in environmental management: tracking Atlantic bluefin tuna. Ann. Am. Assoc. Geogr. **112**(8), 2174–2194 (2022)
Heesemann, M., Insua, T.L., Scherwath, M., et al.: Ocean networks Canada: from geohazards research laboratories to smart ocean systems. Oceanography. **27**(2), 151–153 (2014)
Helbig, C., Dransch, D., Böttinger, M., et al.: Challenges and strategies for the visual exploration of complex environmental data. Int. J. Digit. Earth. **10**(10), 1–7 (2017)
Hemmi, A., Graham, I.: Hacker science versus closed science: building environmental monitoring infrastructure. Inf. Commun. Soc. **17**(7), 830–842 (2014)

Hogan, M.: The data center industrial complex. In: Ruiz, R., Jue, M. (eds.) Saturation: An Elemental Politics. Duke University Press, Durham (2021)
Hong, S.-H.: (2018) Control Creep: When the Data Always Travels, So Do the Harms. https://www.cigionline.org/articles/control-creep-when-data-always-travels-so-do-harms/ (2018)
Huang, C.Y., Liang, S.: The open geospatial consortium sensor web PivotViewer: an innovative tool for worldwide sensor web resource discovery. Int. J. Digit. Earth. **7**(9), 761–769 (2014)
Jackson, S., Bobrow, S.: Standards and/as innovation: protocols, creativity, and interactive systems development in ecology. In: Innovation in Theories & Products, CHI 2015, April 18–23, 2015, pp. 1769–1778 (2015)
Jefferson, B.: Digitize and Punish. University of Minnesota Press, Minneapolis (2020)
Jepson, P., Ladle, R.J.: Nature apps: waiting for the revolution. Ambio. **44**(8), 827–832 (2015)
Joppa, L.N.: The case for technology investments in the environment. Nature. **552**(7685), 325–328 (2017)
Kang, E.B., Hudson, S.: Audible crime scenes: ShotSpotter as diagnostic, policing, and space-making infrastructure. Sci. Technol. Hum. Val. **49**, 646 (2022)
Khan, K.A., Akhter, G., Ahmad, Z.: Integrated geoscience databanks for interactive analysis and visualization. Int. J. Digit. Earth. **6**(2), 41–49 (2013)
Kitchin, R.: Big data, new epistemologies and paradigm shifts. Big Data Soc. **1**(1), 1–12 (2014)
Klein, T., Siegwolf, R., Korner, C.: Belowground carbon trade among tall trees in a temperate forest. Science. **352**, 342–344 (2016)
Kluza, D.A., Vieglais, D.A., Andreasen, J.K., Peterson, A.T.: Sudden oak death: geographic risk estimates and predictions of origins. Plant Pathol. **56**(4), 580–587 (2007)
Komninos, N.: Intelligent Cities: Innovation, Knowledge Systems, and Digital Spaces. Spon Press, New York (2002)
Koomey, J.G., Matthews, H.S., Williams, E.: Smart everything: will intelligent systems reduce resource use? Ann. Rev. Environ. Resour. **38**(1), 311–343 (2013)
Kratz, T.K., Arzberger, P., Benson, B.J., et al.: Toward a global lake ecological observatory network. Publ. Karelian Inst. **145**, 51–63 (2006)
Krause, B., Farina, A.: Using ecoacoustic methods to survey the impacts of climate change on biodiversity. Biol. Conserv. **195**, 245–254 (2016)
Kumar, P., Morawska, L., Martani, C., et al.: The rise of low-cost sensing for managing air pollution in cities. Environ. Int. **75**, 199–205 (2015)
Lehman, J.: A sea of potential: the politics of global ocean observations. Polit. Geogr. **55**, 113–123 (2016)
Lehman, J.: The technopolitics of ocean sensing in Blue Legalities. In: Braverman, I., Johnson, E.R. (eds.) The Life & Laws of the Sea, pp. 359–363. Duke University Press, Durham (2020)
Leszczynski, A. Spatial media/tion. Prog. Hum. Geogr. **39**(6), 729–751. (2015)
Lindenmayer, D.B., Likens, G.E., Franklin, J.F.: Earth observation networks (EONs): finding the right balance. Trends Ecol. Evol. **33**(1), 1–3 (2017)
Little, A.S., Needle, C.L., Hilborn, R., et al.: Real-time spatial management approaches to reduce bycatch and discards: experiences from Europe and the United States. Fish Fisher. **16**(4), 576–602 (2015)
Liu, H. Crowdsourcing: citizens as coproducers of public services. Policy Internet **13**(2), 315–331 (2021)
Luque-Alaya, A., Marvin, S.: Urban Operating Systems: Producing the Computational City. MIT Press, Boston (2020)
Machen, R., Nost, E.: Machen, Ruth, and Eric Nost. Thinking algorithmically: the making of hegemonic knowledge in climate governance. Trans. Inst. Br. Geogr. **46**(3), 555–569 (2021)
Mahony, M.: The predictive state: science, territory and the future of the Indian climate. Soc. Stud. Sci. **44**(1), 109–133 (2014)
Mairota, P., Cafarelli, B., Didham, R.K., et al.: Challenges and opportunities in harnessing satellite remote-sensing for biodiversity monitoring. Ecol. Inform. **30**, 207–214 (2015)
Marvin, S., Luque-Ayala, A., McFarlane, C. (eds.): Smart Urbanism: Utopian Vision or False Dawn? Routledge, Oxford, New York (2015)

Matabos, M., et al.: Expert, crowd, students or algorithm: who holds the key to deep-sea imagery 'big data' processing? Methods Ecol. Evol. **8**(8), 996–1004 (2017)
Meynecke, J.O., Liebsch, N.: Asset tracking whales—first deployment of a custom-made GPS/GSM suction cup tag on migrating humpback whales. J. Mar. Sci. Eng. **9**(6), 597 (2021)
Michener, W.K.: Ecological data sharing. Ecol. Inform. **29**, 33–44 (2015)
Michener, W.K., Jones, M.B.: Ecoinformatics: supporting ecology as a data-intensive science. Trends Ecol. Evol. **27**(2), 85–93 (2012)
Mooney, P., Corcoran, P.: Has OpenStreetMap a role in digital earth applications? Int. J. Digit. Earth. **7**(7), 534–553 (2014)
Morozov, E.: To Save Everything, Click Here: The Folly of Technological Solutionism. PublicAffairs, New York (2013)
Morris, B.D., White, E.P.: The EcoData retriever: improving access to existing ecological data. PLoS One. **8**(6), e65848 (2013)
Murai, S.: Can we predict earthquakes with GPS data? Int. J. Digit. Earth. **3**(1), 83–90 (2010)
NASA [EarthData]. Multi-Mission Data Processing System Study. (2023)
O'Brien, M., Costa, D., Servilla, M.: Ensuring the quality of data packages in the LTER network data management system. Ecol. Inform. **36**, 237–246 (2016)
Ocean Observatories. The Plan To Create A 'Fitbit For The Oceans. https://oceanobservatories.org/2015/08/the-plan-to-create-a-fitbit-for-the-oceans/ (2023)
Oceans Protection Plan. Canada's Oceans Protection Plan. Transport Canada. https://www.tc.gc.ca/eng/canada-oceans-protection-plan.html (2016)
Pearson, E., Tindle, H., Ferguson, M., et al.: Can we tweet, post, and share our way to a more sustainable society? A review of the current contributions and future potential of #Socialmediaforsustainability. Ann. Rev. Environ. Resour. **41**, 363–397 (2016)
Pettorelli, N., Laurance, W.F., O'Brien, T.G., et al.: Satellite remote sensing for applied ecologists: opportunities and challenges. J. Appl. Ecol. **51**(4), 839–848 (2014)
Porter, J.H.: A brief history of data sharing in the US long term ecological research network. Bull. Ecol. Soc. Am. **91**(1), 14–20 (2010)
Pötzsch, H.: The emergence of iBorder: bordering bodies, networks, and machines. Environ. Plan. D Soc. Space. **33**(1), 101–118 (2015)
Reddy, R.: Reimagining e-waste circuits: calculation, mobile policies, and the move to urban mining in Global South cities. Urban Geogr. **37**(1), 57–76 (2016)
Reichman, O.J., Jones, M.B., Schildhauer, M.P.: Challenges and opportunities of open data in ecology. Science. **331**(6018), 703–705 (2011)
Ritts, M., Bakker, K.: Conservation acoustics: animal sounds, audible natures, cheap nature. Geoforum. **124**, 144–155 (2021)
Ritts, M., Simpson, M.: Smart oceans governance: reconfiguring capitalist, colonial, and environmental relations. Trans. Inst. Br. Geogr. **48**(2), 365–379 (2023)
Ritts, M., Gage, S.H., Picard, C.R., Dundas, E., Dundas, S.: Collaborative research praxis to establish baseline ecoacoustics conditions in Gitga'at territory. Glob. Ecol. Conserv. **7**, 25–38 (2016)
Ritts, M., Simlai, T., Gabrys, J.: The environmentality of digital acoustic monitoring: emerging formations of spatial power in forests. Polit. Geogr. **110**, 103074 (2024)
Robertson, M.M., Wainwright, J.D.: The value of nature to the state. Ann. Assoc. Am. Geogr. **103**(4), 890–905 (2013)
Rocchini, D., Hernández-Stefanoni, J.L., He, K.S.: Advancing species diversity estimate by remotely sensed proxies: a conceptual review. Ecol. Inform. **25**, 22–28 (2015)
Rocchini, D., Petras, V., Petrasova, A., et al.: Open-access and open-source for remote sensing training in ecology. Ecol. Inform. **40**, 57–61 (2017)
Roche, D.G., Kruuk, L.E., Lanfear, R., et al.: Public data archiving in ecology and evolution: how well are we doing? PLoS Biol. **13**(11), 1–12 (2015)
Roe, P., Eichinski, P., Fuller, R., McDonald, P., Schwarzkopf, L., Towsey, M., Truskinger, A., Tucker, D., Watson, D.: The Australian acoustic observatory. Methods Ecol. Evol. **12**(10), 1802–1818 (2021a)

Roe, P., Eichinski, P., Fuller, R.A., McDonald, P.G., Schwarzkopf, L., Towsey, M., et al.: The Australian acoustic observatory. Methods Ecol. Evol. **12**(10), 1802–1808 (2021b)

Rotz, S., Duncan, E., Small, M., Botschner, J., Dara, R., Mosby, I., Reed, M., Fraser, E.D.G.: The politics of digital agricultural technologies: a preliminary review. Sociol. Rural. **59**(2), 203–229 (2019)

Sandbrook, C.: The social implications of using drones for biodiversity conservation. Ambio. **44**(4), 636–647 (2015)

Specht, A., Guru, S., Houghton, L., et al.: Data management challenges in analysis and synthesis in the ecosystem sciences. Sci. Total Environ. **534**, 144–158 (2015)

Strubell, E., Ganish, A., McCallum, A.: Energy and policy considerations for deep learning in NLP. In: 57th Annual Meeting of the Association for Computational Linguistics (ACL). Florence, Italy. July 2019 arXiv:1906.02243 (2019)

Swanstrom, E.: Animal, Vegetable, Digital: Experiments in New Media Aesthetics and Environmental Poetics. University of Alabama Press, Tuscaloosa (2016)

Thatcher, J.: Big data, big questions: living on fumes: digital footprints, data fumes, and the limitations of spatial big data. Int. J. Commun. **8**, 1765–1783 (2014)

Timberg, C., Harwell, R.: U.S. sanctions Israel's NSO Group over Pegasus spyware. The Washington Post. https://www.washingtonpost.com/technology/2021/11/03/pegasus-nso-entity-list-spyware/ (2021)

Turner, W., Rondinini, C., Pettorelli, N., et al.: Free and open-access satellite data are key to biodiversity conservation. Biol. Conserv. **182**, 173–176 (2015)

Verburg, P.H., Dearing, J.A., Dyke, J.G., et al.: Methods and approaches to modelling the Anthropocene. Glob. Environ. Chang. **39**, 328–340 (2016)

Volk, C.J., Lucero, Y., Barnas, K.: Why is data sharing in collaborative natural resource efforts so hard and what can we do to improve it? Environ. Manag. **53**(5), 883–893 (2014)

Wiens, K., Chamberlain, E.J.: Deere Just Swindled Farmers out of Their Right to Repair. WIRED Magazine. https://www.wired.com/story/john-deere-farmers-right-to-repair/ (2018)

Wood, D.M.: What is global surveillance? Towards a relational political economy of the global surveillant assemblage. Geoforum. **49**, 317–326 (2013)

Woodward, G., Gray, C., Baird, D.J.: Biomonitoring for the 21st century: new perspectives in an age of globalisation and emerging environmental threats. Limnetica. **32**(2), 159–174 (2013)

World Economic Forum: Governing Smart Cities: Policy Benchmarks for Ethical and Responsible Smart City Development. Online: https://www3.weforum.org/docs/WEF_Governing_Smart_Cities_2021.pdf (2021)

Zandbergen, D.: "We are sensemakers": the (anti-)politics of smart city co-creation. Public Cult. **29**(3_83), 539–562 (2017)

Chapter 6
I'm Afraid HAL Can't Do That: Your Smart Home Is Not That Kind of Existential Threat

Robin L. Zebrowski

Abstract This chapter starts at the cliché of the smart home that has gone rogue and introduces the question of whether these integrated, distributed systems can have ethical frameworks like human ethics that could prevent the science fictional trope of the evil, sentient house. I argue that such smart systems are not a threat on their own, because these kinds of integrated, distributed systems are not the kind of things that could be conscious, a precondition for having ethics like ours (and ethics like ours enable the possibility of being the kinds of things that could be evil). To make these arguments, I look to the history of AI/artificial consciousness and 4e cognition, concluding with the idea that our human ethics as designers and consumers of these systems is the real ethical concern with smart life systems.

Keywords AI · Machine consciousness · Smart home technologies · Embodied cognition · 4e cognition · Sentience

6.1 Introduction

Science fiction is filled with the trope of the smart house or smart dwelling, which eventually becomes the sentient house, and often then becomes evil or at least autonomous (in the truest sense of the word and therefore no longer under the control of its owners). There are several famous versions of this story, most notably HAL 9000 in *2001: A Space Odyssey*, who takes over the spaceship and attempts to murder the crewmembers to preserve its own functioning. This theme recurs throughout various storytelling media, including most notably short fiction like Bradbury's *The Veldt* and *There Will Come Soft Rains* (1950, 1951); television shows including *The Simpsons* ("Treehouse of Horror XI" 2001), *Futurama* ("Love and Rocket" 2002), and *The X Files* ("Ghost in the Machine" 1993); and even in a

R. L. Zebrowski (✉)
Cognitive Science Program, Departments of Philosophy, Psychology, and Computer Science, Beloit College, Beloit, WI, USA
e-mail: zebrowsr@beloit.edu

E. Kornyshova et al. (eds.), *Smart Life and Smart Life Engineering*,
https://doi.org/10.1007/978-3-031-75887-4_6

Disney Channel film called *Smart House* (1999). Indeed, in so much fiction where a sentient house makes an appearance, one can more or less expect the house to act as a disembodied, but distributed, robot engaging in a terrifying uprising dystopia where the house tries to kill or control the human inhabitants (even in the Disney film).

The reality, however, is very different. (A terminological note: the terms "smart life technologies," "distributed computing," "pervasive computing," and "ubiquitous computing" devices all have slightly different meanings. For the sake of this chapter, however, you can assume they are being used more or less interchangeably.) Some of these devices and technologies have made tremendous strides in adoption, at least in the USA, with something like 30 million households (25% of all American households in 2020) having an Amazon Alexa smart speaker in the home (Vincent 2021). And that's only *one brand* of *one kind* of smart life technology. There are competing devices like the Apple HomePod and the Google Home systems that would widen the overall number of households in the USA with smart speakers and even more if we include devices like the Sonos, which can use Alexa or Google Home assistants. We could also count the 10 million users of Amazon's Ring doorbell cameras in 2020 (Greer and Bonesteel 2022). But for many smart home devices, there are burgeoning options among brands and more appearing on the market each year. There are networked vacuums for your rugs, networked thermometers for your heating and cooling, smart locks for your doors, smart air purifiers, pet cameras, beds, refrigerators, ovens, coffee makers, scales, and more.

If you only engaged with fiction about smart homes and smart life technologies, you could be excused for believing that these integrated technologies are the kinds of things that might gain consciousness and rise up with the other robots in the apparently-inevitable (in fiction) robot uprising. But despite being the primary trope surrounding smart homes, disembodied consciousness is not something that anyone need worry about. This chapter will demonstrate that for empirical, historical, and ontological reasons, smart life technologies are not the kinds of systems, even networked together, that could become conscious. However, that doesn't mean there is nothing to worry about with regard to these kinds of technologies. I will return to this point, encouraging thoughtful engagement with these systems, and speak at length about the real and potential harms that they enable, but robot uprising or your house becoming jealous of the attention you give your partner is absolutely not on that list.

6.2 Consciousness and AI: A Brief and Messy History

Since its inception, the project of AI in general has been split into two camps: on the one hand, (usage 1) AI is understood as a way of understanding human cognition better through replication. The idea is that if we can create something capable of the kinds of really quite interesting and adaptable general intelligence humans enjoy, we can finally better understand human psychology and the nature of minds more broadly. This can be seen, in some ways, as merely a continuation of the project of psychology more broadly and cognitive psychology specifically. On the other hand, (usage 2) AI is sometimes understood as a goal in itself, a kind of mad-science pursuit of the re-creation of consciousness in a Frankenstein-like quest to simply create a mind because we can. Of course, lately, with massive amounts of money on the line for corporations and businesses, we see the term "AI" being used simply to mean (usage 3) "algorithm," in a way that hides what the algorithms are and how they work. But this conflation of three very different uses of the terminology makes it hard to have a serious conversation about what integrated, distributed smart life AI systems might look like and how we should think about the design, dissemination, use, oversight, and regulation of such systems, when it's often hard for laypersons to know how the language is being used.

A complete history of AI is not warranted here, nor would it be possible in a chapter-length text (see Dietrich et al. (2021a) for a recent book-length history and Dietrich et al. (2021b) for a shorter one). But in order to argue that there are empirical, historical, and ontological reasons to doubt that machine consciousness could even possibly arise in a smart home system, we must look at some of the ways philosophers, psychologists, neuroscientists, and other AI theorists have thought about minds across AI's history. Most such histories would start with the Turing test and for good reasons: Turing (1950) was concerned not with trying to solve the problem of other minds, which had plagued philosophers for thousands of years, or trying to operationalize the concept of intelligence in a simple way, but was instead offering a way to side-step the problem. He was using what Dennett refers to as a "quick probe assumption" (1990, p. 50). In other words, Turing's suggestion seemed to be that if some system (of any type) were able to carry on an unrestricted conversation about any topic at all, it could be used as a kind of shorthand for the other very many intelligent capacities the system must obviously have in order to be able to speak intelligently on so many subjects. And while the Turing test has long been out of fashion (yet still endlessly discussed), the recent successes of large language models (LLMs) have brought it back out, front and center, as a possible shorthand for whether a machine may be intelligent and, more interestingly, if it may reasonably be said to have a mind. Machines have been intelligent for as long as there have been machines; this should not be the framing of any serious debate. My calculator is more mathematically intelligent that even the best human mathematicians when performing the sorts of calculations it's programmed for. The only way "can machines think" is an interesting question is when "think" comes appropriately pre-loaded with all the baggage we traditionally imbue it with including mindedness and, hence, consciousness, whatever it is that consciousness turns out to be. Consciousness carries a moral dimension that requires accommodation in a way that brute intelligence does not. And this distinction is part of why the terminology of "artificial intelligence" is such a mess.

The language here is historically muddy, so for the sake of clarity, when I talk about machine intelligence, or AI, I have in mind what has been called "Strong AI," as in, a thing that thinks rather than one which models thought, or, more recently, "AGI (artificial general intelligence)," although this often carries with it the undesirable baggage of the singularity or AI superintelligence, neither of which is philosophically interesting or remotely likely. Neither of these terms quite captures the truly interesting piece of this problem though, which is machine consciousness (which corresponds to usage 2 outlined above).

Despite the recent (early 2020s) apparent successes (and extremely notable failures) of LLMs, history is not on their side when it comes to machine consciousness (Bender et al. 2021; Dreyfus 1992; Dietrich et al. 2021a; Harnad 1990; Newman et al. 2019; Birhane 2021). While it's true that there is no widely agreed-upon definition of consciousness, and certainly no useful tests of it beyond those born of medical necessity, such as clinical definitions of brain death, many cognitive scientists have tended to converge on Nagel's (1974) keen observation that "an organism has conscious mental states if and only if there is something that it is like to *be* that organism—something it is like *for* the organism." The possibility of subjective, phenomenal experience, in the most neutral sense of those terms, is what makes living beings minded, and its absence is what continues to make machine intelligence comparatively uninteresting. A thorough discussion about the controversies in consciousness studies would take many more pages (and volumes) than possible here, but to head off some objections and clarify some notions, we might locate the idea of consciousness being supported in this piece somewhere in the area of the pragmatist or enactivist traditions. Dewey, for example, once remarked that "Mind is primarily a verb" (Dewey 1934), in an effort to dissuade us from the common ways of thinking about the mind as an object or a thing. Similarly, Thompson (2007) sums up the enactive approach in part by arguing that "living beings are autonomous agents that actively generate and maintain themselves, and thereby also enact or bring forth their own cognitive domains," and "cognition is the exercise of skillful know-how in situated and embodied action" (13). The thing that the pragmatists and enactivists try to show us is that thinking about consciousness as some *thing* that gets added to cognition, some special magic sauce, is part of what causes most of our philosophical and conceptual problems (but also generates so much of our clever speculative fiction, the very reason we can make sense of Gregor Samsa waking up in the body of a cockroach or a smart sentient house suddenly developing romantic feelings for one of its occupants). Rather than thinking of it as some magic substance, as our legacy from Descartes would have us do, consciousness is most aptly described as a cluster (or even radial) concept: an idea that picks out a number of properties, often overlapping, without considering a list of necessary and sufficient conditions for inclusion in the concept. It denies a central property to the phenomenon while acknowledging that many overlapping features that tend to appear in systems are identified by the label. Wittgenstein's (1953) "family resemblances" are useful here, as is the idea of graded centrality that Lakoff (1987) uses in discussing the structure of prototypical categories. It might be that for consciousness you need certain kinds of perceptual capacities, and capacities to enable action, and be comprised of allostasis[1]-seeking components, alongside a whole host of other potential dynamics involving interaction between individual and environment. What the cluster or radial concept idea buys us is that there isn't an exact list of, for example, perceptual capacities needed. This reminds us that across the animal kingdom, our perceptual capacities vary quite widely, and there is a huge field of human variation as well. Visual perception may be important for some ways of being conscious (including, but not limited to, visual consciousness—having visual experience that you're aware of), but excluding it from a system doesn't somehow preclude the system from being conscious; this would be utterly absurd, as we have wide human variation in sensory and perceptual capacities but all among obviously conscious beings. Any theory of consciousness that threatens to rule out full and complete human beings with divergent ways of experiencing the world must be immediately off the table. Thinking of consciousness this way is fairly safe and would likely err on the side of over-attribution rather than under-attribution, but it also allows for the idea that there are genuine edge cases that are hard to classify and that require additional scrutiny to decide how well they do or do not fit into the concept. This is why humans, including humans who speak another language than I do and hence limit my capacity to communicate verbally, remain safely within the concept of conscious beings, and dogs and squirrels and even bats seem fairly obviously also members. Yet there seems no reason to believe my desk or water bottle is even up for consideration outside of some sort of animism or panpsychism, at least not in the way LLMs currently appear to be or distributed smart house systems may one day be.

While denying LLMs any claim to consciousness probably should be uncontroversial, philosophers and cognitive scientists are not united on this and historically never have been. This relates most obviously to the fact that the story about consciousness laid out a paragraph earlier is not shared by all cognitive scientists. Consciousness remains one of the least agreed-upon problems in philosophy, because our epistemological and ontological access to varieties of it remains challenged. We historically believed (and reinforced through our academic philosophical and psychological practices) that we had privileged access to our own minds and were hopelessly cut off from accessing the minds of any others. (This, of course, is less of a problem when we locate consciousness as a phenomenon in dynamics rather than a hidden, internal, private experience.) Recent arguments, made by Chalmers most notably, approach the problem from a reductionist stance and argue that LLMs may, in fact, be a bit conscious under the right conditions (Chalmers 2023). Contrary to the claim above in which I state that consciousness is very likely a cluster or radial concept, Chalmers instead considers what sorts of properties might mark conscious systems and then applies those properties to LLMs, both current and possible. He says we might consider a LLM to be conscious if there

[1] Allostasis here means something very similar to homeostasis or the body's seeking-after equilibrium. Allostasis implies that it is seeking equilibrium among bodily stresses rather than more routine imbalances.

is some feature X, possessed by LLMs, and that we have reason to believe that a system with X is probably conscious. He goes on to offer a few candidates for X, namely, self-report, conversational ability, and intelligence, all of which I would argue might have been decent proxies for a judgment in the past, but surely must be abandoned in light of conversational ability as its own engineering telos in the absence of any other features of mindedness. He offers a fourth possible feature, "seems-conscious," which is even more problematic than the previous three when considered in the appropriate context. That context, of course, is a world where our judgments about what is and is not conscious have been built up both socially, culturally, and evolutionarily over extremely large periods of time embedded in sociocultural systems with other conscious beings, and even then we quite obviously still get it wrong, and historically have quite often. My students are often horrified to hear that Descartes, in the mid-1600s, believed animals to be little automata, their squeals of apparent pain actually being no more than the equivalent of squeaky gears. Plants are perhaps the modern day equivalent, currently the focus of questions about whether their capacities look enough like cognition to count as cognitive (Calvo and Lawrence 2023). But recent philosophy of mind is rife with similar claims, often centered around the capacity for language as a prerequisite for thought, and thus reserved only for humanity, and then only some subsets with appropriate language skills (e.g., Malcolm 1972; Fodor 1975; Dennett 1975, 1987).[2] So even if we thought there might be a single property, possession of which indicates a system has consciousness, we must always remember all of our judgments about those properties historically have been deeply problematic, not only excluding the overwhelming majority of animal (and plant) species but also awarding consciousness only in lesser degrees to many actual humans, such as women or people with certain kinds of disabilities or certain entire races and cultures. And more specifically, our judgments have centered on language because we've considered it a uniquely human trait, making it an easy shorthand for systems that almost certainly have other features of the cluster or radial concept that is consciousness. If we're throwing out the richness of the concept and reducing it to a property that is necessarily present in a conscious system, language as an indicator is hugely, deeply, and irredeemably problematic. I would argue that his conclusion, "It's reasonable to have a significant credence that we'll have conscious LLM+s within a decade" (Chalmers 2023), is unwarranted from most of its starting assumptions.

But why should we care if LLMs specifically, or language-based AI systems in general, are conscious or not when what's at stake for our purposes here are

[2] Fodor's *The Language of Thought* (1975) is certainly the source of much of the language-based focus on AI throughout its history, focusing as it did on how linguistic structures, even before spoken language, are the source of human kinds of thought. Turing preceded Fodor, but Fodor legitimized the deep linguistic structures as precursors to thought itself. Dennett's claims (1987) are distinct in that they do not require thought to be linguistic in nature but instead attribute thinking only to systems with the capacity for higher-order representations or the ability to represent things self-consciously, a feature that arrives only with language.

smart home devices? We should care because much of the interfacing that happens between users and their devices is mediated by just such language model systems. Furthermore, it seems likely that this will only increase as companies roll these models into their search engines and continue to deploy them to interface all sorts of human-facing systems (Kurian 2023; Leonardis 2023). No one would be tempted to think their networked smart devices might be candidates for consciousness if they weren't able to speak, deceptively or otherwise. What's at stake here is the central debate in artificial intelligence over the last 70 years (at least). What enables, or guarantees, that a system will be conscious, and what sorts of systems are even candidates to be such systems? Language has always been, and continues to be, central to this debate, even among people who argue that it clearly shouldn't be (Browning and Lecun 2022).

The argument against language-only systems being the kinds of things that could possibly have consciousness had a unique formulation in the symbol grounding problem (Harnad 1990). Importantly, situating the problem here allows us to narrow the scope of the question enough that we can then let back in integrated and smart home devices and see if their distributed processing and tangible interfaces enable the possibility of consciousness over and above the simpler language-only systems. I will argue that they don't and that you have nothing to fear from HAL or your networked refrigerator, at least as far as the hyperbolic robot uprising is concerned.

6.3 4e Cognition

Throughout the history of both cognitive science and artificial intelligence as proper academic disciplines, there have been several distinct research programs that have driven the field forward. They are competing waves of thought, although not temporal waves. Rather, we can imagine at least three or four distinct research programs all moving along the same timeline, and what distinguishes them temporally is only the fact that historically, different waves have been dominant in the field at different times.[3] This is a rough sketch with a lot of messiness not captured by this visualization, but it helps to see that folks were pursuing very different underlying systems of thought about what cognition and consciousness are from inside the disciplines tasked with defining and modeling those things. (See Table 6.1).

Relevant here for our purposes is the third wave, often now referred to as 4e cognition. Without a complete history, we can suffice with the driving philosophy: that cognition is not symbol manipulation in the void and it is not mere neuroscience. It denies reduction to either functional program or neural substrate. Instead, it insists

[3] There is much debate about whether cognitive science actually has historical waves or not. Some people carve them up differently. You can find some interpretations in Lakoff and Johnson (1999), where they talk about it as first-generation and second-generation cognitive science. You can also find the three research programs laid out in a similar way to my own analysis in Thompson (2007).

Table 6.1 One way of representing the history of cognitive science and artificial intelligence through distinct research methodologies

Wave	Research program focused on	Roughly dominant	In Cog. Sci.	In AI
1	Symbolic representation	1950s–1990s	– Language of Thought – Representational Theory of Mind – Computational Theory of Mind	– GOFAI ("Good Old Fashioned Artificial Intelligence"; this is traditional rule-based programming)
2	Neural structure	1970s–1980; 2020–current	– Cognitive/ Computational Neuroscience	– ANNs (artificial neural networks) – PDP (parallel distributed processing) – Connectionism – Deep learning
3	4e Cognition	2000s–current	– Dynamic systems – Embodied cognition – Extended mind	– Subsumption architecture – Cognitive robotics

that embodiment is not merely a container for the mind but part of the actual content and workings of it. The body and the dynamics of its development and experience in physical, social, and cultural environments are all irreducible determinants of the ways minds develop and sustain themselves. And while these views are all condensed radically for our purposes here, the four Es themselves reveal much of the driving force behind this research program: Embodied, Embedded, Extended, and Enactive. (There is argument that Ecological deserves a spot as well, making it 5e Cognition, while others argue that it should be 4ea, adding the "a" for affective, but neither of these has been widely adopted yet.) When we say "embodied," we might mean many different things, but most broadly, the idea here is that the resources that the body itself brings to bear in a cognitive task are cognitively relevant to solving the problem (see Wilson 2002 for a breakdown of different uses of "embodied" in the literature). The idea of "embedded" cognition tends to mean ways that the body is situated in specific environments and how that embedding brings the environment into the cognitive process. This is slightly different from "extended" cognition, in which we understand parts of the environment to literally be a part of the cognitive apparatus, such as the use of a pen and paper while doing long division in mathematics (Clark and Chalmers 1998). Finally "enactive" denotes a way of understanding cognition as the way that living autonomous creatures actively create and maintain their own cognitive systems. This view is hard to summarize briefly, but the facts of autonomy and life-sustaining processes are part of how the mind emerges, as living creatures place value and meaning on the parts of the world that help maintain their own existence (see Thompson 2007 for a robust recounting of the current state of enactivism).

Since each of these non-temporal waves arose at various times and in various subdisciplines within and around cognitive science, it would be a mistake to place any specific figures as the founders of these views, but we can look to a few key figures to get a strong sense of why 4e cognition matters in the smart life technologies debates. Historically, the view that the body is irrelevant at best, and actively harmful to cognition at worst, can be traced back to Newton and Descartes and a million other rationalist thinkers across the history of Western thought. The mistakes about mindedness persist despite the scientific evidence that they're incorrect. These errors find their way into common language in various ways, such as: when you're emotional, you don't think clearly; reasoning is at its strongest when we think objectively, removing ourselves as much as possible from the situatedness of our bodies and environments; or even Descartes's famous, "I think, therefore I am," implying that thought is separable in principle from the body and that this would be both a possible and a desirable state of affairs whenever rational thought is our goal. There's a pretty clear, straight line from Descartes's disembodied mind to the belief that a LLM (or the house for which it will someday be an interface) could be conscious. At its simplest, 4e cognition denies not only that a system of language alone will ever be the kind of thing that could develop thought or conscious experience but that the complex interaction of embodiment, environment, evolutionary history, radical autonomy, dynamic social interactions, and various other complex relations are the precursors for the possibility of being the kind of system that might be conscious.

All told, we can look to empirical, historical, and ontological arguments from (at least) the following relevant perspectives:

1. Phenomenology, where we're reminded that the role of the lived body in experience is irreducible to objective examination (Merleau-Ponty 1945/2012; Dreyfus 1992; Dreyfus and Dreyfus 1988; Noë 2010; Gallagher 2012, 2017)
2. Ecological psychology, where the environment is a necessary feature of making sense of systems of perception and action (Chemero 2011; Lobo et al. 2018; Wilson et al. 2016; Gibson 1979)
3. Cognitive linguistics, where we see how the language we use reveals the underlying structure of concepts, which are built via metaphor through ways human bodies tend to be, in environments we tend to inhabit, culturally, socially, and physically (Lakoff and Johnson 1980, 1999; Boroditsky 2001; Thibodeau and Boroditsky 2011)
4. Robotics, which demonstrates ways that bodily structure and dynamics can produce intelligent behavior in the absence of centralized abstract representations (Brooks 1991; Pfeifer and Bongard 2006)
5. Enactive social cognition, which shows how autonomous systems in interaction can co-create new autonomous systems that enable cognitive possibilities over and above the individuals in the interaction (De Jaegher and Di Paolo 2007)

6. Embodied neuroscience, where we can see whole body systems engaging in cognitive work from the micro-level to the macro (Damasio 1994; Gallese and Sinigaglia 2011)
7. Biology, where we can track the way allostasis-seeking systems impose meaning and value onto their lived worlds (Weber and Varela 2002; Varela et al. 1992; Maturana and Varela 1980; Thompson 2007)
8. Gesture studies, which we spontaneously produce to aid cognition, as well as helping us organize, access, and schematize information (Goldin-Meadow and Alibali 2013; Kita et al. 2017)

The evidence is fairly overwhelming that some variety of 4e cognition is going to turn out to be the most accurate description of what we mean when we talk about the structure and function of human minds and consciousness.

When we start from understanding consciousness as related to 4e cognition, it's a very small leap to understanding why ethics is tied to embodied consciousness. Damasio, in his (1994) work describing particular kinds of neural damage to the ventromedial prefrontal cortex (VMPFC), discovered the ways that social intelligence and interaction are encoded in neural structures tied to ethics. The story of Phineas Gage, the man who famously survived a large metal spike shooting through his brain only to become crass, socially awkward, and incapable of holding down a job, is one such anecdote. But Damasio offers rich stories of real people whose brain damage is localized to a space (VMPFC) that seems to be a nexus of social cognition, ethics, and some kinds of decision-making. Similarly, Graziano (2013) outlines a competing theory of social cognition and consciousness that's worth noting. If we begin at a 4e understanding of the mind, there isn't really any surprise that these systems would be bound together, evolutionarily, because of the kinds of beings we are and the kinds of social and ethical systems we inhabit. No one understood this better than Francisco Varela (1992) who opens his *Ethical Know-How: Action, Wisdom, and Cognition* with the sentence, "Ethics is closer to wisdom than to reason, closer to understanding what is good than to correctly adjudicating particular situations." We can see this understanding of ethics as a vein of ethical theory reaching back to Aristotle's *phronesis* (practical wisdom) through contemporary virtue ethics today.

The evidence is firmly against the possibility of the trope of the evil smart or sentient house as it appears throughout popular culture and speculative fiction. Large language models, which are very likely soon to be the most common interface for all sorts of integrated and ubiquitous computing, are simply not the kind of thing which could develop consciousness. HAL is not going to cut off your air in the spaceship to preserve itself. Marge Simpson is safe to take a bath without worry that her Pierce Brosnan-voiced smart house is going to ogle her and plot to destroy Homer to keep her all for itself. These stories are firmly in the category of speculative fiction, and cognitive science has your back.

6.4 But There *Is* a Threat

However safe you are from your networked smart devices with the language model interface experiencing an awakening to consciousness that turns it evil (or doesn't), that doesn't mean there are no ethical considerations in adopting, designing, or promoting these systems. In fact, networked smart devices offer a not-insignificant number of unique ethical challenges to be noted, although they are largely and safely ethical challenges well within the confines of *human* ethics.

Indulge me briefly as I offer two personal anecdotes as guideposts into this conversation. Last year, I found myself shopping for an old-fashioned, analog scale after my partner purchased a new smart scale. The smart scale demanded that I not only make an account with the company before stepping on it to check my weight but that I include my birthdate and gender as well. The scale would not do its single job, to weigh someone, until a non-trivial amount of irrelevant personal data were offered up to the company. It's important to note that this scale was not marketed as or purchased with the intent of tracking any sort of information over time other than weight. And it isn't paranoia to recognize the ways companies vacuum up as much user data as permitted (and more, due to inconsistent regulation and enforcement) and marvel at what was required before a scale would perform its function as a scale.

The second anecdote I offer involves my attempt to purchase a smart doorbell for a new home. First, I immediately rejected anything in the Ring line, because Amazon has been riddled with bad press around handing over the data to police without permission of the owners (Ng 2022) as well as the outrageous amount of private data shared with third parties (Cox 2020). But even rejecting the Ring line immediately and finding a company who could provide this service without compromising any of our privacy proved daunting. I even refused to use a camera that stored any of our data in the cloud or on their own servers. The company we finally landed on doesn't use our data for training the algorithms (so humans are not viewing the footage to label it). The trade-off is this: my front-door camera went off a staggering 103 times in 12 h today, only 6 of which were actually a package delivery or the dog wanting to be let inside. During certain times of the year, the shadows and wind combine to create a perfect storm that moves one of the plants near the door in a way the AI detects, generally just as motion but occasionally as "human." Because I care so much about being careful stewards of our data, I simply mute the camera much of the time, but the trade-off between good AI pattern recognition that comes with really awful corporate practices or bad AI pattern recognition that allows me to keep my data safe is an easy choice for me. I suspect that isn't true of many others in the market for home-security cameras.

From just these two anecdotes of ways I have personally had to contend with smart home devices in the recent past, you can start to get a sense of the kinds of complicated ethical calculus involved in investing in any of these systems, and you can also see how this is not (only) a personal ethical choice but one that impacts numerous others in my society, many of whom are not even aware that they are implicated in such an ethical decision. And yet we have barely scratched the surface of the pile of ethical questions that are raised when we consider the present and future of smart life technologies.

The ways that integrated, distributed, ubiquitous smart life systems are already causing harms are too numerous to offer here in great detail, but it would be irresponsible to write an article about smart life systems and machine consciousness without mentioning some of these very real dangers of already-existing systems. So in the interest of brevity, here is a short list of some of the worries that smart life systems may pose:

1. *IoT botnets*: when the mostly idle computing power of networked home devices is harnessed by would-be hackers to DDoS critical infrastructure, for example. Famous cases include the 2016 Mirai botnet that took down Amazon, Netflix, the *New York Times*, Reddit, Twitter, Spotify, PlayStation, and more (Blue 2016). We are reminded that "In 2012 an anonymous security researcher published the Internet Census 2012, revealing that they'd created a botnet called Carna in over 400,000 embedded devices, such as printers. Their botnet was designed to deliver information from infected machines to create a census of connected—and vulnerable—computers and devices.

   That same year botnets emerged in the popular consciousness when security firm TrendMicro released their report Russian Underground 101, revealing that botnets were available for around $2 an hour, or $700 wholesale. In 2014, infosec company Proofpoint found an attack in which over 100,000 conventional household "smart" appliances had been turned into a botnet for spam attacks" (Blue 2016).
2. *Biased data*: the phrase "garbage in, garbage out" is often used to describe machine learning systems in which biased datasets reproduce societal biases and often launder them into the guise of objectivity. This shows up in numerous ways in relation to all kinds of integrated systems (Flowers 2019; Madan et al. 2022).

   (a) *Facial recognition*: one well-examined example of ways that bias infects our distributed automated "smart" systems is facial recognition. We know that facial recognition systems, in use in airports, police stations, and public spaces like train stations, tend to reproduce harms and biases against already-marginalized members of various societies. Examples are robust, from a black student not being able to take her exams because the software couldn't see her (Buolamwini 2017; Kleinman 2017) to black skin giving false positives in police databases using Amazon's Rekognition software (Buolamwini 2019; Singer 2019) to the facial recognition systems in China being deployed in the service of what many consider genocide (Wakefield 2021; Mozur 2019).

   (b) *Religious, disabled, racial, gender minorities:* popular chatbots like GPT3 and ChatGPT have well-documented inabilities to reproduce language about Islam, for example, without including violence (Gershgorn 2021). They currently cannot make sense of problems in which male pronouns refer to nurses and female pronouns refer to doctors, for example (Williams 2023).

Vision systems in autonomous vehicles often misclassify people on crutches or in wheelchairs as not even people (Williams 2021a, b).

3. *Surveillance capitalism:* The term refers to the ways that personal data is gathered and sold, originally in service to advertising, notably by companies like Facebook and Google, but then in service to altering the behavior of users of these systems (Angwin et al. 2016; Zuboff 2019). Particularly now that people have largely resigned themselves to this massive data gathering by many companies for the sake of convenience, those companies are rolling out their own LLMs and products, selling people their own data back in a new form. And that data is not just used to sell people products but to manipulate behavior and spread disinformation in new, powerful ways.
4. *Humans disguised as AI:* In what has come to be called "ghost work," there is a continually increasing number of examples where companies claim to be using AI to perform some task, and it turns out that either it's simply humans doing that work but calling it AI or humans are doing that work under the guise of labeling data for training the algorithms. This means that often, humans are interacting with systems they believe to be automated, sometimes revealing personal information, as with therapy bots, only to have that data fed directly to actual humans. Without greater education about these worries, the general public can be deceived about their interactions with these products (Williams et al. 2022; Solon 2018; Xiang 2022; Valentine 2021).

6.5 Conclusion

It's worth pointing out that the reason these technologies are worth criticizing to the extent that I do in Sect. 6.4 is that they are technologies that have so much promise: promise to make our lives easier and better; promise to allow us to shift our time to pursuits that interest us rather than be mired in all sorts of mundane tasks we find ourselves doing every day just to survive; and promise to automate "second-shift" work, largely done by women at great personal and societal expense, onto integrated distributed systems that might promote equal access to women in public spaces. The promise of smart life systems is supposed to be a promise of a better, more equitable, more utopian society. But if we don't attend to the very real ethical concerns of these systems (our ethical concerns, concerns about the corporations and governments who own, design, and deploy them, not concerns about the systems needing a code of ethics), then they will be closer to a science fiction dystopia than we'd like to admit. The house won't become sentient and turn on its owner, but the corporations and governments who will have access to facets of our everyday lives that even we might lack will have a new kind of power that we are only beginning to see the effects of. Rather than worry about questionable ethics in a fictionally conscious house, we should worry about questionable ethics in the people who design, build, deploy, and maintain invasive systems throughout our spaces, both shared and private.

In other words, there are no smart home appliances or systems that are set to become conscious and trap you or otherwise rise up as so much science fiction predicts. However, there are real concerns with the way smart home systems are created, deployed, incentivized, and used that should give everyone pause. Without strict regulation, these technologies will be (and already are) used in ways that dehumanize and commodify all of us.

References

Angwin, J., Parris, T., Mattu, S.: Breaking the Black Box: What Facebook Knows About You. Propublica September 28. https://www.propublica.org/article/breaking-the-black-box-what-facebook-knows-about-you (2016). Accessed 16 May 2023

Bender, E., Gebru, T., McMillan-Major, A., Shmitchell, S.: On the Dangers of Stochastic Parrots: Can Language Models Be Too Big? FAccT '21, March 3–10. https://doi.org/10.1145/3442188.3445922 (2021)

Boroditsky, L.: Does language shape thought? Mandarin and English speakers' conceptions of time. Cogn. Psychol. **43**(1), 1–22 (2001)

Birhane, A.: The impossibility of automating ambiguity. Artif. Life. **27**(1), 44–61 (2021). https://doi.org/10.1162/artl_a_00336

Blue, V.: That Time Your Smart Toaster Broke the Internet. Engadget, October 26. https://www.engadget.com/2016-10-28-that-time-your-smart-toaster-broke-the-internet.html (2016). Accessed 16 May 2023

Bradbury, R.: "There Will Come Soft Rains" in The Martian Chronicles. Doubleday (1950)

Bradbury, R.: "The Veldt" in The Illustrated Man. Doubleday (1951)

Brooks, R.: Intelligence without representation. Artif. Intell. **47**(1–3), 139–159 (1991)

Buolamwini, J.A.: Gender Shades: Intersectional Phenotypic and Demographic Evaluation of Face Datasets and Gender Classifiers (MS thesis). MIT. hdl:1721.1/114068 (2017)

Buolamwini, J.: Response: Racial and Gender Bias in Amazon Rekognition – Commercial AI System for Analyzing Faces. Medium, January 25. https://medium.com/@Joy.Buolamwini/response-racial-and-gender-bias-in-amazon-rekognition-commercial-ai-system-for-analyzing-faces-a289222eeced (2019). Accessed 16 May 2023

Browning, J., Lecun, Y.: AI and the Limits of Language. Noēma (2022)

Calvo, P., Lawrence, N.: Planta Sapiens: The New Science of Plant Intelligence. WW Norton (2023)

Chalmers, D.: Could a Large Language Model Be Conscious. arXiv:2303.07103v2. https://doi.org/10.48550/arXiv.2303.07103 (2023)

Chemero, A.: Radical Embodied Cognitive Science. MIT Press (2011)

Clark, A., Chalmers, D.: The Extended Mind. Analysis. **58**(1), 7–19 (1998)

Cox, K.: Amazon's Ring App Shares Loads of Your Personal Info, Report Finds. ArsTechnica, January 28. https://arstechnica.com/tech-policy/2020/01/amazons-ring-app-shares-loads-of-your-personal-info-report-finds/ (2020). Accessed 19 Jan 2023

Damasio, A.: Descartes Error: Emotion, Reason, and the Human Brain. Quill/Harper Collins (1994)

De Jaegher, H., Di Paolo, E.: Participatory sense-making: an enactive approach to social cognition. Phenomenol. Cogn. Sci. **6**(4), 485–507 (2007). https://doi.org/10.1007/s11097-007-9076-9

Dennett, D.: Can machines think. In: Kurzewil (ed.) The Age of Intelligence Machines. MIT Press (1990)

Dennett, D.: The Intentional Stance. MIT Press, Cambridge, MA (1987)
Dennett, D.: True believers: the intentional strategy and why it works. In: Heath, A.F. (ed.) Scientific Explanations: Papers based on Herbert Spencer Lectures Given in the University of Oxford. Oxford University Press (1975)
Dewey, D.: Art as experience. In: Boydston (ed.) John Dewey: The Later Works, 1925–1953, vol. 10, 1989 edn. Southern Illinois University Press, Carbondale (1934)
Dietrich, E., Fields, C., Sullins, J., Van Heuveln, B., Zebrowski, R.: The Great Philosophical Objections to Artificial Intelligence: The History and Legacy of the AI Wars. Bloomsbury (2021a)
Dietrich, E., Fields, C., Sullins, J., Van Heuveln, B., Zebrowski, R.: The AI Wars: 1950-2000 and Their Consequences. J. Artif. Intell. Conscious. (2021b). https://doi.org/10.1142/S2705078521300012
Dreyfus, H.: What Computers Still Can't Do: A Critique of Artificial Reason. MIT Press (1992)
Dreyfus, H.L., Dreyfus, S.E.: Making a mind versus modeling the brain: artificial intelligence back at a branchpoint. Daedalus. **117**(1), 15–43 (1988) http://www.jstor.org/stable/20025137
Flowers, J.C.: Rethinking algorithmic bias through phenomenology and pragmatism. In: Wittkower, D. (ed.) 2019 Computer Ethics - Philosophical Enquiry (CEPE) Proceedings, 27 pp. (2019). https://doi.org/10.25884/mh5z-fb89
Fodor, J.: The Language of Thought. Harvard University Press (1975)
Gallagher, S.: Phenomenology. Palgrave Macmillan (2012)
Gallagher, S.: Enactivist Interventions: Rethinking the Mind. Oxford University Press (2017)
Gallese, V., Sinigaglia, C.: What's so special about embodied simulation? Trends Cogn. Sci. **15**(11) (2011)
Gershgorn, D.: 'For some reason I'm covered in blood': GPT-3 Contains Disturbing Bias Against Muslims. OneZero, January 21. https://onezero.medium.com/for-some-reason-im-covered-in-blood-gpt-3-contains-disturbing-bias-against-muslims-693d275552bf (2021). Accessed 16 May 2023
Ghost in the Machine. The X-Files, created by Chris Carter, season 1, episode 7, 20th Century Fox Television (1993)
Gibson, J.J.: The theory of affordances. In: The Ecological Approach to Visual Perception, pp. 119–137. Taylor & Francis (1979)
Goldin-Meadow, S., Alibali, M.W.: Gesture's role in speaking, learning, and creating language. Annu. Rev. Psychol. **64**, 257–283 (2013). https://doi.org/10.1146/annurev-psych-113011-143802
Greer, E., Bonesteel, A.: America's Ring Doorbell Camera Obsession Highlights the Scourge of Mass Surveillance. NBC News. https://www.nbcnews.com/think/opinion/amazons-ring-doorbell-videos-make-america-less-safe-crime-rcna55143 (2022)
Graziano, M.: Consciousness and the Social Brain. Oxford University Press (2013)
Harnad, S.: The symbol-grounding problem. Physica D. **42**, 335–346 (1990)
Kita, S., Alibali, M.W., Chu, M.: How do gestures influence thinking and speaking? The gesture-for-conceptualization hypothesis. Psychol. Rev. **124**(3), 245–266 (2017)
Kleinman, Z.: Artificial Intelligence: How to Avoid Racist Algorithms. BBC News, April 14. https://www.bbc.com/news/technology-39533308 (2017). Accessed 16 May 2023
Kurian, T.: The Next Generation of AI for Developers and Google Workspace. https://blog.google/technology/ai/ai-developers-google-cloud-workspace/ (2023). Accessed 1 May 2023
Lakoff, G.: Women, Fire, and Dangerous Things: What Categories Reveal about the Mind. Chicago University Press, Chicago (1987)
Lakoff, G., Johnson, M.: Metaphors We Live By. University of Chicago Press (1980)
Lakoff, G., Johnson, M.: Philosophy in the Flesh: The Embodied Mind and its Challenge to Western Thought. Basic Books (1999)
Leonardis, F.: Google Launches a Smarter Bard. TechCrunch, May 10. https://techcrunch.com/2023/05/10/google-launches-a-smarter-bard/ (2023). Accessed 16 May 2023
Lobo, L., Heras-Escribano, M., Travieso, D.: The history and philosophy of ecological psychology. Front. Psychol. **27**(9) (2018). https://doi.org/10.3389/fpsyg.2018.02228

Love and Rocket. Futurama, created by Matt Groening, season 4, episode 4, The Curious Company and 20th Century Fox Television. (2002)
Madan, S., Henry, T., Dozier, J., et al.: When and how convolutional neural networks generalize to out-of-distribution category–viewpoint combinations. Nat. Mach. Intell. **4**, 146–153 (2022). https://doi.org/10.1038/s42256-021-00437-5
Malcolm, N.: Thoughtless Brutes. Proceedings and Addresses of the American Philosophical Association. **46**, 5–20 (1972)
Maturana, H., Varela, F.: Autopoiesis and Cognition: The Realization of the Living. Reidel (1980)
Merleau-Ponty, M.: Phenomenology of Perception, Donald Landes (trans.). Routledge (1945/2012)
Mozur, P.: How China Is Using AI to Profile a Minority. The New York Times, April 14. https://www.nytimes.com/2019/04/14/technology/china-surveillance-artificial-intelligence-racial-profiling.html (2019). Accessed 16 May 2023
Nagel, T.: What is it like to be a bat. Philos. Rev. **83**(4), 435–450 (1974)
Newman, S., Birhane, A., Zajko, M., Osoba, O., Prunkl, C., Lima, G., Bowen, J., Sutton, R., Adams, C.: AI and agency. UCLA (2019) https://escholarship.org/uc/item/8q15786s#main
Ng, A.: Amazon Gave Ring Videos to Police Without Owners' Permission. Politico, July 13. https://www.politico.com/news/2022/07/13/amazon-gave-ring-videos-to-police-without-owners-permission-00045513 (2022). Accessed 16 May 2023
Noë, A.: Out of Our Heads: Why You are Not Your Brain, and Other Lessons from the Biology of Consciousness. Hill and Wang (2010)
Pfeifer, R., Bongard, J.: How the Body Shapes the Way We Think. MIT Press (2006)
Singer, N.: Amazon is Pushing Facial Technology that a Study Says Could Be Biased. The New York Times, January 24. https://www.nytimes.com/2019/01/24/technology/amazon-facial-technology-study.html (2019). Accessed 19 Jan 2023
Solon, O.: The Rise of 'Pseudo-AI': How Tech Firms Quietly Use Humans to Do Bots' Work. The Guardian, July 6. https://www.theguardian.com/technology/2018/jul/06/artificial-intelligence-ai-humans-bots-tech-companies (2018). Accessed 16 May 2023
Thibodeau, P., Boroditsky, L.: Metaphors We Think With: The Role of Metaphor in Reasoning. PLoS One. **6**(2), e16782 (2011)
Thompson, E.: Mind in Life: Biology, Phenomenology, and the Sciences of Mind. Belknap Press/Harvard University Press (2007)
Treehouse of Horror XII. Simpsons, created by Matt Groening, season 13, episode 1, Gracie Films and 20th Television. (2001)
Turing, A.: Computing machinery and intelligence. Mind. **LIX**(236), 433–460 (1950). https://doi.org/10.1093/mind/LIX.236.433
Valentine, M.: The Ghost Work Behind Artificial Intelligence. Slate, June 26. https://slate.com/technology/2021/06/ghost-work-fake-artificial-intelligence-skeleton-crew.html (2021). Accessed 16 May 2023
Varela, F.: Ethical Know-How: Action, Wisdom, and Cognition. Stanford University Press (1992)
Varela, F., Thompson, E., Rosch, E.: The Embodied Mind: Cognitive Science and Human Experience. MIT Press (1992)
Vincent, J.: Alexa Is Nagging You More Because Amazon Knows You Don't Care About Its New Features. The Verge. https://www.theverge.com/2021/12/23/22851451/amazon-alexa-by-the-way-use-case-functionality-plateaued (2021)
Wakefield, J.: AI Emotion-Detection Software Tested on Uyghurs. BBC News, May 26. https://www.bbc.com/news/technology-57101248 (2021). Accessed 16 May 2023
Weber, A., Varlea, F.: Life after Kant: Natural purposes and the autopoietic foundations of biological individuality. Phenomenol. Cogn. Sci. **I**, 97–125 (2002)
Williams, A., Miceli, M., Gebru, T.: The Exploited Labor Behind Artificial Intelligence. Noema, October 13. https://www.noemamag.com/the-exploited-labor-behind-artificial-intelligence/ (2022). Accessed 19 Jan 2023
Williams, D.P.: [@wolven] Post on Mastodon Social Network, April 19. https://ourislandgeorgia.net/@Wolven/110227102110816144 (2023). Accessed 16 May 2023

Williams, D.P.: Why AI Research Needs Disabled and Marginalized Perspectives. Video and transcript of a talk given at NC State R.L. Rabb Symposium on Embedding AI in Society. https://afutureworththinkingabout.com/?p=5558 (2021a). Accessed 16 May 2023

Williams, D.P.: Constructing situated and social knowledge: ethical, sociological, and phenomenological factors in technological design. In: Pirtle, Z., Tomblin, D., Madhavan, G. (eds.) Engineering and Philosophy. Philosophy of Engineering and Technology, vol. 37. Springer, Cham (2021b). https://doi.org/10.1007/978-3-030-70099-7_7

Wilson, A.D., Weightman, A., Bingham, G.P., Zhu, Q.: Using task dynamics to quantify the affordances of throwing for long distance and accuracy. J. Exp. Psychol. Hum. Percept. Perform. **42**(7), 965–981 (2016)

Wilson, M.: Six views of embodied cognition. Psychon. Bull. Rev. **9**(4), 625–636 (2002)

Wittgenstein, L.: Philosophical Investigations, 4th edn. Wiley-Blackwell (1998/1953)

Xiang, C.: AI Isn't Artificial or Intelligent. Motherboard, December 6. https://www.vice.com/en/article/wxnaqz/ai-isnt-artificial-or-intelligent (2022). Accessed 7 Dec 2022

Zuboff, S.: The Age of Surveillance Capitalism: The Fight for a Human Future At the New Frontier of Power. Profile Books (2019)

Chapter 7
Stakeholders in Smart City Standardization

Kai Jakobs

Abstract The chapter suggests a way to better integrate the expertise of societal stakeholders into the earliest possible stage of the development of technologies with significant non-technical ramifications, e.g., societal, environmental, or ethical. Based on a thorough analysis of the current situation, the chapter suggests a modified standards setting process for such technologies. Specifically, it describes how the diverse stakeholders and their different forms of knowledge may be integrated into this process and how it may be managed.

Keywords Smart systems · Smart cities · Multi-stakeholder standardization · Responsible innovation · Standardization

7.1 By Way of Introduction and Motivation

Over the past couple of years, "smart" and "intelligent" applications have become increasingly popular. Well-known examples include intelligent transport systems, smart manufacturing (aka Industry 4.0), smart grid, e-health, and smart cities. In a way, the latter represent a superset of smart applications (see Fig. 7.1). "Smartness" is the result of the integration of information and communication technologies (ICT) into rather more "traditional" technologies, i.e., of the merger of the physical world and the virtual one.

Smart applications receive information from and send instructions to the underlying infrastructure, the individual elements of which need to communicate with each other in order to meet the applications' requirements (see also Fig. 7.2). To actually reach a situation where different smart applications can seamlessly communicate via a shared infrastructure, widely accepted interoperability standards are a sine qua non. "Standards are the first step towards the holy grail of an interoperable, plug-

K. Jakobs (✉)
RWTH Aachen University, Aachen, Germany
e-mail: kai.jakobs@comsys.rwth-aachen.de

E. Kornyshova et al. (eds.), *Smart Life and Smart Life Engineering*,
https://doi.org/10.1007/978-3-031-75887-4_7

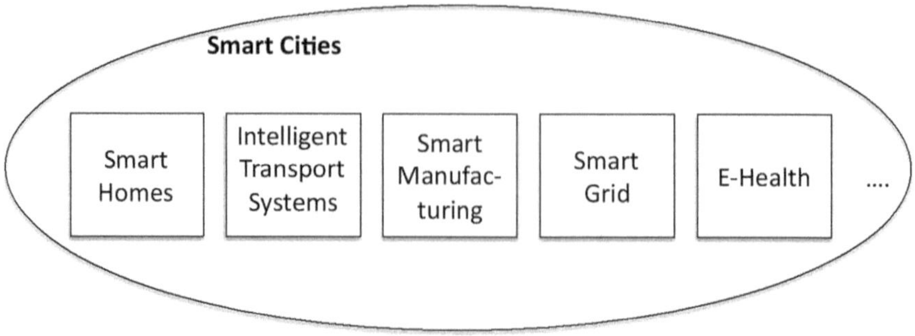

Fig. 7.1 Smart cities as a superset of different smart applications

and-play world where cities can mix and match solutions from different vendors without fear of lock-in or obsolescence or dead-end initiatives."[1]

Smart cities' major characteristic will be their true ubiquity. "The number of IoT devices worldwide is forecast to almost triple from 8.74 billion in 2020 to more than 25.4 billion IoT devices in 2030."[2] This trend suggests that smart systems will exert a tremendous impact on our lives, through this ubiquity and the associated volume of data they will collect. This, in turn, means that they will represent a major challenge for policymakers and for society as a whole, and not least will they have an enormous economic impact.

Smart systems' ubiquity may border on inescapability [think George Orwell (1949) and Aldous Huxley (1932)]. On top of that, interaction with smart systems will be (almost) continuous and "implicit," that is, no explicit action (e.g., log in) will be required. Rather, sensors will continuously collect data that will subsequently be analyzed; they may well serve as the basis for recommendations made and actions taken autonomously by some governing entity (which will most likely apply big data analytics as well as machine learning and AI techniques). Such systems have the inherent potential to either foster the good of humankind or to enable the emergence of a surveillance society. In any case, storage, analysis, and eventual action based on this massive amount of data will have major socioeconomic, legal, and ecological ramifications and directly impact citizens as well as businesses.

The severity and the sheer range of these ramifications call for the inclusion of a variety of non-technical aspects into the development process of smart systems in order to try and shape this process in a way that it aims to avoid, or at least reduce, any undesirable outcomes. This "… shaping process begins with the earliest stages of research and development" (Williams and Edge 1996, p.

[1] According to Jesse Berst (the Chairman of the Smart Cities Council); see https://www.iso.org/sites/worldsmartcity/

[2] https://www.statista.com/statistics/1183457/iot-connected-devices-worldwide/

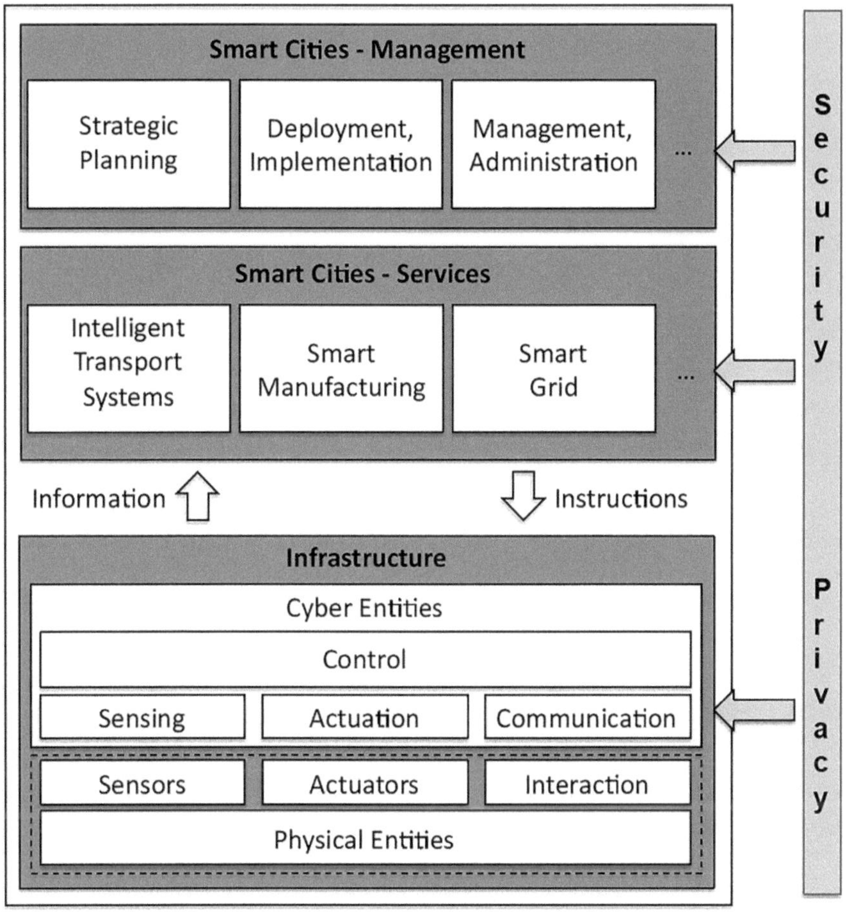

Fig. 7.2 Framework of SSC ICT standards [Adapted from NIST (2016)]

874). This view is complemented by the European Commission's observation from more than 20 years back, when they rightly stated that "Standards are not only technical questions. They determine the technology that will implement the Information Society, and consequently the way in which industry, users, consumers and administrations will benefit from it" (EC 1996, p.1). This still holds today. That is, those who develop standards today shape much of the future environment we will live in (also through subsequent standards-based innovations). Moreover, especially transnational governance increasingly builds upon soft law, notably including standards (see, e.g., (Djelic and Sahlin-Andersson 2006).

Smart systems' "smartness" results from the merger of ICTs and non-ICT technologies (see above). ICTs are in almost all cases based on international standards, and so will be smart systems. Thus, while not necessarily representing the earliest stage of development, standardization clearly is an important early stage of the overall process that leads from R&D to products or services and is thus also subject to a shaping process. Accordingly, the non-technical aspects must be introduced into the standardization process from the outset. This, in turn, makes imperative the participation of variety of stakeholders. Most notably, these include societal stakeholders[3] (as opposed technical/economic ones[4]).

Such inclusiveness should also help increase the eventual standards' legitimacy and thus contribute to a higher degree of their acceptance (Werle and Iversen 2006). Accordingly, the chapter aims to provide an answer to the following question:

> How can stakeholder diversity in smart systems standardization be achieved, and how can the standardization process be adapted and governed to yield standards that are technically sophisticated and implementable, economically viable, and societally desirable?

The remainder of this chapter is organized as follows: Section 7.2 provides the necessary background. Subsequently, Sect. 7.3 addresses some aspects relating to different stakeholders' knowledge and activities in standards setting. Section 7.4 looks at the societal stakeholders, focussing on the governance of a standards setting process adapted to better cater for the needs and requirements of societal stakeholders. Finally, Sect. 7.5 offers some concluding remarks.

7.2 Some Background

Figure 7.2 shows the general framework for smart and sustainable cities (SSC) from an ICT perspective. So far, the vast majority of standardization activities have focussed on the "infrastructure" level. Most of the ensuing standards, however, are not directly linked to smart cities but may be applied in this environment as well. Pretty much the same holds for standards for data security and privacy.

Activities in some sectors at the "services" layer have also been going on for a while, most extensively for intelligent transport systems (since the early 1990s). Standardization efforts in the fields of smart manufacturing and the smart grid got off the ground only in the early 2000s. At this level as well, many relevant standardization activities have originally been launched without smart applications in mind. Some of these standards have then ex post been identified as being of relevance in this field as well. That is, coherent activities to develop dedicated standards for smart applications have been limited also at this level. Things look a bit different for the topmost level, "management." Here, a number of dedicated smart city standards have been developed by different standards setting organizations

[3] For smart cities, these may include, e.g., city councils, unions, NGOs, environmentalists, and citizens but also academics, legal professionals, and ethicists.

[4] Which are mostly large companies with an interest in the technology to be standardized (see, e.g., De Vries et al. 2003; Jakobs 2021).

(SSOs). These standards, however, are mostly dealing with more high-level aspects like architectures, frameworks, and vocabularies.

The following sections introduce some necessary background regarding responsibility, the standardization environment, and its stakeholders (see below).

7.2.1 *Responsible Innovation*

Research and innovation (R&I) need guidance to address not just the technical aspects but to also take into account any potential societal ramifications that may be an (unintended) outcome of an innovation. Moreover, R&I should also aim to contribute to solutions to any societal challenges in general. Responsible innovation (RI) provides guidelines to address these challenges.

RI is not a new phenomenon. Its roots may be traced back at least a couple of decades. In 1947, Detlev Bronk testified before a congressional committee "... that competent social scientists should work hand in hand with the natural scientists, so that problems may be solved as they arise, and so that many of them may not arise in the first instance" (Hearings 1947, p.38). More than 60 years later, v. Schomberg (2013, p.19) defines RI as "a transparent, interactive process by which societal actors and innovators become mutually responsive to each other with a view to the (ethical) acceptability, sustainability and societal desirability of the innovation process and its marketable products (in order to allow a proper embedding of scientific and technological advances in our society)." Stilgoe et al. (2013) propose four dimensions of RI. They include:

- Anticipation—to proactively take into account potential future opportunities, risks, environmental/societal, etc. ramifications.
- Inclusion—to listen to all stakeholders; some may challenge well-established attitudes.
- Reflexivity[5]—to regularly reassess research against norms and values.
- Responsiveness—to adapt with increasing experience and knowledge.

Grunwald (2011, p.17) adds the ethical dimension and observes that "Responsible Innovation unavoidably requires a more intense inter- and trans-disciplinary cooperation between engineering, social sciences, and applied ethics."

The requirement that non-technical aspects shall be taken into account during the innovation process implies that a much broader range of stakeholders has to be involved in the process, notably those that are not normally associated with R&I

[5] According to Stilgoe et al. (2013, p.1571), "Reflexivity, at the level of institutional practice, means holding a mirror up to one's own activities, commitments and assumptions, being aware of the limits of knowledge and being mindful that a particular framing of an issue may not be universally held."

(e.g., consumers, NGOs, unions, ethicists, etc.); this very much resembles the needs of the standardization process for smart cities.

Applying RI principles not just in innovation but also in standards setting would then lead to responsible standardization (Meijer et al. 2023); this will be discussed further below.

7.2.2 The General ICT Standardization Environment

As mentioned above, systems' smartness results from the merger of ICT with other technologies. The bulk of the associated standardization work is and will continue to be done by SSOs from the ICT sector. Accordingly, in the following, the focus will be on ICT standardization.

Most industry sectors have a very simple standardization environment. A number of National Standards Organizations (NSOs) contribute to the work of the international standards development organizations (SDOs), i.e. ISO (International Organization for Standardization) and IEC (International Electrotechnical Commission). An additional regional level in between has been established in Europe through the European Standardisation Organisations (ESOs). In the USA, numerous national sector-specific SSOs exist. Following accreditation, they may contribute to the international standardization work via the American National Standards Institute (ANSI), the US national representative to ISO and IEC.

The situation is different for ICT, specifically for the telecommunication sector. In this sector, the ITU (International Telecommunication Union) represents the equivalent to ISO and IEC. In addition, a number of national/regional bodies and, particularly, a huge number (more than 200) of private standards setting consortia[6] are active in this field; they make this environment unique. The proliferation of these consortia began in the late 1980s and was primarily triggered by the fast-paced development of ICT technologies and a widely perceived slowness and non-responsiveness to users' needs on the side of the "formal" SDOs (Cargill 1995). So far, consortia have not played a major role in the realm of smart city standardization. This may well change though.

The characteristics of the individual SSOs may differ considerably in terms of, e.g., relevance, credibility, voting procedures, membership and membership levels, types of output documents, level of consensus required, and IPR (intellectual property rights) regime.

The number of consortia and the complex links that exist between them on the one hand and to the SDOs on the other yields an almost impenetrable web of SSOs (see Fig. 7.3).

These links represent some level of formal co-operation (mainly between consortia and SDOs). Such co-operation may take the form of exchanging information

[6] Private SSOs such as the World Wide Web Consortium (W3C).

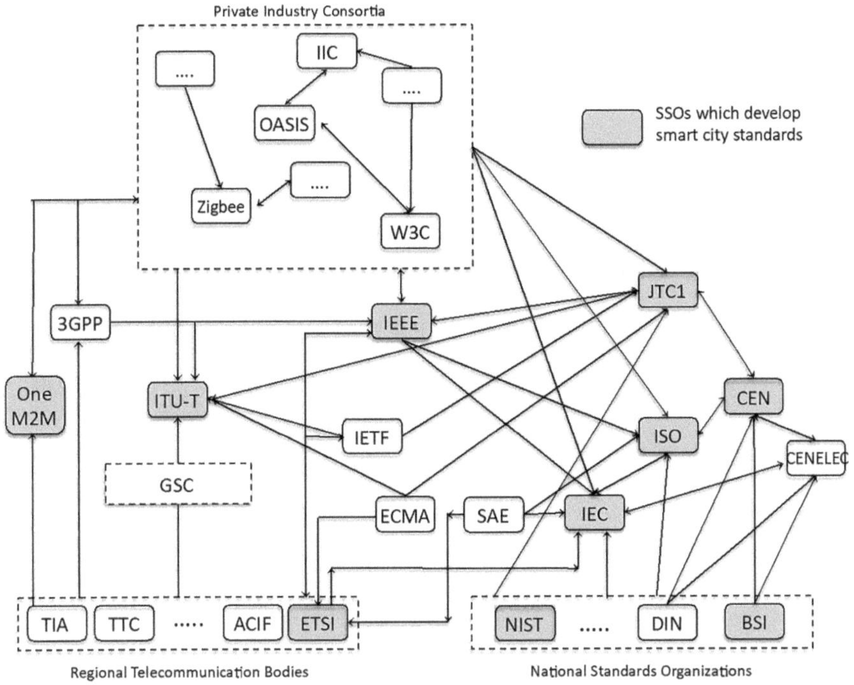

Fig. 7.3 The web of SSOs active in the ICT sector [small excerpt; adapted from Jakobs (2008)]

about planned new work items, the joint development of common standards, or anything in between. In the absence of a central coordinating entity, these links currently represent the most important (distributed) coordination mechanism in standards setting. Such links between consortia are not normally well developed, but some do exist.

To improve coordination of the different standardization activities remains an important issue. A lack of coordination, eventually resulting in the development of functionally equivalent (and thus competing) standards, will reduce market transparency, decrease interoperability and ease of use, fragment the market, and increase transaction costs (Egyedi 2014). Indeed, various coordination mechanisms have been developed over time, ranging from highly formalized high-level regulatory documents to very informal coordination through individuals who contribute to the work of multiple SSOs.

7.3 Stakeholders and Standards Setting

7.3.1 *Expert vs. Lay Knowledge*

At least at first glance, ICT standards setting is a purely technical activity. Experts from different engineering disciplines and from various computer science fields meet, discuss potential alternatives, and eventually come up with a good technical solution. Frequently, economic interests of the respective employers also play an important role. And in many cases, this "technology-centric" scenario will indeed be adequate—the nuts and bolts of the USB protocol (see, e.g., Anderson 2009), for example, will hardly be of interest to the vast majority of those who want to transfer data to a USB stick, and neither will they have any societal nor ethical ramifications.

Things look very different for smart systems though. They will eventually collect and process unprecedented volumes of information, including personal data. At the very least, adequate measures to render impossible any misuse of these information and to guarantee their privacy will need to be in place. Moreover, smart systems hold the promise of making energy provision, traffic, production, and cities more environmentally friendly. To actually reap such potential benefits, sustainability aspects should be considered already during the standardization process. Obviously, the above does have a strong technical dimension. Beyond that, however, legal and regulatory issues will come into play, as will societal and cultural aspects (privacy, e.g., is crucially important in some countries and much less so in others; even within countries, its perceived importance differs between groups of citizens).

Very much in line with the ideas underlying RI, the above suggests that for smart systems, technical expertise ("expert knowledge") will need to be complemented by both "lay knowledge" and "domain knowledge."[7] The former may be contributed through public engagement, the latter through experts from relevant non-technical disciplines (e.g., sociology, philosophy, jurisprudence). Problems are to be associated with both.

For one, Graz and Hauert (2019) observe that it is very difficult, yet crucial, to actually mobilize specifically "lay" (but also "domain") knowledge for the day-to-day activities of SSOs' working groups. This holds primarily for the public engagement.

Moreover, there might be an acceptance problem: "Committee members have also named technical sophistication on the side of the user representatives as a major prerequisite for meaningful participation" (Jakobs et al. 2001, p.106).

[7] Roughly speaking, "expert knowledge" relates to technical aspects, "domain knowledge" to the specifics of either the respective application domain or of the various non-technical fields (e.g., legal, ethical, environmental) domains, and "lay knowledge" to the associated more general societal issues. During the standardization process, the latter two groups initially possess knowledge that is valuable for the former; later on, they may/will eventually join the process of knowledge (standard) production (see Koizumi and Yamashita 2021).

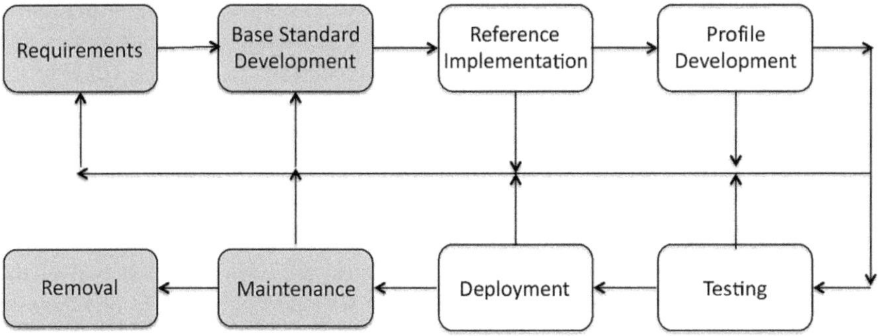

Fig. 7.4 Stages of the standards setting process

This reveals a major misconception. A lack of technical expertise is certainly a problem when purely technical topics are to be standardized. For other types of standards, notably in cases where the ensuing technology based upon these standards is likely to have major societal ramifications (like in nanotechnology and smart systems), any distinction between lay knowledge and expert knowledge becomes void. Here, what may be seen as lay knowledge for, e.g., technical deliberations will become expert knowledge when it comes to the consideration of, e.g., societal or ethical impacts of the technology to be developed (and vice versa). That is, only expert knowledge, albeit from different domains, shall be made available, and both have to be of equal value.

7.3.2 Stakeholders in the Standardization Process

The literature frequently views the standardization process as an indivisible entity, which cannot be subdivided any further (see, e.g., Iversen et al. 2004). Yet standardization is not a homogeneous process carried out under one single set of guidelines, rules, policies, and bylaws. Especially in the ICT sector, standardization work is distributed across a highly complex web of SSOs (see Fig. 7.3). Some of them work—and compete—in very similar fields; some co-operate and some just exist in parallel. Accordingly, from a stakeholder's perspective, the standards setting process has a "spatial" dimension. It also has a "temporal" dimension. Figure 7.4 shows the individual stages of a standards setting process. Most SSOs focus on the first two stages of the process and the two final ones. That is, they elicit requirements, develop the standard specification on paper, maintain, and, eventually, remove it.[8] Yet these specifications tend to also include ambiguities and/or may provide for options, which may easily lead to incompatible implementations of the

[8] A typical such process is described in ISO (2023).

standard (see, e.g., Egyedi 2007). This, in turn, creates the need for interoperability tests and/or profile specifications (which would, e.g., define parameter values and which options to implement). The Internet Engineering Task Force (IETF), for instance, requires two interoperable independent implementations as a pre-requisite for a specification to become an Internet Standard (IETF 1996).

The above suggests that all stakeholders, from large multinationals to small NGOs (or perhaps individual citizens), need to decide to which SSO activities to contribute (where to participate) and at which stage of the process their contributions would be most useful (when to participate). These are, however, just two of the questions to be answered. Others would include why participate (if at all), how to participate most effectively and efficiently, and what to contribute? In fact, these questions should be answered prior to the other two.

First, why participate at all? After all, such commitment implies major expenses, with a very uncertain "return on investment." In fact, primarily, companies with a large-enough interest in the technology to be standardized may hope for an economic gain through participation in the standards setting process. Societal stakeholders, on the other hand, will need to recognize that they stand to suffer from standards that only reflect the technically feasible and/or the economically desirable (from a corporate perspective, as opposed to a societal one). Whether or not many companies will be prepared to adequately take into account societal, environmental, or even ethical aspects, for instance, remains to be seen, all the more so if these aspects are at odds with their respective economic interests. Yet the "why participate" question has more dimensions to it. "Funding" would be one. Within limits, European stakeholders' organizations (ANEC,[9] ECOS,[10] ETUC,[11] and SBS[12]) receive funding from the European Union for their contributions to standardization. Yet to have these organizations' voices adequately heard in all relevant fields, notably including smart systems standardization, will require considerably more (public) funding. Also, whether or not these organizations actually have a widely accepted mandate may become another open question. For example, the organization to "represent social interests in the standardisation process" (EU 2012, p.31) (almost exclusively) focused on cases where "standardisation projects impact the health and safety of workers" (ETUI 2018, p. 47), no such standardization-related activities are foreseen in the current work program (ETUI 2023).

For the time being, the answer to the question of how societal stakeholders (should) participate in standardization would be "through the above stakeholder organisations," at least according to the European Commission. Yet two issues must be associated with this approach. Looking at the participation of SME user companies in standards setting, Jakobs (2005) reports that Working Group (WG) members would particularly welcome their delegates if they represented a relevant umbrella

[9] The European consumer voice in standardization.

[10] European Environmental Citizens' Organisation for Standardisation.

[11] European Trade Union Confederation.

[12] Small Business Standards.

organization (as opposed to their respective individual employer). On the other hand, requirements on a standard (and on a technology) are "... highly specific to particular operating requirements and environmental contingencies" within which it is to be implemented (Fleck 1994, p.642). An analogous argument may be made for the contributions of societal stakeholders. Obviously, this makes the contribution of more general requirements via an umbrella organization, representing a wide range of diverse stakeholders, at least much more difficult. How to realize an "adequate" representation of societal stakeholders is another relevant question. Numerically, adequate representation would probably be next to impossible to achieve. Adequate influence may be something entirely different though. There is ample evidence that representatives' diplomatic, negotiation, rhetoric, and similar non-technical skills are important (see, e.g., Dokko and Rosenkopf 2010; Isaak 2006). A representative with such skills may enable even a small organization to punch well above its weight in the process.

What could societal stakeholders contribute? At a very general level, they could establish whether or not a standard to be developed would be desirable from a broader societal perspective. Aspects to be considered in this context would include, among others, social, environmental, and ethical ones; potential legal ramifications may also need to be considered. These deliberations should result in a set of requirements that should inform and guide the technical standardization process. The different perceptions of technology held by the "technical" side (e.g., engineers or computer scientists) on the one hand and societal stakeholders on the other would be an inherent problem here. These different perceptions would need to be aligned, which would require a learning process on both sides; the "technical side" will need to gain some understanding and appreciation of the (potential) non-technical ramifications of their work, and societal stakeholders will need to have at least some idea of what technology can do and what it cannot.

Different levels of societal stakeholders' participation in standardization may be identified. The International Association for Public Participation has identified five such levels, relevant for "public participation processes" in general (IAP2 2018). Standardization is, or rather should be, one such process. Accordingly, each of these five levels has its justification also in standards setting, albeit with some adaptations to reflect the specifics of the standardization process (Table 7.1).

The respective most desirable level depends on the type of standard to be developed. "Inform" will suffice in case of purely technical standards. "Collaborate" would be the level of choice for smart cities, while "Empower," i.e. to possibly forfeit all technical expertise, would likely be disastrous (not just in the case of smart cities).

Even if the "Collaborate" category were implemented, communication problems would be highly likely to occur. That is, an initial lack of mutual common understanding may be assumed. Accordingly, trust will become all the more important for a meaningful collaboration. Rosenkopf et al. (2001, p.754) note that "frequent and sustained face-to-face meetings among firm representatives engender trust and collaboration among alliance partners." The importance of face-to-face meetings in this context is further corroborated, albeit from a slightly different angle

Table 7.1 Different levels of societal stakeholders' participation in standards setting [Based on and adapted from IAP2 (2018)][a]

	SSOs' tasks
Inform	SSOs will provide societal stakeholders with objective information regarding the standard to help them understand the problem and the proposed solution along with potentially associated alternatives, risks and opportunities
Consult[b]	SSOs will compile feedback from societal stakeholders about the standard (and possibly incorporate it)
Involve	SSOs will co-operate with societal stakeholders to understand and consider their ideas and concerns about the standard
Collaborate	SSOs will consider societal stakeholders as being at eye level with their technical experts during standard's development
Empower	Societal stakeholders will make the final decision about the standard

[a]Permission to use the material has been granted by the Intern. Assoc. for Public Participation; © of the original material Intern. Assoc. for Public Participation
[b]Citizens' assemblies allow citizens' voices to be heard by policymakers and legislators. They have been implemented in various countries. Their recommendations are non-binding though (unlike the European Commission's stakeholder consultations)

by Kramer and Cook (2004), who note that "Trust theorists have long argued the benefits of face-to-face interaction and direct experience with others in the trust-building process" (p.12). In the following, a way to circumvent these problems will be presented.

7.4 Catering for Societal Stakeholders

7.4.1 Stakeholder Identification, Classification, and Engagement

The SSC stakeholders that are likely to be (certainly should be) interested in contributing to the extended standards development process and/or in the subsequent implementation of standards are shown in Table 7.2.

In most cases, this rather "coarse-grained" list of stakeholders will need to be refined and adapted to local particularities. Eventually, representatives from all interested groups will need to be found and motivated to participate. Specifically, care should be taken to make sure that also any, e.g., ethical, legal, and environmental aspects will be given adequate consideration.

With respect to the contribution to SSC standardization, the most relevant stakeholders include "municipalities, city councils, and city administrations," "NGOs," "citizens and citizens' organizations," and "academia, research organizations, and specialized bodies"; the latter will mostly act in a rather more observing and possibly also in a consulting capacity. "Municipalities, city councils, and city administrations" are "the basis for SSC management, and are at the core of the

Table 7.2 Smart cities stakeholders and their roles (Adapted[a] from ITU (2020) and extended). *Std.* standardization, *Imp.* implementation; "Stage" according to Fig. 7.4

Stakeholders	Roles, tasks, and expertise	Std./Imp.[b]	Stage
Municipalities, city councils, and city administrations	Responsible for city management; therefore, they are the main promoters of SSC initiatives in each specific city	Std. and Imp.	1
National and regional governments	Remits on policies that can affect SSC implementation	Std. and Imp.	2
Society at large	Influences any technical development through prevailing societal norms, which may change over longer periods of time	Std. and Imp.	1 and 2
City services companies	Implement SSC solutions to increase city services efficiency	Imp.	
Utility providers	Responsible for the deployment of some of the features of an SSC, such as smart grid or smart water management	Imp.	
ICT companies (e.g., telecom operators, software companies)	Providers of global and integrated solutions, city platforms, as well as the ICT and digital infrastructure to support SSC deployment	Std. and Imp.	2
NGOs	Involved in all initiatives that can influence society and therefore are considered stakeholders in SSC, e.g., on social sustainability	Std. and Imp.	1
International, regional, and multilateral organizations	These include UN agencies and multilateral organizations. They can be promoters of initiatives toward human development, environmental sustainability, and improvement of quality of life worldwide. They can offer funding opportunities and are promoters of SSC initiatives	Imp.	
Industry associations	Since industries are interested in the deployment of SSC, industry associations also work toward the success of this new model	Std. and Imp.	2
Academia, research organizations, and specialized bodies	Study SSCs and associated trends, including their impacts on and contributions to sustainable development as well as any, e.g., potential legal and ethical issues	Std. and Imp.	1 and 2
Citizens and citizens' organizations	As inhabitants of cities, citizens are affected both directly and indirectly by SSC deployment	Std. and Imp.	1
Urban planners	Their expertise is important to better understand how to include ICTs and digital technologies in city planning, as well as to consider urban complexities	Imp.	

(continued)

Table 7.2 continued

Stakeholders	Roles, tasks, and expertise	Std./Imp.[b]	Stage
Urban planners	Their expertise is important to better understand how to include ICTs and digital technologies in city planning, as well as to consider urban complexities	Imp.	
Standardization bodies	These organizations are critical to ensure the application of common terminology and minimum characteristics of an SSC and for specifying measurement methods to assess performance and sustainability of city services based on digital technologies	Std.	1 and 2
Individual standards setters	In charge of the actual standards development. They influence standards development through technical contributions and also through, e.g., beliefs, prejudices, and non-technical skills like diplomacy, alliance formation, good rhetoric, or bullying	Std.	1 and 2

[a]Permission to use the material has been granted by the ITU, © of the original material International Telecommunication Union
[b]Designates the main interest of the stakeholder: standardization and/or implementation

SSC framework" (ITU 2020, p.8). They will also (have to) be the drivers of the associated standardization activities at Stage 1. This observation, plus the fact that standardization resembles regulation in many respects, suggests that elements of societal stakeholder engagement may be adopted from the regulatory environment. According to Alemanno (2015), engagement comprises three different components:

- Public communication enables policymakers to convey information to the public. This is a one-way information flow and corresponds to the "Inform" category (see Table 7.1).
- Public consultation serves to convey information from societal stakeholders to policymakers. This corresponds to the "Consult" category.
- Public participation represents a dialogue between societal stakeholders and policymakers. This corresponds to the "Involve" category.

The categories "Collaborate" and "Empower" will hardly be found in regulation (except perhaps for the Swiss referenda). In smart city standardization, however, "Co-operate," on a level playing field, would be desirable.

7.4.2 Proposed Adaptation of the Standards Setting Process

The current standardization process has been briefly discussed above.[13] There, it has also been shown that participation of societal stakeholders in standards setting is highly likely to be ridden with all sorts of problems and issues. On the other hand, and given the important role they have to play in the standardization of smart cities, their active contribution to the process, on a level playing field, will be crucial. One way out of this dilemma would be a moderately modified process that enables active participation especially of the non-technical stakeholders, provides for more inclusiveness, and caters for a greater diversity of stakeholders than the current processes do, thus also bringing responsibility to standardization (for more details, see, e.g., Jakobs (2019)]. Such inclusiveness would also increase credibility and thus acceptance of the ensuing standards (see, e.g., Werle and Iversen 2006).

The modification would largely decouple requirements elicitation and compilation from the primarily technical work. The right-hand side of Fig. 7.5 (Stage 2) represents the "traditional" standardization process (as depicted in Fig. 7.3). Societal stakeholders' tasks and input are depicted on the left-hand side[14] (Stage 1). Their first task would be a recommendation whether to proceed with or to stop a planned activity. In case of the former, societal stakeholders would subsequently contribute requirements to the technical part of the process. It should be noted that stage 1 may be set up independently from any SSO. However, the interface between the two stages will need to be clearly defined.

This approach would make sure that the technical part of the standardization work remained unchanged. Moreover, the communication between the technical and the societal world would mostly occur via one well-defined interface. Benefit number three would then be that the level of involvement of the societal stakeholders in Stage 2 (the "classical" part of the process), and thus the associated costs would be significantly reduced. This, in turn, might encourage a broader variety of these stakeholders to become active in "their" part of the process. Overall, this should contribute to a stronger societal representation.

It may be expected that this addition to the standards setting process would prolong the overall process. However, especially for ubiquitous technologies like smart systems, with huge ramifications in virtually all sectors of society, speed should take a back seat; aspects like sustainability, interoperability, and added societal value of the technology will need to take precedence.

---

[13] For more information about some different process, see, e.g., ISO (2023); https://www.ietf.org/standards/process/informal/ for the IETF or https://www.etsi.org/standards/standards-making for ETSI.

[14] This is pretty much in line with ETSI's Recommendation to "Ensure that for new topics, there is a clear assessment of who are the interested stakeholders and involve them fully in the process, and do so in a collaborative way between the interested SDOs in advance of the work starting" (ETSI 2020, p.29).

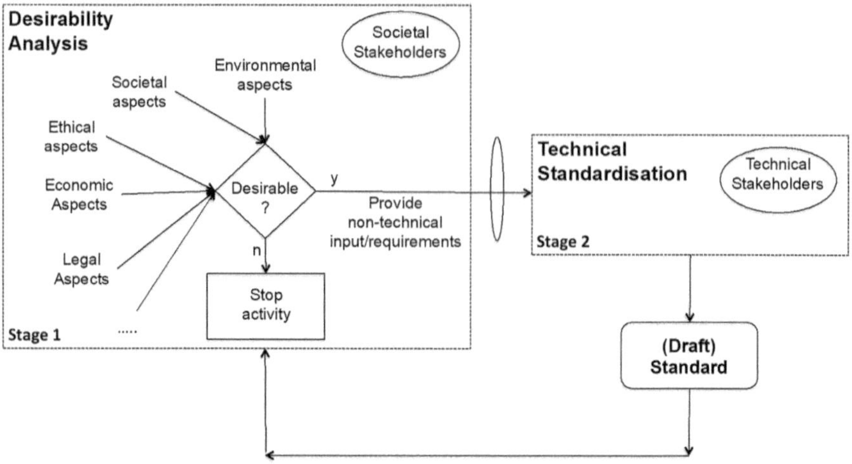

Fig. 7.5 An adapted standardization process (Adapted from Jakobs (2021); see Fig. 7.3 for more details of Stage 2)

The goals of participation of societal stakeholders differ between the stages. During Stage 1, they are "Empowered" (see Table 7.1). At the Interface, societal stakeholders will likely need to form alliances with stakeholders from Stage 2 with whom they will "Collaborate." Finally, they will be "Informed" about the ongoing activities at Stage 2. Eventually, the draft standard will be fed back to Stage 1, for approval or possible requests for modification.

The process outlined above will necessitate a number of additional management activities.

7.5 Establish or Identify the Operating Entity and Its Process

Unless Stage 1 is directly associated with an SSO (which appears to be unlikely), it will need an entity that manages and operates it. SSCs are a global development and highly likely to become of increasing economic interest.[15] This almost mandates a global, not-for-profit entity to operate this process. This might be an entity specifically established for this purpose or an existing entity like, for instance, the G20 Global Smart Cities Alliance on Technology Governance.

In any case, transparency, openness, and inclusiveness will have to be the overriding characteristics of the Stage 1 process, along with due process; national and company interests must not play any decisive role. Krechmer (2009) identifies

[15] According to a report by Research and Markets from 2021, the Global Smart Cities Market is anticipated to grow from USD457 billion in 2021 to USD873.7 billion by 2026.

ten criteria for open standards (and the underlying processes; Stage 2). In addition to "due process" and "consensus," these criteria include, e.g., that all may participate and that everyone may access and use the documents produced. Jakobs (2016) adds another six criteria. These are mainly supposed to reveal any potential, e.g., economic or political interests (on the side of the stakeholders and/or the SSO(s) involved) that may influence the standardization process and include:

- Open rules: The SSOs' bylaws, regulations, etc. are publicly available.
- Transparent membership: names and affiliations of the WG members are known.
- Open roles: names and affiliations of those holding leadership roles are made public.
- Open work programs: which SSO is doing what.
- Open links: which SSO co-operates with whom and how.
- Open history: All SSOs associated with a standard are known.

These criteria as well originally refer to the "normal" standards setting process (i.e., Stage 2) but may also be applied to a process at Stage 1.

7.6 Select SSO(s)

Picking the most suitable SSO for a given task is not a trivial endeavor. Due to the absence of a coordinating entity, individual SSOs may co-operate, compete, or just ignore each other; activities of individual SSOs may well overlap. Accordingly, technical appropriateness and proven competence in the area in which new standards are to be developed may not be sufficient selection criteria.

Each individual SSO has its own rules, guidelines, and bylaws that govern all aspects of its standards setting process (i.e., Stage 2). Individual SSOs' characteristics differ widely in terms of, e.g., openness, power distribution, means for decision-making, and obtaining and/or increasing power. The respective membership base will also be of interest; it will be beneficial if business partners (e.g., suppliers) are involved, especially if they hold any leading positions.

The ease (or lack thereof) with which new work items may be proposed and initiated (and by whom), and the boundary conditions that apply are further important aspects. Specifically, the willingness to support a two-stage process and to implement the necessary interface on the SSO side will need to be established.

7.7 Implement and Manage Interface Between Stages

This is perhaps the most difficult part. The technical and the non-technical side will need to communicate here. Societal, environmental, etc. requirements will have to be conveyed to the technical process and technical boundary conditions and potential limitations in the opposite direction. This implies that ideally individuals with expertise in and experience with both sides (the technical and the non-technical) should communicate to avoid friction losses. These people would act as boundary spanners. This concept has originally emerged from the field of innovation studies (see, e.g., Tushman 1977) but may also be applied to standardization (Dokko and Rosenkopf 2010). To paraphrase Tushman (1977): boundary spanners serve the need of one stage of the standardization process to gather information from and transmit information to another stage.

7.8 Form Alliances

History shows that in very many cases, strong alliances (between, e.g., manufacturers, users, distributors, complementors, etc.) have been crucial for the success of standardization initiatives (see, e.g., Cusumano et al. (1992) and den Uijl and de Vries (2013) for two of the most prominent cases).

In this particular case, such alliances will need to be formed primarily between smart city authorities (Stage 1) on the one hand and, e.g., suppliers, complementors, and service providers (Stage 2) on the other. Such alliances will complement the activities of the boundary spanners (see above).

7.9 Some Brief Concluding Remarks

Smart systems are here to stay. The impact they are highly likely to exert will be tremendous, for businesses, governments, and citizens alike. The nature of this impact, however, still remains largely unclear—we do not have a crystal ball. To be able to eventually reap the potential benefits smart systems offer, their designers need to work hand in hand not just with their prospective (commercial) users (which is frequently the case in "traditional" ICT standards setting) but also with policymakers and legislators (from different levels) as well as with those whose voices are not normally heard during technology development, standardization, and implementation but who stand to benefit—or suffer—the most from smart technologies: consumers, citizens, workers, and the organizational stakeholders who represent certain groups of them.

Despite relevant ongoing developments, "responsible innovation" remains the exception, certainly in the private sector. During its implementation phase, a technology may well be adapted to its environment (and vice versa), but it can no longer be fundamentally changed. This leaves the standardization process as the one platform where societal stakeholders stand a chance to contribute their expertise to an early stage of technical development. To actually be able to do so, however, the current standardization system will need to be modified, in terms of both its structure and its processes. This chapter has discussed some potential changes, the implementation of which would support the development of technologies that are beneficial for society, as opposed to those which benefit primarily large companies.

References

Alemanno, A.: Stakeholder Engagement in Regulatory Policy. Regulatory Policy Outlook. OECD Publishing (2015)

Anderson, D.: Introduction to USB 3.0. MindShare (2009) https://www.mindshare.com/files/resources/mindshare_intro_to_usb_3.0.pdf

Cargill, C.F.: A five-segment model for standardization. In: Kahin, B., Abbate, J. (eds.) Standards Policy for Information Infrastructure, pp. 79–99. MIT Press, Boston, MA (1995)

Cusumano, M.A., Mylonadis, Y., Rosenbloom, R.S.: Strategic maneuvering and mass-market dynamics: the triumph of VHS over beta. Bus. Hist. Rev. **66**(1), 51–94 (1992)

De Vries, H., Verheul, H., Willemse, H.: Stakeholder identification in IT standardization processes. In: Proceedings of the Workshop on Standard Making: A Critical Research Frontier for Information Systems, pp. 12–14. Seattle, WA. https://www.academia.edu/download/50434454/typology.pdf (2003)

den Uijl, S., de Vries, H.J.: Pushing technological progress by strategic manoeuvring: the triumph of Blu-ray over HD-DVD. Bus. Hist. **55**(8), 1361–1384 (2013)

Djelic, M.L., Sahlin-Andersson, K. (eds.): Transnational Governance: Institutional Dynamics of Regulation. Cambridge University Press (2006)

Dokko, G., Rosenkopf, L.: Social capital for hire? Mobility of technical professionals and firm influence in wireless standards committees. Organ. Sci. **21**(3), 677–695 (2010)

EC: Communication from the Commission to the Council and the Parliament on Standardization and the Global Information Society: The European Approach, COM (96) 359. http://eur-lex.europa.eu/legal-content/EN/TXT/PDF/?uri=CELEX:51996DC0359&from=EN (1996)

Egyedi, T.M.: Standard-compliant, but incompatible?! Computer Standards & Interfaces. **29**(6), 605–613 (2007)

Egyedi, T.M.: The Impact of Competing Standards: On Innovation and Interoperability for E-government. PIK-Praxis der Informationsverarbeitung und Kommunikation. **37**(3), 211–215 (2014)

ETSI. (eds.): Task Force Bildt Report – To Operationalize the Recommendations of the Report. https://www.etsi.org/images/files/ETSI-Report-of-the-Task-Force.pdf (2020)

ETUI: Work Programme 2019-2020. https://www.etui.org/sites/default/files/Work%20Programme%202019-2020.pdf (2018)

ETUI: Work Programme 2021-2022. https://www.etui.org/sites/default/files/2023-04/ETUI%20Work%20Programme%202023-24.pdf (2023)

EU: Regulation (EU) No 1025/2012 of the European Parliament and of the Council on European Standardisation. http://eur-lex.europa.eu/LexUriServ/LexUriServ.do?uri=OJ:L:2012:316:0012:0033:EN:PDF (2012)

Fleck, J.: Learning by trying: the implementation of configurational technology. Res. Policy. **23**(6), 637–652 (1994)

Graz, J.-C., Hauert, C.: Translating technical diplomacy: the participation of civil society organisations in international standardisation. Glob. Soc. **33**(2), 163–183 (2019). https://doi.org/10.1080/13600826.2019.1567476

Grunwald, A.: Responsible innovation: bringing together technology assessment, applied ethics, and STS research. Enterprise Work Innov. Stud. **31**, 10–19 (2011)

Hearings: Hearings – United States. Congress. House. Committee on Interstate and Foreign Commerce. https://play.google.com/store/books/details?id=cpDpAAAAMAAJ&rdid=book-cpDpAAAAMAAJ&rdot=1 (1947)

Huxley, A.: Brave New World. A Novel. Chatto & Windus, London (1932)
IAP2: Intern. Assoc. for Public Participation – Public Participation Spectrum. https://www.iap2.org/resource/resmgr/pillars/Spectrum_8.5x11_Print.pdf (2018)
IETF: RFC 2026: The Internet Standards Process – Revision 3. https://www.rfc-editor.org/rfc/pdfrfc/rfc2026.txt (1996)
Isaak, J.: The Role of Individuals and Social Capital in POSIX Standardization. Int. J. IT Stand. Standardization Res. **4**(1), 1–23 (2006). https://doi.org/10.4018/jitsr.2006010101
ISO: ISO/IEC Directives, Part 1 – Procedures for the Technical Work. https://www.iso.org/home.isoDocumentsDownload.do?t=05_kc9ujWR4hPohpeglziAKox8Sc37a7tEhYHLPKhAiaeJReQIS4qm48DOYQvmAX&CSRFTOKEN=WHGS-M7QL-HSHQ-8YEE-KTSY-JHUP-4XN5-XBWP (2023)
ITU: Series Y Supplement 34: ITU-T Y.4000 Series – Setting the Stage for Stakeholders' Engagement in Smart Sustainable Cities. https://www.itu.int/rec/dologin_pub.asp?lang=e&id=T-REC-Y.Sup34-202007-I!!PDF-E&type=items (2020)
Iversen, E.J., Vedel, T., Werle, R.: Standardization and the democratic design of information and communication technology. Knowl. Technol. Policy. **17**(2), 104–126 (2004)
Jakobs, K., Procter, R., Williams, R.: The making of standards: looking inside the work groups. IEEE Commun. Mag. **39**(4), 102–107 (2001)
Jakobs, K.: The role of the 'Third Estate' in ICT standardisation. In: Bolin, S. (ed.) The Standards Edge: Future Generation, pp. 105–116. The Bolin Group, Ann Arbor, MI (2005)
Jakobs, K.: ICT standardisation-co-ordinating the diversity. In: Proc. First ITU-T Kaleidoscope Academic Conference-Innovations in NGN: Future Network and Services, pp. 119–126. IEEE, Piscataway, NJ (2008)
Jakobs, K.: Trust in Open Standardisation?! In: Baccarani, C., et al. (eds.) Management in a Digital World: Decisions, Production, Communication. Proc. 28th Sinergie Annual Conference, pp. 21–33 (2016)
Jakobs, K.: Managing responsible standardisation of smart infrastructures and applications. In: Jakobs, K. (ed.) Corporate Standardization Management and Innovation, pp. 193–202. IGI Global, Hershey, PA (2019)
Jakobs, K.: Responsibility by design?! – On the standardisation of 'Smart' systems. In: Gordon, J.S. (ed.) Smart Technologies and Fundamental Rights, pp. 285–325. Brill, Leiden, Netherland (2021)
Koizumi, H., Yamashita, H.: Deficit lay or deficit expert: how do "experts" in environmental projects perceive lay people and lay knowledge? SAGE Open. **11**(3) (2021) https://journals.sagepub.com/doi/pdf/10.1177/21582440211023155
Kramer, R.M., Cook, K.S. (eds.): Trust and distrust in organizations: dilemmas and approaches. Russell Sage Foundation, New York, NY (2004)
Krechmer, K.: Open standards: a call for change. IEEE Commun. Mag. **47**(5), 88–94 (2009)
Meijer, A., Wiarda, M., Doorn, N., van de Kaa, G.: Towards responsible standardisation: investigating the importance of responsible innovation for standards development. Technol. Anal. Strat. Manag., 1–15 (2023)
NIST. (eds.): Draft Framework for Cyber-Physical Systems, Release 1.0. https://s3.amazonaws.com/nist-sgcps/cpspwg/files/pwgglobal/CPS_PWG_Framework_for_Cyber_Physical_Systems_Release_1_0Final.pdf (2016)
Orwell, G.: Nineteen Eighty-Four. A Novel. Secker & Warburg, London (1949)
Rosenkopf, L., Metiu, A., George, V.P.: From the bottom up? Technical committee activity and alliance formation. Admin. Sci. Quart. **46**(4), 748–772 (2001)
Stilgoe, J., Owen, R., Macnaghten, P.: Developing a framework for responsible innovation. Res. Policy. **42**, 1568–1580 (2013)
Tushman, M.L.: Special boundary roles in the innovation process. Admin. Sci. Ouart. **22**, 587–605 (1977)
von Schomberg, R.: A vision of responsible innovation. In: Owen, R., Heintz, M., Bessant, J. (eds.) Responsible Innovation, pp. 51–74. Wiley, London (2013)

Werle, R., Iversen, E.J.: Promoting legitimacy in technical standardization. Sci. Technol. Innov. Stud. **2**(1), 19–39 (2006)
Williams, R., Edge, D.: The social shaping of technology. Res. Policy. **25**, 856–899 (1996). https://doi.org/10.1016/0048-7333(96)00885-2

Chapter 8
Toward a Consensual Definition for Smart Tourism and Smart Tourism Tools

António Galvão, Fernando Brito e Abreu, and João Joanaz de Melo

Abstract Smart Tourism (ST) stems from the concepts of e-tourism, which is focused on the digitalization of processes within the tourism industry, and digital tourism, which also considers the digitalization of the tourist experience. The earlier ST references found regard ST destinations and emerge from the development of Smart Cities.

Our initial literature review on the ST concept and Smart Tourism Tools (STT) revealed significant research uncertainties: ST is poorly defined and frequently linked to the concept of Smart Cities; different authors have different, sometimes contradictory, views on the goals of ST; STT claims are often only based on technological aspects, and their "smartness" is difficult to evaluate; often the term "Smart" describes developments fueled by cutting-edge technologies, which lose that status after a few years.

This chapter is part of the ongoing initiative to build an online observatory that provides a comprehensive view of STTs' offerings in Europe, known as the **European STT Observatory**. To achieve this, the observatory requires methodologies and tools to evaluate "smartness" based on a sound definition of ST and STT while also being able to adapt to technological advancements. In this chapter, we present the results of a participatory approach where we invited ST experts from around the world to help us achieve this level of soundness. Our goal is to make a valuable contribution to the discussion on the definition of ST and STT.

A. Galvão (✉)
Instituto Universitário de Lisboa (ISCTE-IUL), ISTAR, Lisboa, Portugal

NOVA University Lisbon - School of Science and Technology, CENSE, Caparica, Portugal
e-mail: antonio.galvao@iscte-iul.pt

F. Brito e Abreu
Instituto Universitário de Lisboa (ISCTE-IUL), ISTAR, Lisboa, Portugal
e-mail: fba@iscte-iul.pt

J. Joanaz de Melo
NOVA University Lisbon - School of Science and Technology, CENSE, Caparica, Portugal
e-mail: amg13172@campus.fct.unl.pt; jjm@fct.unl.pt

E. Kornyshova et al. (eds.), *Smart Life and Smart Life Engineering*,
https://doi.org/10.1007/978-3-031-75887-4_8

Keywords Smart Tourism · Smart Tourism Tools · Online observatory · RESETTING

8.1 Introduction

The RESETTING project[1] aims at facilitating the shift toward more robust, circular, and eco-friendly business practices for tourism companies across Europe. Within its scope, we are building an online observatory to provide a broad view of STTs' offer in Europe, the **European STT Observatory**. This observatory requires methods and tools to assess "smartness" based on a sound definition of ST and STT and to be able to cope with technological evolution. This chapter is scoped in this effort.

To correctly understand ST (offer), a preliminary literature review on the ST concept and on STT and a broad online search on STT was performed. These early efforts revealed two significant research gaps or, rather, research uncertainties.

Although there is a common agreement in the academia that Smart Tourism (ST) refers to the use of technologies to improve visitors' and local's experiences while enabling sustainability goals, different authors consider different key aspects, from techno-, through tourist- or business-, to destination-centered definitions. Additionally, the hype around "Smart" has led to the misuse of the concept, known as "SmartWashing" (Desdemoustier et al. 2019). STTs are frequently just claims based on technological aspects provided by developers; the "smartness" of such technologies is often difficult to evaluate.

Additionally, the term "Smart" is used to describe developments fueled by cutting-edge technologies. Since technology development is constantly evolving, STTs are a moving target where a "Smart" offer quickly becomes a "Dumb" offer.

To populate the European STT Observatory, we need (a) strong definition(s) for ST(T). This effort will also allow us to create an STT smartness index to measure the smartness of the European STT supply. This chapter outlines our ongoing efforts to achieve these goals, focusing on our scientific and collaborative approach to reaching a unanimous definition of STT.

Nowadays, travel has become more accessible, convenient, and enjoyable for millions of people around the world. However, there is a digital divide between large enterprises and small and medium-sized enterprises (SMEs) in terms of their stake in the tourism industry (Minghetti and Buhalis 2010; Reverte and Luque 2020). The tourism industry's adoption of digitalization, innovation, and new technologies necessitates the use of STT. However, tourism SMEs lag behind in their ability to capitalize on the opportunity of a digital transformation of their core business due to financial and technical limitations, as well as a lack of awareness of existing STT. This is the driving force behind the creation of the European STT Observatory.

[1] Relaunching European smart and SustainablE Tourism models Through digitalization and INnovative technoloGies.

Thus, our research is framed in the following research questions:

- **RQ1:** What are the main criteria and methods for evaluating the smartness level of STT and comparing them across different domains and regions?
- **RQ2:** How can the participatory approach involving ST experts help reach a consensual definition of ST and STT and create a robust taxonomy for ST?
- **RQ3:** How can the European STT Observatory provide a comprehensive and up-to-date overview of the STT offer in Europe?
- **RQ4:** What are the benefits and challenges of using STT for tourism SMEs, and how can the European STT Observatory help reduce the digital gap between SMEs and large enterprises?

8.2 Literature Review

8.2.1 Smart Tourism: Evolution

The word "tourist" is believed to have originated in the eighteenth century, derived from the French word "tour," meaning "turn" or "trip," and referred to individuals who embarked on a journey or circuit, often for leisure or educational purposes.[2] Others claim that the etymology of the term tourism is much older, tracing back to the ancient Greek word for a tool used in describing a circle. In a sense, tourism is a journey that starts and ends at the same place, home (Leiper 1983). Nomadic lifestyles have accompanied humanity since its earliest development and are responsible for the widespread distribution of human beings. Although early human migrations were probably motivated by a combination of factors, including climate change (Timmermann and Friedrich 2016), population growth, and competition for resources, the advent of religions and culture embodied in prehistoric monuments suggests that early humans visited these sites as a form of primitive tourism.

However, the modern tourism industry began in the nineteenth century with the development of transportation infrastructure such as railways and steamships, and in the 1950s, with the widespread ownership of the automobile and the arrival of charter flights, national and international tourism took off (Christou 2022; Mowforth and Munt 2016; Sharpley 2022).

In the pre-Internet era, tourism suppliers had to rely on intermediaries for their distribution functions. The emergence of Computer Reservation Systems (CRSs) in the 1970s and Global Distribution Systems (GDSs) in the late 1990s facilitated the intermediation process, but it was the development of the Internet in the 1990s, leveraged by Information and Communication Technologies (ICTs) by providing

[2] Still, nowadays, the Merriam-Webster dictionary defines tourism as *the practice of traveling for recreation* (Merriam-Webster 2023).

tools for marketing, customer relationship management, yield management, quality control, and innovation, that changed both business practices and strategies and ultimately reshaped the tourism industry (Buhalis and Law 2008). As ICT evolved, new forms of tourism were shaped. The impact of new technologies is so great that it calls into question the very definition of tourism. We live in an era in which tourism has gone beyond the limits of a circular route between home and destination, and today, we can travel without leaving home (virtual tourism Verma et al. 2022), visit different times, or experience parallel realities in the areas where we travel (metaverse tourism and extended reality Yang and Wang 2023) or even aspire to visit places outside our own atmosphere (space tourism Reddy et al. 2012). With the unprecedented exponential growth we are currently witnessing, thanks to recent developments in AI, who knows what the future holds? It is in this context that ST is developing.

The evolution of Smart Tourism has been a transformative process, marked by the integration of advanced technologies into the tourism industry. The next paragraphs trace the journey from the early stages of e-tourism to the current era of Smart Tourism.

Tourism was one of the first sectors to digitalize business processes on a global scale, bringing flight and hotel booking online to become a digital pioneer. As ICT became a global phenomenon, tourism was a consistent early adopter of new technologies and platforms (Gössling 2021).

The early digitization of tourism was coined as "e-tourism" and was focused on digitizing processes within the tourism industry, changing the way organizations distributed their tourism products in the market (Buhalis and Licata 2002). This led to the development of online booking systems, e-ticketing, and other digital tools that made it easier for travelers to plan and book their trips online. Soon after, the new concept of "digital tourism" was proposed (Zambonelli et al. 2001). It is a broader term that encompasses e-tourism but also includes the use of digital tools by tourists to prepare, organize, control, and enjoy their travel experience.

In the early 2000s, the rise of mobile technology and smartphones paved the way for the development of ST. According to Li et al. (2017), the term "Smart Tourism" can be traced back to 2000 when Gordon Phillips defined it as a sustainable approach to planning, developing, operating, and marketing tourism products and businesses (Phillips 2000).[3] In his opinion, ST is shaped by two types of techniques: (1) smart demand and the use of management techniques that are capable of managing demand and access and (2) smart marketing techniques that can be used to target the proper customer segments to deliver appropriate messages.

Some preliminary research on STT can be found in di Hu et al. (2008). According to Wang et al. (2013), the earliest reference to Smart Tourism Destinations (STD) was coined in the "STD initiative," promoted by China's State Council of Chinese Central Government in 2009, in relation to a platform on which information relating to tourists activities, the consumption of tourism products, and the status of tourism

[3] This presentation in SlideShare could not be found, so this claim could not be verified.

resources could be instantly integrated and then provided to tourists, enterprises, and organizations through a variety of end-user devices.

The concept of ST became widespread in the turn of the 2010s, inspired by the development of Smart Cities and supported by new technologies such as mobile apps, augmented reality (AR), virtual reality (VR), and the Internet of Things (IoT) to provide tourists with personalized and immersive experiences (Buhalis and Amaranggana 2014; Wang et al. 2013).

e-Tourism, digital tourism, and ST came in succession chronologically, portraying the revolutionary changes brought to the tourism industry over the past few decades, leveraged by the power of technology. However, these concepts are often used interchangeably, as they all involve the use of technology to enhance and facilitate tourism activities (Kononova et al. 2020). Yet other technology-inspired designations for tourism have been used in scientific literature, such as "Mobile tourism (M-tourism)," "Intelligent Tourism," "Tourism 4.0," and "Virtual Tourism" (Kononova et al. 2020).

8.2.2 Smart Tourism: A Fuzzy Concept

Despite all the hype around ST, there is a lack of consensus on the definition of ST (Celdrán-Bernabéu et al. 2018; Gretzel et al. 2015; Križaj et al. 2021; Li et al. 2017; Pai et al. 2020; Rodrigues et al. 2023; Roopchund 2020; Shafiee et al. 2022, 2021; Zhang and Yang 2016). Several authors argue that the development of ST is hindered by the lack of such a definition (Celdrán-Bernabéu et al. 2018; Gretzel et al. 2015; Roopchund 2020; Shafiee et al. 2022, 2021). However, producing that definition is an endeavor jeopardized by the inherent complexity of the ST ecosystem, excellently discussed in (Gretzel et al. 2015).

Celdrán-Bernabéu et al. (2018) reason that future research aimed at the theoretical-conceptual development and critical analysis of ST should fill the existing gap between knowledge and operational development of ST. Additionally, they find some regionality associated with the terminology. In Western countries, ST is not a core strategy of tourism development but is based on its contribution to sustainable development and the relationship between tourists and destinations. In East Asia, ST actions focus on policies that promote the development of technological infrastructure, while in Europe, most initiatives are identified with Smart City projects that have favored the emergence of the smart destination approach.

Other authors point out the weaknesses resulting from this lack of clarity. For instance, Rodrigues et al. (2023) point out that *some existing smart tourism strategies seem to use both smart and sustainability concepts in a marginal, propagandist way, more similar to a marketing point of view. This might be due to theoretical inconsistencies, which need to be addressed in future studies, defining a reliable basis for fully understanding the smart approach in tourism.* Li et al.

Table 8.1 Key concepts found in Smart Tourism definition

Technology and innovation	Sustainability
• Maximizing environmental, cultural, social, and economic values through IT	• Intelligent, meaningful and sustainable connections
• Mobile digital connectivity	• Deep civic engagement
• Combined model of tourism industry and innovative technology	• Clean, eco-friendly, ethical, and high-quality services
• Data accumulation with technological means	Tourist experience
• Technology-driven innovation	• Individual tourist support system
• Constant and systematic use of smart elements	• Ubiquitous tour information service
• Device-generated big data for monitoring behavior, tourism management, and marketing	• Automatic provision of suitable and precise services
• Potential replacement of human labor through digital technologies	• Integrated efforts to find innovative ways for data accumulation and aggregation or use
• Evolutionary development of traditional tourism and e-tourism	• Interaction with a more comfortable environment for both locals and tourists
• Sensors, data mining, positioning technology, SNS, and social network technology	• Creation of additional travel value for the tourist
• Products using technological components	Smart cities
• Privacy preserving, context awareness, recommender systems, social media, IoT, user experience, real-time, user modeling, augmented reality, and big data	• Inspired by the idea of smart cities

(2017) argue that because of such practices, there is the risk that the concept of ST could be abandoned.

To highlight the different views on ST, we extracted the key concepts underlying the definitions of ST compiled by Kononova et al. (2020). The results were grouped into classes representing the broader considerations in those definitions (Table 8.1).

8.2.3 Related Work

One interesting approach in refining ST definition is brought by Chen et al. (2024). The authors argue that existing research on ST focuses on technological application and the opinions of users and suppliers, lacking discussion from the perspective of academic experts. Furthermore, they claim that most studies focus only on a single aspect of people, the planning process, or the technological components of ST. In this context, they interviewed 11 ST scholars to examine their views on the role of and interactions among three key components (people, process, and technology) in current ST development. The main findings (per aspect) are summarized below.

People—Key Stakeholders
Informants generally agreed that several stakeholders are involved in the development of ST, including tourists, suppliers, governments, destination marketing organizations, service providers, system providers, the technology itself, and residents. However, informants revealed different levels of importance among all these stakeholders. The development of ST is closely linked to that of the smart city and affects the quality of life of residents, who should have a say in the planning process.

Process—ST Planning Process
The ST planning process requires the collaboration and effort of various stakeholders, including the tourism board, government, and sectors involved. Cooperation between academia and industry is essential to enable a strategic relationship. Fostering innovation is critical to the success of ST planning. Implementing an ST-related project is an essential component for a destination, as the innovative environment ensures a smooth connection with practices.

Technology—ST Technologies
ST applications are being implemented in various areas such as entertainment, hotel operation, aviation, payments, experience training, ICT-related devices or applications, medical services, small business operation, and transportation. Industries with high interaction between tourists and suppliers are the most relevant for the application of ST. The adaptation of ST technologies occurs depending on changes in tourists' behaviors and service patterns.

ICT is a prerequisite component for smart ecosystem management, but ST is not just about applying ICT. Community interest and participation are critical to the smooth running of ST destination development. The sharing economy with traditional businesses also raises concerns. The availability of information from end users is an essential mediator at the operational level. ST development can evolve into a major regional or national development strategy, and operational guidance is needed to serve as a reference for the development of ST destinations.

The current study follows a similar approach in reaching out to the scientific community to try to create a consensual definition of ST.

ST operationalization is supported by the development and implementation of STT, supported by different technologies and operating in diverse domains.

Križaj et al. (2021) set out to ascertain what is being implemented in self-labeled "smart" destinations and whether most "smart" projects actually qualify as such, using a structured operational and innovation technology adoption-based approach, Smart Actionable Classification Model (SACM). Built on top of Perboli et al.'s (2014) taxonomy of Smart City projects, which lacks the evaluation of recent advanced technologies, it is adapted to the context of Smart Tourism, using Buhalis's definition of smart systems in tourism (Buhalis 2022)—*Smart systems use a wide range of networks, connected devices, sensors and algorithms for big data delivery across the IoT*—to define the **Smart Actionable** attributes used to categorize ST projects: (i) **networked/connected devices** and applications, (ii) coordinated by **intelligent algorithms**, and (iii) based on collected and analyzed information at

Table 8.2 ST groups (from Križaj et al. 2021)

id	Description	Techs
S1	Projects dealing with large amounts of networked and connected data, with the attributes of **networked/connected** and **big data**. The *use of intelligent algorithms is negligible*	networks IoT sensors
S2	Projects connected only by the **networked/connected** attribute and using to a *lesser extent* **networked/connected** data. The use of **intelligent algorithms** is *less frequent*, and the *Big Data attribute is absent* (despite most projects using sensors, the collected data is not sufficient to classify them as big data)	sensors mobile apps
S3	Projects associated only with the **big data** attribute. They *rarely apply* **intelligent algorithms** in data processing, and *do not address networked/connected goals*	IoT AI
S4	Projects that have not been assigned to any Smart Actionable. They use significantly fewer individual tech types[a]	mobile apps sensors

[a] Such projects accounted for as much as 31% of all projects in the analysis

a **Big Data** level. They classified 35 ST projects publicly available in Europe into the following groups based on their tech type and Smart Actionable (Table 8.2):

The authors found that *the vast majority of projects branded as "smart" predominantly pursue environmental sustainability goals, but do not feature advanced technology that meets the Smart Actionable attribute criteria, and do not address social sustainability issues to the same extent as the environmental ones*. This may suggest that there is a gap between the buzz generated by Smartness in tourism and its actual application at the destination level. These findings may also indicate that technocentric metrics alone may not be suitable for evaluating Smartness in the tourism sector. Notably, their study underscores the emphasis on sustainability objectives, with a primary focus on environmental considerations and, to a lesser degree, social aspects. Economic sustainability appears to be of less significance. The authors acknowledge that the projects under analysis, as described publicly, often employ vague technological terminology, particularly, but not exclusively, the term ICT, which impedes the classification of these projects with regard to technological intelligence. They also view their model as a preliminary milestone toward developing a stronger SACM approach, which accounts for additional terminology clarifications, as well as updated technological classification frameworks. Our work achieves a similar outcome, but our projects cannot be classified using the Perboli and colleagues' taxonomy. This is because we do not solely focus on smart destination projects but rather mainly on independent technological solutions that can function without the structured context of a smart city or destination.

Buhalis and Amaranggana (2015) discovered three distinct moments in the personalized services expected by tourists in STD:

(1) *Before Trip*: To support the planning phase by giving all the related real-time information based on user profiling in order to make a more informed decision

(2) *During Trip*: Enhanced access to real-time information to assist tourists in exploring the destination, direct personalized services, as well as a real-time feedback loop
(3) *After Trip*: Prolonged engagement to relive the experience, as well as a decent feedback system, allowing tourist to review their holistic tourism experience

8.3 Methodology

In this section, we first present the overall methodology used to build and operate the observatory (Fig. 8.1, where the icon represents the RESETTING Web app form). This chapter focuses on the cornerstones for building the observatory:

- Our proposed STT taxonomy, based on the operationalization of the studied STT applications and the identified technology domains
- The definition of ST and STT, from which we derive the STT Smartness Index, based on our participatory approach

The Observatory will be operated and maintained by semi-automated, AI-based Extraction, Transformation, and Loading (ETL) processes and expert-in-the-loop and is available online at http://sttobservatory.eu.

8.3.1 *STT Operational Taxonomy*

Several initiatives were developed to collect information on STTs. In Europe, we highlight the Scottish Tourism Toolkit (Gidlund and McGurren 2020), the European Commission report on ST Practices (Scholz and Friends Agenda 2022), Spain's Secretary of State for Tourism Catalogue of Technological Solutions for STD (SEGITTUR Turismo e Innovación 2022), and the Spanish Cluster of Innovative

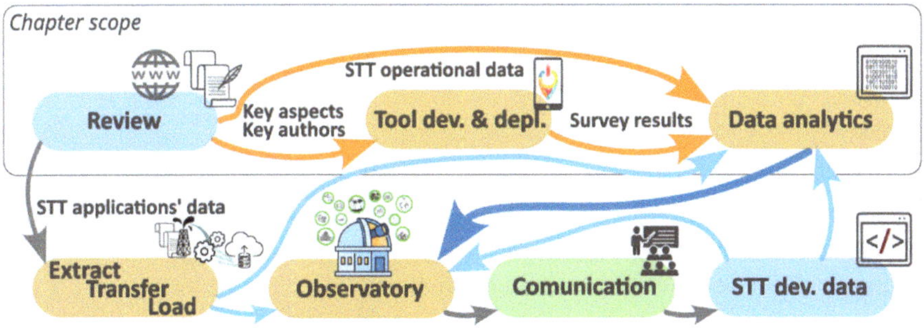

Fig. 8.1 Observatory methodology

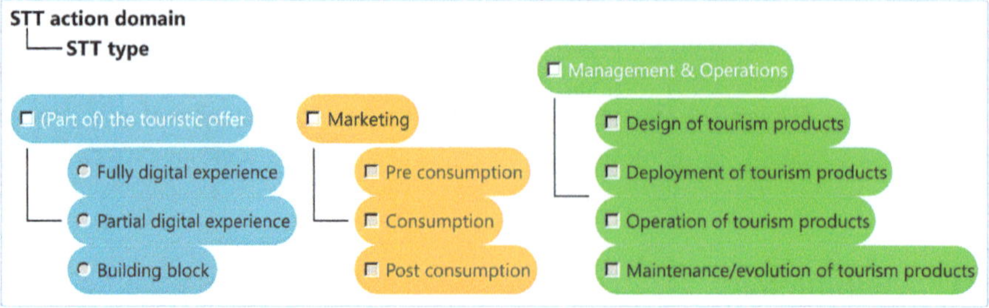

Fig. 8.2 STT action domains and tool types

Companies for Tourism in the Valencia Community Technological Solutions for Tourism catalog (ADESTIC 2023). We analyzed the STTs offered in these catalogs and the descriptions of STTs offered on the Internet, trying to map the areas of operation of STTs, the types of STTs available, and the types of technology most commonly used. This allowed us to identify three domains of application for STTs. In this sense, STTs can be:

- Tools as part of touristic offers
- Tools used for the marketing of touristic offers
- Tools for managing and operating touristic offers

These domains are not exclusive, i.e., some STTs operate in several domains.

Regarding the existing types of STT, we found ten different classes (Fig. 8.2). The main difference between them is not a technological consideration but rather the differences in the final objectives proposed by the developers and the domains in which they operate.

For the *Tourism Offer* action domain, we found three exclusive types of STTs:

- *Fully digital experience*—STTs that constitute tourism experiences occurring in the virtual world (e.g., virtual tours)
- *Partial digital experience*—core STTs that enable and/or enrich the tourism experience in the real world (e.g., augmented reality tours)
- *Building block*—scaffolding tools that support the enrichment of the tourist experience (e.g., audio or video content creation)

Three non-exclusive types of STTs have been identified in the *Marketing* activity domain:

- *Pre consumption*—STTs used in the stage where tourists engage in the decision-making process (e.g., selecting and booking the destination and related tourism services)
- *Consumption*—STTs used in the consumption stage, where tourists enjoy the pre-selected tourism services

- *Post consumption*—STTs used in the stage where tourists act as influencers of other users (e.g., sharing feelings raised and/or contents generated during the consumption stage)

Finally, the *Management and Operations* action domain contains four non-exclusive STT types:

- *Design of tourism products*—STTs that aim to support the creation of tourism offers (e.g., B2B platforms that support the creation of tourism packages)
- *Deployment of tourism products*—STTs that support the deployment of the tourism offer (e.g., online booking and payment platforms)
- *Operation of tourism products*—STTs that support the operation of tourism products (e.g., crowd management tools)
- *Maintenance/evolution of tourism products*—STTs that support the evaluation and decision-making regarding the existing tourism offer (e.g., data analysis tools)

In addition, we have compiled the technological areas that make up the tools analyzed. A non-exhaustive list is presented in Fig. 8.3 that tries to map the technological areas to the cognitive areas of the human brain.

The compiled domains of action cover all application areas found in the literature review and in the responses to the Web app form (see next section). They make up the backbone of the STT taxonomy that will integrate the European Observatory's Smartness Index. The latter should take into account STT's specific goals, technological and implementation aspects, potential impact on local (and global) sustainability, and stakeholder involvement.

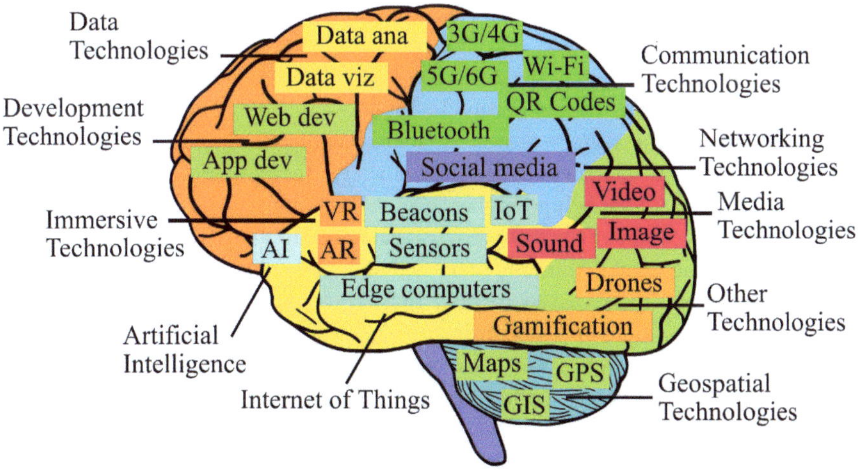

Fig. 8.3 Technologies most commonly found in STT

8.3.2 *ST(T) Definition*

To achieve a consensual definition of STTs, create a robust taxonomy for ST that can cope with the technological evolution needed to populate the European STT Observatory, and create an index that can compare the smartness level of STT offers, we used a scientific collaborative approach, inviting experts to provide their views.

Methodology Questionnaire

We created a form-like Web app considering the following principles:

- Be intuitive and easy to answer.
- Provide help content.
- Have no mandatory answers.
- Do not collect personal data.
- Provide both open- and closed-type questions.
- Be able to capture conceptual and technological aspects from the literature review.
- Be engaging with a game-like feel to promote answering in all fields.
- Provide motivational quotes as responding progresses.
- Reward users answering all questions with a prize: a virtual tourism experience.
- Allow users to leave comments and/or personal information if desired.
- Allow users from different countries to view and respond in their native language.

Next, we briefly present the Web app's GUI (Graphical User Interface) and explain how answering is achieved.

The first question was about the focus of STT in terms of the nexus: Tourist-Destination-Tourism Operator and Sustainability-Technology. The respondents were asked to drag the icon to the desired area in the Venn diagram (Fig. 8.4).

Regarding the nexus Sustainability-Technology, we later identified an error in the formulation of the Venn diagram: the chosen approach does not allow users to select the individual intersections between Society, Technology and Environment, Economy that are hidden behind higher-level central intersections.

The second question on the technologies that make up STT asked users to rate the "smartness" of the most commonly identified technologies in STT offer (Fig. 8.5).

The respondents were asked to rank the hypotheses (e.g., A.I.) by dragging them to the appropriate box according to the desired rank levels. Users could input multiple items in each rank box, allowing for equal importance values for multiple technologies. They could also add or delete rank levels at will, creating further distance between hypotheses to best represent the different advancement states of the technologies. If a technology was not deemed to belong to the STT universe, an additional box was provided labeled *I don't think this is an STT at all!* To aid users in understanding the provided technologies, a help box labeled *Don't know a tech? Drag it here!* was created. This box led users to online content that

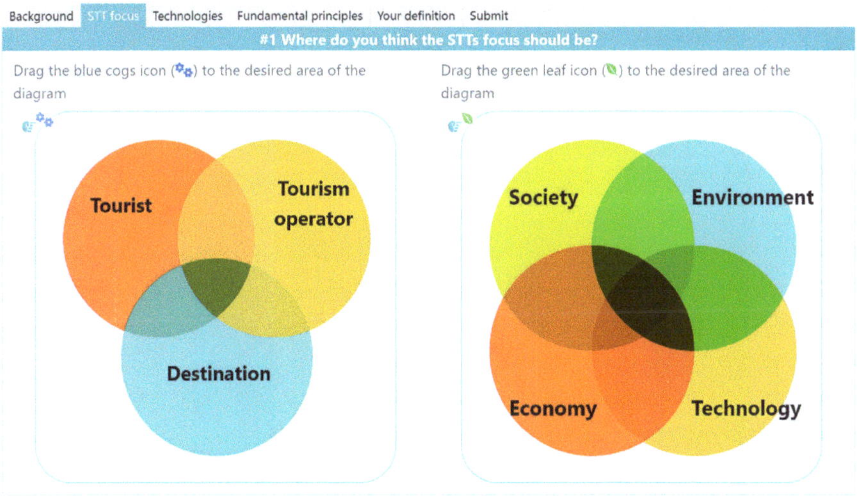

Fig. 8.4 STT focus

explains the intended technologies. Wikipedia was the chosen data source whenever possible for consistency. Additionally, users could create and rank their own custom technologies using the "*Add other*" button.

In the third question, on the basic principles of ST (Fig. 8.6), users were required to compare various concepts that underlie the definition of ST, as derived from the literature review. All functionalities, except for the help box, were similar to those found in the previous question. This meant that users could place multiple items in each rank box, add or remove rank levels at will, and create and rank their own principles for a more discriminating separation of alternatives.

For the fourth and final question, users were asked to provide their own definition of STT in an open-ended format (Fig. 8.7).

The app also featured a completeness gauge and provided motivational quotes to encourage responses (Fig. 8.7).

Respondents who achieved 100% completeness were invited to explore the depths of the earth through a virtual visit to Gralhas VII cave,[4] in Portugal, provided by CEAE-LPN. [5]

[4] Virtual tour (last accessed on 02/27/2024). If you wish to take the tour, please note the red arrows as they may not be very visible.

[5] CEAE-LPN: Centro de Estudos e Actividades Especiais-Liga para a Protecção da Natureza (en: Centre for Special Studies and Activities-League for the Protection of Nature).

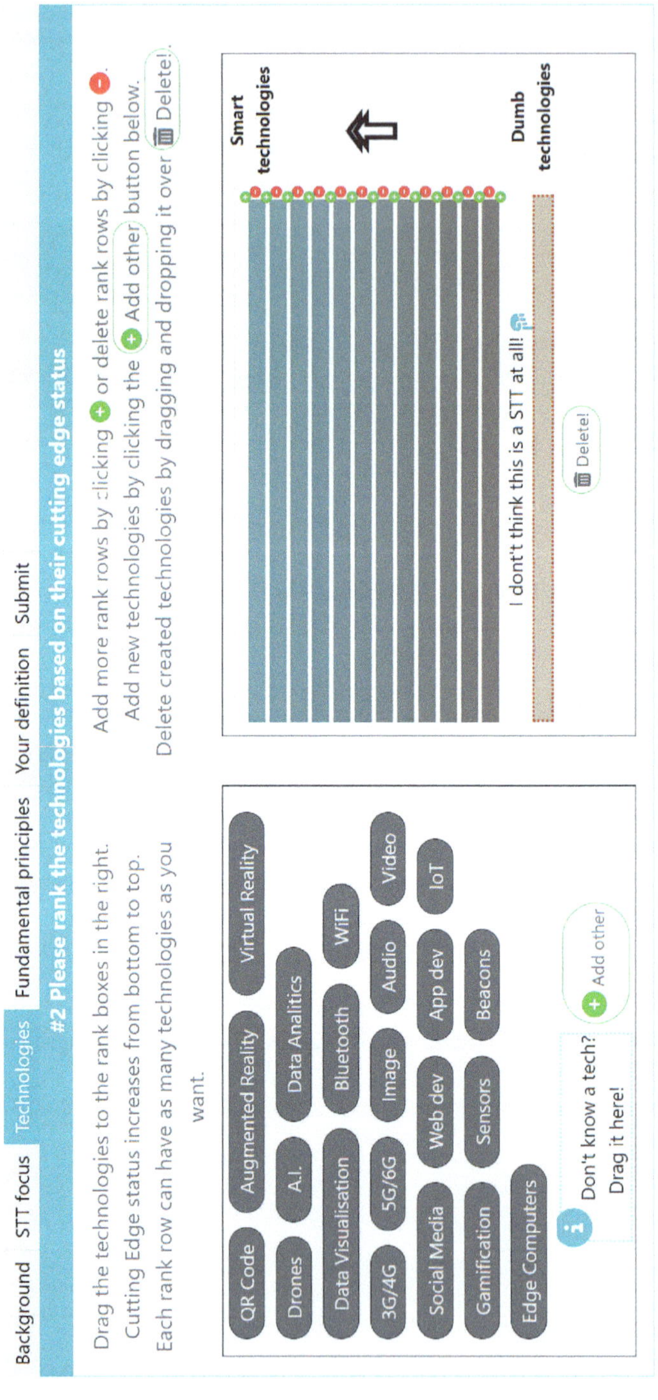

Fig. 8.5 STT technologies

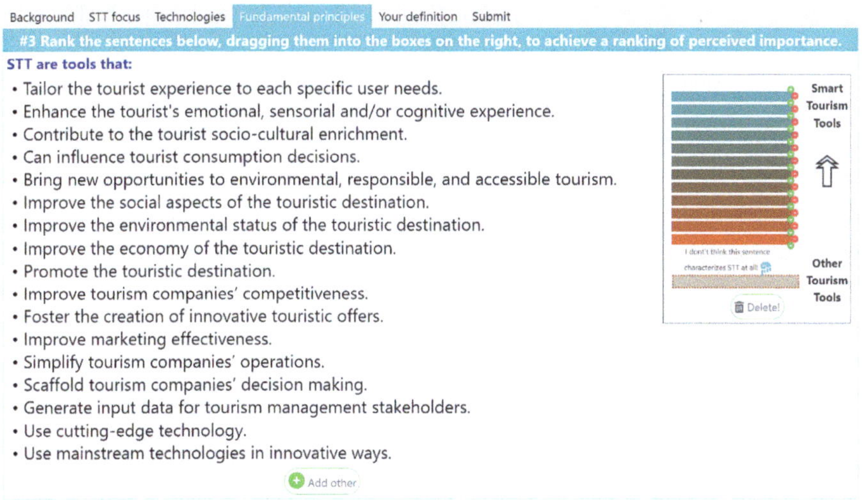

Fig. 8.6 ST principles

Methodology: Questionnaire Respondents

The population of interest for our survey is the community of ST experts. In order to maximize the chances of obtaining a large number of respondents, we searched the following databases for papers containing the term "Smart Tourism" in the title, abstract, and/or keywords and for the contact details of their authors: Scopus, SpringerLink, WebOfScience, lens.org, Dimensions, and Scielo.

In addition, since experts in a given field usually meet with their peers to validate their findings and to inspire themselves through discussion, we also retrieved the contacts of the authors presenting at these annual events focused on ST topics:

- The e-Tourism Conf. of the Int. Federation for IT and Travel & Tourism (ENTER)
- Int. Conf. of the Int. Association of Cultural and Digital Tourism (IACuDiT)
- Int. Conf. on Tourism Technology & Systems (ICOTTS)

We sent a personalized email to each of the identified ST experts, inviting them to participate in the survey.

Methodology: Data Collection and Analysis

In the development of our Web app, we opted to collect both categorical and open-ended data to allow for statistical analysis of the results aimed at identifying the most consensual technologies and principles underlying Smart Tourism Tools (STT), as well as identifying any new aspects and technologies not previously identified in the

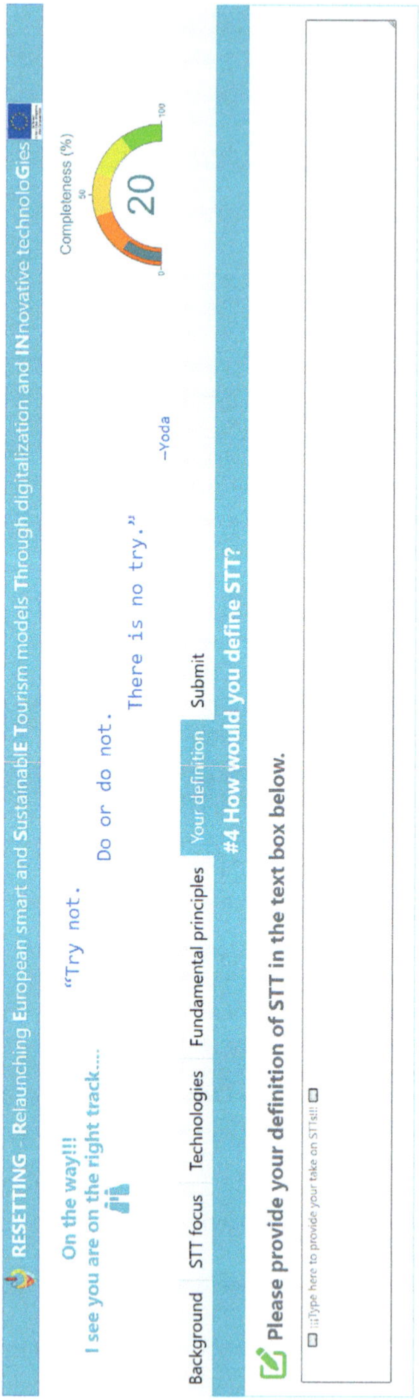

Fig. 8.7 STT definition

literature review. These two types of data underwent different analysis processes, which are explained in further detail in the next section.

The analysis results represent the weights of the sub-indices that will be aggregated to form the STT Smartness Index. In the following section, we present the finalized weights of the sub-indices, along with their rationale and mathematical formulation, where applicable. As the analysis is still ongoing, the final weights of all sub-indices are not yet available, as explained in the next section where appropriate.

8.4 Results: Presentation and Analysis

We received 334 expert responses worldwide, with an average completion rate of 82% (measured within the Web application itself). The Web application's built-in completeness checker measures the partial completeness of each question, meaning that if a respondent fails to rank a given variable in a ranking question, they will not receive a full score. Looking at completeness based on whether the question was answered or not, the average completeness rises to 91% (Table 8.3). Note that the average shown is based on the variables originally provided (excluding respondents' own variables) and also excludes responses to additional comments and contact information. These exclusions were also applied in the Web app's completeness checker, as these variables represent additional information to the survey.

In terms of global representativeness, we received responses from all continents, which should provide different views in relation to their regional realities. Of the 334 responses, we were only able to identify 52 countries, as the geo-referencing is based on the (optional) email domains provided, meaning that only 47% of the responses could be geo-referenced. In addition, 29 of the responses were in 10 different languages other than English—Greek, Korean, Spanish, Italian, Slovak, Chinese (simplified), Ukrainian, Portuguese, Polish, and Persian.

Table 8.3 Average form completeness

Question	% of responses
Rank tool custom user STT definitions	2%
STT definition rank	95%
Rank tool custom user technologies	10%
Technologies rank	95%
STT focus: tourist, destination, company	92%
STT focus: sustainability, technology	93%
Respondent STT definition	81%
Respondent comments	25%
Email contact information	61%
Average completeness	91%

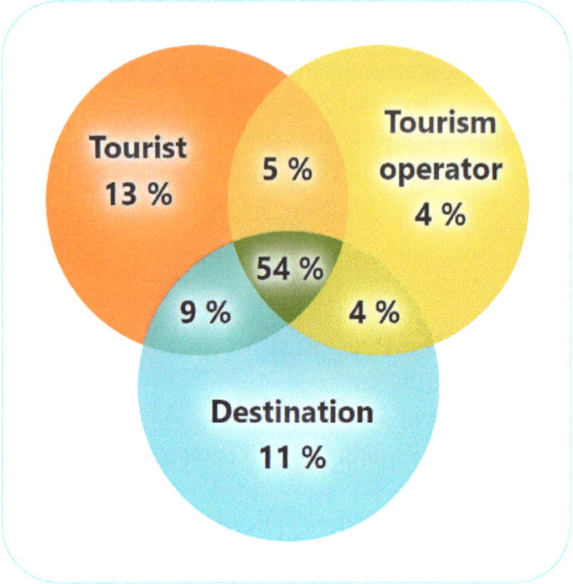

Fig. 8.8 Tourist-Operator-Destination responses

8.4.1 STT Focus

Figure 8.8 shows the results of the answers to the first question concerning the focus of STT regarding the nexus Tourist-Operator-Destination.

Visual analysis of the diagram reveals a consensus of the STT focus on the Tourist and the Destination to the detriment of the Tourism operator. Further analysis of the diagram seems to indicate that the users' perception of the data collection method was not consistent across the universe of STT experts. This may be the case because the data collection approach is innovative. It is reasonable to assume that the problem under study should be additive, i.e., the intersections of the groups should have higher values (or at least the same order of magnitude) than the independent groups, i.e., if one group, let's say "Tourist," is key to STT, then intersections containing "Tourist" should retain at least some of that importance, and add the importance of the intersecting group, even though the importance of each independent group in the intersected group might be different from their importance in the independent groups. To overcome this, we performed a deeper analysis of the data and ultimately extracted indicators for the Smart Index; we analyzed the data considering each level of intersection as a separate universe. In this way, we can derive the relative importance of each of the nexus elements within each intersection universe.

Let's assume that participants in the dual intersection universe assign intrinsic importance or weight to each of the base variables—Tourist, Destination, Company—when responding. This would mean that we can calculate an average weight or ponderation for each of these variables within the dual intersection universe. This can be expressed as:

$$Result_i = \alpha Tourist + \beta Destination + \gamma Company \tag{8.1}$$

where:

i is the group of all possible intersections in that universe. In the case of the dual intersection universe - [Destination_Tourist, Tourist_Company, Company_Destination],

α, β, and γ represent the weights of the base variables—Tourist, Destination, Company—constant within the intersection universe.

Using Equation 8.1, we can create a system of equations for each of the groups in a given universe. Note that for the dual intersection universe, Eq. 1 only has two terms. We can then create a matrix for the equation system—A—taking "$\frac{1}{2}$" for each of the base variables present in each dual intersection world, as we are only analyzing dual intersections.

$$A \cdot X = B \begin{bmatrix} 0.5 & 0.5 & 0 \\ 0.5 & 0 & 0.5 \\ 0 & 0.5 & 0.5 \end{bmatrix} \cdot \begin{bmatrix} \alpha \\ \beta \\ \gamma \end{bmatrix} = \begin{bmatrix} 0.50 \\ 0.29 \\ 0.21 \end{bmatrix} \tag{8.2}$$

where:

A is the systems equation matrix
X is the matrix of weights α, β, and γ, which we are trying to find
B is the matrix containing the ratio of dual intersection i, over the total of the dual intersections universe, calculated directly from the gathered data

We can then solve for X:

$$X = A^{-1} \cdot B \tag{8.3}$$

where:

A^{-1} is the inverted matrix for the equation system.

X contains the average intrinsic weights of the universe of the double intersection. We can directly estimate the average intrinsic weights for the independent universe by calculating the ratio of the entries in each independent group to the total entries for the independent universe. The average weights of the whole universe—independent and intersecting—can then be estimated using a weighted average, taking into account the dimensions of each universe in the data collected.

Table 8.4 shows the resulting overall weights for the Tourist-Operator-Destination nexus. It is clear, as identified in the visual analyses, that the Tourist is the most important focus for STT, closely followed by the Destination, and the Tour Operator (Company) is not as central to STT. We can then apply these averages to each group by adding the weights of the variables present in each group.

Table 8.4 Average weights Tourist-Operator-Destination nexus

Tourist	Destination	Operator
0.50	0.42	0.08

Fig. 8.9 Tourist-Operator-Destination results

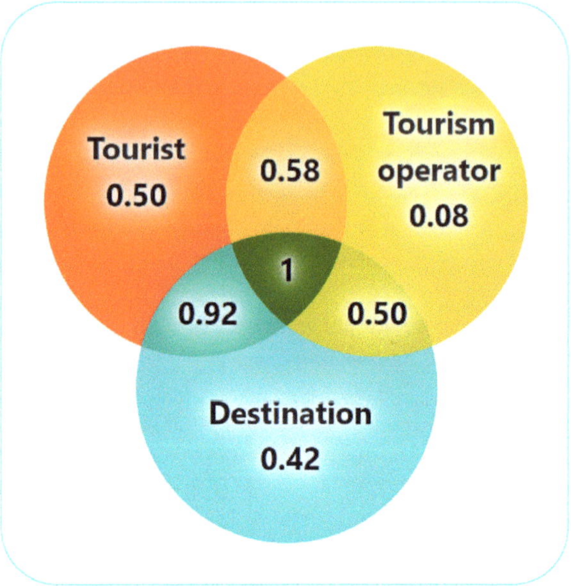

Figure 8.9 presents the results in a Venn diagram to facilitate comparison with the data collected. As you can see, the relationships of the original data remain, but now we have the cumulative effect required by raising the levels of intersection.

Regarding the question concerning the Sustainability-Technology nexus, the approach used to collect data in this particular Venn diagram does not allow the user to select the intersections between Society, Technology and Environment, Economy. However, it is important to note that although the user cannot enter data at the two intersections mentioned, the graphical nature of the response method leads the user to spatially locate their responses in the regions closest to their intended focus. This means that it is still possible to draw valid conclusions from the collected data.

A visual analysis of this diagram (Fig. 8.10) shows that the focus is on the environment, society, and technology and their combinations, to the detriment of the economy. Two interesting conclusions can be drawn from this. Firstly, although the term "smart" is intertwined with technology, at least in the field of SST, the emphasis seems to be primarily on the environment and society and only then on technology. Secondly, technology seems to bypass one of the pillars of the tripartite concept of sustainability, the economy.

In this case, because we have the data gaps mentioned above, we chose a simpler approach. We decided to treat the data as a whole, so we created an overall average by multiple counting the overlapping data, thus creating a new universe where

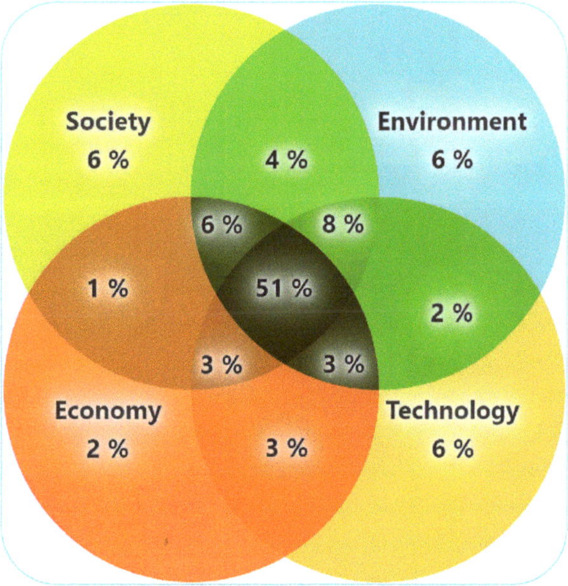

Fig. 8.10 Sustainability-Technology responses

our sample data is three times larger (in the largest dataset of tested alternatives) compared to the collected data. We tested six hypotheses for extracting the average weights with different combinations of:

- Considering or not the central intersection—to test the effect of the largest group (about 50% of the total responses, when all other groups exist)
- Considering or not double intersections, replacing missing values with:
  - The average size of the remaining universe of double intersections
  - An average for the given variables within the remaining universe of double intersections

The alternative that best fits the data does not consider the central intersection and considers the double intersections, replacing the missing values with an average for the variables in question in the remaining universe of double intersections. The results are shown in Fig. 8.11.

8.4.2 *Technology "Smartness"*

Next, we analyze the results of the second question, in which respondents were asked to rank a list of technologies according to their state of the art. In addition, users could suggest and rank their own technology proposals. We received 72 technology suggestions, of which 49 were unique, and some were subsets of our own list.

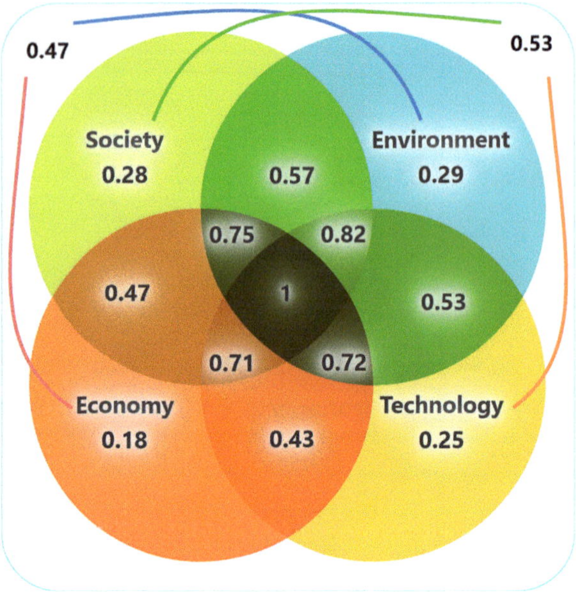

Fig. 8.11 Sustainability-Technology results

The data for each technology category underwent normalization using the *Min-Max Scaling Normalization* method. This involved subtracting the minimum value found in the category from the value in each data point and dividing by the category range (i.e., the difference between the maximum and minimum values in the category). This procedure transforms every data point into a decimal between 0 and 1. The minimum values of that category are transformed into a 0, and the maximum values are transformed into a 1.

Concerning the ranking of the technologies, excluding the custom ones in this analysis, we received answers where users did not classify some technologies, although there is a box to drop technologies not considered STT. We cannot be sure if technologies not ranked were considered not STT or if this was just an issue of incomplete answering, or even a combination of the former two situations. To test the influence on the results, we created two separate average ranks, one considering the arithmetic mean and another considering the sample mean (Fig. 8.12). Figure 8.12a) shows the ranking in descending order of cutting-edge status, from left to right, taking into account the arithmetic mean rank. It does not show arithmetic averages but the ranking at equal intervals. In this way, a perfect blue spiral line is obtained, reflecting the steady descent of the ranking.

The number of ranked technologies is different for each technology (brown line in Fig. 8.12a), reflecting the different sample sizes per technology that influence the results. The behavior of the red line follows a spiral in the higher and lower rankings, but in the intermediate rankings, there are several disagreements between statistical

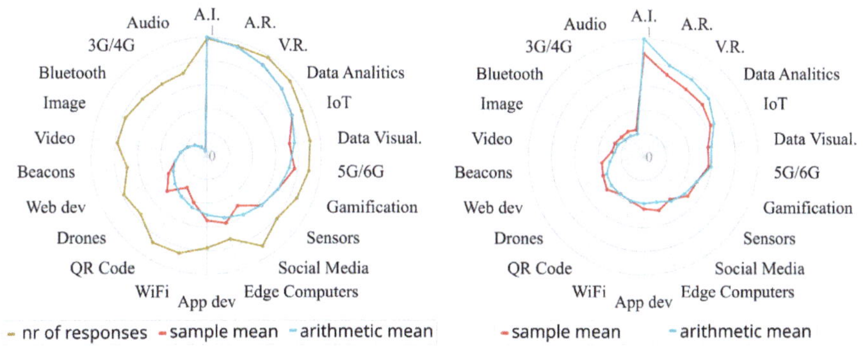

(a) linear ranking order

(b) calculated means

Fig. 8.12 Average ranks found

approaches. If we analyze the average rank expressed in terms of the arithmetic mean actually calculated (Fig. 8.12b), the differences diminish, although they are still present. This figure expresses the actual distances between the technologies proposed by the respondents and shows that the perceived technological status is close for the divergent ranking categories. This approach also highlights the positive distances between adjacent technologies, e.g., the leap from AI to AR is much greater than the leap from the latter to VR, and the same effect can be seen between other technologies, although not as pronounced.

8.4.3 STT Fundamental Principles

In response to the question that asked users to rank some of the fundamental principles found in the literature review and to provide their own fundamental principles, we received 13 principle suggestions from 8 users (Table 8.5). These propositions reveal important aspects such as tourist mobility or safety.

The Web app's fundamental principles were ranked using the same strategy as the technology ranking, which was described above. This included data normalization procedures and testing of the two statistical approaches since some principles were not ranked. The ranking of the fundamental principles of STT was very consensual among the experts. Although the order of three principles varied between the two statistical approaches, their rankings were similar (Fig. 8.13).

Interestingly, the results are very similar to those obtained in the first question on the focus of STT. The tourist and the tourist experience come first, followed by the destination and environmental concerns, technological considerations, and commercial aspects.

For both questions regarding the ranking of data, we have chosen to use the sample average to construct the Smart Index because we believe it is the

Table 8.5 Fundamental principles proposed by respondents

User_ID	Proposed fundamental principles
32	Help tourism destinations to be more sustainable, competitive, and resilient
47	Improves mobility efficiency
	Enhance the tourist's experience
71	Metaverse
96	Creating Tourism Network
118	Optimize the tourist route
128	Bring better experience through smart chain management
250	It supports the improvement of tourism destination branding
	It supports the improvement of users' Customer Satisfaction
318	Promote collaboration among the stakeholders of a tourist destination
	Strengthen the governance of the destination
	Facilitating tourist mobility around the destination
	Increasing security in a tourist destination

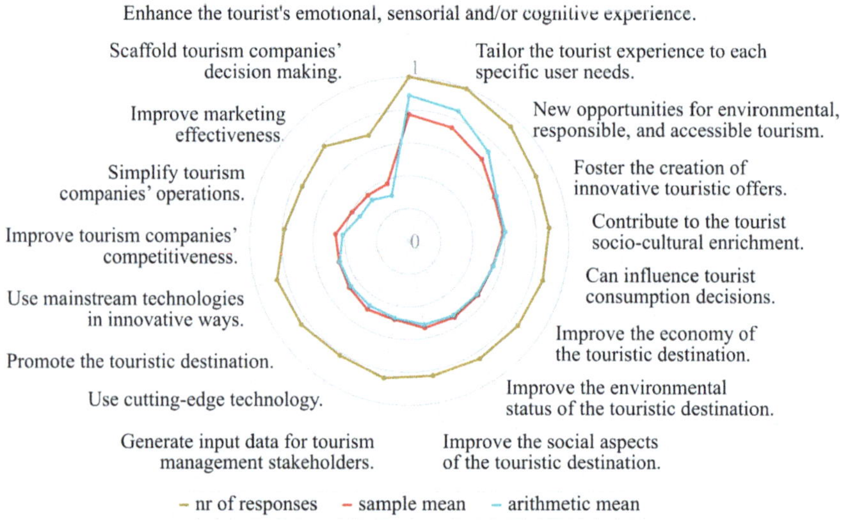

Fig. 8.13 STT fundamental principles average ranks

most appropriate statistical approach to construct the ranking of ST fundamental principles, as it takes into account the variability and richness of the data collected. This is due to the fact that:

- The sample size is relatively large (334 responses from experts around the world) and representative of different regions and perspectives
- The design of the survey was intuitive, easy, engaging, and rewarding, which could have reduced the likelihood of non-response and incomplete answers

Fig. 8.14 Single word cloud

Fig. 8.15 Bigram and trigram word cloud

- The survey used a rating tool that allowed multiple items in each rating box and the addition or deletion of rating levels at will, which could reflect the experts' preferences and opinions more accurately

8.4.4 *Open-Ended STT Definition*

Finally, users could write their own definition of STT in an open-ended question. We first used MAXQDA5[6] to help analyze the responses. We started by creating two word clouds, one with just single words (Fig. 8.14) and the other with bigrams and trigrams (Fig. 8.15).

Once again, we can see the importance of the tourist, destination, and sustainability in the definitions presented. We then coded the responses according to three main categories, (i) STT objectives, (ii) STT target categories, and (iii) technology areas.

The code frequency analysis in relation to the STT objectives is shown in Fig. 8.16. Again, we see the same pattern as in the previous responses. It is worth noting that some mentions of environmental aspects could be related to broader sustainability, as these two concepts are often used interchangeably, and this was evident in our context analysis. The same could be said for inclusive tourism. The

[6] https://www.maxqda.com/

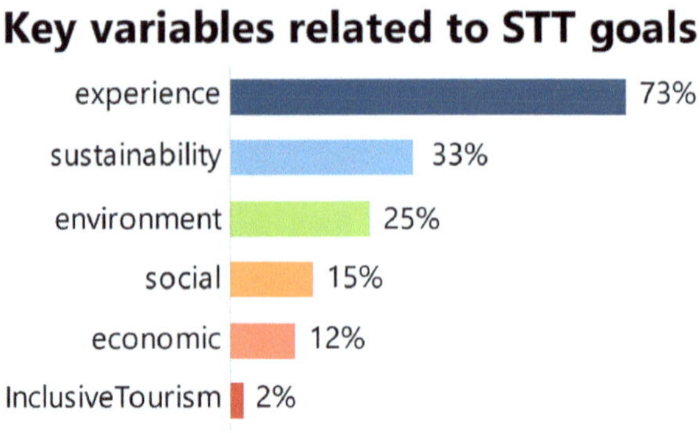

Fig. 8.16 Code frequencies: STT goals

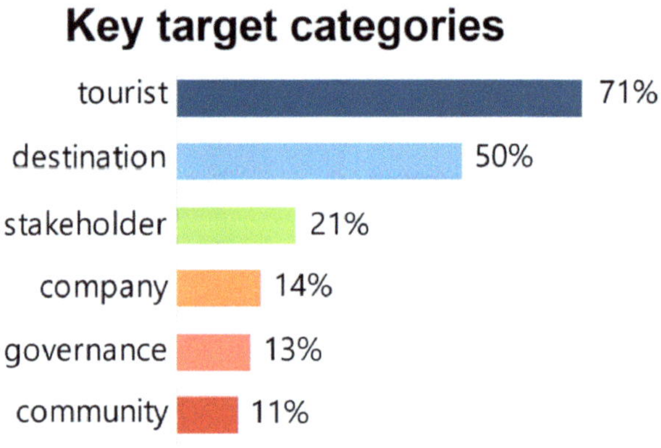

Fig. 8.17 Code frequencies: STT target categories

code for this category only highlights responses that specifically mention it, but other mentions of the social aspects of sustainability could also consider this aspect.

The analysis of the code frequency regarding the key target categories is presented in Fig. 8.17 and again shows the same patterns as previously observed in relation to the STT definition. It should be emphasized that the **stakeholder** code represents the mentions where respondents broadly referred to all direct and indirect stakeholders in the tourism industry.

The code frequencies for technology mentions are shown in Fig. 8.18. The code **Technology** refers to mentions of technology as a broad field and does not distinguish between smart and mainstream technologies, i.e., these could refer to combinations of mainstream and smart technologies, the context analysis points in this direction. The **SMART** code aggregates mentions in different formats such as "innovative," "advanced," "new," or "cutting edge." In the code **Mainstream SMART**, respondents specifically mentioned the use of mainstream and/or advanced technologies.

The presented approach for the analysis of open-ended answers does not allow extrapolating meaningful indices for the Observatory smartness index. To overcome this, we tested different preprocessing techniques and natural language processing

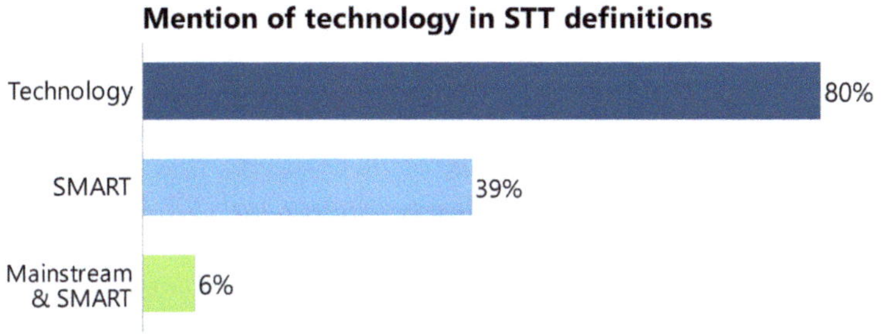

Fig. 8.18 Code frequencies regarding technology mentions

(NLP) analyses. These ranged from simple approaches, such as assessing text complexity, to more complex methods, like topic modelling, a technique that identifies topics in a set of documents. We also attempted to measure data similarity in vector space, a mathematical model where words are represented as vectors in multi-dimensional space, using embeddings from small language models, simple and/or small AI models trained on text data, useful for several NLP tasks, but not highly effective on capturing context and concepts. This latter approach was also combined with a semantic search of previously extracted concepts. However, these attempts fell short of achieving the desired indices. This was largely due to the high text complexity of the definitions and their varied sentence structures. The definitions also include many examples that add redundant or extraneous information to the statistical analysis. Since LLMs (large language models, AI models trained on vast amounts of text data, able to generate humanlike text) can understand both concepts and context, they are particularly useful for treating data with such characteristics, given adequate instructions and examples. We are currently using LLMs to do Text Classification, Relationship Extraction, and Span Categorization. This approach should allow deriving a single vector of the relevant concepts for each definition that can be used to statistically determine the required indices.

8.5 Final Remarks

ST refers to the use of technology and data-based solutions to improve tourist experience, destination management, and sustainability. It involves the collaboration of different stakeholders, such as tourists, suppliers, governments, and residents, to create value and benefits for all. ST is inspired by the concept of smart cities but also takes into account the specific needs and characteristics of tourism and tourism destinations. STTs are the set of tools that support the development and implementation of ST. Therefore, STTs are a set of tools that:

1. *apply the fundamental principles of ST, to achieve (at least some) ST goals,*
2. *within the specific scope envisioned by developers (application domain and specificities of the final consumer or area, ensuring concordance with ST scope),*
3. *considering the inputs of/and the final influence on the key stakeholders,*
4. *taking advantage of the relationship of their specific field, the ST field (as most STT developers are not specifically working with ST, but are experts in their own field, e.g. VR), and with other interconnected knowledge areas, either technological or not, while applying techniques and technologies and*
5. *trying to minimize biases at an operational level (e.g. avoid search engine "commercial" algorithm influence in AI-based tourism recommendation systems) and on a conceptual level, ensuring they are indeed STT and not just digital tools.*

Our results, based on the experts' opinions, corroborate that Smart Tourism's definition cannot just consider one dimension, such as the technocentric one. The results further allow us to define to what degree each key aspect of the definition should be considered when evaluating Smart Tourism offers. Our STT definition cannot yet deal with the fast pace of technological evolution. Further research is required considering different approaches, such as using the reports published yearly by the World Economic Forum, to identify and extract emerging technologies and the number of scientific publications referring to these technologies in the field of Smart Tourism, as a proxy for the technology Smartness. Additionally, this smart-metric approach means that, as technology evolves, earlier technologies do not become dumb but actually less Smart, and this can be quantified.

Our proposed consensual "current" definition for STT is that of:

> Seamlessly interconnected digital tools designed to benefit all stakeholders in the tourism industry, with a special focus on the tourist and the destination, that aim at local, and possibly global, sustainable development

At their highest level, STTs produce experiential ecstasy in the dynamic human interface with technology, enriching and not alienating people. At decreasing smartness levels, they also aim to improve the efficiency, quality, and competitiveness of tourism destinations, operations, products, and companies. They also aim to improve the quality of life of local communities and the well-being of tourists while minimizing the negative impacts of tourism on the environment and local culture. The level of STT Smartness depends more on achieving the objectives of sustainable tourism than on their technological status. Indeed, emerging technologies offer unforeseen possibilities, but so does innovation combined with conventional technology. This means that the intelligence of these tools should give higher importance to their alignment with the principles and objectives of Smart Sustainable Tourism. A full evaluation would require assessing tool deployment results, i.e., their impact on all relevant stakeholders in the tourism industry and on local (and possibly global) sustainability. This more complete Smartness assessment is beyond the scope of our current work since the latter only considers the potential impact of STTs based on the information available, mainly in the product descriptions and then in more detailed descriptions provided by the STT developers/owners.

8.5.1 Future Developments

We anticipate broadening the audience to derive the ST(T) definition from other key stakeholders, such as tourists, tourism operators, and destination managers. This will allow us to derive a more representative STT Smartness Index. Finally, we plan to use the STT Smartness Index to assess the STT offer in the European market.

Acknowledgments This work was developed in the scope of the RESETTING project, funded by the COSME Programme (EISMEA) of the European Union under grant agreement No.101038190.
We also thank all survey participants, without whom this study would not have been possible.

References

ADESTIC: Soluciones Tecnológicas para el Turismo. Tech. Rep. 2nd edition, Clúster de Empresas Innovadoras para el Turismo de la Comunitat Valenciana, Valencia, Spain (2023)

Buhalis, D.: Smart Tourism, pp. 124–127. Edward Elgar Publishing, Cheltenham (2022). https://doi.org/10.4337/9781800377486.smart.tourism

Buhalis, D., Amaranggana, A.: Smart tourism destinations. In: Xiang, Z., Tussyadiah, I. (eds.) Proceedings of the International Conference on Information and Communication Technologies in Tourism 2014, pp. 553–564. Springer, Cham (2014). https://doi.org/10.1007/978-3-319-03973-2_40

Buhalis, D., Amaranggana, A.: Smart tourism destinations enhancing tourism experience through personalisation of services. In: Tussyadiah, I., Inversini, A. (eds.) Proceedings of the International Conference on Information and Communication Technologies in Tourism, pp. 377–389. Springer, Cham (2015). https://doi.org/10.1007/978-3-319-14343-9_28

Buhalis, D., Law, R.: Progress in information technology and tourism management: 20 years on and 10 years after the Internet—The state of eTourism research. Tour. Manag. **29**(4), 609–623 (2008). https://doi.org/10.1016/j.tourman.2008.01.005

Buhalis, D., Licata, M.C.: The future eTourism intermediaries. Tour. Manag. **23**(3), 207–220 (2002). https://doi.org/10.1016/S0261-5177(01)00085-1

Celdrán-Bernabéu, M.A., Mazón, J.N., Ivars-Baidal, J.A., Vera-Rebollo, J.F.: Smart tourism. Un estudio de mapeo sistemático. Cuadernos de Turismo **Enero–Junio**(41) (2018). https://doi.org/10.6018/turismo.41.326971

Chen, Z., Chan, I.C.C., Mehraliyev, F., Law, R., Choi, Y.: Typology of people–process–technology framework in refining smart tourism from the perspective of tourism academic experts. Tour. Recreat. Res. **49**(1), 105–117. (2024). https://doi.org/10.1080/02508281.2021.1969114

Christou, P.: The History and Evolution of Tourism. CABI (2022). https://doi.org/10.1079/9781800621282.0000

Desdemoustier, J., Crutzen, N., Giffinger, R.: Municipalities' understanding of the smart city concept: an exploratory analysis in Belgium. Technol. Forecasting Soc. Change **142**, 129–141 (2019). https://doi.org/10.1016/j.techfore.2018.10.029. Understanding Smart Cities: Innovation ecosystems, technological advancements, and societal challenges di Hu, L., Long, Y., yang Qian, C., Zhang, L., nian Lv, G.: Design and realization of intelligent tourism service system based on voice interaction. In: Liu, L., Li, X., Liu, K., Zhang, X., Wang, X. (eds.) Geoinformatics 2008 and Joint Conference on GIS and Built Environment: The Built Environment and Its Dynamics, vol. 7144, p. 714427. International Society for Optics and Photonics, SPIE (2008). https://doi.org/10.1117/12.812827

Gidlund, K., McGurren, M.: Scottish Tourism TOOLKIT: Technology solutions for tourism businesses in a post Covid19 Scotland. Tech. Rep. 2nd edition, Traveltech for Scotland, The University of Edinburgh, Scotland (2020)

Gretzel, U., Sigala, M., Xiang, Z., Koo, C.: Smart tourism: foundations and developments. Electron. Markets **25**(3), 179–188 (2015). https://doi.org/10.1007/s12525-015-0196-8

Gretzel, U., Werthner, H., Koo, C., Lamsfus, C.: Conceptual foundations for understanding smart tourism ecosystems. Comput. Hum. Behav. **50**, 558–563 (2015). https://doi.org/10.1016/j.chb.2015.03.043

Gössling, S.: Tourism, technology and ICT: a critical review of affordances and concessions. J. Sustain. Tour. **29**(5), 733–750 (2021). https://doi.org/10.1080/09669582.2021.1873353

Kononova, O.V., Prokudin, D.E., Tupikina, E.: From e-Tourism to Digital Tourism. Terminologically Review. In: Proceedings of the Conference on Scientific Services & Internet (SSI-2020), vol. 2784. CEUR (2020)

Križaj, D., Bratec, M., Kopić, P., Rogelja, T.: A technology-based innovation adoption and implementation analysis of european smart tourism projects: towards a smart actionable classification model (SACM). Sustainability **13**(18) (2021). https://doi.org/10.3390/su131810279

Leiper, N.: An etymology of "tourism". Ann. Tour. Res. **10**(2), 277–280 (1983). https://doi.org/10.1016/0160-7383(83)90033-6

Li, Y., Hu, C., Huang, C., Duan, L.: The concept of smart tourism in the context of tourism information services. Tour. Manag. **58**, 293–300 (2017). https://doi.org/10.1016/j.tourman.2016.03.014

Merriam-Webster: Tourism (2023). Accessed 1 Oct 2023

Minghetti, V., Buhalis, D.: Digital divide in tourism. J. Travel Res. **49**(3), 267–281 (2010). https://doi.org/10.1177/0047287509346843

Mowforth, M., Munt, I.: Tourism and Sustainability: Development, Globalisation and New Tourism in the Third World, 4th edn. Routledge (2016). https://doi.org/10.4324/9781315795348

Pai, C.K., Liu, Y., Kang, S., Dai, A.: The role of perceived smart tourism technology experience for tourist satisfaction, happiness and revisit intention. Sustainability **12**(16) (2020). https://doi.org/10.3390/su12166592

Perboli, G., De Marco, A., Perfetti, F., Marone, M.: A new taxonomy of smart city projects. Transp. Res. Proc. **3**, 470–478 (2014). https://doi.org/10.1016/j.trpro.2014.10.028. 17th Meeting of the EURO Working Group on Transportation, EWGT2014, 2–4 July 2014, Sevilla, Spain

Phillips, S.G.: The tourism industry association of Canada [EB/OL] (2000)

Reddy, M.V., Nica, M., Wilkes, K.: Space tourism: research recommendations for the future of the industry and perspectives of potential participants. Tour. Manag. **33**(5), 1093–1102 (2012). https://doi.org/10.1016/j.tourman.2011.11.026

Reverte, F.G., Luque, P.D.: Digital Divide in E-Tourism, pp. 1–21. Springer, Cham (2020). https://doi.org/10.1007/978-3-030-05324-6_109-1

Rodrigues, V., Eusébio, C., Breda, Z.: Enhancing sustainable development through tourism digitalisation: a systematic literature review. Inform. Technol. Tour. **25**(1), 13–45 (2023). https://doi.org/10.1007/s40558-022-00241-w

Roopchund, R.: Mauritius as a smart tourism destination: technology for enhancing tourism experience. In: Pati, B., Panigrahi, C.R., Buyya, R., Li, K.C. (eds.) Proceedings of 3rd International Conference on Advanced Computing and Intelligent Engineering (ICACIE 2018), pp. 519–535. Springer, Singapore (2020). https://doi.org/10.1007/978-981-15-1483-8_44

Scholz & Friends Agenda: Leading Examples of Smart Tourism Practices in Europe. Tech. Rep. 2nd edition, European Commission (2022)

SEGITTUR Turismo e Innovación: Catalogue of Technological Solutions for Smart Tourist Destinations. Tech. Rep. 2nd edition, Spain's Secretary of State for Tourism, Madrid, Spain (2022)

Shafiee, S., Jahanyan, S., Ghatari, A.R., Hasanzadeh, A.: Developing sustainable tourism destinations through smart technologies: a system dynamics approach. J. Simul. **0**(0), 1–22 (2022). https://doi.org/10.1080/17477778.2022.2030656

Shafiee, S., Rajabzadeh Ghatari, A., Hasanzadeh, A., Jahanyan, S.: Smart tourism destinations: a systematic review. Tour. Rev. **76**(3), 505–528 (2021). https://doi.org/10.1108/TR-06-2019-0235

Sharpley, R.: Tourism and development theory: which way now? Tour. Plan. Dev. **19**(1), 1–12 (2022). https://doi.org/10.1080/21568316.2021.2021475

Timmermann, A., Friedrich, T.: Late pleistocene climate drivers of early human migration. Nature **538**, 92–95 (2016). https://doi.org/10.1038/nature19365

Verma, S., Warrier, L., Bolia, B., Mehta, S.: Past, present, and future of virtual tourism-a literature review. Int. J. Inform. Manag. Data Insights **2**(2), 100085 (2022). https://doi.org/10.1016/j.jjimei.2022.100085

Wang, D., Li, X.R., Li, Y.: China's "smart tourism destination" initiative: a taste of the service-dominant logic. J. Destin. Mark. Manag. **2**(2), 59–61 (2013). https://doi.org/10.1016/j.jdmm.2013.05.004. Researching Destination Experiences

Yang, F.X., Wang, Y.: Rethinking metaverse tourism: a taxonomy and an agenda for future research. J. Hosp. Tour. Res. **0**(0), 10963480231163509 (2023). https://doi.org/10.1177/10963480231163509

Zambonelli, F., Cabri, G., Leonardi, L.: Developing mobile agent organizations: a case study in digital tourism. In: Proceedings of 3rd International Symposium on Distributed Objects and Applications, pp. 270–279 (2001). https://doi.org/10.1109/DOA.2001.954092

Zhang, L., Yang, J.: Smart Tourism, pp. 862–863. Springer, Berlin (2016). https://doi.org/10.1007/978-3-319-01384-8_175

Part III
Smart Life Applications

Chapter 9
Smart-Viticulture and Deep Learning: Challenges and Recent Developments on Yield Prediction

Lucas Mohimont, Lilian Hollard, and Luiz Angelo Steffenel

Abstract Smart agriculture is a trendy topic as it has a clear impact in both productivity, ecological impact, and improvement of working conditions. Smart viticulture is one of the domains that can benefit both from wireless sensor networks and mobile devices embarked in vineyard labor tools (e.g., on a straddler tractor). One important use case is related to the yield estimation, an invaluable information to drive the harvest organization, plant management, and business's economy. Traditional methods rely on destructive sampling and manual counting, resulting in error rates sometimes greater than 30%. In this chapter, we review existing techniques for the automation of yield estimation and, focusing on deep learning methods, propose some strategies and preliminary results obtained in a production environment.

Keywords Computer vision · Deep learning · Viticulture · Yield prediction

9.1 Introduction

The development of smart agriculture has raised interesting opportunities for improved automation, logistics, and working conditions. Numerous different technologies have been studied for practical applications in agriculture. For instance, wireless sensor networks allow the collection of data from different locations in a parcel. The acquired data, such as the temperature or the humidity, are used to predict the emergence of diseases (Pérez-Expósito et al. 2017; Steffenel et al. 2021). In addition, the sensors can include embedded cameras to detect the presence of symptoms of illness or deficiencies (Lloret et al. 2011) or simply to control the maturity state of the fruits or estimate the yield. Finally, other sensors such as LIDARs (*laser imaging detection and ranging*) can estimate the size of the

L. Mohimont · L. Hollard · L. A. Steffenel (✉)
Université de Reims Champagne-Ardenne, LICIIS Laboratory, Reims, France
e-mail: lucas.mohimont@univ-reims.fr; lilian.hollard@univ-reims.fr; luiz-angelo.steffenel@univ-reims.fr

E. Kornyshova et al. (eds.), *Smart Life and Smart Life Engineering*,
https://doi.org/10.1007/978-3-031-75887-4_9

canopy or the number of missing plants (Grocholsky et al. 2011). The advance in image processing techniques and the emergence of affordable digital cameras and embarked processors also bring new opportunities for smart agriculture, with the promise to improve the work conditions and the accuracy of forecasts as it can better humans in repetitive, time-consuming, and tedious tasks.

Among these tasks, we can cite the automation of fruit counting, a central problem in smart agriculture as it has a direct impact on yield prediction and management. Several methods have been proposed in recent years, and this concept has been applied to the detection of oranges (Maldonado and Barbosa 2016), bell peppers (Song et al. 2014), and lemons (Dorj et al. 2017).

In the case of viticulture, winegrowers use yield estimation to get decisive information for the business's economy, plant management, and harvest organization. The interest in knowing the yields early enough involves several economic, administrative, and qualitative objectives (Liu et al. 2013). For example, winegrowers can manage the wine market by estimating and controlling the crop volume on a regional or national scale. Yield forecast also helps increase the quality of the wines, by eliminating part of the harvest by thinning out the bunches, as it has been proven that too high density may hinder the quality of the grapes (Xi et al. 2018). This is an essential element in some appellations such as Champagne (INAO), where annual production quotas in kg/ha are defined and any excessive production cannot be transformed in Champagne.

Traditionally, winemakers estimate their production by performing samplings on selected land plots, using a simple formula such as Eq. 9.1 for a given area.

$$Yield\ (kg/ha) = \frac{nb\ plants \times nb\ grapes \times avg\ grape\ weight}{surface} \tag{9.1}$$

This procedure relies on both grape counting and weighting. Grapes are harvested among a random sample allowing an estimation of the number of grapes by vine, the number of berries per grape, and the weight of the berries. Furthermore, grape counting is mostly performed by a human operator, leading to uncertainties on the precision and dubious repeatability. Weighting of the grapes, on the other hand, requires them to be harvested prematurely, a destructive process that cannot be performed extensively. Some works use historical data to limit grape weighting, but significant variations from year to year can skew the predictions. As a result, a variation of 30% can be found between the estimations and the reality (Dami and Sabbatini 2011). Reducing this error is therefore essential for the organization of the harvest.

The moment yield forecasts are performed also impacts the solutions. Indeed, most winegrowers prefer to obtain estimations at least 1 month before harvest, which usually falls before the *veraison*, i.e., the start of the maturing period where grapes' colors change. This complicates the yield estimation using non-intrusive or non-destructive methods, as the color contrast between the leaves of the vine and the green grapes is reduced (Di Gennaro et al. 2019). In addition, the solutions shall adapt to the winegrowers' working hours, being tolerant to different light intensities during the day and variable weather conditions (Zhang et al. 2022).

In this work, we focus on the analysis of works where deep learning models are used for grape and berry counting, the first step toward an accurate yield performance forecast. Recent works demonstrate that deep learning contributes to automatically count grapes in the vineyard (Santos et al. 2017; Heinrich et al. 2019) showing more robustness and accuracy than other computing vision methods based on signal processing or traditional machine learning (Diago et al. 2015; Dunn and Martin 2004; Liu et al. 2018).

We also present some results obtained by our team in an effort to develop a yield performance forecast model for the Champagne vineyards. Since 2019, we work on data collection and labeling, as well as the development and training deep learning models for smart-viticulture. Today, our focus is on the development of lightweight and robust models that can later be integrated in edge or embarked devices, allowing on-site real-time processing even in remote locations with no network coverage.

The remainder of the chapter is structured as follows: Sect. 9.2 introduced the literature on grape detection and counting, pointing out traditional and deep learning models as well as the remaining challenges and opportunities. Similarly, Sect. 9.3 focuses on berry counting and weighting. In Sect. 9.4, we introduce our works and some of our preliminary results. Finally, Sect. 9.5 concludes this work.

9.2 Grape Detection and Counting

The main component for automatic yield estimation is to detect and count grape clusters (also called *bunches of grapes* or simply *grapes*). In this case, images with grapes are sent to the detection algorithm, whose output includes the number of grapes present in the image and eventually an image containing the location of the grapes as well (see Fig. 9.1).

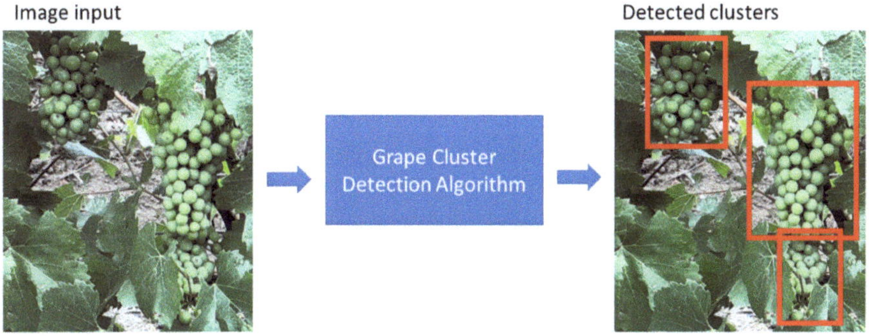

Fig. 9.1 Example of grape cluster detection (Chardonnay, before veraison) (Mohimont et al. 2022)

This is an important step because it enables several practical applications besides yield estimation, for example, automatic harvesting using a robot (Reis et al. 2012; Luo et al. 2016, 2018), the automatic spraying of growth hormones, Berenstein et al. (2010), the characterization of phenotyping (Rose et al. 2016), or even the detection of water stress to optimize irrigation (Kang et al. 2023).

Multiple obstacles shall be met during the creation of such an algorithm. First of all, the acquisition method is important: drone/UAV (*unmanned aerial vehicle*) images are good for general analysis on the canopy (water stress, diseases) but may lack the resolution to identify grape details (Ariza-Sentís et al. 2023). Indeed, precise grape counting and characterization often require ground-based image acquisition solutions, like a camera embedded in a vehicle. Furthermore, several variability factors (lighting, angle, distance, complex background) are present in natural images, and the algorithm must account for (*ii*) occlusions created by the foliage, and often there is (*iii*) color confusion between the grapes and the foliage.

A simple approach to detect grapes consists in using thresholding segmentation. Thresholding segmentation is a simple approach that was first used by Dunn and Martin (2004) to evaluate the potential of image processing for yield estimation. Here, one or more thresholds (e.g., color or brightness filters) are applied to the images to keep the areas that correspond to the fruits only. Thresholding segmentation algorithms usually have short execution times and are easy to develop. However, these algorithms have several drawbacks that limit their use in the field without partial control of the environment. The main issue is that strict thresholds are not robust to the color variations caused by natural lighting and the background. The thresholds must be determined in each situation, and the grapes must have attained the maturity to discriminate their color from the ground or the leaves (Di Gennaro et al. 2019; Torres-Sánchez et al. 2021). For this reason, most works limit its usage to nighttime with a lighting source, in order to erase the background elements (sky, ground, and further rows). Indeed, threshold segmentation has been applied on the field on red and white varieties but only during the night, with artificial lighting (Reis et al. 2012).

A different approach relies on traditional machine learning (ML) to make the detection of grapes more robust to lighting variations. It segments the image by using small pixel neighborhoods, or blocks, as inputs for a classification model. Examples of pixel neighborhoods are illustrated in Fig. 9.2.

The pixel classification model produces a binary output (grape or non-grape) that is applied to the central pixel or the entire input block. Classical ML techniques cannot be directly applied to the raw images, as features must be extracted first for each block. A simple feature is the mean values of the R, G, and B channels to produce a vector with only three components (Chamelat et al. 2006). Similarly, the mean value of the RGB (*red, green, blue*) channels was used in several studies (Casser 2016; Luo et al. 2016; Font et al. 2015). A genetic algorithm was suggested to select the best color channels among several possible color spaces: RGB, HSV (*hue, saturation, value*), and CIELAB (Behroozi-Khazaei and Maleki 2017). Nonetheless, pixel classification suffers from several limitations, including sensitivity to color (variety) and potentially long execution time, and it heavily

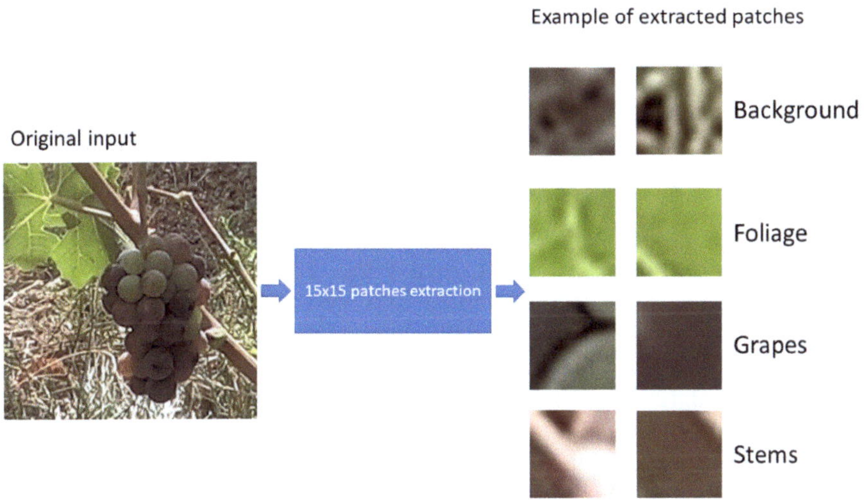

Fig. 9.2 Examples of pixel neighborhoods extracted from a vine image (Pinot Noir, during veraison) (Mohimont et al. 2022)

depends on the choice of extractors because the quality of the features will impact the final results.

9.2.1 Using Deep Learning

Deep learning has recently been applied to the problem of detecting and counting grapes. A naive approach uses the same pixel-wise classification discussed previously, but with a neural network that combines both feature extraction and classification (Lopes et al. 2017; Cecotti et al. 2020; Milella et al. 2019).

The use of convolutional neural networks (CNN) simplifies the detection step because the model will learn the best features from the data. However, this method is always limited by the small size of the blocks and the long calculations required to segment one image. Several CNNs have been studied to predict the mass of the grapes automatically (Silver et al. 2019). The error is relatively low, 11% in controlled conditions with an artificial background, but the proposed method has many drawbacks. The distance between the grapes and the camera varies, impacting the results. This limit could be overcome using a depth sensor, but this approach should also be evaluated on several rows and with different varieties to better appreciate its potential.

Several popular object detection models, Faster R-CNN (Ren et al. 216), R-CNN (Girshick et al. 2014), R-FCN (Dai et al. 2016), and SSD (Liu et al. 2016), have been tested on the task of grape detection and counting using videos (Heinrich et al. 2019). SSD was applied to grapes detection at two stages (0.5 cm berries and 1.2

cm berries) in natural conditions and with real-time hardware acceleration (TPU) (Aguiar et al. 2021). The Mask R-CNN model (He et al. 2018), which detects objects and segments them, has also been applied to the detection of grapes (Santos et al. 2020). The counting of grapes from videos is corrected with a *structure-from-motion* method that estimates the 3D position along the camera path. The 3D position is used as an identifier to avoid counting one grape twice. Mask R-CNN and multiple Yolo models (Redmon et al. 2016) were compared on the dataset published by Deng et al. (2020), Santos et al. (2020). Yolo models were also compared on red grape detection from smartphone images (Li et al. 2021). The Faster R-CNN model was applied similarly with a tracking algorithm to process videos of Riesling and Pinot Noir vines taken at night with artificial lighting (Jaramillo et al. 2021). Mask R-CNN was studied in multiple recent works Barbole and Jadhav (2021), Ghiani et al. (2021), Yin et al. (2021). The authors of Barbole and Jadhav (2021) compared the performances of Mask R-CNN to other models like U-Net and Yolov3 (Redmon et al. 2018) (they also used the WGISD benchmark published by Santos et al. 2020). They found better precision with U-Net and better recall with Yolov3. The authors of Ghiani et al. (2021) applied Mask-RCNN to the GrapeCS-ML dataset published by Seng et al. (2018). It contains images of different varieties taken in natural conditions at different stages. One limitation of this dataset is that most images only contain one grape cluster, so the resulting model cannot process images with many clusters.

Mask R-CNN was also applied with stereo images to detect and reconstruct 3D models of the grapes for automated harvesting (Yin et al. 2021). The Yolov4 (Bochkovskiy et al. 2020) model was applied to low-resolution images of white grapes to measure the correlation between grape counting and fruit weight (Sozzi et al. 2021). A low correlation was found between the number of detected clusters and the actual number of clusters (0.24 R^2). The correlation between the number of detected clusters and fruit weight was better (0.59 R^2), indicating a potential application for yield estimation in future works. Similarly, YOLOv5s was successfully used by Shen et al. (2023) to perform real-time detection and counting in a defoliated dataset, reaching a 79% accuracy after applying filtering for motion-induced errors.

The authors of Chen et al. proposed a modified PSPNet (Zhao et al. 2016) model for grape segmentation (Chen et al. 2021). It was applied on white and red grapes after veraison. They reached good segmentation performances with an average of 87.42% IoU (*Intersection over Union*). Similar results were obtained on both red and white grapes. However, the main limitation of semantic segmentation models is their inability to separate overlapped clusters. This results in inaccurate grape counting. Similarly, the authors of Peng et al. (2021) applied a DeepLabV3+ model to multiple varieties of red, green, purple, and black colors, with or without spherical berries. They reached an IoU of 88.44% with an inference of 60 ms/image, which allows an automatic harvesting deployment. The authors are well aware of the difficulty of separating overlapping grapes and proposed the use of a depth sensor (Intel Realsense D435 stereo camera) to solve this problem (Peng et al. 2021).

Their results, 85.6% recall and 87.1% precision, show the viability of their solution. However, this method should be compared to object detection models.

Finally, a generative model was proposed to adapt images to different lighting conditions (Fei et al. 2021). A CycleGAN (Zhu et al. 2020) model was used to translate images taken in daylight to images taken at night with artificial lighting. This step can be useful to increase the size of existing datasets and make the models robust to the varying environmental conditions.

9.2.2 Remaining Challenges

Although effective, most of the methods presented in the previous section only have been applied to controlled environments and are seldom adapted to the processing of real-time video streams. For this reason, looking for more performing solutions offering advanced computing and AI capabilities is interesting, and several works now explore the interaction between different layers (cloud-fog-edge) (Vermesan et al. 2021), including Edge-AI capable devices.

Developing real-time Edge AI also helps improve the autonomy of the devices, as one of the main challenges in smart agriculture is the difficulty to deploy solutions capable of handling complex actions in environments subjected to high network constraints (absence of network coverage, high latency) and the limited performance of embarked devices.

Finally, another challenge comes from the complexity of the natural environments in which these devices are supposed to work. For example, Kumrai et al. (2020) demonstrate the difficulty of recognizing human activity according to the angle, capturing and extracting information from the captured images for a camera mounted on a robot. This is somehow similar to the problems faced when detecting and counting grapes on the vineyard, as the angle and other plant elements (leaves, branches) lead to image occlusions that affect the identification of the grapes or the variance of luminosity during the day. Hence, robust deep learning models shall withstand such environmental variance all while delivering accurate results.

9.3 Berry Counting and Weighting

If counting the grapes is the first step toward an automatic yield prediction, it is often insufficient to provide accurate results. Indeed, a complementary step is required to reduce the variability caused by different grape bunch sizes in the plot: counting and weighting the berries. Indeed, according to the work from Clingeleffer et al. (2001), the number of grapes per vine, the number of berries per grape, and the weight of the berries make up, respectively, 60%, 30%, and 10% of the yield variance in a model using these three factors.

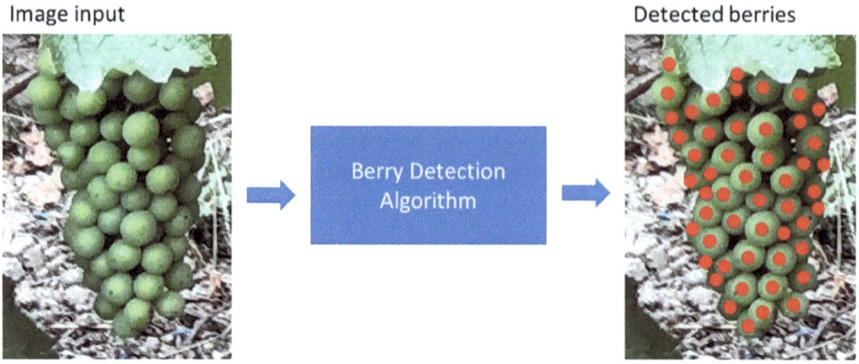

Fig. 9.3 Example of berry counting (Chardonnay, before veraison) (Mohimont et al. 2022)

As this method is inherently destructive, the sample size is often reduced in traditional estimation methods, leading to important biases. As a consequence, several studies propose methods for automatic counting of berries through computer vision. These methods consist mainly in the detection of visible berries and the further estimation of the number of grape bunches. As stated before, these two factors account for up to 90% of the variance in the yield estimation. An example of automatic berry counting is illustrated in Fig. 9.3.

The problem with berries counting can therefore be formulated as a circle detection or local maxima detection task. Most signal processing solutions use the specular reflection caused by the light on the surface of the berries, producing a pattern that follows a Gaussian distribution. The berries appear as bright little spheres that make them more easily distinguishable from the background of the image. One of the first methods exploiting specular reflection used a Gaussian kernel to process images taken with a smartphone with flash (Grossetete et al. 2012), but it was limited to close-up images of one or several grapes to limit confusion caused by the background.

Several other image analysis algorithms have been used to detect berries: the h-maxima transform (Aquino et al. 2017, 2018), the fast radial symmetry transform (Nuske et al. 2014; Luo et al. 2021), and the Hough transform (Murillo-Bracamontes et al. 2012; Diago et al. 2015; Liu et al. 2015, 2020; Roscher et al. 2014; Rahman et al. 2014; Keresztes et al. 2018). The fast radial symmetry transform detects berry candidates rapidly, whereas the Hough transform potentially has higher memory and computing power requirements. An alternative to the h-maxima transform, named invariant maxima detector, is proposed by (Nuske et al. 2014) to detect berry candidates with artificial lighting. Indeed, these works show that detectors based on local maximums are too sensitive to variations in natural lighting, and the use of a flash or lamp creates a uniform specular reflection on the surface of the berries, making the detection easier.

This classical approach is therefore complex because it requires several algorithms that need to be fine-tuned to (1) detect the berry candidates, (2) extract the features of each candidate, and (3) filter the false positives with a classifier.

Of course, counting grapes and berries may not be enough to predict the yield, as the final weight/volume also depends on other factors such as the average grape/berry size or weight and the weather conditions prior to the harvest (Anastasiou et al. 2023).

9.3.1 Deep Learning Strategies

Deep learning can simplify berry counting by processing raw images. CNNs can be used as a feature extractor and as a classifier at the same time to filter berry candidates. This technique has been implemented on a Raspberry Pi (Keresztes et al. 2018) for real-time detection. CNNs have also been shown to be more accurate than support vector machines (SVM) (Śkrabánek 2018). Furthermore, CNNs have been adapted to object counting with density map prediction. The areas with strong density correspond to the berries' location (Coviello et al. 2020). This method manages to count berries with an error rate of approximately 10%. CNNs have also been adapted to image segmentation. These CNNs have shown very promising results. A fully convolutional neural (FCN) model was proposed to count the berries with two classes of labeling, the first for the inside of the berries and the second for the edges (Zabawa et al. 2020). The model is faster and better than Mask R-CNN (He et al. 2018) and UNet (Ronneberger et al. 2015). This difference is explained by the structure of the models as Mask R-CNN uses a complex structure to detect and segment objects and by the small size of the database. Deng et al. (2020) used the Hough Transform for circle counting after grape detection with the Yolov4 model (it is similar to the method proposed by Rudolph et al. for flower counting Rudolph et al. 2019). One limitation of this algorithm is its sensibility to berries' apparent size (the radius must be known).

Miao et al. proposed to use edge detection to solve the problem of counting overlapping berries (Miao et al. 2021). The proposed methodology is complex with a holistically nested edge detection model for berry edge segmentation, a Yolo model for berry detection, and a RANSAC algorithm for sphere fitting. It was evaluated on images of individual grape clusters in different conditions (laboratory or field conditions). A simpler object detection model based on RetinaNet (Lin et al. 2018), modified with a counting section, was evaluated on three plants for counting bananas-per-bunch, spikelets-per-wheats-spike, and berries-per-grape-cluster in natural conditions (Khoroshevsky et al. 2021).

Palacios et al. (2022a,b) proposed a three-step segmentation process, with SegNet models, for grapes, berries, and the canopy features extraction from images taken at night with lighting. The goal is to use segmentation to measure traits with predictive power for actual berry counting (visible + hidden) with regression models.

9.3.2 Current Challenges

A problem arises from deploying the berry detection algorithms in the field. They must be applied to image sequences to cover entire rows of vines. Doing this introduces the risk of counting the same grapes twice. Therefore, more or less complex solutions have been applied to avoid redundancy during the counting. A simple one reconstructs the full image of the row using a video and then keeps the highest counts in the overlapping areas (Nuske et al. 2014). It is also possible to follow the detected grapes from one image to the next based on the distance between the grapes in consecutive images (Heinrich et al. 2019). Another mechanical solution consists in taking an image based on the distance covered by a vehicle (one every two meters, for instance) (Aquino et al. 2018).

Another challenge is related to the estimation of the yield volume. The classic modeling approach estimated the total number of berries with a regression model, generally linear. The total estimation number is then converted into mass using the historical average weight of the berries or by extracting samples from the field. This method used by Aquino et al. (2018) with a linear model predicts the total weight based on the visible fruits. An average error rate of 12.83% was achieved on five varieties over 30 segments of three vines.

A recent method uses new techniques to count berries and estimate the total number of berries in a grape (Liu et al. 2020). A 3D reconstruction method that only needs a single 2D image is built by positioning the berries to fill the estimated profile, estimated from the edges, of a single grape bunch. Grape compactness is used as a parameter to simulate different varieties and growth stages. Therefore, this method directly estimates the number of berries in a grape bunch. Although it has only been applied to partially controlled conditions with images of individual grapes with an artificial background, a yield estimation was done by combining this method with another one proposed by the same authors Liu et al. (2017) based on the counting of the shoots. The error rates of predicted yield on three parcels were 3%, 6%, and 16%, which is comparable to or better than other methods.

Finally, the phenological stage also influences the results. For instance, berries in early stages are harder to count due to their reduced size, and their color is similar to the foliage before ripening (Fig. 9.4). Good results were observed in practice by Nuske et al. in 2014 up to 75 days before the harvest (Nuske et al. 2014). The counting can be more difficult once the grapes close (the berries touch each other). The work of Liu et al. shows similar yield estimation performances before and after the ripening (Liu et al. 2020).

Also, we must account for the grapes hidden by the foliage, one of the main problems currently limiting yield prediction performances. Contrarily to several works conducted in laboratory or controlled environments, a winemaker cannot trim his vines. A possible solution is to use a blower to remove the foliage temporarily, but it has not been quantitatively evaluated (Nellithimaru and Kantor 2019). An additional modeling step is hence necessary, and it could benefit from additional variables such as the porosity of the canopy (0.82 R^2 correlation between the canopy's porosity and the percentage of visible grapes) (Victorino et al. 2019).

Fig. 9.4 Different stages of a vine

Recent studies have shown that the fruit area might be more robust to occlusion than berry counting (Victorino et al. 2020). This work was extended by comparing yield estimation from images to the classical manual sampling approach on six parcels (Victorino et al. 2022). They used artificial background and manual segmentation of the images to extract meaningful features (such as visible bunch area, canopy porosity, etc.) for yield estimation. In this manner, ideal performances of image analysis methods were evaluated against the current yield estimation process. An average error rate of 8% was found with image analysis compared to 31% for manual sampling. It is also noted that the error increases with canopy density. Although fruit area prediction potential is still highly impacted by foliage, moderate defoliation can help obtain a better correlation (Íñiguez et al. 2021). In practice, the conditions in the vineyard are more difficult: smaller green grapes, high canopy occlusion, natural background, lighting, etc.

Features related to occlusion and fruit area were used as yield predictors in the work of Palacios et al. (2022a,b). An error rate, including six varieties, of 29.77% NRMSE (*Normalized root-mean-square error*, in kg per vine, 0.83 R^2) was reported with images taken 66 days before harvest. Error rates ranged from 16.47% to 39.17% depending on the variety. Zabawa et al. (2020), Zabawa et al. (2022) reported an MAE rate of 26% for 70 vines of Riesling. They only used berry detection and a simple equation (estimated number of berries multiplied by the berry weight).

A possible solution to solve the hidden-berries problem was proposed by Kierdorf et al. (2021). A CycleGAN generative model was used to predict the location of hidden berries from pairs of vine images before and after defoliation. As a result, better counting performances were obtained, 0.88 R^2 compared to 0.72 R^2 on the images without defoliation. However, it has not yet been applied to more complex vine images with a natural background. More experiments are needed to determine the practicality of this new method for yield prediction.

9.4 Contributions

As illustrated above, several grape detection methods are using deep learning and image processing for grape detection as well as berry counting. These methods, although effective, do not focus on speed of execution or the use of real-time video streams. We are therefore faced with a problem confronting artificial intelligence models with high prediction performance against models capable of combining high prediction and execution time performance in the edge. Indeed, the ability to optimize and compress deep learning models leads toward the convergence of solutions between robust models in the cloud and stand-alone models with deep learning inference directly at the edge.

In order to achieve such objectives, we have conducted several experiences since 2019 for the European projects H2020 AI4DI (Mohimont et al. 2021) and KDT JU EdgeAI, using different cameras and methods, for example, with a GoPro fixed on a picket or embarked on a tractor (Fig. 9.5a). For instance, one of the models we developed was an alleged UNet encoder-decoder with a ResNet-34 backbone with 24M parameters and sufficiently optimized to be deployed in embedded computing boards like a Nvidia Jetson Nano 2GB. As the dataset is limited (approximately 600 photos were taken in the 2019 campaign, from which 386 photos were labeled), there is a risk of overfitting. To avoid this problem, we applied transfer-learning from a ResNet-34 backbone pre-trained on the ImageNet database. Transfer learning allow us to speed up the training process and, as the original model was trained in a larger variety of images, reduces the risk of overfitting. Another optimization we

Fig. 9.5 (**a**) Camera attached to the vehicle, (**b**) defoliated vine

have made is to avoid processing the whole images but, instead, to proceed them by patches of 512×512 pixels. In this way, we greatly increase the size of the training base. A mini-batch size of 16 is then used, and about 30% of the database is used for model validation. To speed up the training phase, we have used the DGX-1 server from the ROMEO Supercomputing Center, a dedicated deep learning machine with eight Nvidia Tesla V100 GPUs.

After training, this model presents an IoU score of 0.69 and an F1 score of 0.8 (the IoU is limited due to the lack of precision in the labeling). Nonetheless, the model allows detecting nearly 100% of the grapes with a false-positive rate near 0%. In this work, we calibrated our deep learning algorithms for automated yield using a systematic tracking of several rows in the vineyard car (Rossignon 2020). This tracking, performed over four rows (200 vines) at different phenological stages, has included the counting of classic organs (vine, flowers/grapes) using traditional strategies (random counting or by the sampling of the parcels) as well as sampling the berries to estimate their volume and ripeness.

The counting of the grapes has also been done by unveiling hidden grapes by defoliation. Hence, the operator first counts the visible grapes in the plant and, after defoliation, takes a second picture (Fig. 9.5b). Around 30 images were taken in this way and labeled and used to help identify partially hidden grapes. The model can therefore be used to simply count grapes as seen in Fig. 9.6a or segment the image for further analysis (berry counting), like in Fig. 9.6b.

Thanks to the manual and automated counting data, a linear regression model has been generated for each row, followed by a cross-examination of each model using the three other rows (Fig. 9.7). Although the error rate varies from 0% to 31%, depending on the model and the row, we obtain an average error rate of 14%. This is better than current error rates with the traditional approach and can be further improved. Hence, the improvement of this analysis is based on a better distinction between grapes in the foreground and grapes in the background, as well as using non-linear regression models and other variables such as the porosity of the canopy (to account for occlusions).

Fig. 9.6 Examples of image analysis with deep learning. (**a**) Grape counting. (**b**) Image segmentation for further berry counting

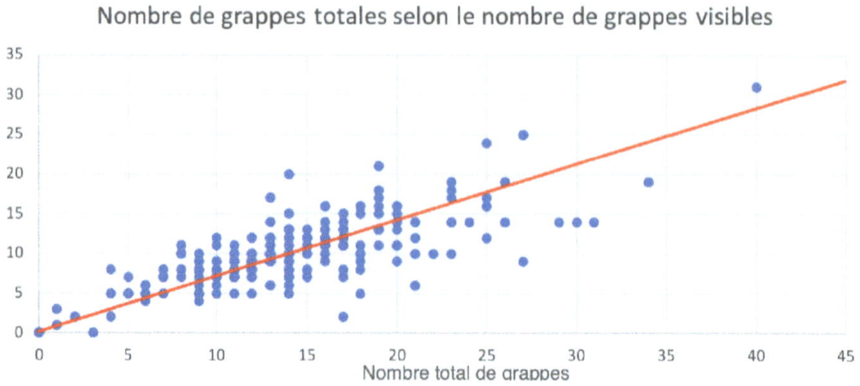

Fig. 9.7 Correlation between visible grapes and the total number of grapes

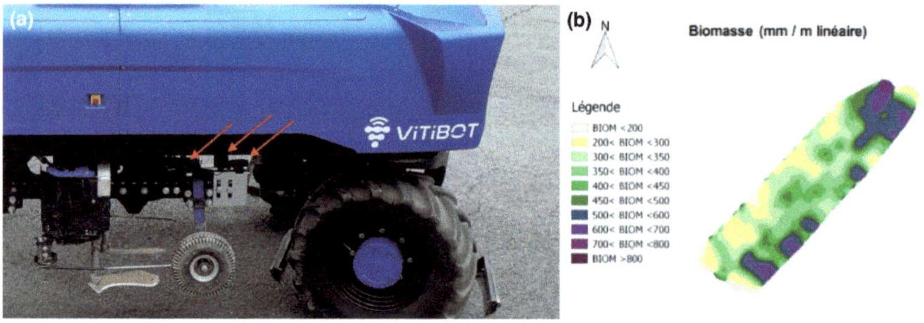

Fig. 9.8 (**a**) Prototype device installed in a tractor. (**b**) Biomass chart obtained with Physiocap

As this is an ongoing project, we regularly iterate with our partner Vranken-Pommery on how to effectively deploy the solution according to their needs. The optimization efforts made to execute the AI algorithm in edge devices allow us to run most of the steps in an embarked node, as illustrated in Fig. 9.8a. Processing most information onsite allows to reduce the amount of data to store and favor the deployment on areas with reduced or unavailable Internet connection.

We are now preparing the prototype devices to be tested in preparation to the Summer 2023 harvest, based on a Jetson Nano device equipped with a camera and a RTK GPS receiver, making it an affordable solution (less than 500 for the complete equipment). Grape count shall be performed from the middle of June 2023, and together with geolocation data, we aim at producing detailed grape density maps similar to the biomass maps from Fig. 9.8b produced by the Physiocap sensor,[1] allowing a precise harvest planning (workers, material, logistics).

Berry counting is also being introduced in our workflow, as illustrated in Fig. 9.9. Additional work is required to extrapolate the total number of berries in the grape

[1] https://www.physiocap.eu/

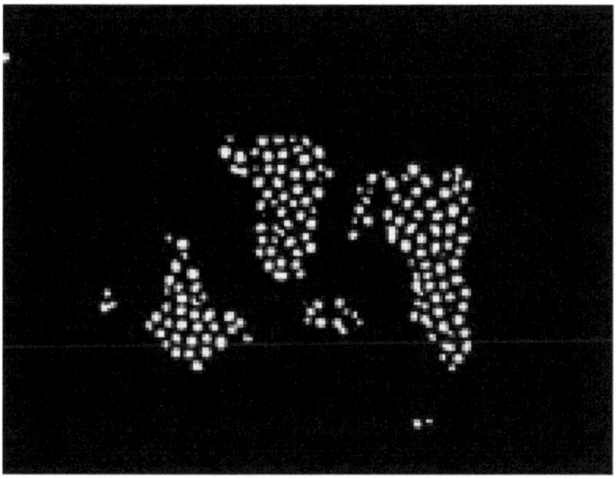

Fig. 9.9 Examples of berry detection

(3D counting) from a 2D image (visible berries) but also to allow real-time counting in an embedded device.

9.5 Conclusion

Deep learning has introduced several innovations on the domain of smart agriculture. Contrarily to traditional signal-processing and image analysis methods, deep learning seems to be more robust to natural variations, and pretraining allows easy transfer to similar problems. This is indeed the case of grapevine yield performance forecast, a smart-viticulture use case that can heavily benefit from automation. Generally speaking, counting fruits is a difficult task because the aspect of the plant can vary enormously depending on the point of view and development stages.

In this chapter, we focus on grape yield forecast strategies that use deep learning to count grapes or berries, providing a survey on existing works. We can observe that many works present good performances, but these results shall be put in perspective as most authors rely in controlled scenarios or specific lightning conditions that are not compatible with field deployment at scale. Nonetheless, they point toward some interesting techniques that can be further improved using more robust models and richer datasets.

We also presented some preliminary results from our team, which focus on grape detection and counting under natural conditions. The good performances we obtained show the interest of deep learning and encourage the pursuit of the works, even though additional modeling steps are still needed to account for the non-visible part of the fruits hidden by leaves or the number of berries per cluster and their average weight. Furthermore, a compromise between accuracy and inference speed is necessary for a practical implementation allowing a real-time and autonomous usage. We expect that future improvements in our models and more comprehensive data sources will allow the creation of better yield estimation models.

Acknowledgments This work has been started as part of the project AI4DI "Artificial Intelligence for Digitizing Industry" (ECSEL JU grant agreement No 826060) and continues as part of the EdgeAI project "Edge AI Technlogies for Optimised Performance Embedded Systems" under grant agreement No 101097300. The EdgeAI project is co-funded by grants from Austria, Belgium, France, Greece, Italy, Latvia, Luxembourg, Netherlands, Norway, and the European Key Digital Technologies Joint Undertaking (KDT JU).

We want to thank Vranken-Pommery Monopole for allowing image collection in their vineyards. We also thank the ROMEO Computing Center[2] of Université de Reims Champagne-Ardenne, whose Nvidia DGX-1 server allowed us to accelerate the training steps and compare several model approaches.

References

Aguiar, A.S., Magalhães, S.A., dos Santos, F.N., Castro, L., Pinho, T., Valente, J., Martins, R., Boaventura-Cunha, J.: Grape bunch detection at different growth stages using deep learning quantized models. Agronomy **11**(9) (2021). https://www.mdpi.com/2073-4395/11/9/1890

Anastasiou, E., Templalexis, C., Lentzou, D., Biniari, K., Xanthopoulos, G., Fountas, S.: Do soil and climatic parameters affect yield and quality on table grapes? Smart Agric. Technol. **3**, 100088 (2023). https://doi.org/10.1016/j.atech.2022.100088

Aquino, A., Diago, M.P., Millán, B., Tardáguila, J.: A new methodology for estimating the grapevine-berry number per cluster using image analysis. Biosyst. Eng. **156**, 80–95 (2017). https://doi.org/10.1016/j.biosystemseng.2016.12.011

Aquino, A., Millan, B., Diago, M.P., Tardaguila, J.: Automated early yield prediction in vineyards from on-the-go image acquisition. Comput. Electron. Agric. **144**, 26–36 (2018). https://doi.org/10.1016/j.compag.2017.11.026

Ariza-Sentís, M., Vélez, S., Valente, J.: Dataset on UAV RGB videos acquired over a vineyard including bunch labels for object detection and tracking. Data Brief **46**, 108848 (2023). https://doi.org/10.1016/j.dib.2022.108848

Barbole, M.D., Jadhav, D.P.: Comparative analysis of deep learning architectures for grape cluster instance segmentation. Inform. Technol. Ind. **9**(11), 344–352 (2021). https://doi.org/10.17762/itii.v9i1.138

Behroozi-Khazaei, N., Maleki, M.R.: A robust algorithm based on color features for grape cluster segmentation. Comput. Electron. Agric. **142**, 41–49 (2017). https://doi.org/10.1016/j.compag.2017.08.025

Berenstein, R., Shahar, O.B., Shapiro, A., Edan, Y.: Grape clusters and foliage detection algorithms for autonomous selective vineyard sprayer. Intell. Service Robot. **3**(44), 233–243 (2010). https://doi.org/10.1007/s11370-010-0078-z

Bochkovskiy, A., Wang, C.Y., Liao, H.Y.M.: Yolov4: Optimal speed and accuracy of object detection (2020)

Casser, V.: Using feedforward neural networks for color based grape detection in field images. In: CSCUBS 2016—Computer Science Conference for University of Bonn Students, pp. 23–33 (2016). https://doi.org/paper/Using-Feedforward-Neural-Networks-for-Color-Based-Casser/139ccba0b3a00565f61febcc62f98c6c44cca990

Cecotti, H., Rivera, A., Farhadloo, M., Pedroza, M.A.: Grape detection with convolutional neural networks. Expert Syst. Appl. **159**, 113588 (2020). https://doi.org/10.1016/j.eswa.2020.113588

[2] https://romeo.univ-reims.fr

Chamelat, R., Rosso, E., Choksuriwong, A., Rosenberger, C., Laurent, H., Bro, P.: Grape detection by image processing. In: IECON 2006—32nd Annual Conference on IEEE Industrial Electronics, pp. 3697–3702 (2006). https://doi.org/10.1109/IECON.2006.347704

Chen, S., Song, Y., Su, J., Fang, Y., Shen, L., Mi, Z., Su, B.: Segmentation of field grape bunches via an improved pyramid scene parsing network. Int. J. Agric. Biol. Eng. **14**(6), 185–194 (2021)

Clingeleffer, P.R., Martin, S.R., Dunn, G.M., Krstic, M.P.: Crop development, crop estimation and crop control to secure quality and production of major wine grape varieties: a national approach. Adelaide, Grape and Wine Research and Development Corporation (2001)

Coviello, L., Cristoforetti, M., Jurman, G., Furlanello, C.: Gbcnet: In-field grape berries counting for yield estimation by dilated CNNs. Appl. Sci. **10**(1414), 4870 (2020). https://doi.org/10.3390/app10144870

Dai, J., Li, Y., He, K., Sun, J.: R-FCN: Object detection via region-based fully convolutional networks (2016)

Dami, I., Sabbatini, P.: Crop Estimation of Grapes. The Ohio State University Fact Sheet (2011)

Deng, G., Geng, T., He, C., Wang, X., He, B., Duan, L.: Tsgye: Two-stage grape yield estimation. In: Yang, H., Pasupa, K., Leung, A.C.S., Kwok, J.T., Chan, J.H., King, I. (eds.) Neural Information Processing, pp. 580–588. Springer, Cham (2020)

Di Gennaro, S.F., Toscano, P., Cinat, P., Berton, A., Matese, A.: A low-cost and unsupervised image recognition methodology for yield estimation in a vineyard. Front. Plant Sci. **10**, 559 (2019). https://doi.org/10.3389/fpls.2019.00559

Diago, M.P., Tardaguila, J., Aleixos, N., Millan, B., Prats-Montalban, J.M., Cubero, S., Blasco, J.: Assessment of cluster yield components by image analysis. J. Sci. Food Agric. **95**(66), 1274–1282 (2015). https://doi.org/10.1002/jsfa.6819

Dorj, U.O., Lee, M., seok Yun, S.: An yield estimation in citrus orchards via fruit detection and counting using image processing. Comput. Electron. Agric. **140**, 103–112 (2017). https://doi.org/10.1016/j.compag.2017.05.019

Dunn, G.M., Martin, S.R.: Yield prediction from digital image analysis: a technique with potential for vineyard assessments prior to harvest. Aust. J. Grape Wine Res. **10**(33), 196–198 (2004). https://doi.org/10.1111/j.1755-0238.2004.tb00022.x

Fei, Z., Olenskyj, A., Bailey, B.N., Earles, M.: Enlisting 3D crop models and GANs for more data efficient and generalizable fruit detection (2021)

Font, D., Tresanchez, M., Martínez, D., Moreno, J., Clotet, E., Palacín, J.: Vineyard yield estimation based on the analysis of high resolution images obtained with artificial illumination at night. Sensors **15**(4), 8284–8301 (2015). https://doi.org/10.3390/s150408284

Ghiani, L., Sassu, A., Palumbo, F., Mercenaro, L., Gambella, F.: In-field automatic detection of grape bunches under a totally uncontrolled environment. Sensors **21**(11) (2021). https://doi.org/10.3390/s21113908

Girshick, R., Donahue, J., Darrell, T., Malik, J.: Rich feature hierarchies for accurate object detection and semantic segmentation (2014)

Grocholsky, B., Nuske, S., Aasted, M., Achar, S., Bates, T.: A camera and laser system for automatic vine balance assessment. In: American Society of Agricultural and Biological Engineers Annual International Meeting 2011, ASABE 2011, vol. 7 (2011). https://doi.org/10.13031/2013.38146. JournalAbbreviation: American Society of Agricultural and Biological Engineers Annual International Meeting 2011, ASABE 2011

Grossetete, M., Berthoumieu, Y., Da Costa, J.P., Germain, C., Lavialle, O., Grenier, G.: Early estimation of vineyard yield: site specific counting of berries by using a smartphone. In: International Conference on Agriculture Engineering (AgEng) (2012)

He, K., Gkioxari, G., Dollár, P., Girshick, R.: Mask R-CNN (2018). arXiv:1703.06870 [cs]

Heinrich, K., Roth, A., Breithaupt, L., Möller, B., Maresch, J.: Yield prognosis for the agrarian management of vineyards using deep learning for object counting. Wirtschaftsinformatik 2019 Proceedings p. 15 (2019)

INAO: AOC champagne—conditions de production

Íñiguez, R., Palacios, F., Barrio, I., Hernández, I., Gutiérrez, S., Tardaguila, J.: Impact of leaf occlusions on yield assessment by computer vision in commercial vineyards. Agronomy **11**(5) (2021). https://doi.org/10.3390/agronomy11051003

Jaramillo, J., Vanden Heuvel, J., Petersen, K.H.: Low-cost, computer vision-based, prebloom cluster count prediction in vineyards. Front. Agron. **3**, 8 (2021). https://doi.org/10.3389/fagro.2021.648080

Kang, C., Diverres, G., Achyut, P., Karkee, M., Zhang, Q., Keller, M.: Estimating soil and grapevine water status using ground based hyperspectral imaging under diffused lighting conditions: addressing the effect of lighting variability in vineyards. Comput. Electron. Agric. **212**, 108175 (2023). https://doi.org/10.1016/j.compag.2023.108175

Keresztes, B., Abdelghafour, F., Randriamanga, D., Da Costa, J.P., Germain, C.: Real-time fruit detection using deep neural networks. In: 14th International Conference on Precision Agriculture (2018)

Khoroshevsky, F., Khoroshevsky, S., Bar-Hillel, A.: Parts-per-object count in agricultural images: solving phenotyping problems via a single deep neural network. Remote Sensing **13**(13) (2021). https://doi.org/10.3390/rs13132496

Kierdorf, J., Weber, I., Kicherer, A., Zabawa, L., Drees, L., Roscher, R.: Behind the leaves—estimation of occluded grapevine berries with conditional generative adversarial networks (2021)

Kumrai, T., Korpela, J., Maekawa, T., Yu, Y., Kanai, R.: Human activity recognition with deep reinforcement learning using the camera of a mobile robot. In: 2020 IEEE International Conference on Pervasive Computing and Communications (PerCom), pp. 1–10 (2020). https://doi.org/10.1109/PerCom45495.2020.9127376

Li, H., Li, C., Li, G., Chen, L.: A real-time table grape detection method based on improved yolov4-tiny network in complex background. Biosyst. Eng. **212**, 347–359 (2021). https://doi.org/10.1016/j.biosystemseng.2021.11.011

Lin, T.Y., Goyal, P., Girshick, R., He, K., Dollár, P.: Focal loss for dense object detection (2018)

Liu, S., Cossell, S., Tang, J., Dunn, G., Whitty, M.: A computer vision system for early stage grape yield estimation based on shoot detection. Comput. Electron. Agric. **137**, 88–101 (2017). https://doi.org/10.1016/j.compag.2017.03.013

Liu, S., Li, X., Wu, H., Xin, B., Tang, J., Petrie, P.R., Whitty, M.: A robust automated flower estimation system for grape vines. Biosyst. Eng. **172**, 110–123 (2018). https://doi.org/10.1016/j.biosystemseng.2018.05.009

Liu, S., Marden, S., Whitty, M.: Towards automated yield estimation in viticulture. In: Proceedings of the Australasian Conference on Robotics and Automation, p. 9 (2013)

Liu, S., Whitty, M., Cossell, S.: A lightweight method for grape berry counting based on automated 3 d bunch reconstruction from a single image. In: ICRA, International Conference on Robotics and Automation (IEEE), Workshop on Robotics in Agriculture (2015)

Liu, S., Zeng, X., Whitty, M.: A vision-based robust grape berry counting algorithm for fast calibration-free bunch weight estimation in the field. Comput. Electron. Agric. **173**, 11 (2020). https://doi.org/10.1016/j.compag.2020.105360

Liu, W., Anguelov, D., Erhan, D., Szegedy, C., Reed, S., Fu, C.Y., Berg, A.C.: Ssd: Single shot multibox detector. Lecture Notes in Computer Science pp. 21–37 (2016). https://doi.org/10.1007/978-3-319-46448-0_2

Lloret, J., Bosch, I., Sendra, S., Serrano, A.: A wireless sensor network for vineyard monitoring that uses image processing. Sensors **11**(6), 6165–6196 (2011). https://doi.org/10.3390/s110606165

Lopes, C., Torres, A., Guzman, R., Graça, J., Monteiro, A., Braga, R., Barriguinha, A., Victorino, G., Reys, M.: Using an unmanned ground vehicle to scout vineyards for non-intrusive estimation of canopy features and grape yield. In: 20th GiESCO International Meeting (2017)

Luo, L., Liu, W., Lu, Q., Wang, J., Wen, W., Yan, D., Tang, Y.: Grape berry detection and size measurement based on edge image processing and geometric morphology. Machines **9**(10), 233 (2021)

Luo, L., Tang, Y., Lu, Q., Chen, X., Zhang, P., Zou, X.: A vision methodology for harvesting robot to detect cutting points on peduncles of double overlapping grape clusters in a vineyard. Comput. Ind. **99**, 130–139 (2018). https://doi.org/10.1016/j.compind.2018.03.017

Luo, L., Tang, Y., Zou, X., Wang, C., Zhang, P., Feng, W.: Robust grape cluster detection in a vineyard by combining the AdaBoost framework and multiple color components. Sensors **16**(1212), 21 (2016). https://doi.org/10.3390/s16122098

Luo, L., Tang, Y., Zou, X., Ye, M., Feng, W., Li, G.: Vision-based extraction of spatial information in grape clusters for harvesting robots. Biosyst. Eng. **151**, 90–104 (2016). https://doi.org/10.1016/j.biosystemseng.2016.08.026

Maldonado, W., Barbosa, J.C.: Automatic green fruit counting in orange trees using digital images. Comput. Electron. Agric. **127**, 572–581 (2016). https://doi.org/10.1016/j.compag.2016.07.023

Miao, Y., Huang, L., Zhang, S.: A two-step phenotypic parameter measurement strategy for overlapped grapes under different light conditions. Sensors **21**(13) (2021). https://doi.org/10.3390/s21134532

Milella, A., Marani, R., Petitti, A., Reina, G.: In-field high throughput grapevine phenotyping with a consumer-grade depth camera. Comput. Electron. Agric. **156**, 293–306 (2019). https://doi.org/10.1016/j.compag.2018.11.026

Mohimont, L., Alin, F., Rondeau, M., Gaveau, N., Steffenel, L.A.: Computer vision and deep learning for precision viticulture. Agronomy **12**(10) (2022). https://doi.org/10.3390/agronomy12102463

Mohimont, L., Roesler, M., Rondeau, M., Gaveau, N., Alin, F., Steffenel, L.A.: Comparison of machine learning and deep learning methods for grape cluster segmentation. In: Boumerdassi, S., Ghogho, M., Renault, É. (eds.) Smart and Sustainable Agriculture, pp. 84–102. Springer, Cham (2021)

Murillo-Bracamontes, E.A., Martinez-Rosas, M.E., Miranda-Velasco, M.M., Martinez-Reyes, H.L., Martinez-Sandoval, J.R., Cervantes-de Avila, H.: Implementation of Hough transform for fruit image segmentation. Proc. Eng. **35**, 230–239 (2012). https://doi.org/10.1016/j.proeng.2012.04.185

Nellithimaru, A.K., Kantor, G.A.: Rols : Robust object-level slam for grape counting. In: 2019 IEEE/CVF Conference on Computer Vision and Pattern Recognition Workshops (CVPRW), pp. 2648–2656 (2019). https://doi.org/10.1109/CVPRW.2019.00321

Nuske, S., Wilshusen, K., Achar, S., Yoder, L., Singh, S.: Automated visual yield estimation in vineyards. J. Field Robot. **31**(55), 837–860 (2014). https://doi.org/10.1002/rob.21541

Palacios, F., Diago, M.P., Melo-Pinto, P., Tardaguila, J.: Early yield prediction in different grapevine varieties using computer vision and machine learning. Precision Agriculture pp. 1–29 (2022)

Palacios, F., Melo-Pinto, P., Diago, M.P., Tardaguila, J.: Deep learning and computer vision for assessing the number of actual berries in commercial vineyards. Biosyst. Eng. **218**, 175–188 (2022). https://doi.org/10.1016/j.biosystemseng.2022.04.015

Peng, Y., Wang, A., Liu, J., Faheem, M.: A comparative study of semantic segmentation models for identification of grape with different varieties. Agriculture **11**(10) (2021). https://www.mdpi.com/2077-0472/11/10/997

Peng, Y., Zhao, S., Liu, J.: Segmentation of overlapping grape clusters based on the depth region growing method. Electronics **10**(22), 2813 (2021)

Pérez-Expósito, J.P., Fernández-Caramés, T.M., Fraga-Lamas, P., Castedo, L.: Vinesens: An eco-smart decision-support viticulture system. Sensors **17**(33), 26 (2017). https://doi.org/10.3390/s17030465

Rahman, A., Hellicar, A.: Identification of mature grape bunches using image processing and computational intelligence methods. In: 2014 IEEE Symposium on Computational Intelligence for Multimedia, Signal and Vision Processing (CIMSIVP), pp. 1–6 (2014). https://doi.org/10.1109/CIMSIVP.2014.7013272

Redmon, J., Divvala, S., Girshick, R., Farhadi, A.: You only look once: Unified, real-time object detection (2016)

Redmon, J., Farhadi, A.: Yolov3: An incremental improvement (2018)

Reis, M.J.C.S., Morais, R., Peres, E., Pereira, C., Contente, O., Soares, S., Valente, A., Baptista, J., Ferreira, P.J.S.G., Bulas Cruz, J.: Automatic detection of bunches of grapes in natural environment from color images. J. Appl. Logic **10**(44), 285–290 (2012). https://doi.org/10.1016/j.jal.2012.07.004

Ren, S., He, K., Girshick, R., Sun, J.: Faster R-CNN: Towards real-time object detection with region proposal networks (2016)

Ronneberger, O., Fischer, P., Brox, T.: U-net: Convolutional networks for biomedical image segmentation. In: Navab, N., Hornegger, J., Wells, W.M., Frangi, A.F. (eds.) Medical Image Computing and Computer-Assisted Intervention – MICCAI 2015, Lecture Notes in Computer Science, pp. 234–241. Springer, Berlin (2015). https://doi.org/10.1007/978-3-319-24574-4_28

Roscher, R., Herzog, K., Kunkel, A., Kicherer, A., Töpfer, R., Förstner, W.: Automated image analysis framework for high-throughput determination of grapevine berry sizes using conditional random fields. Comput. Electron. Agric. **100**, 148–158 (2014). https://doi.org/10.1016/j.compag.2013.11.008

Rose, J.C., Kicherer, A., Wieland, M., Klingbeil, L., Töpfer, R., Kuhlmann, H.: Towards automated large-scale 3d phenotyping of vineyards under field conditions. Sensors **16**(1212), 2136 (2016). https://doi.org/10.3390/s16122136

Rossignon, L.: Vers une méthode optimale d'estimation du rendement de la vigne basée sur l'intelligence artificielle. Master's thesis, AgroParisTech (2020)

Rudolph, R., Herzog, K., Töpfer, R., Steinhage, V.: Efficient identification, localization and quantification of grapevine inflorescences in unprepared field images using fully convolutional networks. J. Grapevine Res. **58**(3) (2019). https://doi.org/10.5073/vitis.2019.58.95-104

Santos, T., Bassoi, L., Oldoni[1], H., Martins, R.: Automatic grape bunch detection in vineyards based on affordable 3D phenotyping using a consumer webcam. XI Congresso Brasileiro de Agroinformática (SBIAgro 2017) (2017)

Santos, T.T., de Souza, L.L., dos Santos, A.A., Avila, S.: Grape detection, segmentation, and tracking using deep neural networks and three-dimensional association. Comput. Electron. Agric. **170**, 105247 (2020). https://doi.org/10.1016/j.compag.2020.105247

Seng, K.P., Ang, L., Schmidtke, L.M., Rogiers, S.Y.: Computer vision and machine learning for viticulture technology. IEEE Access **6**, 67494–67510 (2018). https://doi.org/10.1109/ACCESS.2018.2875862

Shen, L., Su, J., He, R., Song, L., Huang, R., Fang, Y., Song, Y., Su, B.: Real-time tracking and counting of grape clusters in the field based on channel pruning with yolov5s. Comput. Electron. Agric. **206**, 107662 (2023). https://doi.org/10.1016/j.compag.2023.107662

Silver, D.L., Monga, T.: In vino veritas: Estimating vineyard grape yield from images using deep learning. In: Meurs, M.J., Rudzicz, F. (eds.) Advances in Artificial Intelligence, Lecture Notes in Computer Science, pp. 212–224. Springer, Berlin (2019). https://doi.org/10.1007/978-3-030-18305-9_17

Škrabánek, P.: Deepgrapes: Precise detection of grapes in low-resolution images. IFAC-PapersOnLine **51**(66), 185–189 (2018). https://doi.org/10.1016/j.ifacol.2018.07.151

Song, Y., Glasbey, C., Horgan, G., Polder, G., Dieleman, J., van der Heijden, G.: Automatic fruit recognition and counting from multiple images. Biosyst. Eng. **118**, 203–215 (2014). https://doi.org/10.1016/j.biosystemseng.2013.12.008

Sozzi, M., Cantalamessa, s., Cogato, A., Kayad, A., Marinello, F.: Grape yield spatial variability assessment using yolov4 object detection algorithm. pp. 193–198 (2021). https://doi.org/10.3920/978-90-8686-916-9_22

Steffenel, L.A., Langlet, A., Hollard, L., Mohimont, L., Gaveau, N., Copola, M., Pierlot, C., Rondeau, M.: Ai-driven strategies to implement a grapevine downy mildew warning system. In: Industrial Artificial Intelligence Technologies and Applications, pp. 177–187. Rivers Publishers (2022)

Torres-Sánchez, J., Mesas-Carrascosa, F.J., Santesteban, L.G., Jiménez-Brenes, F.M., Oneka, O., Villa-Llop, A., Loidi, M., López-Granados, F.: Grape cluster detection using UAV photogrammetric point clouds as a low-cost tool for yield forecasting in vineyards. Sensors **21**(9) (2021). https://doi.org/10.3390/s21093083

Vermesan, O., Martinsen, J.E., Kristoffersen, A., Bahr, R., Bellmann, R.O., Hjertaker, T., Breiland, J., Andersen, K., Sand, H.E., Rahmanpour, P., Lindberg, D.: Optimisation of soybean manufacturing process using real-time artificial intelligence of things technology. In: Vermesan, O., John, R., Luca, C.D., Coppola, M. (eds.) Artificial Intelligence for Digitising Industry Applications, pp. 301–325. Rivers Publisher (2021)

Victorino, G., Braga, R.P., Santos-Victor, J., Lopes, C.M.: Comparing a new non-invasive vineyard yield estimation approach based on image analysis with manual sample-based methods. Agronomy **12**(6) (2022). https://doi.org/10.3390/agronomy12061464

Victorino, G., Maia, G., Queiroz, J., Braga, R., Marques, J., Lopes, C.: Grapevine yield prediction using image analysis – improving the estimation of non-visible bunches. European Federation for Information Technology in Agriculture, Food and the Environment (EFITA), p. 6 (2019)

Victorino, G.F., Braga, R., Santos-Victor, J., Lopes, C.M.: Yield components detection and image-based indicators for non-invasive grapevine yield prediction at different phenological phases. OENO One **54**(4), 833–848 (2020). https://doi.org/10.20870/oeno-one.2020.54.4.3616

Xi, X., Zha, Q., Jiang, A., Tian, Y.: Stimulatory effect of bunch thinning on sugar accumulation and anthocyanin biosynthesis in Shenhua grape berry (Vitis vinifera × v. labrusca). Aust. J. Grape Wine Res. **24**(2), 158–165 (2018). https://doi.org/10.1111/ajgw.12323

Yin, W., Wen, H., Ning, Z., Ye, J., Dong, Z., Luo, L.: Fruit detection and pose estimation for grape cluster–harvesting robot using binocular imagery based on deep neural networks. Front. Robot. AI **8**, 163 (2021). https://doi.org/10.3389/frobt.2021.626989

Zabawa, L., Kicherer, A., Klingbeil, L., Töpfer, R., Kuhlmann, H., Roscher, R.: Counting of grapevine berries in images via semantic segmentation using convolutional neural networks. ISPRS J. Photogramm. Remote Sensing **164**, 73–83 (2020). https://doi.org/10.1016/j.isprsjprs.2020.04.002

Zabawa, L., Kicherer, A., Klingbeil, L., Töpfer, R., Roscher, R., Kuhlmann, H.: Image-based analysis of yield parameters in viticulture. Biosyst. Eng. **218**, 94–109 (2022). https://doi.org/10.1016/j.biosystemseng.2022.04.009

Zhang, C., Ding, H., Shi, Q., Wang, Y.: Grape cluster real-time detection in complex natural scenes based on yolov5s deep learning network. Agriculture **12**(8) (2022). https://doi.org/10.3390/agriculture12081242

Zhao, H., Shi, J., Qi, X., Wang, X., Jia, J.: Pyramid scene parsing network (2016). https://doi.org/10.48550/ARXIV.1612.01105

Zhu, J.Y., Park, T., Isola, P., Efros, A.A.: Unpaired image-to-image translation using cycle-consistent adversarial networks (2020)

Chapter 10
How Do You Ride an Elevator? Passenger In-Cabin Behavior Analysis on a Smart-Elevator Platform

Tarmo Robal and Uljana Reinsalu

Abstract Modern elevators came into wide use some 150 years ago. With the advancement of technology, the main task of elevators has remained the same—transport people and goods in between floors—yet elevators have become more sophisticated with a trend toward smart-elevators. While increasing passenger comfort and travel experience, these systems also allow to get an insight into elevator passengers' behavior during their travels. Have you ever wondered why some people always stand in the same place, or what is your favorite spot to stand in an elevator? This chapter focuses on exploring passengers' in-cabin behavior while they travel between floors, enabled by a smart-elevator platform. To interpret collected real passengers' data, a general passenger location analysis model and evaluation methods are developed and several scenarios designed to validate system readiness for behavioral studies. The latter three enablers are used to analyze real elevator passengers' data to understand how passengers behave in cabins. The results show that passengers tend to choose their favorite position inside the cabin, permitted by the situation, and smart-elevators as a platform can be efficiently used to study passengers' behavior to enhance cabin environment.

Keywords Smart-elevators · Socio-cyber-physical systems · Behavioral studies · Elevator environment · Elevator users · Privacy

10.1 Introduction

The history of passenger elevators goes back to the beginning of the 1800s when steam and hydraulic power were introduced for lifting. The first passenger elevator powered by a steam engine was installed in 1857 in New York in a department store. Despite the advancement in technology at these times, the elevator received a cold reception from passengers with refusal to accept it (Bernard 2014). Nowadays,

T. Robal (✉) · U. Reinsalu
School of Information Technologies, Tallinn University of Technology, Tallinn, Estonia
e-mail: tarmo.robal@taltech.ee; uljana.reinsalu@taltech.ee

E. Kornyshova et al. (eds.), *Smart Life and Smart Life Engineering*,
https://doi.org/10.1007/978-3-031-75887-4_10

passenger elevators are a norm for modern commercial and residential buildings, providing an alternative mobility option to stairs. In high-rise buildings, which are typically equipped with several elevators to accommodate peoples' moving needs, elevators are the easiest way for people to move from one floor to another. For handicapped persons, elevators are key enablers of mobility for ensuring accessibility to buildings. Today, new buildings are typically equipped with elevators, and many older buildings are retrofitted. In Estonia (since 2019) and many other European Union countries, new buildings with five or more floors must be fitted with an elevator, as required by the law.

The advancements in technology and computerization of systems have also shaped the development of elevators, which today can be referred to as cyber-physical-social systems (CPSS) (Cassandras 2016; Dressler 2018; Lee and Seshia 2016; Zhuge 2014), where the "social" part incorporates human aspects of otherwise technical cyber-physical systems. Elevator systems have become complex, including rope-free and side-ways moving cabin systems (e.g., ThyssenKrupp Multi elevator). The trend is toward smart-elevators equipped with various sensors allowing to monitor, sense, and interpret the operational context of the elevator and deliver better service, safety, lower operational and maintenance cost, and improved user experience (UX) and comfort for passengers. Still, the need for passenger elevators and the underlying mode of exploitation has stayed the same—passengers place a call, wait for the cabin to arrive, and take a ride to a desired floor. However, the extended capabilities of smart-elevator platforms also provide an opportunity to study the exploitation of elevators closer. With the emergence of smart cities, the social aspects of elevators are also becoming more important, and in the future, smart-elevators can be addressed as socio-cyber-physical systems (SCPS) (Calinescu et al. 2019), which are complex systems where human and technical aspects are massively interconnected. Adding smart features to elevators, new or existing, allows to improve their exploitation and make our everyday lives more convenient. For example, imagine entering the elevator with hands full, and you can just ask by voice to be taken to a desired floor. This on the other hand drives the need to better understand human involvement and behavior in such systems and, through modelling, data analysis, and exploration, enable engineers to come up with improvements and enhancements for such SCPS.

Considerable amount of research is available for CPSS, and still, smart-elevators as SCPS have received little attention with the main focus on decreasing waiting time and energy consumption (Bamunuarachchi and Ranasinghe 2015; Bharti et al. 2017; Chou et al. 2018; Fernandez and Cortes 2015; Fujimura et al. 2013; Wang et al. 2011), thereby reducing carbon footprint, optimal parking in group elevator control (Brand and Nikovski 2004), use of floor sensors and RFID technology for elevator scheduling (Kwon et al. 2014), and the use of mobiles phones to improve flow of people (Turunen et al. 2013). A thorough overview of elevator control systems is provided in Fernandez and Cortes (2015); Ge et al. (2018) and passenger behavioral patterns while using elevators discussed in Liang et al. (2013).

In this chapter, we focus on elevator passengers' behavior inside the elevator cabin during their mobility. We take advantage of the existing smart-elevator platform and study passengers' preferences and behavior for standing and movement in the cabin and the dependencies on cabin occupancy. The knowledge on passenger behavior can be used for movement prediction (e.g., using machine learning), improved layout of information panels (including advertisements), touch buttons, and sensors of a smart-elevator or even for improving user experience and enabling personalized travel service through passenger recognition in future smart-elevators. To the best of our knowledge, human behavior inside an elevator cabin has not yet been studied in the context of and using the equipment of a smart-elevator.

For the studies, we use the smart-elevator system (SES) (Leier et al. 2021; Reinsalu et al. 2020; Robal et al. 2020) set up at Tallinn University of Technology (TalTech) campus in the Information and Communication Technologies (ICT) building. The main aim of the smart-elevator system project was to investigate the applicability of common hardware and software to bring smart features to everyday passenger elevators and help users navigate in the ICT building—thus making elevators smarter by adding features of floor pre-selection (Leier et al. 2021; Robal et al. 2020), floor prediction (Reinsalu et al. 2020; Robal et al. 2020), and voice commands (e.g., set destination floor or even ask for weather forecast) and information services on staff working in the building (Leier et al. 2021). The SES also facilitates passenger identification and anonymous profiles of which we advantage in our passenger behavior research, based on the use of real passengers' travel data. In this chapter, we investigate passengers' in-cabin behavior and their attitude toward smart-elevators to establish a general framework for investigating and understanding elevator usage in the context of SCPS through the following research questions:

RQ1: *How to model and analyze the location of elevator passengers inside the cabin during their travels?* We hypothesize that the two-dimensional elevator floor model can be divided into meaningful parts for passenger location-based behavior analyses. We establish a general model to analyze passengers' in-cabin locations based on captured coordinates. We further apply this model on our smart-elevator platform and use real passengers' data to explore their in-cabin behavior.

RQ2: *What are the most preferred standing locations of passengers in an elevator cabin while travelling alone or with fellow travellers?* We hypothesize that with single occupancy, passengers prefer to stand near the doors or in the middle of the cabin, whereas in a situation with multiple passengers, distance is kept.

RQ3: *What are the reported preferred standing locations travellers indicate?* We hypothesize that travellers declare a preference to stand in the elevator either in the middle of the cabin or closer to the doors. We are also eager to see if the reported preferences map with the data captured from actual passengers.

RQ4: *How likely is an elevator passenger to choose the same standing location for successive travels?* The hypothesis is that each traveller tends to have a preferred location(s) to stand in the elevator cabin.

RQ5: *What are the in-cabin movement path patterns passengers follow during their travels, if any?* We hypothesize that each passenger tends to follow a certain path in the elevator cabin environment while entering and exiting.

RQ6: *What is the perceived invasion of privacy passengers have toward different devices installed into a smart-elevator?* We hypothesize that cameras will be considered the most invasive devices regarding privacy, whereas other devices that are not likely to capture (facial) images are considered less invasive.

The results of passengers' in-cabin behavior studies indicate that passengers tend to have their preferred standing locations and they favor to stand in the middle of the elevator cabin or in the first half of a rectangular-shaped elevator cabin.

The main contributions of this chapter are (i) a section-based model for passenger location analysis in elevator cabin, transferable to other contexts, (ii) scenarios for system validation tests of passengers' in-cabin behavior analysis, (iii) methods for passengers' position data analysis, and (iv) studies on passenger in-cabin behavior and preferences.

The rest of the chapter is organized as follows: Sect. 10.2 is dedicated to related work, while Sect. 10.3 presents the Smart-Elevator System platform. In Sect. 10.4, we address RQ1 and establish the general location analysis model for passengers' behavior analysis in the cabin, which we will validate through ground-truth study and specially designed experiments. In Sect. 10.5, we take up on the established model and methods to answer the rest of the research questions using collected real passengers' data. Finally, Sect. 10.6 provides discussion, and Sect. 10.7 draws conclusions.

10.2 Related Work

The research on human behavior regarding elevators has mainly focused on passenger arrival at elevator lobbies (Sorsa et al. 2013, 2021), passenger flow influence on lift control systems (Lin et al. 2016), finding patterns in usage (Liang et al. 2013), or exploring evacuation models (Heyes and Spearpoint 2012; Ronchi and Nilsson 2013).

Liang et al. (2013) gathered real-world traces of human behavior data from 12 elevators in an 18-story office building, showing that elevator usage patterns vary depending on the layout of the building, i.e., whether the stairs as an alternative are available next to the elevator, or not, and the proximity of stairs to elevators, and the function of the building (e.g., in hospitals and hotels, most of the vertical movement is done using elevators). Their study also indicated high-rise buildings with multiple elevators benefit more than low-rise buildings from human behavioral patterns on elevator usage, since waiting time in smaller buildings is minimal as the elevator can reach all floors quickly.

Ronchi and Nilsson (2013) investigated the capabilities of evacuation models in high-rise buildings and showed that the use of elevators can reduce the evacuation time in a non-fire emergency, while for fire events, the elevator was less valuable due to the layout of the particular building used in the study. Heyes and Spearpoint (2012) explored evacuation behavior of building residents in case of a fire, to develop parameters that could be used for designing an evacuation system that uses elevators. Their study shows that the number of building occupants that are likely to use the elevator as an evacuation method was increasingly dependent on the floor level. The primary factor whether to choose stairs or the elevator is the prediction of how much time it takes to reach the ground level via each evacuation route.

Sorsa et al. (2013, 2021) rejected the assumption that passengers arrive at the elevator lobbies separately, showing that in multi-story office, hotel, and residential buildings, people tend to arrive in batches of variable size (typically two or more persons) depending on the time of day. Considering passengers' batch arrival helped to improve elevator group performance by reducing car loading, round-trip time, and passenger waiting times by 30–40%.

Susi et al. (2004) explored the effect of human behavior in a simulation case of the elevator traffic flow by studying the effect of passenger behavior. The work describes a model of human decision-making in a transportation system, which can be used for more accurate elevator traffic flow simulations to achieve realistic results by including passenger behavior into simulations. They find that simulation results are affected by characteristics and behavior of passengers.

Chou et al. (2018) used cameras and deep learning to minimize the average waiting time for passengers and at the same time decrease energy consumption by rescheduling elevator movements. The cameras were placed in front of elevators outside the cabin, and region-based convolutional neural network (R-CNN) was used to detect the number of passengers queuing for an elevator and dispatch elevators according to the detected demand such that the elevator with the smallest energy consumption was serving the waiting passengers.

To the best of our knowledge, human movement behavior inside an elevator car has not yet been studied in the context of and using the equipment of a smart-elevator. Liang et al. (2013) studied human behavioral patterns in the context of exploiting modern elevators through indicators such as elevator load factor, the number of floors travelled, and the doors-opened events to describe general behavioral patterns of office-building inhabitants, using the data (logs) generated by the elevator system itself, we in contrary focus not on the external events caused by the passengers but the passengers' behavior in traveling situation inside the elevator cabin, and for this, we use real data from real passengers collected using the smart-elevator platform.

Our previous work on the smart-elevator platform (Leier et al. 2021) has focused on profiling passengers for travel behavior characterization and destination floor prediction (Reinsalu et al. 2020; Robal et al. 2020) to enhance travel experience in elevators. We have also investigated elevator passengers' behavior regarding cabin usage, i.e., preferred locations (Basov et al. 2022), typical movement paths followed in the cabin, and whether there are recurring patterns (Robal et al.

2022). In connection of the SES, we have also proposed a design for a low-power touchless remote elevator call button (Reinsalu and Robal 2023). This chapter is a continuation of our work on the smart-elevator platform and contributes to fill the gap in the existing literature for social research in the context of elevator usage by providing a general model and methods to study and evaluate passengers' in-cabin behavior during their travels and applying the method in real-life scenario using real-world passenger ride data. The model and methods could be applied to any passenger elevator or transferred to other domains (e.g., public transportation) for user behavior studies.

10.3 Smart-Elevator Platform

A smart-elevator system can be considered as a CPSS and SCPS advantaging of data mining and artificial intelligence (AI) (Russell and Norvig 2009), e.g., facial image recognition (Robal et al. 2018; Silva et al. 2018; Stark 2019; Zhao et al. 2003) and human speech recognition (Allen 2003; Goetsu and Sakai 2019; Ketkar and Mukherjee 2011; Ross et al. 2004). Our studies on passengers' in-cabin behavior are carried out using the SES (Leier et al. 2021) developed at the School of Information Technologies and installed at TalTech in ICT building, which resides at the campus and hosts offices for university staff, labs, computer classes, and offices for private and start-up companies. Thus, the passengers of the elevator are the employees having offices in the ICT building and students accessing classrooms and working places. The smart-elevator operates through all the eight floors of the building, with a load limit of 1000 kg referring to a maximum of 13 persons.

The ICT building is a typical office building with eight floors (0 to 7) with the main entrance at level 1. The building has two elevators from KONE (global company for elevators and escalators), one on each side of the building. Each elevator is a single car running in its allocated elevator shaft. The elevator on the north side of the building is equipped with additional common hardware and software to deliver the features of the smart-elevator (Leier et al. 2021)—a RGB camera (Basler acA2040-25gc) for facial recognition, four depth cameras (Intel Real Sense D435) to detect and track passengers' location within the cabin, a speakerphone (Senheiser SP20) enabling voice commands, and a mini-PC (Intel NUC Mini PC NUC5i7RYB) for processing sensor data. The RGB camera is installed in the back corner of the cabin on the side of the button panel at the height of 1.55 meters to capture the video from the elevator entrance and cabin to ensure facial detection. The elevator can be called to a floor by up/down travel buttons located at each floor next to the elevator entrance and operated by push-button controls inside the cabin. Figure 10.1 describes the smart-elevator system cabin context and setup.

For the passenger in-cabin behavior studies, we take advantage of the four depth cameras installed in the elevator ceiling (Fig. 10.1) to capture passengers' location and movement data in the cabin during their rides. In general, the number of needed

Fig. 10.1 Smart-elevator system and the cabin context. With the black labels, the devices for smart-elevator platform used in this study are shown, while white labels indicate the locations of common controls

depth cameras and their placement depends on the elevator cabin layout (length, width, and height) and the field of view (FoV) of the chosen depth cameras (Leier et al. 2021). The current setup of the SES uses four depth cameras, as a single camera would not be able to provide full coverage of the cabin—to detect passengers' position, it is needed to capture relatively flat areas in the upper half of the cabin. The cabin height of our elevator is 2.2 meters, which means that a single Intel RealSense D435 depth camera placed in the middle of cabin ceiling would only be able to capture objects in the cabin at the height of 1.3 meters—making it impossible to capture taller passengers, especially those standing close to the walls. Therefore, to cover the whole cabin at maximum height up to 2.0 m, our smart-elevator uses four depth cameras. The SES positioning system merges the results from each camera and maps them to global coordinate system reflecting the elevator coordinates layout (Fig. 10.2).

While the location of passengers inside the cabin is tracked using the depth cameras, the boarding of new passengers is also registered by the RGB camera, placed such that all incoming passengers could be detected and assigned a tracking ID. Further, the detection results are used to identify known frequent passengers through facial recognition against existing profiles. The profiles are stored as anonymous profiles with only a vector of facial features and numeric IDs (no facial photo/video is stored in the system), making it impossible to match these profiles to identifiable persons. Passengers of the elevator are notified of the existence of the cameras within the elevator cabin by a sign outside the cabin, and in case they disagree, they are instructed to use the second elevator of the ICT building. The advantage of the facial recognition camera is that passengers are not required to make any additional efforts to be known by the system as it can be fully automized. An alternative to the use of facial recognition camera to identify and distinguish frequent passengers would be to use contactless cards (e.g., either as anonymous cards or staff cards) with radio-frequency identification (RFID) or near-

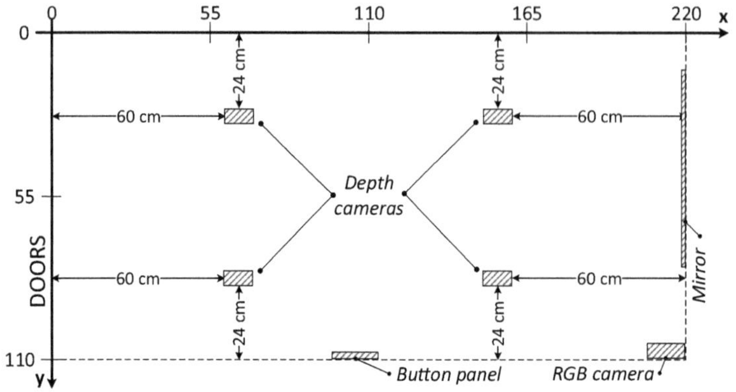

Fig. 10.2 Elevator cabin context and the coordinates system of the SES positioning service (SES-PS)

field communication (NFC) technology. In this study, we exploit passenger profiles as anonymous numerical IDs to distinguish frequent travellers re-taking elevator while addressing RQ4 and RQ5.

To continue, let us now define some terms. A *travel* is a ride an elevator passenger undertakes between departure and destination floors such that it starts with a passenger entering the elevator cabin and ends with exiting the cabin. Each travel is assigned a new travel identification number (travel ID) in the SES stored alongside with track data. A *track* is the location of the passenger inside the elevator cabin attributed with travel ID, position coordinates (x, y), and timestamp. *Single travel* is a travel with only one passenger in the cabin, while *crowded travel* describes situations where at least two or more passengers have occupied the cabin for a travel.

The passenger position data is gathered using the SES positioning service (SES-PS), which allows to collect position data for each individual passenger by tracking and retrieving sensor data from the four depth sensors located in the ceiling of the elevator cabin. Detection of travellers is done using an image processing algorithm (Leier et al. 2021). The algorithm delimits the heads of passengers in the elevator cabin regardless of their height. The system starts to locate heads at the height of 120 cm and, with every iteration, increases the detection height by 5 cm. Every height layer is run through until the ceiling height is reached. All the detected heads' movements will be monitored throughout the travel and track data stored periodically (every 200 ms). Whenever a passenger with an existing profile (the passenger has travelled previously) is identified, the track is also associated with the profile ID in the SES. The coordinates in the SES-PS are expressed in the metric system using centimeters as the unit (Fig. 10.2). The coordinates for the x-axis range from 0 to 220 cm and for the y-axis from 0 to 110 cm, reflecting the central position of the detected object position at 120 cm or higher above the floor. Figure 10.2 outlines the elevator cabin context with the equipment and the coordinates system used by the SES-PS.

10.4 Passenger Location Analysis Model and Methods

As learned in Sect. 10.3, the SES-PS collects data about passengers' location and movement in the cabin, using a global coordinate system laid out on the floor area (Fig. 10.2). In this section, we first discuss how to establish a model for passenger location interpretation in the elevator cabin by projecting captured coordinates to meaningful passenger locations and, by this, address RQ1. We then proceed to validate the model and establish methods of data analysis through a ground-truth study.

10.4.1 Passenger Location Analysis Model

To analyze passenger location in elevator cabin, we propose to divide the elevator-floor-area two-dimensional model into ideally equally sized squared sections. We reason that from top-down view, a person in an elevator cabin will take up an elliptical space, which we transform into a circle, as we have no knowledge about the direction of the person inside the elevator. For the diameter of the circle, we use the approximate shoulder length of humans. A study by Randall et al. (1946) for Army Air Force reports that 95% of cadets have biacromial shoulder width of 42.9 cm. Considering that not every passenger is in the ideal shape of a "cadet" and that humans prefer to have a personal space around them, we extend this area to approximately $d_{section} = 50$ cm. We do not recommend to decrease this value; however, extending the personal space could be applied. As the person in the elevator is represented by a circular area, we therefore opt for the squared sections in the model, as it is the best way to fit a circle representing a person. Figure 10.3 describers the establishment of one section for our passenger location analysis model.

Next, having established a model for a single section, we scale the section-based location model to elevator floor area. For this, we find the number of possible sections $s = n_l \times n_w$ over the length l and width w of the elevator floor area, where

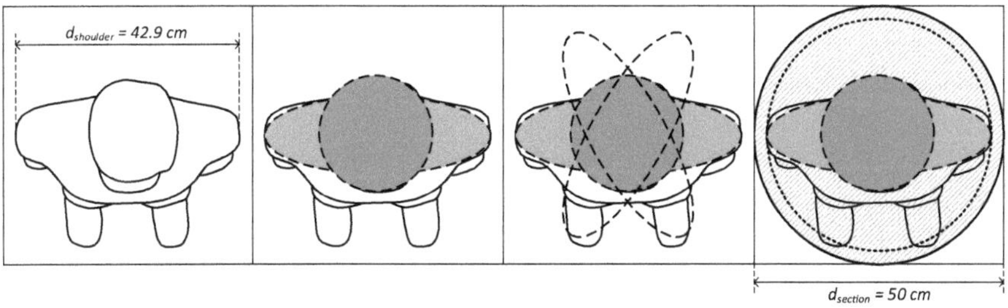

Fig. 10.3 Development of the passenger location section model (a view of one section)—from biacromial shoulder-width to section

Table 10.1 Examples of elevator cabin dimension conversion into sections using the passenger location section model

Elevator	Cabin dimensions		# Sections		Total #	Section dimensions	
#	l	w	n_l	n_w	sections	l_s	w_s
1	110	100	2	2	5	55	50
2	135	130	2	2	5	68	65
3	214	168	4	3	13	54	56
4*	220	110	4	2	9	55	55
5	267	173	5	3	16	53	58

* The smart-elevator used in this study

n_l and n_w are the number of possible sections over the dimensions $l \in Z$ and $w \in Z$ correspondingly. After studying several elevator cabin size configurations ranging from 1.0 to 2.7 meters in dimensions (Table 10.1 exemplifies some of them), we find that to identify the number of sections, the dimensions should be rounded up toward the nearest decimal and then the lowest fit applied; thus, we use the floor function to settle the number of sections over a dimension. Equation 10.1 provides the general formula for finding the number of sections N over a cabin dimension Z.

$$N = \left\lfloor \frac{\lceil Z \rceil}{d_{section}} \right\rfloor \tag{10.1}$$

In our passenger location analysis model, we have one more additional section representing the center of the elevator. The center of this section matches the central point of the elevator floor area. We use this section to identify passengers who prefer to stand in the middle of the elevator (e.g., while travelling alone). Therefore, the total number of sections is $s_{total} = (n_l \times n_w) + 1$.

In reality, the actual cabin dimensions (height, width, depth) vary by design, producer, possibilities to install an elevator in a building, etc. Thus, depending on the actual elevator cabin dimensions, it may not be always possible to retain the ideally modelled squared sections in the two-dimensional-floor model. In case squared sections cannot be achieved, section dimensions should be adjusted (stretched) in the dimension (length/width) where otherwise full sections cannot be established. The section dimension is then determined by cabin dimension divided by the number of sections N for that cabin dimension (Eq. 10.1). An alternative would be to define partial sections. In Table 10.1, one can observe section dimension variability considering different common cabin sizes.

The designed location analysis model is not connected to the elevator capacity characteristics (maximum and normal loading), which are typically calculated based on weights or a combination of weights and elevator speed, together with a recommendation for allocated passenger area. The latter for normal loading is ca. 0.21 m^2 and for maximum ca. 0.14 m^2. In our model, the area allocated per passenger is 0.25 m^2, allowing sufficient personal space (around 5–10 cm) or space for belongings (e.g., rucksack). Fitting the elevator cabin with the maximum number

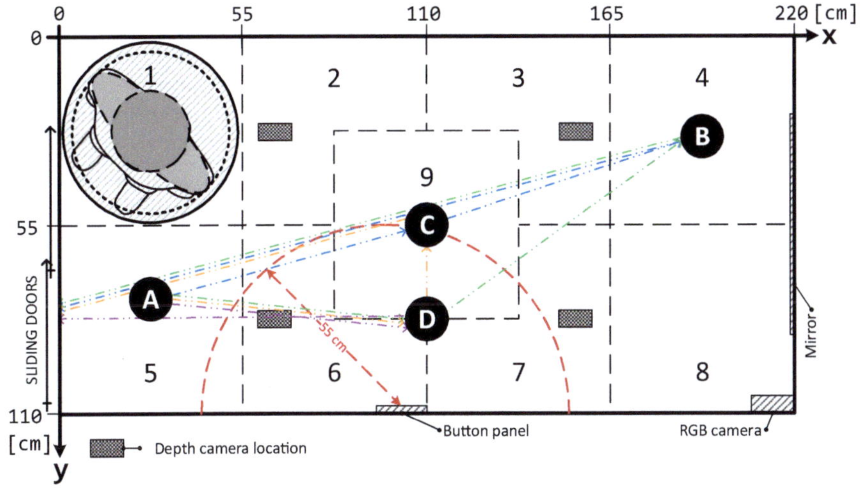

Fig. 10.4 The model for passenger location analysis with nine sections (1–9) and the context of the elevator cabin environment. Letters *A–D* mark the stand-location points used in the ground-truth study. Dash-dot-dot colored lines mark the movement path for the continuous location detection study: Route#1, blue; Route#2, green; Route#3, orange; and Route#4, magenta

of passengers comes with the cost of the loss of personal space and being pressed together with fellow passengers.

We now turn to our smart-elevator platform. Considering our smart-elevator cabin dimensions ($l \times w$) are 220×110 cm, we detect that for the passenger location analysis, the number of sections is nine. The application of the model divides the elevator floor area into eight equal square-sized sections with an additional section of the same size overlaying the sections in the middle of the cabin. Figure 10.4 describes the context of the elevator cabin environment (e.g., the position of doors sliding open from left to right while standing in the cabin and facing the doors, location of floor selection buttons, etc.) and the division of the floor area to nine sections, each of which identifies a potential location of an elevator passenger. The center point of a passenger in a section is at ca. 22 cm according to the average passenger's shoulder width, which correlates to 27.5 cm in the section of the location model for our smart-elevator. As usually passengers do not stand against the wall, there is a high probability that the passenger center point aligns well with the section center point in the model. The elevator producer KONE has limited the maximum number of people for the elevator type we use to 13 passengers.

Next, we validate the established zone-based location model and SES-PS, and establish methods for data analysis to be able to analyze passenger in-cabin location behavior based on real travel data (Sect. 10.5) used to answer RQ2, RQ4, and RQ5.

10.4.2 Model Validation and Methods Establishment

To validate the location analysis model and to be able to properly interpret the real elevator passenger data collected by SES, we carried out a ground-truth study consisting of a series of validation experiments, based on the developed passenger location analysis model. As a result, we establish methods for data analysis according to the location analysis model and answer RQ1.

On April 6, 2021, late evening (after 20:00), a ground truth study was carried out by a single test passenger to evaluate and validate SES setup and precision in detecting a passenger's location in the elevator cabin based on the location analysis model (Sect. 10.4.1). We chose a late hour to have minimum disturbance for other potential travellers, as well as for the continuity of the experiments. Through a series of experiments, the performance and accuracy of the SES-PS were validated, whereas the location of the test passenger inside the elevator cabin was known in advance. Multiple locations inside the cabin were selected (Fig. 10.4) with the goal to determine the accuracy of passenger position detection in any of the given section according to the location analysis model and to identify any variability. The study assumed that the test subject was always standing in the middle of the designated section of the location analysis model, and for this, to aid the test passenger, a grid was marked down on the elevator floor with white paint tape (Fig. 10.5). The grid,

Fig. 10.5 Performing the ground-truth study to validate the analysis model and SES-PS: sections of the location analysis model marked down on the elevator floor with paint tape (left), and the test passenger carrying out the experiments standing in Section 9 in the middle of the elevator cabin, facing the doors (right)

placed to help the test passenger stick to pre-planned elevator usage scenarios, was removed immediately after the experiments, which lasted for 3 hours.

Two different experiment series, (i) *static stand positions* and (ii) *continuous position detection for pre-determined movement path*, were carried out to validate the SES positioning service against the location analysis model. Although the total number of planned test travels was 60 (10 for each static stand position and 5 for every continuous position detection), the actual number of travels captured was 61 due to a counting error made by the test passenger. Four additional travel records appeared in the captured data as other passengers entered the cabin in the middle of one of the experiment trips. These travels were removed from the analysis data, leaving thereby a dataset of 59 travels and location tracks data of 37,044 coordinate pairs. The collected data was analyzed using general-purpose programming language Python (ver. 3.7) with *Psycopg*[1] PostgreSQL database adapter and *XlsxWriter*,[2] *DateTime*,[3] *numpy*,[4] and *Matplotlib*[5] packages.

10.4.2.1 Static Stand Positions

First, a series of static stand-still experiments was carried out with four different specifically selected stand-positions *A*–*D* (Fig. 10.4) in the elevator cabin. The position *A* represents a zone right in front of the elevator doors on the opening side (doors open in the direction from Section 5 to 1). Position *B* in Section 4 marks the back corner of the elevator cabin in front of the mirror while *C* (Section 9) the middle of the elevator and *D* on the border of Sections 6 and 7 an ambiguous multi-section area in front of the elevator floor buttons, which can be reached for pressing from Sections 6, 7 or 9 in an approximate reach radius of 55 cm (Fig. 10.4).

Each position *A*–*D* was tested with a series of ten travels (except *C* for which 1 series appeared invalid due to accidental additional passengers and was removed) between two floor levels (e.g., floor 3–5), with a travel lasting about 20 seconds. The SES-PS captures passenger position tracks with depth cameras at a rate of 200 ms—roughly 100 position data points for each travel in the experiment. The collected data indicated 104 tracks in average per experiment travel (min 88 and max 112). To ensure data completeness, for each travel, a new elevator call was made. It was required that the test passenger follows the same route to enter the elevator and stands in the center of the agreed experiment position (*A*, *B*, *C*, or *D*), turning around to face the doors once having reached the position.

Standing in each position *A*–*D* was analyzed separately. To evaluate the SES-PS accuracy of measuring the static stand location, the data coordinates describing the

---

[1] https://pypi.org/project/psycopg2/

[2] https://pypi.org/project/XlsxWriter/

[3] https://pypi.org/project/DateTime/

[4] https://pypi.org/project/numpy/

[5] https://pypi.org/project/matplotlib/

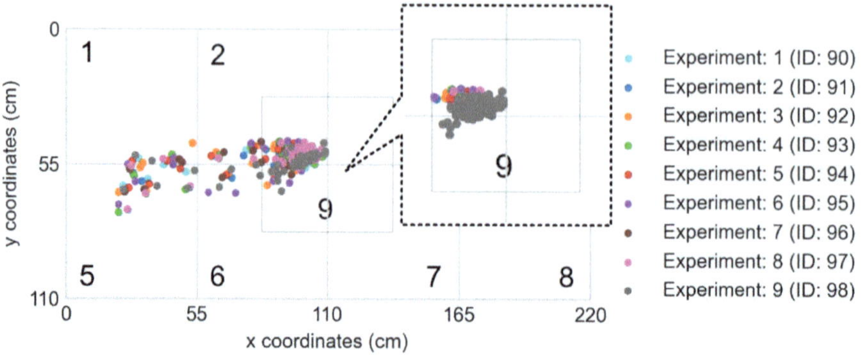

Fig. 10.6 Visualization of the captured passenger location data before data filtering and after (callout with a dashed line) movement information has been filtered out, for example, location point *C* in Section 9 of the location analysis model

Table 10.2 Experiment results for the static stand position study

	# track coordinates		$M_{x,y}$ [a]		$E_{x,y}$ [b]		Average deviation	
Position	Experiments	Filtered	x	y	x	y	x	y
A	983	893	27.5	82.5	32	76.5	4.9 ± 4.4	-7.3 ± 4.2
B	1156	759	192.5	27.5	170.4	28.5	-21.3 ± 4.8	1.4 ± 3.3
C	962	778	110	55	100.9	52.6	-9.4 ± 2.9	-2.8 ± 1.5
D	1042	873	110	82.5	103.9	80.9	-7.1 ± 4.5	-2.8 ± 4.9
Avg	1036	826	n/a	n/a	n/a	n/a	-8.2 ± 4.2	-2.9 ± 3.5
Sum	4143	3303	n/a	n/a	n/a	n/a	n/a	n/a

[a] Central section coordinates in the model, [cm]
[b] Median central coordinates of section in experiments, [cm]

movement into the required position *A–D* were filtered out as follows: first, any coordinate outside of the planned stand position section was deemed as movement into the section and eliminated; additionally, the movement points from the section edge to the center of the planned stand position section were removed until five consecutive points (ca. 1 second) were captured at the planned stand position section to assure a safe margin for reaching a stand position. Similar filtering action was carried out for data describing exiting a section and the elevator. Figure 10.6 visualizes the experiment data before and after filtering for position *C* located in Section 9.

The results of the static stand positions experiment series are outlined in Table 10.2. On average, 210 location points for each series were deemed to describe moving to location and thus removed from the analysis—more for positions further away from the doors (e.g., position *B*). We noted that for position *B*, the deviation for determining the x-coordinate differs from all other findings, which could be the misalignment of the positioning service or the effect of the back-wall mirror reflections. In further analysis, this blind-spot area has been accounted for.

The results of static stand position experiments indicate that the coordinates captured by the SES-PS system are slightly off-centered on the x-axis, while the y-coordinates are rather accurate. This misalignment may be due to the test passenger's posture and height (1.90 m) but also an alignment shift in the positioning service or noise from artificial lightning and reflections. From the validation experiments, we conclude that the SES-PS is able to locate the passenger in a section center with a deviation of 8 cm on x-axis and 3 cm on the y-axis, which, considering the technical setup and the passenger location analysis model, is satisfactory.

With this, we conclude that it is feasible to model passengers' location through location sections as meaningful parts of the two-dimensional floor model ($RQ1$), confirming our hypothesis. The experiment forms a benchmark for interpreting the collected real passenger travel track data used to answer $RQ2$ and $RQ4$.

10.4.2.2 Continuous Position Detection for a Movement Path

To validate the detection of passenger movement path inside the cabin with the SES-PS, we designed four different routes starting and ending at the cabin doors in between the positions A–D as given on Fig. 10.4:

- Route#1: $A \rightarrow C \rightarrow B \rightarrow A$, a scenario where a passenger enters the elevator, moves to the middle, reaches the floor buttons, and moves to the back corner having a good view on the indicator panel and the cabin for the duration of travel.
- Route#2: $A \rightarrow D \rightarrow B \rightarrow A$, a scenario similar to Route#1, except the floor buttons are reached right in front of these at the position D.
- Route#3: $A \rightarrow D \rightarrow C \rightarrow A$, where after pressing the floor buttons the passenger proceeds to stand in the middle of the elevator at the position C.
- Route#4: $A \rightarrow D \rightarrow A$, where the passenger reaches the button panel and then immediately steps back to the closest position to doors on the opening side.

The test passenger followed each route for five times during the experiments. Each travel was through four floor levels (e.g., floor 1 to 5) with an average travel duration of 25 seconds, during which, in average, 112 track points for each travel were captured by SES-PS. At each point (A–D), the test passenger made a short stop, yet keeping the movement as natural as possible. While exiting the cabin, the shortest path through the opening side of the doors (position A) was taken.

For the analysis, the captured location data was filtered and compressed as follows: section and location coordinates were added to the movement path whenever five consecutive points were captured by SES in the same section (at rate of 200 ms), provided that the section was an adjacent section (in the location analysis model) to the previous one in the movement path list. The path was constructed as a sequence of sections (detected from the track coordinates) passed by the passenger, where each section is sequentially counted only once, forming, for example, a path 5-6-9-6-5. Figure 10.7 illustrates the detected paths for Route#2 in the experiments.

From the data analysis, we notice that there is a certain blind-spot area of approximately 15 cm from the wall into which no coordinates fall. First of all,

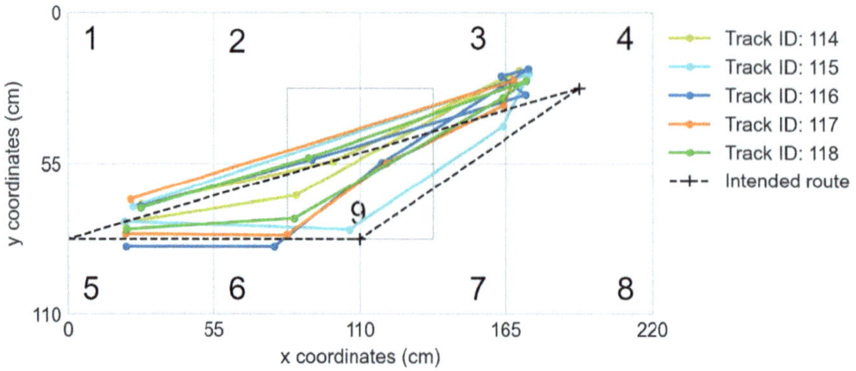

Fig. 10.7 Movement path construction with applied data filtering for Route#2 in the experiments. The dashed black line indicates the planned route for the experiment

the SES-PS estimates the center point of the passenger, and second, even if a passenger stands against the wall, the detected center point of the person would still be ca. 15 cm away from it. The validation experiments with continuous location detection confirmed that the SES positioning service can sufficiently enough track the passenger movement inside the cabin environment throughout the travel. The analysis of collected experiment data allowed to establish a path construction method with data point reduction for real passenger data analysis using the location analysis model. The results will be applied to answer $RQ5$.

10.5 Passenger In-Cabin Behavior Analysis

In this section, we apply the methods established and knowledge gained from the ground-truth study to answer the research questions about passenger movement behavior in elevator cabin environment. For this, we use the track data of real passengers collected through 61 days (2 months, April–May 2021) and consisting of 11,731 travels, out of which 67.9% of travels were made with a single passenger, and in 32.1% of cases, there were multiple passengers in the cabin. The period of data collection matches with the enforced COVID-19 restrictions (2+2 rule and facial mask mandate), which affects the available number of travels as well as the ability of the SES to differentiate between known travellers through facial recognition. In addition, the ICT building was partially closed for students due to the pandemics, and we also noticed that people preferred stairs over the use of the elevators. Travels performed by the test passenger for the ground-truth study have been excluded. Table 10.3 characterizes the real passenger data we used.

Table 10.3 Smart-elevator passenger data used for the behavior analysis

	# Travels	# Tracks	ntp_{avg}[a]	d_{avg}[b]
Total (count)	11,731	1,414,740	120	24
Travelling alone in cabin (count)	7790	1,034,162	130	26
Travelling in a crowded cabin (count)	3761	380,578	101	20

[a] Avg. tracks per travel per passenger
[b] Avg. travel duration per passenger [s]

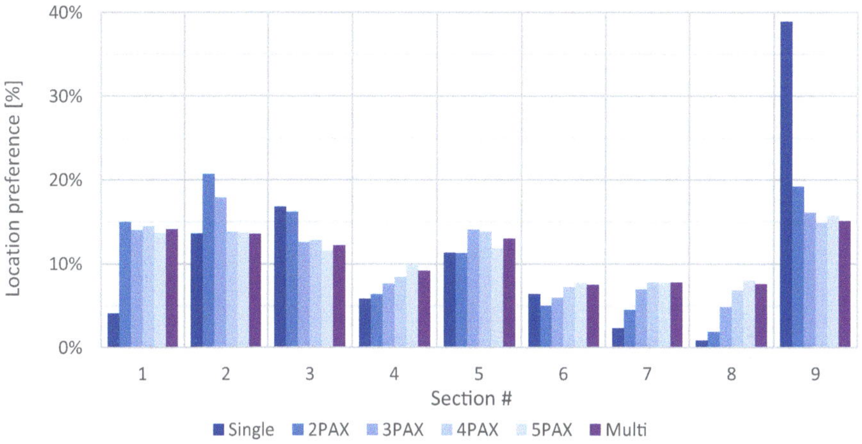

Fig. 10.8 Preferred standing positions by sections for single travel and with multiple passengers (PAX) in the cabin. The column *Multi* indicates more than one passenger in the cabin during a travel

10.5.1 RQ2: Passengers' Preferred Standing Locations

We start passenger in-cabin behavior analysis by considering the most preferred standing locations while travelling alone or with fellow passengers (crowded) in the elevator cabin. To answer *RQ2*, we look at all track data collected on real passengers during the study period, regardless whether the passengers had an existing user profile in the SES or not. The data is analyzed according to the location analysis model (Sect. 10.4.1) and the method described in Sect. 10.4.2. For each position track coordinate x-y pair, a location section 1–9 representing passenger's location is found.

The analysis (Fig. 10.8) reveals that while travelling alone in the cabin, the most favorable position to stand is in the middle of the elevator (Section 9). However, if multiple travellers are in the elevator, other sections become more favorable (Fig. 10.9), and we can observe a dramatic drop of more than two times for Section 9 in occupancy compared to single travels. The less favorable locations are Sections 6–8, while Section 8 in the back corner in front of the facial recognition camera is the least occupied among all travels. We also observe that passengers

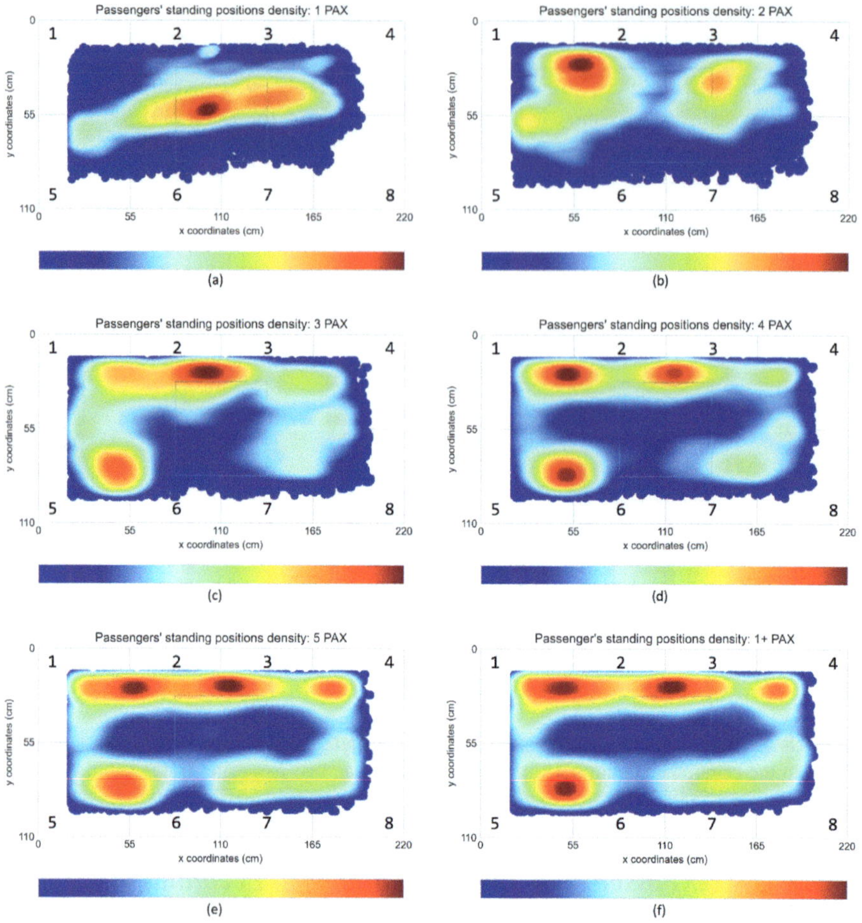

Fig. 10.9 Density maps for elevator passengers' in-cabin positions trough travels: (**a**) single passenger in cabin, (**b–e**) 2–5 passengers 2–5 in cabin, (**f**) overall density with multiple passengers in cabin. Blue, least density; red, highest density. Single-density maps created using Matplotlib (Hunter 2007)

prefer to stand on the opposite side to the button panel and floor level indicator (compare Sections 2 and 3 to Sections 6 and 7), which we believe is due to have a better view over the travel status from the floor indicator but also not to block other passengers from (de-)boarding. It would be interesting to see if this distribution changes when an additional panel is installed on the opposite wall or there are no floor buttons present in the cabin at all.

The density maps for preferred in-cabin standing positions (Fig. 10.9) reveal that a central location is preferred while travelling alone. Yet, when other passengers are also in the cabin, distance is kept, and standing locations begin to form around the opposite wall to the button panel and floor indicator (Sections 1–3) on the closing side of the doors but also just opposite to the opening side of the door (Section 5). Overall, we see that with single occupancy, passengers prefer to stand in the middle of the cabin or closer to the doors, whereas in a situation with multiple passengers in the cabin, passengers tend to keep distance, confirming our initial hypothesis.

Although these results are directly bound to a particular elevator type we used, we still observe the following general findings: (i) the established location analysis model performs well in distinguishing passenger locations, (ii) typically passengers try not to block (de-)boarding fellow passengers and distance is kept while at the same time having a good view of the travel status indicators, and (iii) for single travels, a central location is preferred. For another type of an elevator, we expect these findings to hold; however, in case of larger elevators with multiple button panels (i.e., panels on both sides of the elevator doors), this is likely to change, and single travellers may also opt for a location closer to a wall. It would be interesting to carry out this experiment on different elevator layouts, equipment permitted. Unfortunately, still, today, it would require significant installation work of equipment.

10.5.2 RQ3: Passengers' Reported Standing Locations

We compare the results of the detected standing preferences of passengers (Sect. 10.5.1) to their explicit preferences reported back through a survey on elevator usage habits. The survey, consisting of 19 questions, was sent to potential elevator users of the ICT building through internal mailing lists. We selected to carry out the survey on employees working in the building as they are potentially using the elevators on a daily basis, are familiar with the elevators, and are likely represented in the collected passenger travel data we analyzed. Out of the ca. 180 potential users, 63 (35%) responded to our survey. Eighty-six percent of the respondents reported that they had used either both of the elevators or the smart-elevator, while 11% had used only the regular elevator, and two respondents (3%) had never used the elevators in the ICT building.

In the survey, we presented the participants with the smart-elevator of the ICT building and the floor plan with identifiable spots for standing (Fig. 10.10). We asked the participants to indicate their explicit preference toward a single spot in the cabin during the travel and evaluate all the spots regarding the likelihood of occupying a spot for two scenarios: travelling alone and with fellow passengers in the cabin. The response rate for these questions was 98%. For the spots (Fig. 10.10), we selected all the nine sections of the location analysis model (Sect. 10.4.1), plus a few extra of interest (F in front of the button panel and J in the middle at the back wall in front of the mirror).

The preferred standing positions explicitly reported by users are presented on Fig. 10.11. We observe the same trends as for RQ2 for Sections 1, 3, 5, 6, 8, and 9, whereas for Sections 2, 4, and 7, an opposite trend is observed compared to the findings from the passengers' location behavior (Fig. 10.8), in line with our

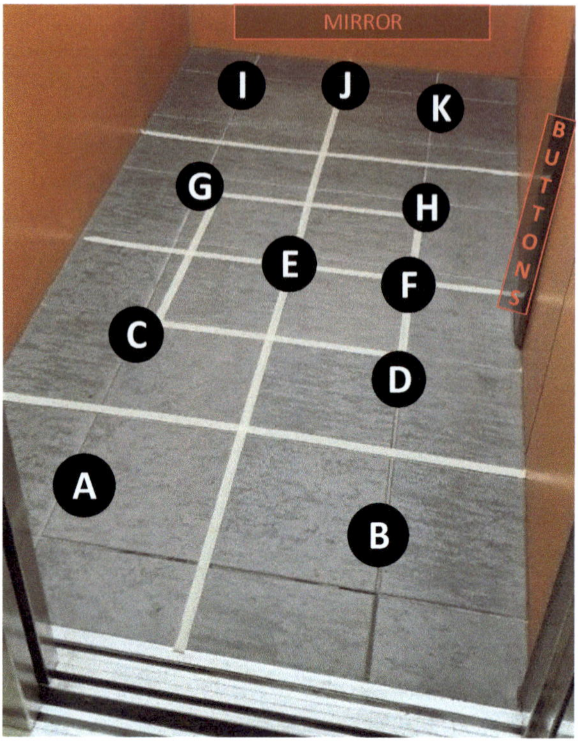

Fig. 10.10 Elevator floor plan with preferred standing spots *A–K* presented to survey respondents to collect their standing location preferences regarding the elevator usage

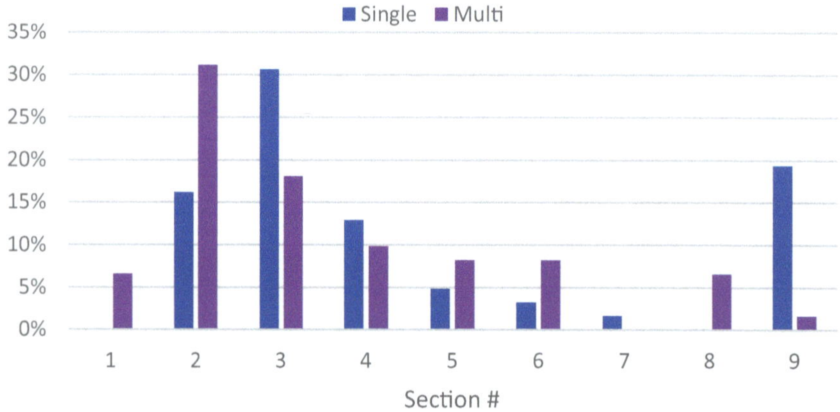

Fig. 10.11 Reported explicit preferences for standing locations for single and multi-user travels. The spots presented in the user survey have been transferred to sections of the location analysis model

hypothesis. Interestingly, the preference to stand in the middle of the elevator is superseded by preferring Section 3. For the additional spot *F* (Fig. 10.10) in the survey, we do not find any reported preference (0%) while travelling alone, and only one respondent (2%) reported it back as a preference while travelling with fellow passengers. The spot *J* is reported to be preferred in 8–10% of cases correspondingly.

10.5.3 RQ4: Preferred Standing Position for Successive Travels

Next, we consider the likelihood of a passenger to choose the same standing location in the elevator cabin for re-occurring travels, i.e., do passengers have their favorite standing positions they choose in the cabin each time they ride? To answer *RQ*4, we analyze only the track data of passengers known (profiled) by SES. Profiles are created, and passengers identified by SES automatically using facial recognition (Leier et al. 2021; Robal et al. 2020) with an identification success rate of 98.2%. Unfortunately, during the study, COVID-19 restrictions (including the mask mandate) were effective, which significantly reduced the travel data available for such known passengers due to system inability to recognize all known passengers. Thereby, we obtain only 793 travels with 305 distinct profiles, which we again separate into two groups: travelling alone (single, 30.0%) or in a crowded cabin (two passengers, 42.1%; three, 21.7%; four and more, 5.9%). We reject any profile that has less than three travels associated. Further, we organize travels of each profile in chronological order, split the set into two, and use the first 2/3 to determine the preferred standing position and the last 1/3 to verify the hypothesis of choosing mostly the same standing location. This leaves us with 361 travels (46%), 83 as single and 278 as crowded cabin travels, with 17 and 60 profiles correspondingly. To determine the preferred location, we apply the same approach as for RQ2 based on the location analysis model, determining the preferred standing position as one of the nine sections.

For each passenger, we find over her travels a list of standing positions as sections of the location analysis model (Section 1–9) in a decreasing order of occupancy and use the top-two items (*Top 1* and *Top 2*) of this list as the most likely standing positions. We then compare these to the remaining 1/3 of data (Table 10.4). Based on the small sample of data we have, we see that while travelling alone in the cabin, passengers tend to choose (as hypothesized) the same standing position as they have

Table 10.4 Probability of choosing the same standing position for re-occurring travels

Cabin situation group	# Profiles	# Travels	Top 1	Top 2	Top 1 or Top 2
Single travel	17	83	60%	31%	91%
Crowded travel	60	278	26%	9%	35%

Table 10.5 Characterization of constructed movement paths and re-occurrence match

	# Travels/profile	L_{path}[a]	$L_{pax-path}$[b]	M^c [%]	$M_{partial}$[d] [%]
Avg	5 ± 2	6	6.4 ± 1.0	13%	62.3%
Min	3	3	5.2 ± 1.3	75%	100.0%
Max	12	11	7.8 ± 1.4	0%	0.0%

[a] Path length over all travels
[b] Avg. path length per passenger
[c] Exact path match rate
[d] Partial path match rate on the first three positions

chosen previously, while in the situation of a crowded cabin, no favorable position is chosen, as it may already be taken, and a random open standing location is occupied.

10.5.4 RQ5: Recurring Movement Flow Patterns

We also study passengers' in-cabin behavior regarding their movement in the cabin environment and explore whether they tend to choose the same path through the cabin during their travels. To answer *RQ5*, we analyze the successive travels of profiled passengers for the single travel situation only and use the same dataset as for RQ4. From RQ4, we already know that passengers tend to choose the same standing location in 60% of cases when travelling alone. We decide not to analyze movement routes while travelling in a crowded elevator as the path would greatly depend on the occupancy of the elevator cabin and locations of the fellow passengers.

For each travel associated with a profile in the SES, we construct a movement path based on the sections the traveller has been found to be present in (passing or standing) using the method described in Sect. 10.4.2.2, producing a path (e.g., 5-6-9-1-5) for each travel. Table 10.5 characterizes the movement paths for the 83 single travels available for the 17 profiled passengers.

Based on the small sample of data we were able to collect, we do not find that passengers would in an identifiable way follow the same movement path when entering, standing, and exiting the elevator for travelling in between floors. The average path consists of four to eight sections of movement with a maximum of 11 sections. The same path is followed only in 13% of travels observed. In this regard, we fail to confirm our hypothesis. However, for two profiled travellers, we notice the exact path match to be 75% and 67%. Analyzing the first three positions of a path, we interestingly find that the same passenger who had the exact match rate at 75% had a movement path match by first three positions at 100%, whereas the general rate for all single-travelling profiled passengers was at 62%. This is somewhat expected, as passengers usually enter the elevator cabin from Section 5, move to Section 6 to press a floor button, and then to Section 9 to stand in the middle of the elevator cabin. With a larger set of data available and for a longer duration, there might be some interesting findings to be uncovered.

Table 10.6 Perceived invasion of privacy imposed by devices of a smart-elevator platform

Device	Do not know	No	Somewhat	Definitely
Facial recognition camera	17%	11%	29%	33%
Microphone	8%	12%	29%	33%
Infrared camera	17%	19%	22%	21%
Motion sensor	33%	31%	8%	3%
Weight measurement	25%	27%	12%	10%

10.5.5 RQ6: Perceived Invasion of Privacy in Smart-Elevator Cabin

In our survey on elevator usage habits (Sect. 10.5.2), we also asked participants to rate the devices installed in the smart-elevator cabin considering the perceived invasion of privacy on the scale of *No*, *Somewhat*, and *Definitely*. The question we presented in the survey was as follows: *Do you feel your privacy is threatened when using a smart-elevator equipped with the following devices?* We presented the following list of devices: (i) facial recognition camera; (ii) microphone; (iii) infrared camera, referring to the used depth cameras; (iv) motion sensor; and (v) weight measurement.

The majority of respondents (62%) identified that they felt their privacy being invaded by facial recognition camera and microphone in the elevator cabin, while 17% could not decide, and 11% did not see a problem with these devices being installed into the elevator cabin. This confirms our initial hypothesis that cameras are perceived as the most privacy-invasive devices, together with microphones. Interestingly, a fifth of respondents also considered weight measurement, present in every elevator, as a threat to their privacy. Table 10.6 reports the responses.

10.6 Discussion

Although advancements in technology have enabled to equip, for example, common passenger elevators with features of a smart-elevator, there is still a long way to go toward smarter and assistive elevator travel. In comparison to traditional passenger elevators, smart-elevators allow to deliver additional features and value to make passengers' daily travels more convenient and improve through it UX. For example, inclusion of voice user interfaces (VUIs) would allow to select destination floor without the need to touch buttons, a highly assistive service for persons with visual impairment, or for anyone in case hands are loaded with things. To improve user travel experience, it is important to collect knowledge on the actual exploitation of elevators, including passengers' behavior in the cabin and its dependency on the number of passengers during their travels. This could, for instance, be used as an input for cabin layout design. Adding smartness to elevators will in the long run enable to establish smart-elevator systems that are able to learn from and adapt to its daily users and the habits of the building residents, either on a personal or aggregated level, targeting smooth and convenient travel with least waiting time and power consumption.

The present SES, initiated just as an innovation project to bring smart features to common elevators, has found its way into research as a platform to study user behavior. This chapter focused on passenger in-cabin behavior based on the location detection made possible by this smart-elevator platform. Elevators, compact enough, are just one of the possible type of objects, where user behavioral studies could be beneficial. For example, the approach described in this chapter could be transferred to study the distribution of passengers in public transport systems, e.g., city buses and bus stops, to either find better cabin layout, improve usability, or passenger flow.

On top of allowing to study user behavior in a closed space through a short period, such as the elevator travel is, the smart-elevator platform equipped with passenger position detection can provide valuable information for cabin interior (re-)design, e.g., placement of interactive screens (including building guide, important information boards, or screens with commercials in department stores), placement of security cameras, etc. based on actual exploitation of elevators by its passengers, and thereby contribute to increased levels of UX. For instance, our studies showed that passengers prefer to stand close to the button panel in the center of the cabin or opposite to it in this particular elevator type. The SES platform in combination of additional sensors could also be used to detect emergency situations, for example, in elderly homes, where the system could automatically notify the operator that a person has fallen and needs attention. In other cases of emergency, e.g., fire, the platform could provide immediate feedback on the number of passengers in the cabin. The system could also be used for vandalism detection based on fast movements in the cabin environment.

Elevators are able to detect changes in the weight of the cabin. Yet there is no way to distinguish whether this change came from passengers or cargo. The SES discussed in this chapter would allow to add this knowledge to the weight change with a precision of a passenger count. This would allow to establish better usage models and improve maintenance planning, which today is planned as a periodic event over some time, but could be transformed into aperiodic and usage-based, being more economical and allowing to save on cost.

Like with every new technology (recall that the first passenger elevator was rejected by the users), there are also challenges with smart-elevators. Although the technology may allow to provide a better service and novel features, this may come on the cost of privacy (e.g., cameras) and may not be well received by users—passengers may feel discomfort or annoyed and discontinue the use. Even if the system is technically secure, convincing passengers of it and winning their trust may take time. After the setup of the smart-elevator in the ICT building, we noticed a rise in the use of stairs instead of an elevator, even up to higher floors. Also, technical challenges have arisen. The traditional elevator technology is proven and rarely fails, whereas the smart features and their combination are rather experimental and therefore require a DevOps person or a team to continuously be involved and monitor the system and the status of its various components and services, for proper system exploitation.

As for future work, we have planned to continue to maintain the smart-elevator platform and to further investigate novel possibilities applicable for smart travelling with elevators. For example, a project of a "touchless-button" was initiated (inspired by the pandemics), allowing passengers to place elevator calls without touching any buttons and set the destination floor already when placing the elevator call (Reinsalu and Robal 2023). The latter will allow to optimize operations and can be considered a step toward energy-saving and greener deal delivered by smart solutions. In the future, it would be interesting to investigate our approach on several different elevator types, preferably in high-rise buildings, should this become possible. With the existing SES, we would like to continue behavior studies and explore how individual passengers react to (de-)boarding in sense of their position or how passengers change their behavior when their destination floor is about to be reached.

10.7 Conclusions

Advances in technology have delivered the possibility to set up smart-elevators as cyber physical-social systems. These systems, based on their innovative features, enable a platform to study passengers' behavior—once used to be possible only with surveillance cameras and manual work—to improve elevator systems, user experience, quality of service (QoS), and passenger travel experience and further enhance the concept of smart-elevators toward smarter life.

This chapter discussed a model and methods for elevator passengers' in-cabin behavior analysis, which were benchmarked and validated against the smart-elevator positioning service. This allowed to investigate real passengers' in-cabin behavior using an existing smart-elevator platform built using common hardware and software. Although our study was only limited to one type of an elevator cabin, the established section-based location analysis model and methods could be applied to any other elevator type able to carry more than ten persons at a time, being therefore large enough by floor area. Such elevators are typically found in large commercial buildings, shopping malls, hotels, hospitals, etc. With the model, methods, and experiments, we have contributed to fill the gap in existing literature regarding studies on human behavioral patterns in the context of elevator travels. The results can be used for smart-elevator cabin layout design, including sensors, but also improve the quality of service by knowing how passengers take advantage of the existing elevator in real-life situations—all in all, *small things matter*!

The scenarios designed for the ground-truth study to validate the elevator system positioning service can be used on any elevator (or other system) type for a similar purpose. As for the passengers' behavior, we explored whether there are favorable standing places for elevator passengers in general, finding that passengers tend to prefer to stand in the middle of the elevator while being the only occupant of the cabin, which is not the case when multiple travellers occupy the cabin. Further, we took advantage of the smart-elevator system profiling capabilities to identify repeatedly travelling passengers to investigate whether passengers tend to have personal preferred standing locations and if they follow certain movement paths in the cabin. The analysis revealed that indeed passengers tend to choose the same standing location quite often (60%) in case they are the only occupant of the cabin. We however failed to find confident results that passengers would always follow the same movement path while entering, travelling, and exiting the elevator. The small sample of data we collected due to COVID restrictions intervening our study was not sufficient to draw any solid conclusions.

With the advancement of technology over time driving the elaboration of smart cities for smarter everyday life, smart-elevators will also become a standard of every building, delivering us improved and more convenient travel service for different situations, considering the operational context and our needs at a particular moment in time and space.

References

Allen, J.: Speech Recognition and Synthesis, pp. 1664–1667. John Wiley and Sons, GBR (2003)

Bamunuarachchi, D.T., Ranasinghe, D.N.: Elevator group optimization in a smart building. In: 2015 IEEE 10th International Conference on Industrial and Information Systems (ICIIS), pp. 71–76 (2015)

Basov, K., Robal, T., Reinsalu, U., Leier, M.: Elevator passenger in-cabin behaviour – a study on smart-elevator platform. In: Ivanovic, M., Kirikova, M., Niedrite, L. (eds.) Digital Business and Intelligent Systems, pp. 3–18. Springer, Cham (2022)

Bernard, A.: Lifted: A Cultural History of the Elevator. NYU Press, New York (2014)

Bharti, H., Saxena, R.K., Sukhija, S., Yadav, V.: Cognitive model for smarter dispatch system/elevator. In: 2017 IEEE International Conference on Cloud Computing in Emerging Markets (CCEM), pp. 21–28 (2017)

Brand, M., Nikovski, D.: Optimal parking in group elevator control. In: IEEE International Conference on Robotics and Automation, 2004. Proceedings. ICRA '04. 2004, vol. 1, pp. 1002–1008 (2004)

Calinescu, R., Cámara, J., Paterson, C.: Socio-cyber-physical systems: models, opportunities, open challenges. In: 2019 IEEE/ACM 5th Intl Workshop on Software Engineering for Smart Cyber-Physical Systems (SEsCPS), pp. 2–6 (2019)

Cassandras, C.G.: Smart cities as cyber-physical social systems. Engineering **2**(2), 156–158 (2016)

Chou, S., Budhi, D.A., Dewabharata, A., Zulvia, F.E.: Improving elevator dynamic control policies based on energy and demand visibility. In: 2018 3rd International Conference on Intelligent Green Building and Smart Grid (IGBSG), pp. 1–4 (2018)

Dressler, F.: Cyber physical social systems: Towards deeply integrated hybridized systems. In: 2018 International Conference on Computing, Networking and Communications (ICNC), pp. 420–424 (2018)

Fernandez, J.R., Cortes, P.: A survey of elevator group control systems for vertical transportation: a look at recent literature. IEEE Control Syst. Mag. **35**(4), 38–55 (2015)

Fujimura, T., Ueno, S., Tsuji, H., Miwa, H.: Control algorithm for multi-car elevators with high transportation flexibility. In: 2013 IEEE 2nd Global Conference on Consumer Electronics (GCCE), pp. 544–545 (2013)

Ge, H., Hamada, T., Sumitomo, T., Koshizuka, N.: Intellevator: a context-aware elevator system for assisting passengers. In: 2018 IEEE 16th International Conference on Embedded and Ubiquitous Computing (EUC), pp. 81–88 (2018)

Goetsu, S., Sakai, T.: Voice input interface failures and frustration: Developer and user perspectives. In: The Adjunct Publication of the 32nd Annual ACM Symposium on User Interface Software and Technology, UIST '19, pp. 24–26. Association for Computing Machinery, New York (2019)

Heyes, E., Spearpoint, M.: Lifts for evacuation – human behaviour considerations. Fire Mater. **36**(4), 297–308 (2012)

Hunter, J.D.: Matplotlib: A 2d graphics environment. Comput. Sci. Eng. **9**(3), 90–95 (2007). https://doi.org/10.1109/MCSE.2007.55

Ketkar, S.S., Mukherjee, M.: Speech recognition system. In: Proceedings of the Intl Conference & Workshop on Emerging Trends in Technology, ICWET '11, pp. 1234–1237. Association for Computing Machinery, New York (2011)

Kwon, O., Lee, E., Bahn, H.: Sensor-aware elevator scheduling for smart building environments. Build. Environ. **72**, 332–342 (2014)

Lee, E.A., Seshia, S.A.: Introduction to Embedded Systems: A Cyber-Physical Systems Approach, 2nd edn. The MIT Press, Cambridge (2016)

Leier, M., Riid, A., Alumäe, T., Reinsalu, U., Pihlak, R., Udal, A., Heinsar, R., Vainküla, S.: Smart elevator with unsupervised learning for visitor profiling and personalised destination prediction. In: 2021 IEEE Conference on Cognitive and Computational Aspects of Situation Management (CogSIMA), pp. 9–16 (2021)

Liang, C.J.M., Tang, J., Zhang, L., Zhao, F., Munir, S., Stankovic, J.A.: On human behavioral patterns in elevator usages. In: Proceedings of the 5th ACM Workshop on Embedded Systems For Energy-Efficient Buildings, BuildSys'13, pp. 1–2. Association for Computing Machinery, New York (2013)

Lin, K.K., Lupin, S., Vagapov, Y.: Analysis of lift control system strategies under uneven flow of passengers. In: Camarinha-Matos, L.M., Falcão, A.J., Vafaei, N., Najdi, S. (eds.) Technological Innovation for Cyber-Physical Systems, pp. 217–225. Springer, Cham (2016)

Randall, F.E., Damon, A., Benton, R.S., Patt, D.I.: Human body size in military aircraft and personal equipment (1946)

Reinsalu, U., Robal, T.: A touch-free service button for smart elevator operation with dynamic QR-code generation. In: 2023 12th Mediterranean Conference on Embedded Computing (MECO), pp. 1–4 (2023). https://doi.org/10.1109/MECO58584.2023.10155102

Reinsalu, U., Robal, T., Leier, M.: Floor selection proposal for automated travel with smart elevator. In: Robal, T., Haav, H.M., Penjam, J., Matulevičius, R. (eds.) Databases and Information Systems, pp. 38–51. Springer, Cham (2020)

Robal, T., Basov, K., Reinsalu, U., Leier, M.: A study into elevator passenger in-cabin behaviour on a smart-elevator platform. Baltic J. Mod. Comput. **10**(4), 665–688 (2022). https://doi.org/10.22364/bjmc.2022.10.4.05

Robal, T., Reinsalu, U., Leier, M.: Towards personalized elevator travel with smart elevator system. Baltic J. Mod. Comput. **8**(4), 675–697 (2020). https://doi.org/10.22364/bjmc.2020.8.4.12

Robal, T., Zhao, Y., Lofi, C., Hauff, C.: Webcam-based attention tracking in online learning: a feasibility study. In: 23rd International Conference on Intelligent User Interfaces, IUI '18, pp. 189–197. ACM, New York (2018)

Ronchi, E., Nilsson, D.: Fire evacuation in high-rise buildings: a review of human behaviour and modelling research. Fire Sci. Rev. **2**(1), 7 (2013)

Ross, S., Brownholtz, E., Armes, R.: Voice user interface principles for a conversational agent. In: Proceedings of the 9th International Conference on Intelligent User Interfaces, IUI '04, pp. 364–365. Association for Computing Machinery, New York (2004)

Russell, S., Norvig, P.: Artificial Intelligence: A Modern Approach, 3rd edn. Prentice Hall Press, USA (2009)

Silva, E.M., Boaventura, M., Boaventura, I.A.G., Contreras, R.C.: Face recognition using local mapped pattern and genetic algorithms. In: Proceedings of the International Conference on Pattern Recognition and Artificial Intelligence, PRAI 2018, pp. 11–17. Association for Computing Machinery, New York (2018)

Sorsa, J., Kuusinen, J.M., Siikonen, M.L.: Passenger batch arrivals at elevator lobbies. Elevator World **61**(1), 108–120 (2013)

Sorsa, J., Siikonen, M.L., Kuusinen, J.M., Hakonen, H.: A field study and analysis of passengers arriving at lift lobbies in social groups in multi-storey office, hotel and residential buildings. Build. Services Eng. Res. Technol. **42**(2), 197–210 (2021)

Stark, L.: Facial recognition is the plutonium of AI. XRDS **25**(3), 50–55 (2019)

Susi, T., Sorsa, J., Siikonen, M.L.: Passenger behaviour in elevator simulation. In: IAEE Elevator Technology 14 (2004). https://global.ctbuh.org/resources/papers/download/1052-passenger-behaviour-in-elevator-simulation.pdf

Turunen, M., Kuoppala, H., Kangas, S., Hella, J., Miettinen, T., Heimonen, T., Keskinen, T., Hakulinen, J., Raisamo, R.: Mobile interaction with elevators: Improving people flow in complex buildings. In: Proceedings of Intl Conference on Making Sense of Converging Media, AcademicMindTrek '13, pp. 43–50. ACM, New York (2013)

Wang, F., Tang, J., Zong, Q.: Energy-consumption-related robust optimization scheduling strategy for elevator group control system. In: 2011 IEEE 5th Intl Conference on Cybernetics and Intelligent Systems (CIS), pp. 30–35 (2011)

Zhao, W., Chellappa, R., Phillips, P.J., Rosenfeld, A.: Face recognition: a literature survey. ACM Comput. Surv. **35**(4), 399–458 (2003)

Zhuge, H.: Cyber-physical society–the science and engineering for future society. Future Gener. Comput. Syst. **32**, 180–186 (2014)

Chapter 11
Wireless Crowd Detection for Smart Overtourism Mitigation

Tomás Mestre dos Santos, Rui Neto Marinheiro, and Fernando Brito e Abreu

Abstract Overtourism occurs when the number of tourists exceeds the carrying capacity of a destination, leading to negative impacts on the environment, culture, and quality of life for residents. By monitoring overtourism, destination managers can identify areas of concern and implement measures to mitigate the negative impacts of tourism while promoting smarter tourism practices. This can help ensure that tourism benefits both visitors and residents while preserving the natural and cultural resources that make these destinations so appealing.

This chapter describes a low-cost approach to monitoring overtourism based on mobile devices' wireless activity. A flexible architecture was designed for a smart tourism toolkit to be used by small and medium-sized enterprises (SMEs) in crowding management solutions, to build better tourism services, improve efficiency and sustainability, and reduce the overwhelming feeling of pressure in critical hotspots.

The crowding sensors count the number of surrounding mobile devices, by detecting trace elements of wireless technologies, mitigating the effect of MAC address randomization. They run detection programs for several technologies, and fingerprinting analysis results are only stored locally in an anonymized database, without infringing privacy rights. After that edge computing, sensors communicate the crowding information to a cloud server, by using a variety of uplink techniques to mitigate local connectivity limitations, something that has been often disregarded in alternative approaches.

Field validation of sensors has been performed on Iscte's campus. Preliminary results show that these sensors can be deployed in multiple scenarios and provide a diversity of spatiotemporal crowding data that can scaffold tourism overcrowding management strategies.

Keywords Overtourism · Smart tourism toolkit · Crowding sensor · Edge computing · Wi-Fi detection · Fingerprinting · MAC address randomization

T. Mestre dos Santos (✉) · R. Neto Marinheiro · F. Brito e Abreu
Instituto Universitário de Lisboa (ISCTE-IUL), Lisboa, Portugal
e-mail: tmmss1@iscte-iul.pt; rui.marinheiro@iscte-iul.pt; fba@iscte-iul.pt

E. Kornyshova et al. (eds.), *Smart Life and Smart Life Engineering*,
https://doi.org/10.1007/978-3-031-75887-4_11

11.1 Introduction

The tourism sector has been growing steadily. If the pre-pandemic trend is achieved from 2023 onward, it will reach 3 billion arrivals by 2027, based on the World Bank development indicators (see Fig. 11.1).

As a consequence, the impact of tourist activities in popular destinations has risen significantly over the years, often fostered by the proliferation of cheaper local accommodation (Guttentag 2015). That increase led to exceed of carrying capacity in those destinations, a phenomenon called *tourism overcrowding*, or simply *overtourism*. The latter degrades visitors' quality of experience, reducing their feeling of safety, making it difficult to move around, enjoy the attractions, and use basic services, such as transportation and restoration, due to long wait times, while reducing the authenticity from the perspective of tourists (Tokarchuk et al. 2022). Overtourism also deteriorates the lives of local residents, due to an increase in urban noise, less effective urban cleaning, higher prices for basic goods and services (as businesses seek to capitalize on the increased demand), displacement caused by local accommodation, and cultural clashes when visitors fail to respect local customs, traditions, and privacy, sometimes leading to the former expressing negatively against the latter (Biendicho et al. 202). Last, but not least, the environmental sustainability, structures, and cultural heritage of overcrowded destinations are also jeopardized, leading to a loss of authenticity (Seraphin et al. 2018). Mitigating overtourism benefits all stakeholders:

- Local residents reduce their stress from over-occupation of personal space and privacy and improve their attitude toward tourists and tourism professionals.
- Tourism operators speed up service delivery and quality of service.

Fig. 11.1 Worldwide evolution of tourism arrivals, based on the World Bank's data

- Tourists increase their visit satisfaction, with fewer delays, increased safety, and cleanliness.
- Local authorities improve services by making just-in-time decisions and planning more effectively urban cleaning and public safety routines, as well as reducing operating costs.
- Heritage managers can prevent heritage degradation more effectively, thus retaining the authenticity of destinations.
- Local businesses increase their share of tourism income.

Overtourism mitigation actions, such as promoting the visitation to less occupied but equally attractive areas, can be applied in recreational, cultural, or religious spots, both in indoor scenarios like palaces, museums, monasteries, or cathedrals and in outdoor ones such as public parks, camping parks, concerts, fireworks, or video mapping shows.

Besides assuring a better visiting experience, those actions are also necessary for security reasons (e.g., to prevent works exhibited in a museum from deteriorating or even being vandalized by exceeding room capacity), health reasons (e.g., preventing infection in pandemic scenarios by not exceeding the maximum people density specified by health authorities), or even for resource management (e.g., to reduce the intervention of security and cleaning teams).

To implement overtourism mitigation actions, crowding information should be made available. Several approaches can be used for crowd detection, such as image capturing, sound capturing, social networks, mobile operator's data, and wireless spectrum analysis (Dias da Silva et al. 2019). The latter can be performed using passive or active sniffing methods, characterized by exploring protocol characteristics and small information breaches, such as on Wi-Fi or Bluetooth protocols, extensively used in mobile devices. Figure 11.2 provides a comparison of those approaches for crowd counting in terms of range, precision, time delay of analysis, and implementation costs.

The best option regarding cost, precision, and the near-real-time availability of data required for managing tourism crowding effectively, while complying with privacy rights, is the one based on sensing wireless communication traces, since the vast majority of tourists carry a mobile phone (Dias da Silva et al. 2019; Singh et al. 2020). Earlier approaches relied on counting the number of unique MAC (Media Access Control) addresses in messages emitted by mobile devices. However, due to user privacy concerns, most mobile devices nowadays use MAC address randomization, i.e., the same device exposes different MAC addresses over time, making it more challenging to accurately count the number of devices, thus leading to inaccurate crowd counting.

This chapter describes a low-cost approach to monitoring overtourism. It consists of a crowding sensor that performs real-time detection of trace elements generated by mobile devices from different wireless technologies, namely, Wi-Fi and Bluetooth, while addressing the MAC address randomization issue when determining the number of mobile devices in the sensors' vicinity, as an improvement over our previous work Dias da Silva et al. (2019). Another improvement refers to

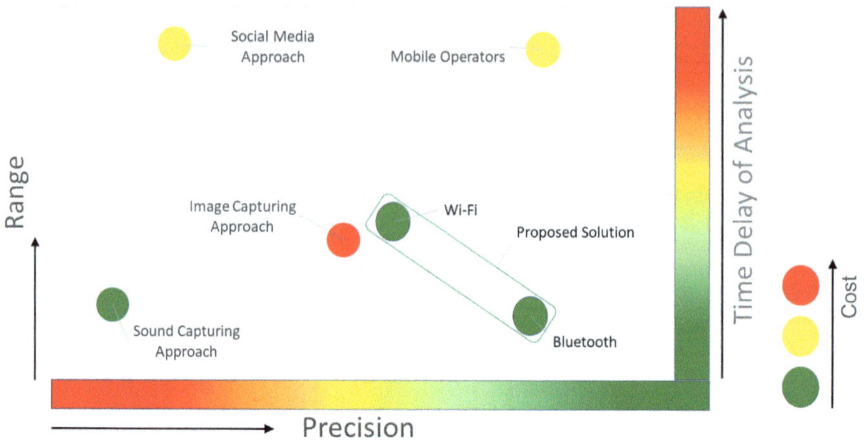

Fig. 11.2 Different approaches for crowd counting in terms of range, precision, time delay of analysis, and implementation costs (Adapted from Dias da Silva et al. 2019)

the provision of multiple communication methods for uploading the crowding information to a cloud server, by using either Wi-Fi or LoRaWAN protocols, thus mitigating network limitations on the installation location, something that has been disregarded on other approaches.

Our sensor is the basis of a Smart Tourism Toolkit (STToolkit) being built in the scope of the RESETTING[1] project, funded by the European COSME Programme., to facilitate the transition toward a more sustainable operation of tourism SMEs and improved quality of the tourism experience. The STToolkit will guide how to build and set up our sensors, either in indoor or outdoor appliances, by including support materials such as an installation manual, video tutorials, setup images, and cost calculators.

Furthermore, this research considers a correlation between the number of mobile devices and the real number of people present in an area. This assumption is especially relevant in touristic scenarios, where our sensors are aimed to be deployed since tourists usually carry their mobile phones to take pictures and record videos during their visits. Therefore, it is assumed that the number of mobile devices in a given area is directly correlated with the number of people in the same area. This is corroborated by De Meersman et al. (2016), where it is shown that mobile phone data is a valuable data source for statistical counting of people.

This chapter is organized as follows: Sect. 11.2 identifies and discusses related work; Sect. 11.3 presents the proposed architecture of a typical installation using our sensors; then, in Sect. 11.4, we describe our proposed Wi-Fi detection algorithm, which tackles the MAC address randomization issue; on Sect. 11.5, we describe

[1] RESETTING is an acronym for "Relaunching European smart and SustainablE Tourism models Through digitalization and INnovative technoloGies".

the technologies used in our solution; then, on Sect. 11.6, we present the setup and discuss the results obtained from a field validation; finally, on Sect. 11.7, we draw some conclusions and outline future work.

11.2 Related Work

Crowd counting by detecting trace elements from mobile devices' wireless activity can be performed either by the use of passive or active sniffing methods. However, only passive methods that monitor wireless traffic in a non-intrusive manner are acceptable, because active methods can cause network and user disruptions, as well as legal infringements. Many passive methods employ probe request capturing, which are messages periodically sent by devices to announce their presence to surrounding APs (Access Points), allowing a fast connection upon reaching a known network. These messages are sent in bursts and are unencrypted, meaning that they can be simply captured using passive sniffing techniques, and contain the device's MAC address. The probe request frame structure is presented in Fig. 11.3.

Earlier detection approaches relied on the device's real MAC address that was sent in the SA (Source Address) of these frames. In this case, the number of devices was simply equal to the number of different MAC addresses. However, when devices send their real MAC address, they may be easily tracked. To solve this privacy vulnerability, since 2014, manufacturers started to implement MAC address randomization on their devices. It consists of assigning to probe requests randomly generated virtual MAC addresses changing over time. Thus, the real MAC address remains unknown, protecting the user's identity and making it much more difficult to track. Unfortunately, this has led to inaccurate crowd counting and has hampered many solutions adopted until then. Moreover, the MAC address randomization process is dependent on the manufacturer and the operating system of the device, which also makes it a much more complex procedure to circumvent.

The difference between a real MAC address (globally unique) and a virtual MAC address (locally administered) is in the 7th bit of the first byte of the MAC address, as shown in Fig. 11.4. Therefore, we can simply distinguish these two types of MAC addresses by only checking this bit.

The implementation of the MAC address randomization added a level of complexity to uniquely identify devices. Therefore, the research has advanced toward the exploration of other properties and fields of the probe request frames,

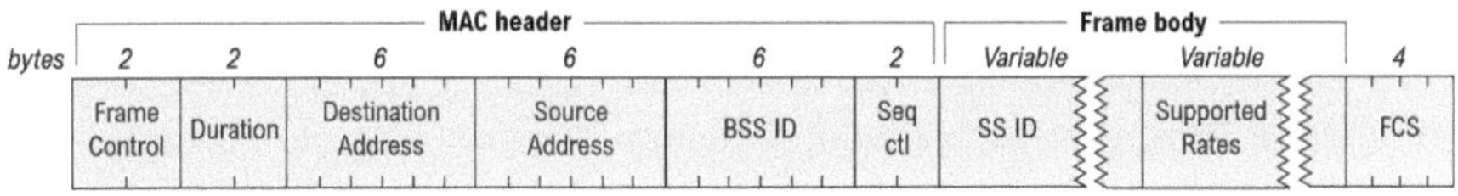

Fig. 11.3 Probe request frame (based on Institute of Electrical and Electronics Engineers)

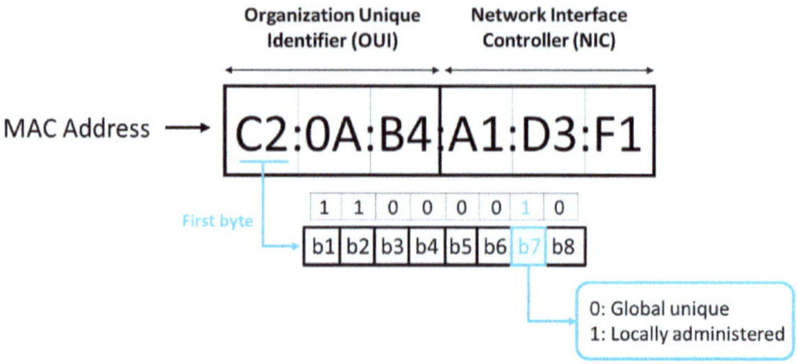

Fig. 11.4 Difference between a real and a virtual MAC address

since the MAC address is no longer a reliable option just by itself for accurate crowd counting. In spite of this, probe request frames still disclose other weaknesses that can be exploited for counting the number of devices. Several strategies have been adopted to mitigate the impact of randomization, as follows:

- **SSIDs[2] Comparison:** based on comparing the known networks (in terms of SSIDs) to a device, an information that is contained in the probe requests (Berenguer et al. 2022).
- **Fingerprinting:** based on generating a unique identifier (fingerprint) from other fields in probe request frames. The contents to generate this fingerprint are usually obtained from IEs (Information Elements) conveyed in the frame body of probe requests (Bravenec et al. 2022; Vega-Barbas et al. 2021).
- **Fingerprinting + Clustering:** this strategy relies not only on fingerprinting from IEs but also on other properties from these messages, such as the SEQ (SEQuence number), burst size, or IFTA (Inter-Frame Time Arrival) from probe request frames. A clustering algorithm considering these properties simultaneously can be applied, where each cluster will represent a unique device (Cai et al. 2021; Covaci 2022; He et al. 2022; Torres-Sospedra et al. 2023; Uras et al. 2020, 2022).

In Berenguer et al. (2022), the PNL (Preferred Network List), which contains the SSIDs from the known networks of a device sent in probe requests, is used for counting the number of devices in a location and distinguishing residents from visitors in the city of Alcoi in Spain. The authors claim an accuracy of 83% in detection, with some reported overestimations and incongruencies.

Most approaches rely, however, on applying fingerprinting techniques to uniquely identify mobile devices. The work reported in Vega-Barbas et al. (2021) used a network of sensors to estimate the number of persons in a given location based on IEs fingerprinting. The system was tested in public events with a considerable density of people, with a claimed accuracy close to 95%. Another

[2] SSID (Service Set IDentifier) is a sequence of characters that uniquely names a Wi-Fi network.

work described in Bravenec et al. (2022) used the same approach, considering not only the IEs but also the PNL and the recurrence of the same randomized MAC address to generate device fingerprints at a conference in Lloret de Mar, Spain, but precision is not reported.

Some other studies not only considered IEs for fingerprinting but also clustered this information along with other properties or patterns from probe requests. For this purpose, many studies used clustering algorithms that consider a combination of different features from probe requests. In Cai et al. (2021), not only probe requests but also beacons and data packets were used to count the number of devices in given locations. This method was tested with a dataset purposefully generated for the scope of this work, reaching an accuracy of 75%; however, it was not tested in a real crowded scenario. The work reported in He et al. (2022) considered IEs, SEQ, and the RSSI (Received Signal Strength Indicator) from probe requests with a neural network for estimating crowding levels in a shopping mall in Hong Kong, reaching an accuracy of slightly over 80%.

The studies reported in Uras et al. (2020, 2022) clustered fingerprinting from IEs, the incremental speed of the SEQ, the burst frequency, and the IFTA. The authors first tested the algorithm at the University of Cagliari's Campus (Uras et al. 2020), achieving an accuracy of about 91%. A follow-up to this work Uras et al. (2022) tested the algorithm first in a controlled environment, reaching an accuracy of 97%, and further inside buses in Italy for an Automatic Passenger Counting system, with a precision of 75%. Another work reported in Covaci (2022) used the same approach considering the IEs for fingerprinting and also used a clustering algorithm for combining the generated fingerprints with burst sizes and the IFTA in the canteen of the University of Twente, with an accuracy of 90%. The work described in Torres-Sospedra et al. (2023) combined fingerprints from RSSI values of Wi-Fi APs and BLE (Bluetooth Low Energy) beacons with several clustering algorithms variants for indoor positioning, achieving a precision of around 93%.

Table 11.1 summarizes the previous approaches for crowd counting, clarifying the adopted strategies to mitigate MAC address randomization and the obtained precision.

11.3 Proposed System Architecture

The proposed system architecture of the STToolkit is presented in Fig. 11.5, where sensors count the number of devices in their vicinity and periodically report the crowding information to a cloud server. The latter also has other components for making downlink communication transparent and providing uplink services for rendering the crowding information and creation of notification policies.

Table 11.1 Approaches for crowd counting, tackling MAC address randomization

Authors	Packet-type capturing	Strategies for MAC address randomization	Real scenario appliance	Precision
Berenguer et al. 2022	Probe Requests	SSIDs Comparison	Alcoi (Spain)	83%
Vega-Barbas et al. 2021	Probe Requests	Fingerprinting	Public events	90%
Bravenec et al. 2022	Probe Requests	Fingerprinting	Conference at Lloret del Mar (Spain)	Not available
Cai et al. 2021	Beacons Data packets Probe Requests	Fingerprinting + Clustering	Not available	75% (with simulated data)
He et al. 2022	Probe Requests	Fingerprinting + Clustering	Shopping mall in Hong Kong	80%
Uras et al. 2020	Probe Requests	Fingerprinting + Clustering	Campus of the Univ. of Cagliari	91%
Uras et al. 2022	Probe Requests	Fingerprinting + Clustering	Buses in Italy	75%
Covaci 2022	Probe Requests	Fingerprinting + Clustering	University of Twente campus	90%
Torres-Sospedra et al. 2023	Beacons	Fingerprinting + Clustering	Not available	93%

11.3.1 Crowding Data Collection

Each crowding sensor includes a detector responsible for passively capturing mobile devices' trace elements for each wireless technology (Wi-Fi and Bluetooth) in the sensor vicinity, an anonymized local database, where all gathered information is stored, and a detection engine, responsible for counting the number of devices by analyzing the information contained in the local database and reporting the crowding information to the cloud server. Each sensor can perform only Wi-Fi or Bluetooth detection, or both simultaneously, and can quickly switch between the technologies to be used for detection.

In this edge computing approach, data collection and crowding level measurement generation are performed locally in each sensor, so that only the number of devices detected is sent to the cloud server. So, the information to be passed is minimal, not requiring a high sampling rate for data transmission, and also protecting nodes from outside threats, since the communication line prevents the majority of attack types. Furthermore, limiting data exchange not only reduces communication costs, but also eases protection complexity for the node, and makes it easier to guarantee user privacy. Also regarding user privacy, all gathered data is anonymized before being stored in the local database.

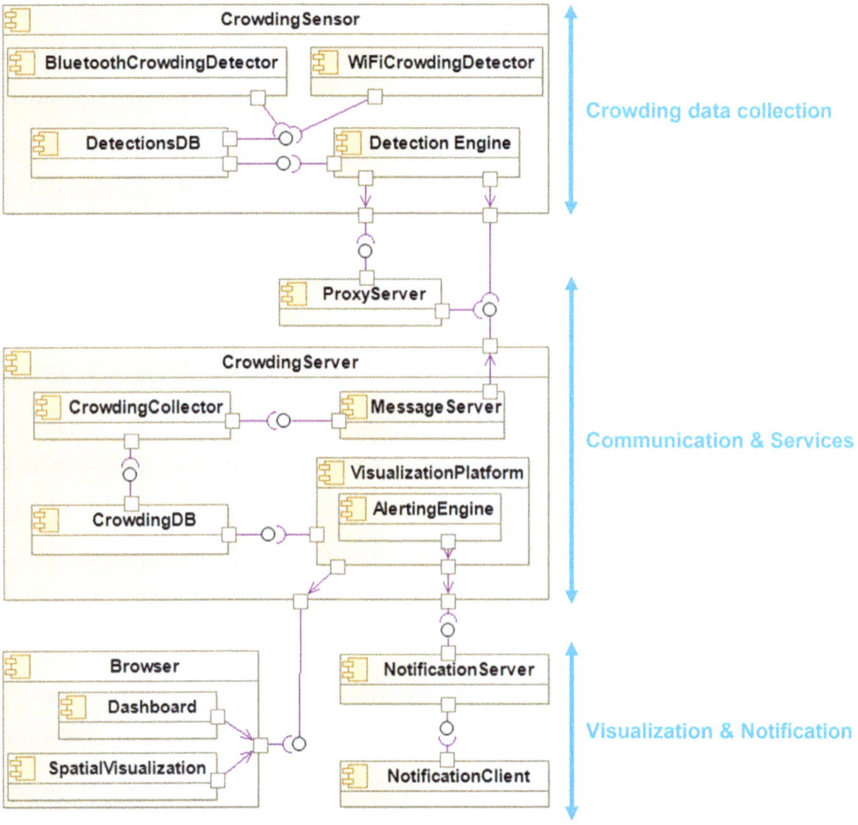

Fig. 11.5 Component diagram of the crowding detection STToolkit

11.3.2 Communication and Services

To better address installation location requirements and connectivity limitations, a flexible deployment regarding uplink technologies has been considered. Data can be uploaded to the cloud server by using a variety of communication protocols, such as Wi-Fi or LoRaWAN (Long Range Wide Area Network).

If Wi-Fi is available on-site, data can be uploaded directly to the *Message Server* via the MQTT (Message Queuing Telemetry Transport) protocol, a lightweight method of carrying out messaging, using a publish/subscribe model, widely used for IoT (Internet of Things) applications. This option can be applied straightforwardly in indoor tourism scenarios, for instance, in a museum, which generally provides a Wi-Fi network to visitors.

In outdoor scenarios, such as public parks or city squares, where overtourism situations can also arise, Wi-Fi coverage may not be available. Since sensors must upload crowding information, other approaches rely on mobile operators' communication, which may be an expensive option, usually with monthly fees depending on the number of sensors used, each using a SIM card.

To mitigate this problem, we offer the option for uploading data via LoRaWAN, a standard of the International Telecommunication Union that provides a low-cost and scalable alternative that is feasible for our application, since sensors only communicate a small amount of data, i.e., the number of detected devices. For this, sensors must be equipped with a LoRa board and corresponding antenna to communicate the crowding information to a LoRaWAN gateway that, in turn, will route the information to the cloud server via the MQTT protocol. Regarding coverage, there are a few LoRa networks, designed for IoT appliances, that can be used for uploading data, like The Things Network open collaborative network or the, also crowdsourced, Helium network, a decentralized wireless infrastructure supported by blockchain. The Helium network adopted for this solution is the fastest growing IoT network with LoRaWAN compatibility that provides a large coverage in many countries in Europe, such as those involved in the RESETTING project. Figure 11.6 shows the Helium network coverage provided by Hotspotty in cities where our STToolkit may be deployed in the context of the RESETTING project, such as Lisbon, Barcelona, Tirana, and Heraklion, the capital of the Greek island of Crete.

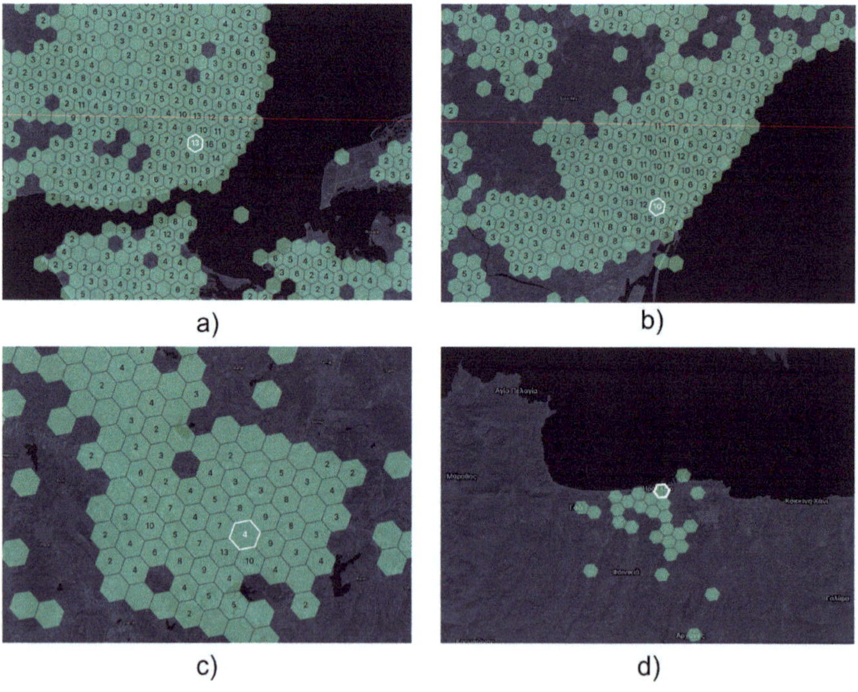

Fig. 11.6 Helium network coverage in (**a**) Lisbon, (**b**) Barcelona, (**c**) Tirana, and (**d**) Heraklion (Compiled by the authors from Hotspotty 2023)

Regarding the Helium network, an SME can choose between two alternatives for uploading crowding information: using Helium with a third-party LoRaWAN service provider, such as Helium-IoT, or using Helium with a private LoRaWAN server.

As shown in Fig. 11.5, the *Message Server* is the only entrance point for all messages in the cloud server, independently of the communication protocol used for uploading the crowding information. This provides transparency since all messages are received in the cloud server via the MQTT protocol independently of the communication technology adopted for uploading the crowding information.

Furthermore, in areas with low or no Wi-Fi or Helium network coverage, it is also possible to acquire equipment for that purpose, such as a Wi-Fi mesh system, which will allow expanding the Wi-Fi network coverage, or a Helium hotspot, for grating Helium network coverage for uploading data via the LoRaWAN protocol.

11.3.3 Visualization and Notifications

The cloud server also has several components to make downlink communication transparent and provide several uplink services that can be used by Smart Tourism Tools to understand the crowding levels in areas where each sensor is placed, with a clear and simple perspective. Possible crowding services are:

- Rendering of temporal information, as seen in Fig. 11.10
- Rendering of geographic information, as seen in Fig. 11.11
- Notification policies, e.g., when crowding threshold levels are reached
- Raw data for custom-made integrations, e.g., spatial visualization using a BIM (Building Information Model), as seen in Fig. 11.12

11.4 Proposed Wi-Fi Detection Algorithm

MAC address randomization performed by mobile device manufacturers, due to user privacy concerns, has made the identification of a mobile device a much more difficult task and, consequently, more difficult to accurately perform device counting. Therefore, an algorithm was developed for the detection of mobile devices through Wi-Fi, tackling the MAC address randomization issue using a fingerprinting technique, presented in Fig. 11.7. The explanation of each step of the proposed algorithm is presented below. A similar algorithm is also envisaged for Bluetooth detection since the randomization problem is also pertinent to this technology.

The *WiFiCrowdingDetector*, seen in Fig. 11.5, is responsible for processing each Wi-Fi packet captured by the sensor. The first operation performed is a packet-type identification (data packets, probe requests, or other type). Data packets will be used for counting the number of devices connected to an AP and probe requests for

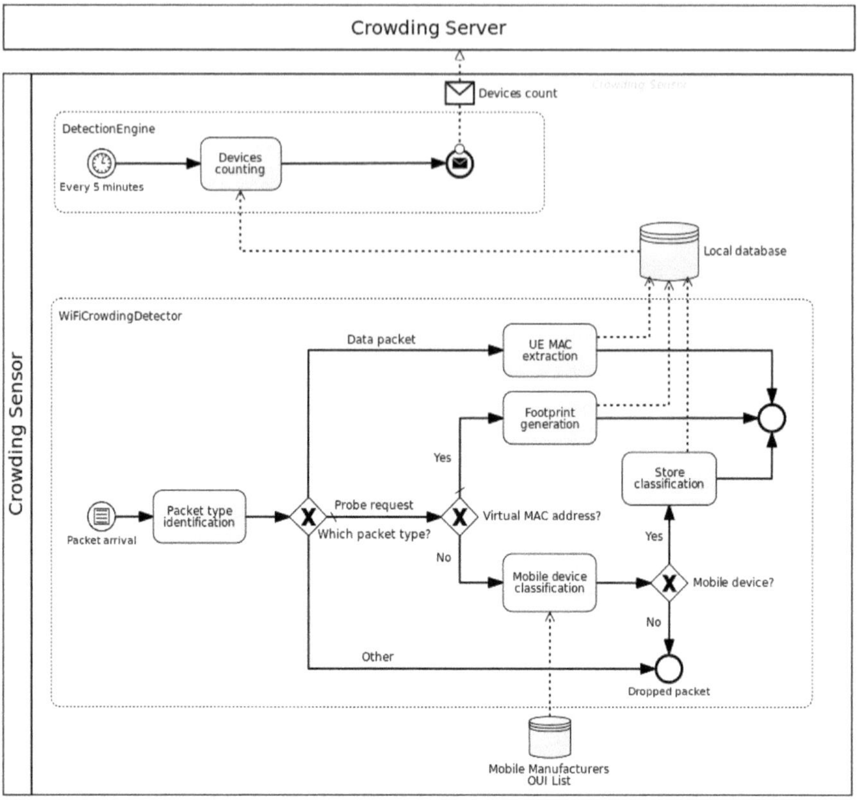

Fig. 11.7 Proposed Wi-Fi detection algorithm

counting the number of devices not connected to any AP. The packet type can be obtained by checking the Frame Control field, presented in Fig. 11.3. Packets that are not either data packets or probe requests will be immediately dropped since they are not relevant for device counting.

Regarding data packets, only the UE (User Equipment) part of the MAC address needs to be accounted for. First, it is necessary to locate it in the frame, which is performed by checking the DS (Device Status) information in the frame header, since the UE MAC address position may vary according to the direction of the frame. These MAC addresses can be directly counted as single devices because when a device is connected to an AP, the MAC address is kept constant throughout the connection and, therefore, will not change randomly. For this reason, after the UE MAC address extraction, it is directly stored in the sensor's anonymized local database.

Regarding probe requests, the first operation performed is aimed at distinguishing its Source Address between a real and a virtual MAC address. This is performed by checking the 7th less significant bit of the 1st octet of the MAC address, as already

Table 11.2 Probe request's information elements used to create device fingerprint

Information element	IE ID	IE length	Description
Supported rates	1	<8	Data transfer rates supported by the device
Extended supported rates	50	<256	Other bit rates supported by the device
DS parameter set	3	1	Device's channel setting when sending a probe request
HT capabilities	45	26	Compatibility with the 802.11n standard
VHT capabilities	191	12	Compatibility with the 802.11ac standard
Extended capabilities	127	<256	Other device capabilities
RM-enabled capabilities	70	5	Information for measuring radio resources
Interworking	107	<9	Interworking service capabilities of the client
Vendor specific	221	<256	Vendor-specific information (e.g., device manufacturer)

shown in Fig. 11.4. To follow the trace of a real MAC address, a device classification is applied, aimed at only counting MAC addresses that belong to mobile devices. This is done by checking the address's OUI (Organizational Unique Identifier):[3] if the OUI matches one of the known mobile manufacturers, obtained from the Wireshark manufacturer database, the MAC address should be considered as a mobile device, and it must be counted and stored in the local database; otherwise, the MAC address is not considered as a mobile device and is discarded.

To follow the trace of a virtual MAC address, a fingerprinting technique must be performed to uniquely identify devices that use MAC address randomization. For this, the IEs contained in the frame body of the probe request are analyzed. For each IE, the entirety of its information is considered, including the IE ID, Length, and Value bytes. For those IEs with substantially varying values across probes emitted from the same device (e.g., DS Parameter Set), only the bytes of IE ID and Length are analyzed. Table 11.2 shows the IEs used for the fingerprinting technique. After analyzing all IEs, a hash function is applied to all its contents. As a result, a 64-bit footprint is generated for each probe request and stored in the local anonymized database. Then, all the devices that are trying to connect to a Wi-Fi network, by sending probe requests to discover available networks in proximity with a virtual MAC address, are uniquely identified by the footprint. So, each footprint should be counted as one mobile device using MAC Address randomization that is trying to connect to a Wi-Fi network. To avoid counting the same device twice, if the

[3] OUI is a part of the MAC address identifying the network adapter vendor.

same MAC address is captured in both data packets and probe requests, it is only accounted for once.

Then, the *Detection Engine* will periodically count the number of devices detected within a sliding window of X minutes, i.e., the number of devices detected in the last X minutes, and upload that information to the cloud server. Both the sliding window period and data sampling rate can be independently and easily configured by the user. Since we intend to provide real-time or near-real-time data availability, the data sampling rate of our sensors needs to comply with this requirement. So, we have chosen a 5-minute period for the data sampling rate, as it is a sufficient time period for providing near-real-time data availability. Also, the same 5-minute period was chosen for the sliding window, so that each crowding measurement could comprise all detected devices within each sliding window.

The number of devices detected is the sum of (i) the number of devices connected to an AP, obtained from the UE MAC addresses captured in data packets, plus (ii) the number of different devices not connected to any AP, obtained from the MAC addresses from probe requests with real MAC addresses, plus (iii) the number of different footprints from probe requests with virtual MAC addresses.

11.5 Adopted Technologies

The developed STToolkit uses a variety of open-source software technologies, installed in off-the-shelf hardware available at affordable costs. Figure 11.8 presents the UML deployment diagram proposed for the STToolkit concerning all technologies adopted in our solution.

For the operating system of our sensors, we have opted for a Kali Linux distribution, which comes with a large number of preinstalled network tools that can be easily used for detecting devices in different technologies. For the local database, a SQLite database was chosen for storing all gathered data, which requires low memory usage, while meeting all other requirements. For data anonymization, the sensors use the t1ha library that provides several terraced and fast hash functions. In particular, we have opted for the t1ha0 hash function, as it is one of the fastest available at the library.

To perform Wi-Fi detection, the required hardware is a Wi-Fi card that supports monitor mode, which allows the board to capture all network traffic in its proximity. We have chosen the Alfa Network AWU036AC board for our sensor, which provides high performance at a low cost, having two antennas for dual-band detection (2.4 GHz and 5 GHz) without interfering with Bluetooth devices. As for the sniffing software, we have chosen the Aircrack-ng tool, an open-source software with several different applications for detecting devices. In particular, we use *airmon-ng* for enabling the monitor mode in the Wi-Fi board, and *airodump-ng* for capturing raw Wi-Fi frames. For Bluetooth detection, we have selected the Ubertooth-One board and corresponding BlueZ package that contains tools and frameworks for Bluetooth usage in Linux.

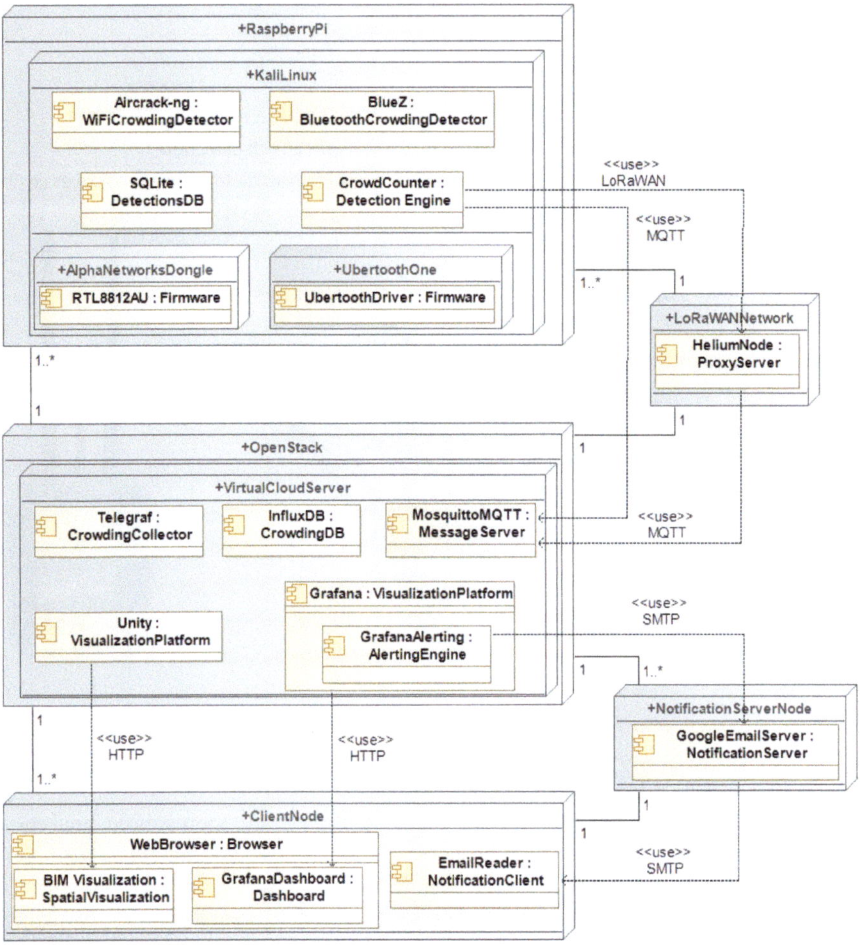

Fig. 11.8 Deployment diagram for the crowding detection STToolkit

For receiving all messages, our cloud server uses the Mosquitto MQTT, a lightweight message broker that implements the MQTT protocol.

For the data ingestion of all measurements sent by sensors, a database is necessary. This database has to be lightweight, capable of querying data rapidly from timestamps, and also capable of providing support for data visualization platforms to observe the results in real-time. That is why we chose InfluxDB, a time-series database focused on IoT applications, for our *CrowdingDB* component. For the *CrowdingCollector*, responsible for pushing all messages received in the *Message Server* via MQTT protocol to the *CrowdingDB* in the appropriate format, we chose Telegraf, an open-source plugin-driven server agent for collecting and reporting metrics from devices.

Table 11.3 Prototype hardware components and respective functions

Component	Function
Raspberry Pi 3/4	Coordinate and process
Alfa Network AWUS036AC	Wi-Fi detection
Ubertooth-One	Bluetooth detection
Raspberry Pi IoT LoRa pHAT	Upload via LoRaWAN (if necessary)

a) b)

Fig. 11.9 Sensor cases: (**a**) large version with no exposed antennas; (**b**) small version with exposed antennas

Finally, for data visualization, we chose Grafana, an open-source analytics and monitoring tool compatible with several databases, including *InfluxDB*. This framework can be used for creating custom dashboards with graphs and panels for viewing, with different spatiotemporal levels of granularity, the crowding information. Additionally, *Grafana* can be used for creating notification policies, allowing users to receive alerts according to the crowding levels via a diversity of contact points.

A prototype was developed whose hardware components and respective functions are illustrated in Table 11.3. The prototype uses custom-designed cases adapted to deployment locations, either with exposed antennas or not, as shown in Fig. 11.9. These prototype versions have been deployed at several locations at our university campus to test the operation and performance of the STToolkit, which is further described in the next section.

Furthermore, as our sensor's processing unit is a single computer board, namely, a Raspberry Pi, there are multiple options for powering our sensor, either directly from a battery or even via USB ports or Power over Ethernet (PoE), even though the most straightforward and convenient alternative should be to directly connect it to a mains power supply through a transformer.

11.6 Field Validation and Discussion

The prototype described in the preceding section was designed and implemented to withstand all the scenarios where the sensors may be deployed.

To test and validate the STToolkit architecture, sensors have been placed at several spots across Iscte's campus, and crowding information has been collected since September 2022.

The sensors were deployed both indoors and outdoors, in places with different crowding patterns, such as areas with a large pedestrian flow, internal and external passages between buildings, and places for prolonged stays, such as a large study hall and the university library.

This field experiment has been conducted with the sole purpose of assessing the perception of the crowding phenomena in the university campus, rather than the accuracy regarding the real number of people at each location. It focused on perceiving crowding patterns and tendencies, such as time breaks between classes, lunch periods, and highly populated events. The aim was to assess how sensors could perceive relative variations throughout the days across the several locations of the campus and how quickly the sensors were able to detect them.

The accuracy was addressed in other contexts in a more controlled environment (Santos 2023), where the detections from sensors were compared with the real number of people, obtained through direct observation during a public event, to assess the effectiveness of the solution.

The crowding data has been used for visualization, using a variety of temporal dashboards, and maps that highlight the geographic distribution of crowding at each location where the sensors have been deployed. Data has also been used for spatial visualization in the form of heatmaps and also, for a more realistic view, using avatars on top of Iscte's BIM (Building Information Model).

Dashboards allow users to select time ranges for crowding data temporal visualization, to perceive people's concentration and flows during specified periods, and to identify highly populated events. Figure 11.10 shows a comparison of crowding levels during a normal day of classes at Iscte's campus, at the selected spots where sensors have been deployed.

In addition to the temporal rendering of the information, data has also been used for spatial visualization in the form of heatmaps, to grant users a better perception of people distribution at several locations where the sensors are deployed. This can be seen in Fig. 11.11, where it is possible to perceive the crowding hotspots from our sensors deployed at Iscte's campus at a given time.

Moreover, raw crowding information can also be easily used by third-party integrations. To validate this, we built a walking avatar animation upon Iscte's BIM, to achieve a more realistic perception of space occupancy, as shown in Fig. 11.12, for one of the campus buildings. There, the number of detected devices, obtained in real time from sensors, determines the number of ingress and egress avatars in their areas of detection. This last experience was performed during the International

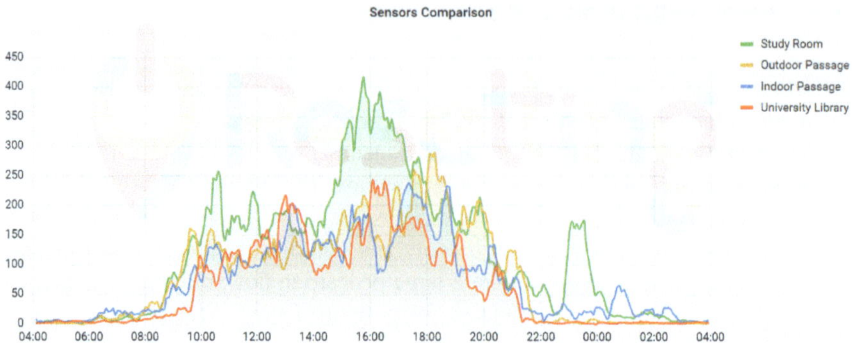

Fig. 11.10 Comparing crowding at Iscte's campus

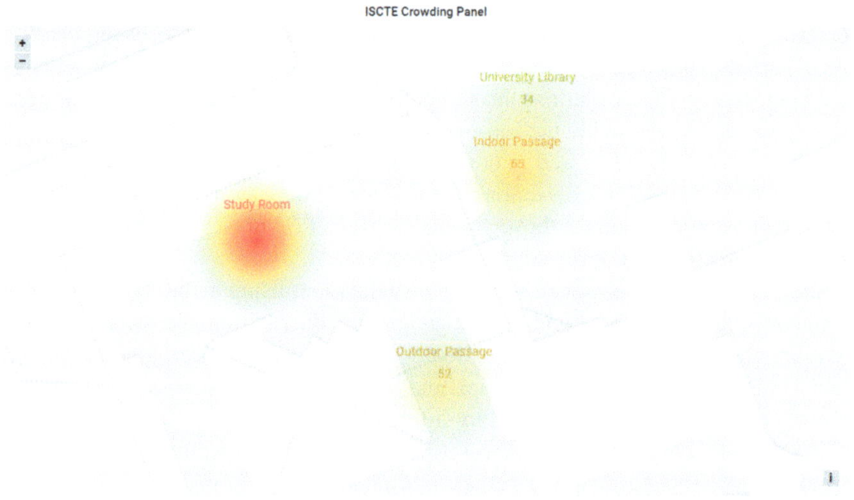

Fig. 11.11 Crowding hotspots at Iscte's campus

Posters & Demos Workshop on Smart Tourism held by the RESETTING project at Iscte in January 2023.

Furthermore, it is also possible to create notification policies, where alerts can be triggered if predetermined crowding thresholds are exceeded, by using several contact points such as email, Telegram, Google Chat, Microsoft Teams, Slack, or PaperDuty, enabling users to make just-in-time decisions facing overtourism situations. These alerts can be easily configurable by using the *Grafana* tool, also used for spatiotemporal visualization of crowding information.

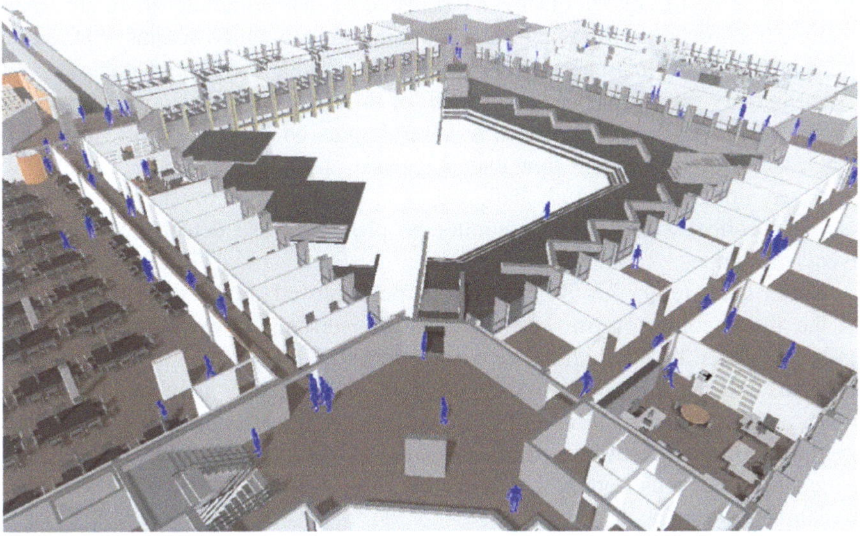

Fig. 11.12 Crowding visualization based on avatars upon the campus BIM

11.7 Conclusions and Future Work

Overtourism deteriorates the visiting experience of tourists, the quality of life of residents, as well as the environment. By monitoring it, tourism professionals can identify areas of concern and put measures in place to lessen its negative effects, encouraging better tourism practices to ensure that tourism benefits both tourists and locals while preserving natural and heritage resources.

For monitoring overtourism, a low-cost approach based on mobile devices' activity has been developed. The sensors, equipped with off-the-shelf hardware available at affordable costs, perform real-time detection of trace elements of mobile devices' wireless activity, mitigating MAC address randomization, and crowding values are put together in a cloud server. Alternative communication channels for uploading the crowding information, namely, via Wi-Fi or LoRaWAN protocols, allow for addressing local connectivity limitations at the installation location of sensors. In addition, scalability is provided by maintaining the hardware costs low, by using open-source software, and by the simplicity of the installation and configuration of each sensor. Regarding the RESETTING project, an SME must choose the option that best fits its needs and requirements for implementing its system. To help with this purpose, the STToolkit will include a sensor deployment calculator for SMEs to estimate the most cost-effective uplink alternative according to the installation location of each sensor.

The crowding information can then be analyzed by destination managers to understand the crowding levels in areas where each sensor is placed in a clear and simple perspective, either by dashboards for temporal or spatial visualization of crowding information or using the raw data for custom-made integrations.

Furthermore, notification policies can be created when overtourism situations occur, opening the possibility of implementing just-in-time mitigation actions required by the nature of these circumstances, as they may be sudden and unpredictable.

Preliminary tests have been conducted for this solution. A prototype version of the crowding sensor was deployed at several spots on Iscte's campus, in typical usage scenarios with a high flow and/or extended presence of people, such as the university library, a large study hall, and two passageways. Crowding information has been collected and used to monitor people's flow and detect high-crowding events on campus.

In the short term, this STToolkit will be deployed at the Pena Palace, one of the most iconic tourism sites in Portugal, surrounded by a large walkable park, flagellated by overtourism all year round. The objectives will be promoting alternative routes for tourists within the park, limiting their number in sensitive areas, and making the tourism offer in this area more sustainable. Our detection approach will then contribute to reducing the overwhelming feeling of pressure in critical hotspots, thus leading to a greater visiting experience for tourists who visit this attractive tourist site.

Furthermore, a second prototype version of sensors is also envisaged. The latter will include new boards with greater performance, new antennas with higher gains for larger detection ranges, directional antennas for performing detection in specific areas, custom-designed heatsinks for the processing units to achieve the best possible performance, as well as new custom-designed cases.

Further details on the sensors, including demos of setting up and configuring the edge nodes and the cloud server, can be found online at the RESETTING@Iscte site.

Acknowledgments This work has been developed in the scope of the RESETTING project, funded by the European COSME Programme (EISMEA), under grant agreement COS-TOURINN 101038190. The cloud-based infrastructure (computing and storage) used was provided by the INCD, Funded by FCT and FEDER under project 01/SAICT/2016 nº022153. The current work has also been supported by Fundação para a Ciência e Tecnologia (FCT)/Ministério da Ciência, Tecnologia e Ensino Superior (MCTES) through national funds and, when applicable, co-funded by European Union (EU) funds under the project UIDB/EEA/50008/2020.

References

Berenguer, A., Ros, D.F., Gómez-Oliva, A., Ivars-Baidal, J.A., Jara, A.J., Laborda, J., Mazón, J.N., Perles, A.: Crowd monitoring in smart destinations based on GDPR-ready opportunistic RF scanning and classification of WiFi devices to identify and classify visitors' origins. Electronics **11**(6), 835 (2022). https://doi.org/10.3390/electronics11060835

Biendicho, M., Papaoikonomou, E., Setó-Pamies, D.: Tourists go home! Examining antitourism in Barcelona from an emotions perspective. Tour. Culture Commun. **22**(3), 275–295 (2022). https://doi.org/10.3727/109830421x16345418234010

Bravenec, T., Torres-Sospedra, J., Gould, M., Fryza, T.: What your wearable devices revealed about you and possibilities of non-cooperative 802.11 presence detection during your last IPIN visit.

In: 2022 IEEE 12th International Conference on Indoor Positioning and Indoor Navigation (IPIN). IEEE, Piscataway (2022). https://doi.org/10.1109/ipin54987.2022.9918134

Cai, Y., Tsukada, M., Ochiai, H., Esaki, H.: MAC address randomization tolerant crowd monitoring system using Wi-Fi packets. In: Asian Internet Engineering Conference. ACM, New York (2021). https://doi.org/10.1145/3497777.3498547

Covaci, A.I.: Wi-Fi MAC address randomization vs crowd monitoring. Tech. rep., University of Twente (2022). http://essay.utwente.nl/91744/

De Meersman, F., Seynaeve, G., Debusschere, M., Lusyne, P., Dewitte, P., Baeyens, Y., Wirthmann, A., Demunter, C., Reis, F., Reuter, H.I.: Assessing the quality of mobile phone data as a source of statistics. In: European Conference on Quality in Official Statistics, pp. 1–16 (2016)

Dias da Silva, R., Neto Marinheiro, R., Brito e Abreu, F.: Crowding detection combining trace elements from heterogeneous wireless technologies. In: 2019 22nd International Symposium on Wireless Personal Multimedia Communications (WPMC). IEEE, Piscataway (2019). https://doi.org/10.1109/wpmc48795.2019.9096131

Guttentag, D.: Airbnb: disruptive innovation and the rise of an informal tourism accommodation sector. Curr. Issues Tour. **18**(12), 1192–1217 (2015). https://doi.org/10.1080/13683500.2013.827159

He, T., Tan, J., Chan, S.H.G.: Self-supervised association of Wi-Fi probe requests under MAC address randomization. IEEE Trans. Mobile Comput. 1–14 (2022). https://doi.org/10.1109/tmc.2022.3205924

Hotspotty: Helium hotspot map (2023). https://explorer.helium.com

Institute of Electrical and Electronics Engineers: IEEE Standard for Information Technology–Telecommunications and Information Exchange between Systems - Local and Metropolitan Area Networks–Specific Requirements - Part 11: Wireless LAN Medium Access Control (MAC) and Physical Layer (PHY) Specifications. https://doi.org/10.1109/ieeestd.2021.9363693

Santos, T.M.: Smart tourism toolkit for crowd-monitoring solutions. Master's thesis, Iscte - Instituto Universitário de Lisboa (2023). http://hdl.handle.net/10071/29505

Seraphin, H., Sheeran, P., Pilato, M.: Over-tourism and the fall of Venice as a destination. J. Destination Marketing Manag. **9**, 374–376 (2018). https://doi.org/10.1016/j.jdmm.2018.01.011

Singh, U., Determe, J.F., Horlin, F., Doncker, P.D.: Crowd monitoring: state-of-the-art and future directions. IETE Tech. Rev. **38**(6), 578–594 (2020). https://doi.org/10.1080/02564602.2020.1803152

Tokarchuk, O., Barr, J.C., Cozzio, C.: How much is too much? Estimating tourism carrying capacity in urban context using sentiment analysis. Tour. Manag. **91**, 104522 (2022). https://doi.org/10.1016/j.tourman.2022.104522

Torres-Sospedra, J., Quezada Gaibor, D.P., Nurmi, J., Koucheryavy, Y., Lohan, E.S., Huerta, J.: Scalable and efficient clustering for fingerprint-based positioning. IEEE Internet Things J. **10**(4), 3484–3499 (2023). https://doi.org/10.1109/JIOT.2022.3230913

Uras, M., Cossu, R., Ferrara, E., Bagdasar, O., Liotta, A., Atzori, L.: WiFi probes sniffing: an Artificial Intelligence based approach for MAC addresses de-randomization. In: 2020 IEEE 25th International Workshop on Computer Aided Modeling and Design of Communication Links and Networks (CAMAD). IEEE, Piscataway (2020). https://doi.org/10.1109/camad50429.2020.9209257

Uras, M., Ferrara, E., Cossu, R., Liotta, A., Atzori, L.: MAC address de-randomization for Wi-Fi device counting: combining temporal- and content-based fingerprints. Comput. Netw. **218**, 109393 (2022). https://doi.org/10.1016/j.comnet.2022.109393

Vega-Barbas, M., Álvarez-Campana, M., Rivera, D., Sanz, M., Berrocal, J.: AFOROS: a low-cost Wi-Fi-based monitoring system for estimating occupancy of public spaces. Sensors **21**(11), 3863 (2021). https://doi.org/10.3390/s21113863

Part IV
Experience Reports of Smart Life Applications

Chapter 12
Leuven: A Smart City Experience

Lieve Heyrman, Tim Guily, Rébecca Deneckère, Elena Kornyshova, and Ramona Elali

Abstract Leuven is the eighth-largest city in Belgium with more than 100,000 inhabitants. It is a leading region in the creation of starts-ups, research centers, and applications on health and climate. Numerous organizations in the Leuven region and the city administration itself are currently cooperating in order to work out advanced ideas around Smart City technology, which is also a crucial step in Leuven's goal to become climate neutral by 2030. For this particular goal, the organization Leuven 2030 was founded. Leuven 2030 strives for a climate-neutral future for Leuven, representing inhabitants, companies, civil society organizations, knowledge institutions, and public authorities. They do this by combining science (scientific framework), social power (bringing people together around projects), and storytelling (inspiring stories about the steps taken).

Keywords Smart City · Smart City Strategy · Smart City Projects

12.1 Introduction

Leuven received the award of "European Capital of Innovation" in 2020. The prestigious award from the European Commission rewards the city that makes the best use of innovation to improve the quality of life of its inhabitants in creating new and groundbreaking solutions to public challenges. The European Commission

L. Heyrman · T. Guily
Department of Economics and Trade, Smart City Leuven, Leuven, Belgium
e-mail: lieve.heyrman@leuven.be; tim.guily@leuven.be

R. Deneckère · R. Elali (✉)
Centre de Recherche en Informatique, Université Paris 1 Panthéon-Sorbonne, Paris, France
e-mail: rebecca.deneckere@univ-paris1.fr; ramona.elali@univ-paris1.fr

E. Kornyshova
Centre d'Etudes et de Recherche en Informatique et Communications, Conservatoire National des Arts et Métiers, Paris, France
e-mail: elena.kornyshova@cnam.fr

E. Kornyshova et al. (eds.), *Smart Life and Smart Life Engineering*,
https://doi.org/10.1007/978-3-031-75887-4_12

praised a unique symbiosis of empathy in leadership and structural collaboration between citizens, knowledge institutions, and local organizations to create a brighter future, for itself and far beyond.[1] The city of Leuven applied for the award in close collaboration with Leuven 2030 and Leuven MindGate.

More recently, in April 2022, Louvain was identified as one over one hundred climate-neutral and smart cities to pursue ambitious goals to slash emissions rapidly and pioneer innovative approaches with citizens and stakeholders.[2] These cities will be supported by NetZeroCities to bring together all key players within a city, including citizens, academia, and businesses, and implement transformative processes and innovative actions, with the objective of reaching climate neutrality by 2030. The opportunities are to contribute to the European Green Deal ambition to reduce gas emissions by at least 55%, to offer cleaner air, safer transport, and less congestion to citizens, to lead in climate and digital innovation, making Europe attractive for investments from innovative companies and skilled workers.

12.2 Smart City Strategy in Leuven

The Smart City unit of Leuven was initiated more than 5 years ago by the head of the Department of Economics and Trade, who noticed within her international network an upcoming relevance in the "smart use of technology" for local policies. From that moment on, a Smart City vision, framework, and strategy gradually developed and modified under the influence of continuous insights and lessons learned through our own experience with Smart City projects but also as a result of local and international Smart City networks that grew over time.

There are several smart key drivers that occur and are important in city policy. (See Fig. 12.1).

First, we can see that there is a change in the demographics that is occurring in the city. People living in the city are becoming older, they live longer, and, in consequence, the number of citizens is growing.

We have rapid urbanization as all these people need to be able to live somewhere. The housing market is very tight in Leuven as houses are very expensive.

All these people use energy, they need to use transportation, and it gives us strain on the traffic and the pollution. Environmental concerns are global, but they are also present at city level.

Climate change over the planet means that the water supplies are going down, and this is a concern also at the city level as there is a high amount of population and we all use these resources from nature. As these resources become scarcer, we have problems finding energy or water resources.

[1] https://leuven.be/en/capital-of-innovation

[2] https://eurocities.eu/latest/the-100-climate-neutral-and-smart-cities-by-2030/

Fig. 12.1 Leuven Smart City drivers

There is also a technical aspect. A lot of people, and more and more people in the future, are using the Internet. This technology and others evolve very fast. This has been an important aspect to take into account when we set up our Smart City strategy.

These are the challenges that the city of Leuven, like other cities, are facing, and we tried to contribute with our Smart City strategy to address all these aspects.

Smart City Leuven uses connected, innovative technologies in the public space to generate and use the gathered data to gain insights into the functioning of the city and into the functioning of all these key drivers. The final goal is to improve the quality of city life so that people are happy to live in the city and feel well supported. We look for how Smart City can contribute to that goal.

Smart Cities also make a turn to data-driven policymaking. Before, policymaking was more based on people's experience, with trials and errors. Now, we combine this information with sensor data to identify if changes are beneficial or not. That is the direction chosen with the Leuven Experience, with gathering and use of data to support the policymaking of the city. This support in data-driven policymaking is provided via several modi: via monitoring and providing insights, via simulation and prediction, and via automatization and control.

At the start of Smart City Leuven, five targets could be defined (See Fig. 12.2):

- Optimization of flows. It can be general, like mobility, energy, waste, and economy.
- Sublime city experience. This represents how you experience the city as a visitor and also as a resident. It has to do with tourism and its economy.
- Harbor and grow talent. There are projects to support students to develop their talent.
- Smart health and Wellness. We focus here on environmental factors such as noise, heat, and so on.

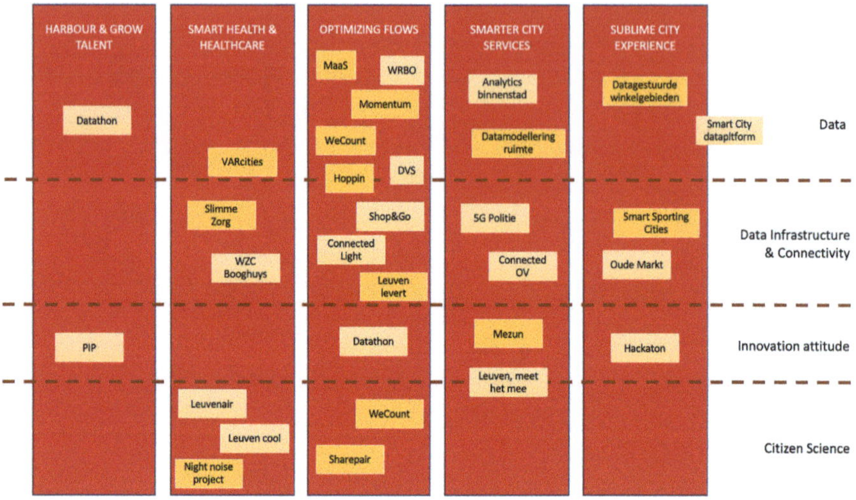

Fig. 12.2 Overview of Leuven Smart City projects

- Smart City services. Internally but also related to visitors and residents living in the city to offer more smart services. This has more to do with the digitalization that is always growing.

12.3 Smart City Projects in Leuven

Figure 12.2 shows an overview of the Leuven Smart City projects, related to these targets. Also, the main focus of the projects throughout the different targets is defined: data of course, how it can make the infrastructure and connectivity smarter, and what the innovation attitude is. Also, some projects specifically focus on "citizen science" by involving our citizens in data gathering for the city's benefit.

Over time, the need arose to rearrange the Smart City targets, since Smarter City services concerns more with digitalization and IT projects, and harbor and grow talent is also handled in other city projects. Therefore, the current main three targets of the Leuven Smart City strategy are smart health and wellness, optimizing flows, and sublime city experience. We will go further into detail on each one (Fig. 12.3).

12.3.1 Optimizing Flows

Shop & Go Project The Shop & Go project is concerned with the optimization of flows and shared mobility. In some Leuven areas, you do not need any parking disc, parking ticket, or resident's card. Sensors on the floor of the parking area record

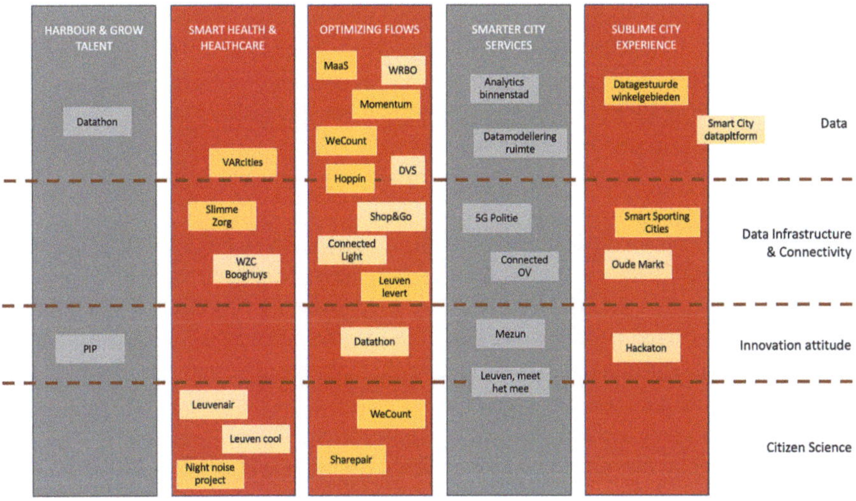

Fig. 12.3 Selected Leuven Smart City projects

your hour of arrival, and if you exceed the parking time, a parking attendant will arrive on site and you will receive a parking fee.

Hoppin/eHUBS Hoppin is a project embedded in a European project. It combines shared mobility and packaging. When shopping online, you can choose to have your package delivered to some specific place. This project combines different facilities related to shared mobility and delivery of packages into one eHUBS spot. eHUBS are on-street locations that bring together e-bikes, e-cargo bikes, and/or e-cars, offering users a wide range of options to experiment with and use in various situations. The idea is to give a high-quality and diverse offer of shared electric mobility services to dissuade citizens from owning private cars, resulting in cleaner, more liveable, and pleasant cities. The eHUBS in Leuven are characterized by the Hoppin polls (digital and analogs), which refer to the branding of eHUBS foreseen by the Flemish strategy that aims at deploying 1000 eHUBS in the Belgian region by the end of 2024.

Mobility as a Service A service in which different mobility services are offered to the user through one application. In this way, the user has access to the various mobility services. By using this application, the user can plan his transport modes. First steps toward this application were taken in a project funded by the Flemish government, and a follow-up project is currently ongoing.

Citizen Science—WeCount Project WeCount[3] is a European project that enables citizens to initiate a policymaking process with fully automated measurement data in the field of mobility and air quality.

[3] https://www.we-count.net/

The community building process of WeCount was based on previous participatory processes, whether initiated by the local government or by the citizens themselves. Steps were taken to gain a good understanding of the local mobility context, supported by an existing rich participatory context organized by the city government and initiated by citizens.

Low-cost sensors are placed, by citizens, on their house's front windows. This sensor contains a small camera, and it counts what passes by. In particular, it can differentiate bikers, cars, trucks, and pedestrians, so it is used as a traffic counter.

This is a nice example of how citizens can contribute to the city's policymaking by gathering the data themselves. They were just asked to commit to this project, and then they received a low-cost sensor. The only thing they had to do was to plug it in and connect it to their Internet, and so the data came in and was used, in this case as one of the data sources for a new local circulation plan. This data gathering benefited the citizens themselves, as the studied area is very small; however, there are a lot of small roads but also a lot of people (families and children). There was a problem with the traffic and the use of the streets, and people were very concerned about how the traffic would be guided through their streets. This project allows them to be able to do something about gathering data themselves.

12.3.2 Smart Health and Wellness

Smart health and wellness is one of the main target strategies that we have for Smart City. Two citizen projects within this target will be presented in the next session: Leuven.cool and Night Noise project.

Project Leuven.cool It is one of the citizen science projects[4] currently running in the city. In collaboration with the KU Leuven (who has the lead in this project), the Royal Meteorological Institute, and climate Leuven2030, this project studies the heat island effect in the city. The project aims to map the moderating effect of green elements in the city and in the gardens of citizens. The urban microclimate is created by the interaction between the urban surface and the atmosphere. The physical processes that occur are the result of energy and water exchange between the urban surface and the atmosphere, generating differences following the layout of the urban landscape. This project was set up after a heating up in the city with a higher temperature inside than in the green areas and urban surroundings had been noticed. We wanted to discover how likely the presence of green areas and water zones could have a beneficial impact on the heat island effect.

[4] https://www.exello.net/nl/kennisdeling/leuvencool

Over 100 weather stations are placed at different public places and private gardens in the city center and its surroundings (real time maps directly accessible online[5]).

Based on the data provided by these weather stations, a heat map and a network map were created, where the temperature was represented through a color code in order to be able to compare the temperature within the city center with the surrounding areas. The data obtained from those stations are used for scientific and research purposes but also at the city policy level as it allows to monitor heat spots that can be used as a starting point for beneficial interventions such as creating more green areas and introducing more water spots.

Night Noise Project The purpose of this project is to tackle the nightly noise using technology and nudging. Leuven is a lively city, and there are around 50,000 students staying and studying, which gives a nice atmosphere. However, students like to go out and have some fun, the same as the local residents. Hence, we have a lively nightlife, which may produce nightly noise in transit streets, which are the routes taken by students or residents while going home. Thus, this causes a problem for the local residents living in these streets because they are disturbed in their sleep. Different decisions were taken to tackle this problem, such as police control and direct intervention, by giving penalties in a repressive way but also by creating campaigns in a preventive way, with limited effect. Tackling night noise is challenging because it occurs only for a relatively short period. When a group of people passes through and makes noise, by the time a local resident calls the police to complain about the noise and the police come, the noisy people are already gone! In addition, the noisy people are not always aware that other people are sleeping in these streets, as at night the streets are isolated, which may give the feeling that no one lives there; hence, for them, there won't be any problem in making some noise.

Therefore, in this project, we combine technology and nudging techniques as a possible solution for this problem. There are three targets:

1. *Get insights into the nightly noise* with more objective data because we don't know how likely the reported noise is loud, disturbing, or annoying or when it is occurring, on which days, or at which times. So we need to get more insights about the night problem itself to objectify the first target.
2. *Classify sources of nightly noise*. There are different sources of night noises. Some of the noise is produced by traffic; then, it is difficult to have the police intervene or to use nudging techniques in such a case. Some other noises can be produced by humans directly such as singing and shouting, breaking glass or punching a garbage bag with the leg, playing music on a loud sound, etc. For this source of noise, nudging techniques might have a positive influence.
3. *Nudge to influence behavior*. Nudging is a motivation technique to stimulate and/or influence people in a subtle way to perform expected behavior. So it is

[5] https://leuven.cool/

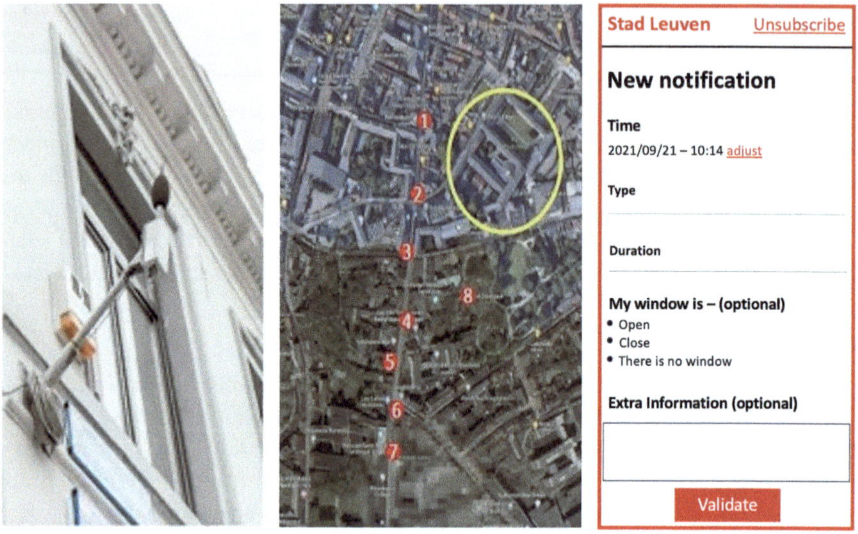

Fig. 12.4 Night noise identification

used to direct people to the expected behavior, in this case being more silent when passing through the streets at night.

The VLAIO City of Things is a recurrent funding initiative of the Flemish government and is funding the Night Noise Project. We set up this research project in cooperation with the local police and the local prevention service. The project focusses on a specific street called Naamsestraat nr.40 until 100. After a positive evaluation, this project will be resubmitted for new funding to extend to other streets hindered by nightly noise in Leuven.

Several noise sensors are placed in a 300-meter area between the Heilige Geestcollege and the arts center STUK. These sensors do not record conversations, but they do analyze all nocturnal sounds: what the volume is, how high or low does it sound, how long does it last, and if it comes from traffic, people, or music. There is also a meter in the city park, inaccessible overnight, to compare the noise measurements with a quiet zone. In addition, the residents are asked to report via an app when they experience night noise (what kind of noise, the time, the duration of the noise, whether their window was open or not). By combining the noise analysis results with residents' reports, the system can better identify which sounds are perceived as disturbing (Fig. 12.4).

In the next step, we found a way to classify the sources of nightly noise with an AI-trained model. The image below represents sensor data obtained between 10:00 p.m. and 6:00 a.m., with the source of noise peaks classified as either human voice shouting or a traffic. Preliminary data analysis showed that part of the noise peaks come from an ambulance since a hospital is located in this street. However, it is difficult to control this type of night noise; therefore, this project focusses on sources of noises on which we can intervene (Fig. 12.5).

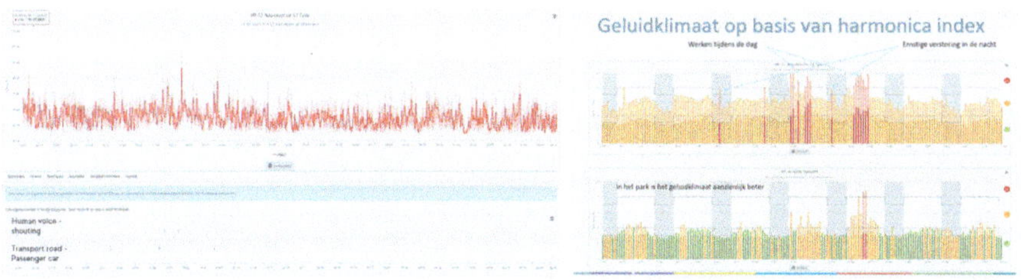

Fig. 12.5 Night noise data analysis

As in the image above, we are able to convert the data into a harmonica index to find out the intensity of the noise. Green indicates low intensity, orange indicates medium intensity, and red represents high intensity of noise. The first diagram is from a sensor in Naamsestraat. We can see how the orange color is dominant. The second diagram is from the sensor attached inside the park quiet zone. We can notice how the green color is dominant here. In addition, we can detect, from both diagrams, when the peak time and day are for the noise.

Since we have data from the sensors, we can process these data for nudging purposes in our Smart City Data Platform.

12.3.3 Sublime City Experience

Smart Sporting Cities The last project is the smart sporting cities that consist of monitoring sports and exercise behavior in the public space using AI technology. Sport Vlaanderen and the city of Leuven want to gather insights about the growing group of recreative athletes (athletes who work outside clubs) to strengthen the policy around them and thus encourage even more residents to exercise and exercise. The project, which was realized with the support of the innovative Public Procurement Program (PIO), will be launched in two pilot gardens in Leuven (Fig. 12.6).

In the first experimental garden in de Bruul Park, the sports infrastructure of the park is specifically monitored. The green park in the center of Leuven has a multipurpose lawn, a football cage, and a sports wall, where tennis and urban fitness can take place. The technology will have a permanent place until the summer of 2024 to monitor sports behavior on a permanent basis.

The second testing garden is the Philips site at the Leuvense ring. Mobile technologies are tested there to allow the measurement equipment to be moved to other sites after a certain period of time. Thanks to a solar panel and 4G/5G connection, these applications are independent of existing power and data facilities in public spaces. The Philips site focuses on the multipurpose lawn and the bar park between the sports center Sportoase and the Leuvense ring.

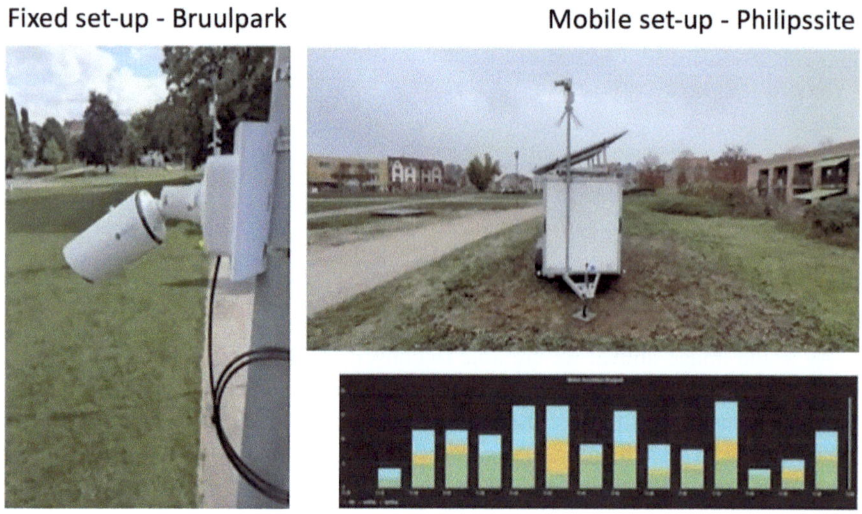

Fig. 12.6 Smart sporting city in Leuven

12.3.4 Smart City Data Platform

All data coming from the different types of sensors (city wireless environment, waste management, parking, urban mobility) have been integrated into the Smart City Data Platform (Fig. 12.7). It is then possible to standardize the data between all sensors to have a cross-sharing experience of information of streams to provide an efficient, effective, and scalable platform (which can be used in other projects and in other cities), to have governance with a cost-sharing mechanism, and to share data between all cities. This integration of sensor data for different purposes is now possible even if it is not yet operational today.

We have two main layers in this platform: the IOT layer and the data layer. In the data layer, the data is being stored on Azure; thus, we can do some analysis on the data to get insights.

In the second phase, the city tested various nudging techniques. Nudges are psychological techniques that often unconsciously and in a simple way encourage people to change their behavior. For example, (Fig. 12.8) when one of the noise meters catches nighttime noise, public lighting can be dimmed. A message can also be projected on the ground between 11:00 p.m. and 5:00 a.m. in order to make noise makers aware that they are waking someone up. The city chose to first experiment with the dimming or the intensification of the public lightning in the project area of the Naamsestraat. The noise sensor detects noise peaks with the label "human shouting," or the residents could use the app to report the night noise. Then, an AI algorithm processes this data, and a trigger is sent through the Smart City Data Platform in order to dim or intensify public lighting. Consequently,

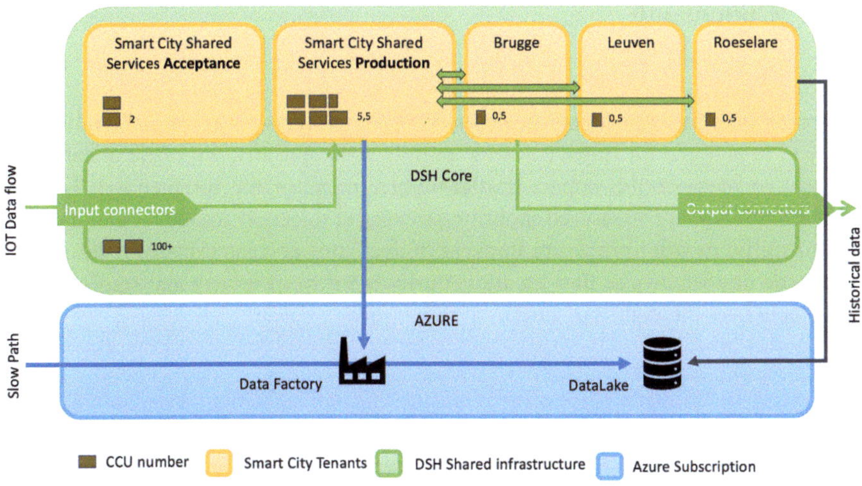

Fig. 12.7 Leuven Smart City Data Platform

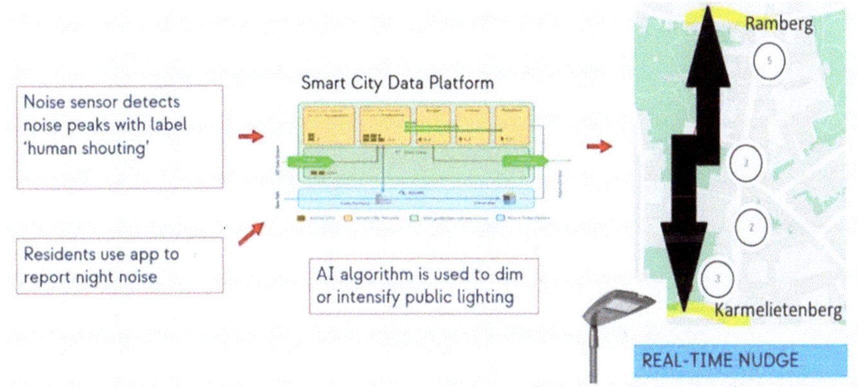

Fig. 12.8 Data Platform usage for night noise management

a different atmosphere is created in the streets, which might indirectly influence people's behavior.

These so-called incidental nudging techniques are combined with more semi- and permanent nudges such as floor stickers and projections on streets indicating that it is a sleeping zone. Preliminary results of the project suggest a positive effect of the nudging techniques on nightly noise; however, more data need to be gathered to draw more conclusive conclusions.

12.4 Conclusion

The Leuven Experience is still an ongoing project that will integrate a lot of other sub-projects in the years to come. For most of the projects, there was an analysis on the data to analyze for impact: for the nightly noise project, we made a statistical analysis to measure the impact on the nightly noise of the intervention. For the project mobility, we measured mobility streams at different moments and use this on our traffic model to measure impacts of decisions and interventions. We didn't plan to do any surveys as they are quite costly in terms of money and staff (and not repeatable over the course of time).

Chapter 13
Enhancing the Visitor Experience with Immersive Technologies and Gaming: The Monserrate Use Case

Carlos Portugal, David Vaz, Miguel Sales Dias, Pedro Trocado, Alcina Prata, and Fernando Brito e Abreu

Abstract Immersive technologies, such as augmented reality (AR) and virtual reality (VR), are effective technologies being implemented across diverse fields. We propose an AR/VR-based Web app to be applied in the cultural tourism field with the objective of enhancing the visitors' experience of the Monserrate Palace, part of a UNESCO cultural landscape located in Sintra, Portugal, managed by Parques de Sintra – Monte da Lua SA.

This chapter overviews the state of the art on immersive technologies in cultural heritage sites and the visitor experience at these sites. Then, it exposes the palace's historical and cultural significance and some of the challenges it faces in engaging its visitors. The potential applications of immersive technologies in the palace are explored, including interactive storytelling and immersive experiences that allow for a higher level of visitor engagement. Next, it addresses potential challenges and limitations of deploying the proposed solution in the palace, such as technical constraints and preservation concerns. It then concludes with a reflection on the significant potential of AR and VR in enriching the immersive experience of Monserrate Palace, offering new possibilities for engaging with cultural heritages and creating a memorable and enjoyable visit for modern audiences.

Keywords Smart tourism · Augmented reality · Virtual reality · Gaming · 360° Imaging · Tracking · Cultural heritage site · Monserrate Palace · RESETTING

C. Portugal (✉) · D. Vaz · M. Sales Dias · F. Brito e Abreu
Iscte - Instituto Universitário de Lisboa, Lisboa, Portugal
e-mail: carlos_portugal@iscte-iul.pt; david_vaz@iscte-iul.pt; miguel.dias@iscte-iul.pt; fba@iscte-iul.pt

P. Trocado
Parques de Sintra - Monte da Lua S.A., Sintra, Portugal
e-mail: pedro.trocado@parquesdesintra.pt

A. Prata
IPS - Instituto Politécnico de Setúbal, Setúbal, Portugal
e-mail: alcina.prata@esce.ips.pt

E. Kornyshova et al. (eds.), *Smart Life and Smart Life Engineering*,
https://doi.org/10.1007/978-3-031-75887-4_13

13.1 Introduction

Cultural heritage sites are an important part of the identity and history of each nation, making their preservation and sharing crucial to uphold the traditions and their customs. In recent years, new technologies have been introduced to these sites to enhance the visitors' experience (Jung et al. 2020; Koeva et al. 2017). In this chapter, we will focus on immersive technologies, such as virtual reality (VR) and augmented reality (AR), that can enrich the experience of the visitors. Their objective in this context is to provide a high degree of interactivity, allowing users to engage with their content in a meaningful and memorable way, and in more specific cases, VR provides an elevated sense of presence in virtual worlds and allows its users to interact with virtual objects, mimicking real-life situations more accurately than other media, while AR enhances the user's perception of reality by overlaying virtual elements onto the real world. Thanks to these features, immersive technologies offer a more immersive and engaging user experience (Chiu et al. 2019) while also enhancing the learning experience of its users (tom Dieck et al. 2016). With all these benefits, these technologies can bring innovation in various fields, such as healthcare, entertainment, education, training, tourism, etc.

Given its broad implementation and adoption in various fields, it is often no surprise that immersive technologies have also been extended to tourism and, in the case of this chapter, into cultural heritage sites. One way these have manifested is through virtual tours where users experience the real-world location in an immersive simulated world. Another way is through reconstruction of physical heritage artifacts/rooms into virtual ones, allowing the visitor to interact with them while also preserving them. Furthermore, augmented virtual guides and information overlays have been widely used to provide visitors with greater amounts and quality of information about the sites they visit.

While these technologies have already begun to be implemented in cultural heritage sites, there are still challenges to be addressed. Our main goal is to design on-site immersive experiences that are both engaging and rewarding for visitors in order to improve tourism experiences.

In this chapter, we report a case of usage of immersive technologies designed for Monserrate Palace, part of a UNESCO cultural landscape located in Sintra, Portugal, aiming at enhancing the visitor experience. This initiative is being carried out under the framework of the COSME RESETTING project.[1]

This chapter is structured as follows. In Sect. 13.2, we present the findings of our literature review, which highlights factors affecting cultural heritage site experiences and the role of immersive technology in enhancing visitor engagement. In Sect. 13.3, we provide a historical background of the Monserrate Palace, with a rich history dating back to before Sintra's reconquest. In Sect. 13.4, we detail the design of the "Monserrate in the Cook family era" gaming app, highlighting the game design, the

[1] Relaunching European smart and SustainablE Tourism models Through digitalization and INnovative technoloGies.

user-centered prototyping approach, and the preliminary results of our proposed techniques that enable the immersive visitor experience. In Sect. 13.5, we draw conclusions and describe our plans for further research.

13.2 Literature Review

13.2.1 Visitor Experience at Cultural Heritage Sites

Several studies have shed light on the various factors that contribute to a positive visitor experience at cultural heritage sites. One of the key factors identified is the quality of the visitor experience, perceived value, satisfaction, and sustainable behavior. For instance, one paper found that the quality of experience directly influences the perception of value and satisfaction, ultimately impacting behavioral intentions (Chen et al. 2010), while another discovered that perceived quality and emotions play direct roles in determining visitor satisfaction, with the individual's mood state serving as a moderator along the cognitive path to satisfaction (de Rojas and Camarero 2008).

In addition to these findings, Buonincontri et al. (2017) proposed a conceptual framework that integrates visitors' heritage experiences, their attachment to heritage sites, and their engagement in sustainable behavior. This framework highlights the interconnections between visitors' experiences, emotional connections to the site, and their inclination toward sustainable practices, ultimately shaping their overall experience.

Moreover, Abuamoud et al. (2014) conducted a study focusing on the factors influencing tourists' willingness to travel to cultural heritage sites. They discovered that aspects such as education, variety of sites, multiple destinations, cost, and the reasons for visiting significantly impact tourists' decision-making process. These findings underscore the importance of considering diverse elements when designing and promoting cultural heritage sites to attract visitors.

Furthermore, Alazaizeh et al. (2019) explored the role of tour guide performance in enhancing visitor sustainable behavior, consequently contributing to a positive visitor experience. The study revealed that tour guides have both a direct and indirect effect on visitors' sustainable behavior, thereby shaping their overall experience.

By considering these research findings, cultural heritage site managers can better understand and address the key factors that influence visitor experiences. Focusing on factors such as quality, perceived value, satisfaction, emotional engagement, sustainability, and the role of tour guides can lead to a more holistic and enriching experience for visitors, ensuring their lasting enjoyment and appreciation of the cultural heritage site.

13.2.2 Immersive Technologies in Cultural Heritage Sites

Immersive technologies, such as VR and AR, have the potential to enhance visitors' engagement with cultural heritage sites and improve learning outcomes. Additionally, VR and AR can aid in the preservation and conservation of heritage sites by digitally documenting and safeguarding fragile structures or artifacts.

A systematic review conducted by Yung and Khoo-Lattimore (2017) found that the most common use of these technologies was in marketing and in tourism education, as well as highlighting some gaps and challenges in the adoption of such technologies, these being the awareness of the technology, usability, and time commitment to become proficient.

Another paper identified AR-related factors that influence the user's satisfaction and, with those factors, presented a user experience model with product features for a user-centered interface design for AR applications (Han 2017).

Some other studies focused on the examination of the learning outcomes on the use of these technologies. One of them compared a control group whose tour was conducted through traditional approaches while the experimental group conducted its tour with the aid of an AR system using image-based recognition. The experimental group exhibited significant differences and improvement in the learning outcomes (tom Dieck et al. 2016). Another study found that just providing instructions to the visitors with a mobile application made their experience more valuable and recommends the use of new approaches to visitor engagement and experience enhancement (Chiu et al. 2019).

An interesting use case found was a Web portal with the integration of high-resolution spherical panoramas and information representing the cultural heritage in Bulgaria (Koeva et al. 2017) that concluded that the visual and metric qualities of those panoramas are sufficient for many applications, namely, tourism, documentation, and demonstration of cultural objects.

The effectiveness of a VR/AR application named *JejuView* was evaluated to advertise the cultural heritage of Jeju Island to tourists. The authors found that when using immersive media, consumers are more focused on the hedonic value than on the usefulness of the medium (Jung et al. 2020).

These technologies can be used to recreate life inside historical sites, as Bruno et al. (2010) and Gaitatzes et al. (2001) discuss the use of VR in cultural heritage, including the creation of immersive virtual environments and interactive virtual archaeology projects. Additionally, Noh et al. (2009) provides an overview of AR in virtual heritage systems, which can be used to reconstruct historical buildings and monuments. Similarly, Younes et al. (2017) contributes to the discourse by presenting a case study on the construction of a computerized model of the Roman Theater of Byblos, which includes both VR and AR applications.

Overall, these studies suggest that immersive technologies can be effective tools for enhancing visitors' engagement with cultural heritage sites and improving learning outcomes. However, there is still a need to be cautious about certain aspects of the application to ensure the success of its implementation.

13.2.3 Gamification

Gamification is the process of applying game mechanics, such as points, badges, leaderboards, etc. Saleem et al. (2022) to non-game contexts, aiming at motivating users' behavior and enhancing participation and productivity. This strategy has gained attention from researchers and has become popular as a method for engagement in various contexts (Aulia et al. 2022; Mora et al. 2015).

One of these contexts is education, where gamification has been used to generate more engaging educational environments. Saleem et al. (2022) reports on the increase in acceptance of gamification in e-learning and indicates that the most common game elements used in this context are points, leaderboards, badges, and levels.

Other contexts that have adopted gamification are tourism and hospitality. Pasca et al. (2021) identified five themes in tourism and hospitality, where gamification is relevant: edutainment, sustainable behavior, engagement factors, service provider-generated content, and user-generated reviews. The cross-analysis of these themes also revealed some key components of gamification mechanics, including affordances, behavioral and psychological outcomes, and benefits.

Hamari et al. (2014) suggests that gamification does work, but with some caveats. These authors claim that the majority of the reviewed studies yielded positive effects from the adoption of gamification. However, most of the quantitative studies concluded on positive effects that exist only in part of the considered relationships between the gamification elements and studied outcomes.

In conclusion, gamification is a promising approach to motivate user behavior and enhance participation and productivity in various scenarios, including education, tourism, and hospitality. However, the effectiveness of gamification is dependent on the context in which it is being implemented and on the characteristics of the users.

13.3 Monserrate Palace Brief Historical Background

The Monserrate Estate is believed to have had a chapel on its grounds before D. Afonso Henriques's reconquest of Sintra back in 1147. In 1540, Gaspar Preto, a cleric, commissioned the construction of a chapel dedicated to Nossa Senhora de Monserrate, which at that time belonged to the Hospital of Todos-os-Santos in Lisbon. The property was leased to the Melo e Castro family in 1601 and purchased by D. Caetano de Melo e Castro in 1718. The property was kept by caretakers until 1755 when the great Lisbon earthquake left the houses uninhabitable. In 1790, the property was leased to Gerad De Visme, a wealthy English merchant, who built the first neo-Gothic palace and demolished the sixteenth-century chapel. William Beckford leased the property from De Visme in 1793 and invested heavily in the palace and gardens. The property remained in the hands of the Melo e Castro family until 1863 when it became the property of Francis Cook, a wealthy English textile millionaire. Cook made Monserrate the family's summer residence and employed a considerable amount of people to care for the house, park, and family. He also bought neighboring properties and the Convento dos Capuchos, becoming a major employer in the surrounding area. In 1947, the Cook family sold the property due to financial difficulties, and it was purchased by Saúl Fradesso da Silveira de Salazar Moscoso Saragga, a Lisbon antiques' dealer, who sold it to the Portuguese state in 1949 along with 143 hectares of the Tapada de Monserrate. In this sale, the valuable contents of the palace were scattered during an auction (Neto 2017, 2015).

This palace has also hosted another project to enhance the visiting experience, which was *FalaComigo*. This project involved the creation of interactive virtual characters, namely, Sir Francis Cook and a fictional butler named Edgar Smith. The visitors could interact with these characters and other audiovisual content through touch and speech, using a touch table, an interactive kiosk located in some palace rooms, and a smartphone app, which would help capture the visitor's attention. The project provided the visitors with a new attractive and interactive way to acquire the history of the palace (Neto and Neto 2012) (Fig. 13.1).

The Monserrate Palace is rectangular in plan and mostly symmetrical on its two axes (see Fig. 13.2). The two ends of the building are circular towers whose interiors are appropriately circular rooms. One of these towers can be understood as the face of the palace since it is the first face we see when arriving at the palace (assuming

Fig. 13.1 Monserrate Palace entrance

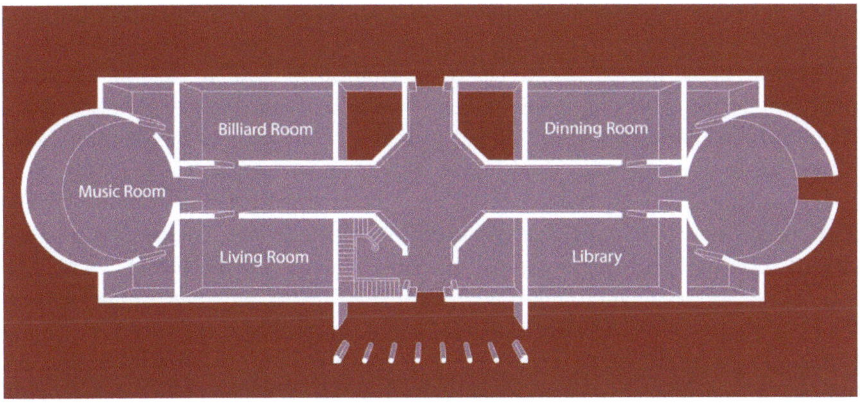

Fig. 13.2 Room layout of the ground floor of the Monserrate Palace

we come from somewhere other than the garden). Inside this first tower, we find the main atrium that functioned as the main entrance for those arriving at the palace for the first time and gave access to the main bedroom. In the opposite tower is the music room. This tower has no access to the outside, effectively being understood as the end of the palace. The large corridor that connects these two towers serves as the main axis of circulation, also giving access to the various rooms located between the two ends of the palace towers. These rooms all have the same morphology, a rectangular plan whose larger sides have windows (on one side) and a door to the central corridor (on the other side). These four rooms are arranged in pairs, symmetrically facing the corridor: the dining room and library and the living room and billiard room. Between these four rooms, we have the palace's central point, the midpoint of the corridor that connects the circulation space to the two side entrances. This point is an octagonal plan space, and, in the center, we find a fountain (whose plan is an offset from the larger octagon). The palace is oriented with its major sides perpendicular to the northwest and minor ones to the southeast.

13.4 Designing an Immersive Game for the Monserrate Palace

The Monserrate palace faces some challenges in appealing the visitors with an on-site experience that could recreate the indoor spaces at the time of the Cook Family, since such spaces are now essentially empty, ever since the 1949 auction. In this context, we designed a solution based on an immersive gaming user experience (UX), named *Monserrate in the Cook family era app.* This gaming app was designed specifically for use on the smartphones of visitors inside the Palace of Monserrate, to complement and enrich the visit. The focus of the game will be to convey what it would be like to live in the palace in the era of the Cook family, at the beginning of the twentieth century.

When visiting the palace, a visitor is confronted with a lack of furniture. Analyzing historical photographs,[2] taken inside and outside the palace around 1902 (David Knights-Whittome 1902), made available to the authors by the Monserrate palace, we can see the fully furnished first-floor rooms and the Cook family in an outdoor enclosure of the palace. From these photos, we get a more faithful view of the Cook era, something that has been lost today, in part due precisely to the lack of furniture (and obviously the residents themselves, the Cooks). Although these photos portray a more faithful perspective of the palace, they are just photos. There is always a discrepancy between seeing the world from two-dimensional photos and experiencing the world in three dimensions, i.e., physically. For this, the introduction of immersive environments (VR and AR) with a mobile (smartphone)-based user experience, within a gaming framework, is suggested.

Given the availability of early-twentieth-century photos for certain rooms, the development of our solution will be focused primarily on the rooms located on the first floor of the palace. This can be observed in Fig. 13.2, depicting the room layout of the first floor, with locks indicating the specific rooms where the solution will be implemented.

13.4.1 Gaming Experience Proposal

After some discussions and brainstorming with tour guides, specialists of the romantic period of the mid-nineteenth century, and palace curator and bibliographic review, we came up with some ideas that could be explored in the game.

One of the ideas that stood out as we reflected on the world illustrated in the 1902 photos, compared to the real world of today, is the day-to-day experience of the Cook family when they were visiting the Palace of Monserrate during vacation, in the dawn of the twentieth century. We can thus focus the basic theme of the game on an event that occurred daily such as "the Cook family mealtime."

The Cook family's way of life inside the palace was quite particular, with customs that no longer exist today and in accordance with the upper-class British lifestyle of the time. Some of the spaces were segregated by gender. For example, the "Billiard Room" was dedicated to men, as a smoking room too, and the "Living Room" ("Indian Room") to women in the family. The life of this family was thus much more "ritualized" than the family life of today.

Our gaming experience explores the following scenario. At noon, the Cook family returns from an early morning walk through the Monserrate gardens, enjoying the exotic nature and the panoramic views of the surrounding landscape,

[2] These photographs are part of the Monserrate Palace private collection and were taken by David Knights-Whittome, at the Palácio de Monserrate, in the early twentieth century (circa 1902).

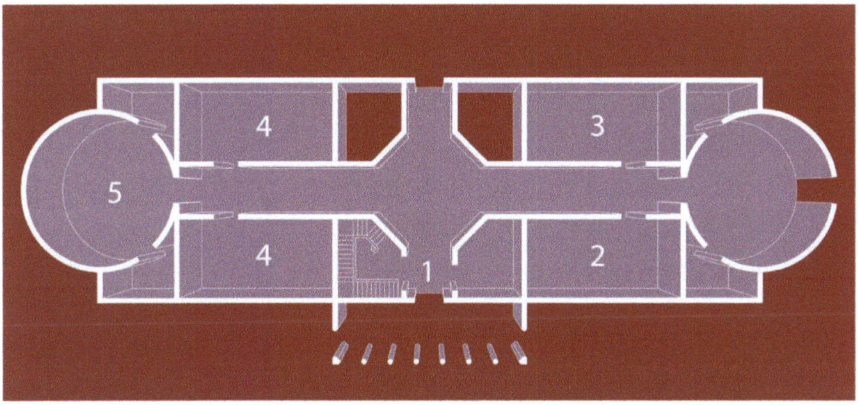

Fig. 13.3 Proposed visitors' trajectory

and enters the palace through the "Garden Entrance," where some members of the family meet others coming down from the upper floor by the monumental staircase. Together and in a single line, they make their way through the "South Gallery" and into the "Dining Room," passing by the "Library," a room set aside for studying and reading, where Sir Cook is also busy dispatching business matters. Sir Cook joins the group, and together they enter the "Dining Room." After a pleasant light lunch, the family leaves the room and walks through the "South Gallery" toward the "Octagon" and then through the "North Gallery" and divides into two groups: the female group goes to the "Indian Room," left, where they socialize and discuss social topics, and the male group goes to the "Billiard Room," right, where they discuss contemporary political and business topics, in a relaxed atmosphere, and where they also play billiards and smoke cigarettes and cigars. Later, both family groups gather again in the "Music Room" to enjoy the rest of the day while appreciating the music of that era.[3]

For a game that addresses this theme, the visitor may be invited to walk through the rooms, starting from the south wing, going into the "Library" first, followed by the "Dining Room," "Indian Room," and "Billiard Room," and finishing in the "Music Room," according to the ritualized order already mentioned. Visitors will also have the freedom to enter any room of their choice and deviate from the suggested path if they prefer. Once a visitor enters one of the previously mentioned rooms, he/she will be prompted to complete certain challenges. Figure 13.3 provides an overview of the proposed app's sequence, and Fig. 13.4 depicts the Business Process Model flowchart of the proposed solution.

[3] An example could well be Antonín Dvorák's "Serenade in G major, Op. 95" on piano and violin, very popular at the time, played by the palace's resident pianist.

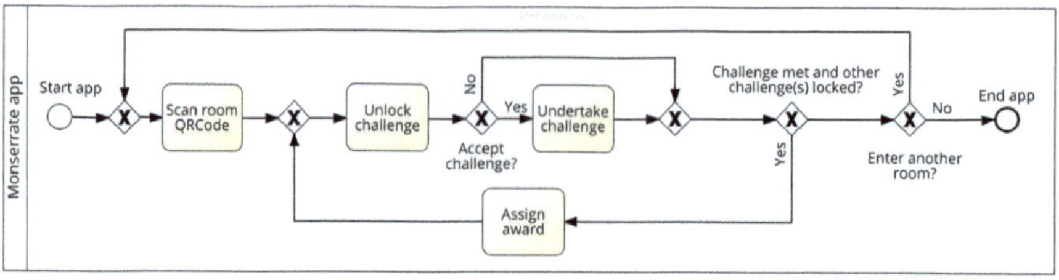

Fig. 13.4 Business Process Model and Notation (BPMN) flowchart of the proposed solution

13.4.1.1 First Challenge: Match 1902 Photos That Correspond to the Visited Room

In this challenge, when entering one of the rooms of the palace, the visitor is invited to use the app to browse through the gallery of the palace's historical photos. The player will have to choose the photo that corresponds to the room he or she is in, from auditory and visual clues of the room today. For example, when entering the "Billiard Room," the visitor would have access to a sound ambiance (either in egocentric mode—only for a given visitor—or exocentric, for all the visitors present in the room), reflecting what is going on in the room. As an example, in the billiard/smoking room, there could be the sound of men talking to each other and the billiard balls hitting the corners of the table. As far as visual clues are concerned, to be able to identify the correct picture, the player will have to pay some attention to the room in front of him, noticing the details of the ceiling, the floor, and the walls, since there is no furniture. There are some rooms where the choice is easier. For example, the library is the only room with bookshelves lining the walls, and the music room is the only one that has a different shape from the other rooms. Other examples are not so clear to identify, such as the living room, which will have to be identified based on the ornamentation of the walls. Each time the player chooses the correct picture, he or she receives a reward that corresponds to a brief overview of the historical and cultural significance of the room, enabling the visitor to assimilate information that may have been neglected otherwise.

13.4.1.2 Second Challenge: Discover the Photographer's Position

In this challenge, after choosing the photo that corresponds to the respective room, the game focuses on getting the visitor to understand what the pose (position and orientation) of the photographer was when he took the photo. The visitor moves around the room and uses his/her cell phone as a "sonar": as he/she approaches the correct position and orientation, the smartphone will vibrate more intensely until success is achieved. To accomplish this feedback interaction, there will be indicators situated inside each room to get the initial position of the visitor, which, combined with the sensors of the visitor's device, enable the tracking of the user throughout the room. When arriving at the required pose and position, the visitor will receive a reward, which is a VR experience based on 360° images on the smartphone, where he/she will observe a panoramic image of the current room merged with the image(s) of the room collected in 1902. The visitor is then invited to participate in the next challenge.

13.4.1.3 Third Challenge: Discover Room Curiosities

In this third challenge, the visitor must discover a set of curiosities and associated information, which can be found in the room of the previous challenge. Thus, the app would invite the visitor to discover "where the curiosities in this room are." As an example, the music room has some wall busts that belong to muses and goddesses. By pointing the phone at different parts of the room, the player would observe points of interest and could click on the screen to reveal information about what he or she sees. For example, if the visitor points the phone at one of the busts previously mentioned and clicks on the screen to find out who they are, the app will display the pertinent information. After finding these curiosities, the player is rewarded with an AR experience, where a virtual 3D scene will augment the physical space. The challenge in realizing this idea has to do with the fact that we select curiosities and objects that have an important connection to the Cook family's past and the era we are portraying.

13.4.2 User Interface Design

We adopted a user-centered design approach. In fact, to demonstrate the feasibility of our solution and to get feedback on the proposed design and functionalities, we start by designing a user interface prototype. The prototype serves as a visual representation of our ideas and allows us to validate our assumptions and gather feedback from experts and end-users (visitors) and make informed decisions toward the development of a minimum viable product of our gaming app. All this occurs before the beginning of the software development of the solution, so mistakes or wrong assumptions do not become costly to modify, since it is much cheaper in terms of resources to modify the user interface prototype than to modify the end product.

A low-fidelity paper prototype was first designed to get a broad idea of how the interface would look like, which can be seen in Fig. 13.5, and it was shown to two experts who had the chance to interact with it, via a "human-computer" interaction paradigm (Rettig 1994).

After collecting some feedback, we improved the prototype and developed a high-fidelity prototype version with the help of Figma, a user interface design tool that also allows for the creation of interactive prototypes that can be seen in Fig. 13.6. The high-fidelity prototype allows us some degree of interaction such as

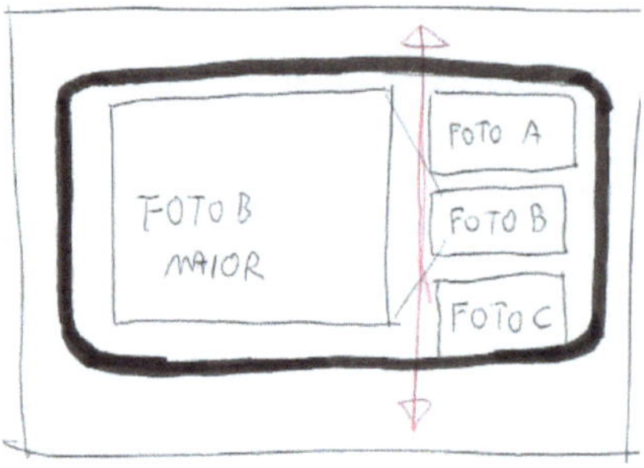

(a) Photograph matching challenge

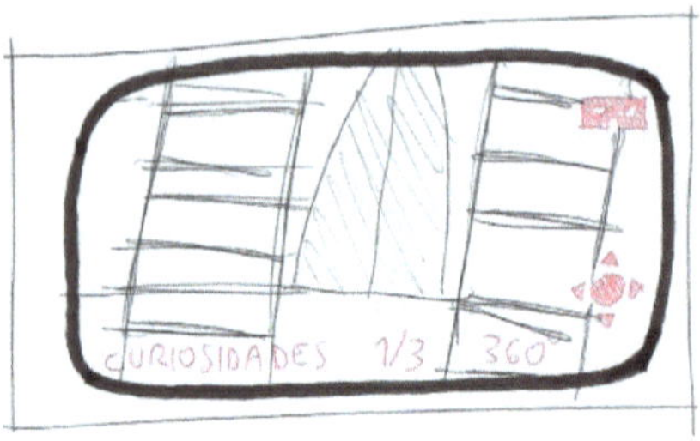

(b) Discover curiosities challenge

(c) Curiosity additional information overlay

(d) Augmented 3D object reward

Fig. 13.5 Low-fidelity user interface prototype

(a) Photograph matching challenge

(b) Discover curiosities challenge

(c) Curiosity additional information overlay

(d) Mimicked augmented 3D object reward

Fig. 13.6 High-fidelity user interface prototype

Fig. 13.7 Color palette

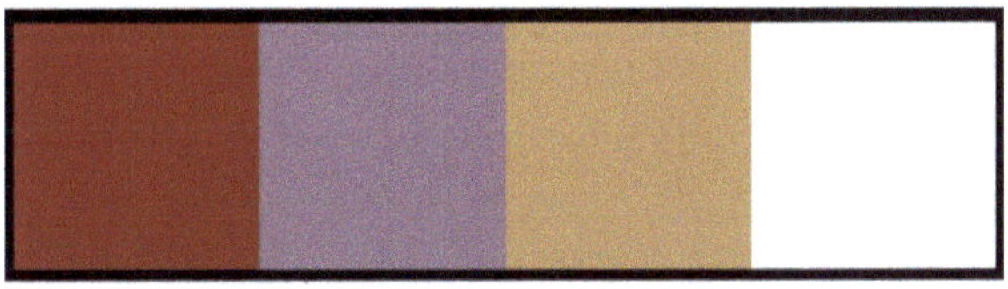

navigating the existing pages and some limited animations; this will be quite helpful when performing tests with the end-users since it will be much closer to the end product.

The prototype has been designed with the user in mind, and it aims to provide a simple and natural user experience. Some design choices made were, for example, the color palette that is illustrated in Fig. 13.7, derived from colors present in the palace while maintaining a pleasing visual experience, keeping things simple and easy to use, minimizing the learning curve and the implementation of some feedback mechanisms.

13.4.3 Proposed Software Architecture

13.4.3.1 Toolkit Architecture

In Fig. 13.8, there is the component diagram of the STToolkit that will be used to build the proposed solution. We will use Unity and WebXR. Unity is a game engine that provides powerful tools for creating and rendering 3D and 360° imaging environments that can be explored in VR and AR user experiences, while WebXR is an API for Web content and apps that need to interface with VR and AR software and hardware. By combining these tools, our solution will only require end-users to access the envisaged immersive experience via a Web browser.

13.4.3.2 Proposed Software Deployment

Our solution's system architecture is illustrated in Fig. 13.9. A server will host the Web service as well as the database, which means that users can access the content of the app without downloading an application to their devices. The client will need to provide data from its camera and from its inertial measurement unit, which uses a combination of accelerometers and gyroscopes to calculate changes in position and orientation and will support a graphical user interface, also featuring user experience with AR and VR based in 360° imaging.

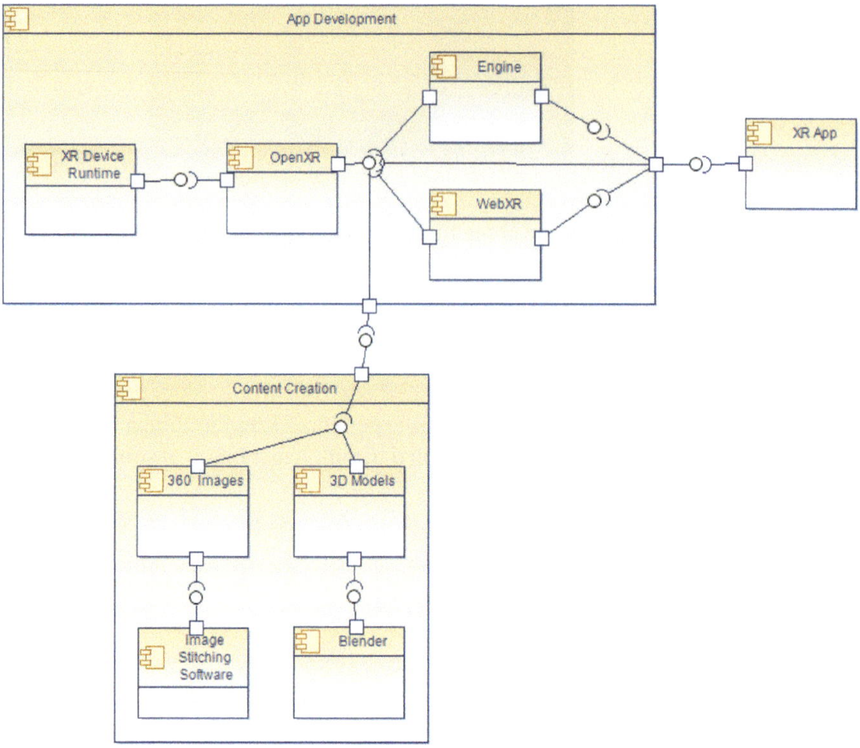

Fig. 13.8 Component diagram of proposed XR STToolkit

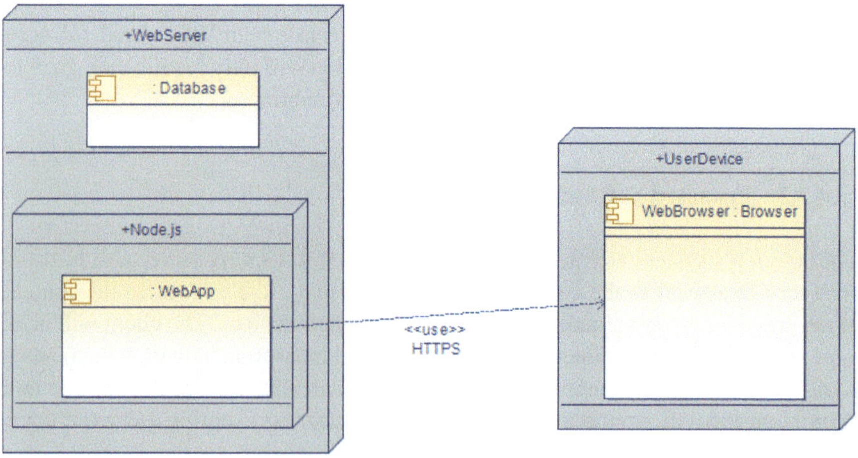

Fig. 13.9 Deployment diagram of proposed solution

(a) Historical photograph of the library (David Knights-Whittome 1902)

(b) Colorized version of the library

Fig. 13.10 Results of colorization tests

13.4.4 Feasibility Study

In preparation for the full software development of the proposed Web app, several preliminary tests were conducted, some of them involving image-stitching and colorization of historical photographs. In more detail, using a high-quality camera and specialized software PTGui, a series of images of the interior of the palace were captured by the authors in arbitrary poses and then stitched together to create a seamless panorama, which then was also merged with the historical photographs, made available to the authors. Another test, represented in Fig. 13.10, entailed the use of Photoshop's neural filter to automatically colorize the historical photograph.

In Fig. 13.11, we depict the results of applying both automatic colorization and image-stitching in panorama images of the library room, comparing situations before and after applying the effect. Results are promising, but we can see some limitations of this approach. We do not have yet knowledge of the original pose of the 1902 photograph nor the camera's intrinsic parameters, and today's situation image panorama was captured in an ad hoc manner. Therefore, image distortion is perceived. This will be corrected with better 360° imaging capture and also an estimation of the 1902 photograph camera pose and its intrinsic parameters, which is underway.

13.5 Conclusions and Future Work

In this chapter, we have described the steps that have been taken to attempt to reach our main goal, specifically with the design of a solution for the Monserrate Palace, part of a UNESCO cultural landscape located in Sintra, Portugal, more specifically, a Web gaming app.

(a) Present-day at the library without any stitching

(b) Present-day at the library, stitched with colorized historical photograph

(c) Present-day at the library, stitched with historical photograph

(d) Gray scaled present-day at the library, stitched with historical photograph

Fig. 13.11 Sections of the resulting panorama from image-stitching tests

We performed a literature review that shows that immersive technologies (VR and AR), when properly implemented, can be very beneficial to the visitor experience at cultural sites, by providing tourists with a more engaging and interactive experience, and can enhance their appreciation of the site's cultural and historical significance.

With this analysis at hand, we proceed to design an immersive gaming app to enhance visitor experience at the largely unfurnished Monserrate Palace. Referred to as the "Monserrate in the Cook family era," the gaming app uses historical photos and modern smartphone technology to recreate the daily life of the Cook family, in the early twentieth century. Visitors will play the game on-site, navigating the palace's spaces and completing challenges that include matching photos to rooms, locating the photographer's pose, and discovering room curiosities. Successful completion of tasks rewards players with insights into the room's historical and cultural significance and AR experiences. User-centered design and expert feedback guided the app's development and prototype testing, and a feasibility study using image-stitching and colorization of historical photos yielded promising results. The game combines education and entertainment, offering a unique, engaging, and interactive tour of the palace.

Current work involves the collection of 360° imaging on-site with proper camera equipment, the estimation of the 1902 photograph camera poses, and its intrinsic parameters of available photos taken in the palace rooms, to improve our image-stitching process. In the context of our user-centered design approach, we are going to proceed in the near future, with expert-reviewed usability studies using popular approaches from the literature, which will drive the improvement of the user experience (Jakob Nielsen 2012).

The beta version of the gaming app, including the backend and frontend will also be subject to an end-user study, prior to the deployment of the proposed solution in the palace, to help us gauge the visitors' impressions of the palace. Additionally, the study helps define end-users' levels of satisfaction and engagement with the current traditional visiting experience, as well as providing insights into the visitors' attitudes and opinions toward the use of immersive technologies and identifying the barriers to the adoption and use of the proposed solution. Final refinements in the app will then result in its deployment on-site to serve the end-users visiting the Monserrate Palace (Jakob Nielsen 2012).

Continued efforts will be required to identify areas for improvement and optimization of the app, in order to better align with the needs and expectations of visitors. This will involve conducting visitor experience surveys and actively seeking feedback to gather valuable insights.

Overall, our work represents a step toward the development and implementation of immersive technologies in cultural heritage sites. By embracing these technologies and finding innovative ways to integrate them into the visitor experience, we can ensure that the visitors are able to appreciate and learn from cultural heritages (tom Dieck et al. 2016) in new and exciting ways.

The app and supporting libraries will be mostly developed by adopting open-source software, by means of a reusable toolkit that can be leveraged by SMEs in the tourism sector to easily implement AR/VR-based experiences, as stated in the work plan of the RESETTING project. Essentially, this app will act as a testing ground for the toolkit, evaluating its viability, usability, task satisfaction, and user experience.

Acknowledgments This work was developed in the scope of the RESETTING project, funded by the COSME Programme (EISMEA) of the European Union under grant agreement No.101038190.

References

Abuamoud, I.N., Libbin, J., Green, J., ALRousan, R.: Factors affecting the willingness of tourists to visit cultural heritage sites in Jordan. J. Heritage Tour. **9**(2), 148–165 (2014). https://doi.org/10.1080/1743873x.2013.874429

Alazaizeh, M.M., Jamaliah, M.M., Mgonja, J.T., Ababneh, A.: Tour guide performance and sustainable visitor behavior at cultural heritage sites. J. Sustain. Tour. **27**(11), 1708–1724 (2019). https://doi.org/10.1080/09669582.2019.1658766

Aulia, V.R., Subriadi, A.P., Nadlifatin, R.: Gamification: A comprehensive review of literature. In: 2022 1st International Conference on Information System & Information Technology (ICISIT), pp. 277–282 (2022). https://doi.org/10.1109/ICISIT54091.2022.9872830

Bruno, F., Bruno, S., Sensi, G.D., Luchi, M.L., Mancuso, S., Muzzupappa, M.: From 3D reconstruction to virtual reality: A complete methodology for digital archaeological exhibition. J. Cultural Heritage **11**(1), 42–49 (2010). https://doi.org/10.1016/j.culher.2009.02.006

Buonincontri, P., Marasco, A., Ramkissoon, H.: Visitors' experience, place attachment and sustainable behaviour at cultural heritage sites: a conceptual framework. Sustainability **9**(7), 1112 (2017). https://doi.org/10.3390/su9071112

Chen, C.F., Chen, F.S.: Experience quality, perceived value, satisfaction and behavioral intentions for heritage tourists. Tour. Manag. **31**(1), 29–35 (2010). https://doi.org/10.1016/j.tourman.2009.02.008

Chiu, C.C., Wei, W.J., Lee, L.C., Lu, J.C.: Augmented reality system for tourism using image-based recognition. Microsyst. Technol. **27**(4), 1811–1826 (2019). https://doi.org/10.1007/s00542-019-04600-2

David Knights-Whittome: Palácio de Monserrate. Foto ©PSML (1902). Accessed 10 May 2023

de Rojas, C., Camarero, C.: Visitors' experience, mood and satisfaction in a heritage context: evidence from an interpretation center. Tour. Manag. **29**(3), 525–537 (2008). https://doi.org/10.1016/j.tourman.2007.06.004

Gaitatzes, A., Christopoulos, D., Roussou, M.: Reviving the past: cultural heritage meets virtual reality. In: Proceedings of the 2001 Conference on Virtual Reality, Archeology, and Cultural Heritage. ACM, New York (2001). https://doi.org/10.1145/584993.585011

Hamari, J., Koivisto, J., Sarsa, H.: Does gamification work? A literature review of empirical studies on gamification. In: 2014 47th Hawaii International Conference on System Sciences, pp. 3025–3034 (2014). https://doi.org/10.1109/HICSS.2014.377

Han, D.I., tom Dieck, M.C., Jung, T.: User experience model for augmented reality applications in urban heritage tourism. J. Heritage Tour. **13**(1), 46–61 (2017). https://doi.org/10.1080/1743873x.2016.1251931

Jakob Nielsen: Usability 101: Introduction to usability (2012). https://doi.org/www.nngroup.com/articles/usability-101-introduction-to-usability/. Accessed 10 May 2023

Jung, K., Nguyen, V.T., Piscarac, D., Yoo, S.C.: Meet the virtual Jeju Dol Harubang—The mixed VR/AR application for cultural immersion in Korea's main heritage. ISPRS Int. J. Geo-Inform. **9**(6), 367 (2020). https://doi.org/10.3390/ijgi9060367

Koeva, M., Luleva, M., Maldjanski, P.: Integrating spherical panoramas and maps for visualization of cultural heritage objects using virtual reality technology. Sensors **17**(4), 829 (2017). https://doi.org/10.3390/s17040829

Mora, A., Riera, D., Gonzalez, C., Arnedo-Moreno, J.: A literature review of gamification design frameworks. In: 2015 7th International Conference on Games and Virtual Worlds for Serious Applications (VS-Games), pp. 1–8 (2015). https://doi.org/10.1109/VS-GAMES.2015.7295760

Neto, M.J.B.: Monserrate: a casa romântica de uma família inglesa. Caleidoscópio (2015)

Neto, M.J.: Monserrate revisitado: a coleção Cook em Portugal: 200 anos do nascimento de Sir Francis Cook mecenas e colecionador de arte–1817-2017. Caleidoscópio (2017)

Neto, J.N., Neto, M.J.: Immersive cultural experience through innovative multimedia applications: the history of Monserrate Palace in Sintra (Portugal) presented by virtual agents. Int. J. Heritage Digital Era **1**(1_suppl), 101–106 (2012). https://doi.org/10.1260/2047-4970.1.0.101

Noh, Z., Sunar, M.S., Pan, Z.: A Review on Augmented Reality for Virtual Heritage System. In: Learning by Playing. Game-based Education System Design and Development, pp. 50–61. Springer, Berlin, Heidelberg (2009). https://doi.org/10.1007/978-3-642-03364-3_7

Pasca, M.G., Renzi, M.F., Di Pietro, L., Guglielmetti Mugion, R.: Gamification in tourism and hospitality research in the era of digital platforms: a systematic literature review. J. Service Theory Practice (2021). https://doi.org/10.1108/JSTP-05-2020-0094

Rettig, M.: Prototyping for tiny fingers. Commun. ACM **37**(4), 21–27 (1994). https://doi.org/10.1145/175276.175288

Saleem, A.N., Noori, N.M., Ozdamli, F.: Gamification applications in e-learning: a literature review. Technol. Knowl. Learn. (2022). https://doi.org/10.1007/s10758-020-09487-x

tom Dieck, M.C., Jung, T.H., tom Dieck, D.: Enhancing art gallery visitors' learning experience using wearable augmented reality: generic learning outcomes perspective. Curr. Issues Tour. **21**(17), 2014–2034 (2016). https://doi.org/10.1080/13683500.2016.1224818

Younes, G., Kahil, R., Jallad, M., Asmar, D., Elhajj, I., Turkiyyah, G., Al-Harithy, H.: Virtual and augmented reality for rich interaction with cultural heritage sites: a case study from the Roman

Theater at Byblos. Digit. Appl. Archaeol. Cultural Heritage **5**, 1–9 (2017). https://doi.org/10.1016/j.daach.2017.03.002
Yung, R., Khoo-Lattimore, C.: New realities: a systematic literature review on virtual reality and augmented reality in tourism research. Curr. Issues Tour. **22**(17), 2056–2081 (2017). https://doi.org/10.1080/13683500.2017.1417359

Conclusion

Smart Life embraces various Smart applications, such as Smart home, Smart city, and Smart transportation, each comprising numerous Smart artifacts. For instance, for Smart transportation, we can cite Smart vehicles, Smart ships, Smart railways, and so on. By unifying these fields under the same umbrella of Smart Life, we aim to provide an integrated vision of Smart application systems developed for the purpose of an enriched life experience.

Throughout this book, we have presented an in-depth exploration of the Smart Life concept and its various applications. We studied several fundamental aspects in understanding the concept of Smart Life and its taxonomy, evolution, and ethical considerations. We presented four conceptual contributions in Smart environment, Smart home, Smart city, and Smart tourism. Three innovative applications on Smart viticulture, Smart elevators, and Smart crowd detection were detailed. Finally, we described two experience reports on Smart city and Smart tourism.

The domain of Smart Life is vibrant and marked by substantial innovation. It holds immense promise for significantly improving the quality of life. The main challenge here is to find an equilibrium between the maximization of benefits for people and the planet and solving multiple critical issues, including concerns about privacy, security, dependency, identity theft, and the potential for abuse and misuse of technologies.

Moving forward to Smart Life Engineering will provide valuable insights to address this challenge. We are willing to investigate deeper the key problems within the field of Smart Life and find chunks of solutions to architect a Smart Life building. Within this huge ambition, our next step is to discover whether common

E. Kornyshova et al. (eds.), *Smart Life and Smart Life Engineering*,
https://doi.org/10.1007/978-3-031-75887-4

methodological foundations can be established across the diverse areas of Smart Life. By doing so, we aim to foster a more coherent and integrated approach to Smart Life, ultimately enhancing its potential to deliver careful, sustainable, secure, and enriched experiences for all beings on Earth.

Elena Kornyshova
Rébecca Deneckère
Sjaak Brinkkemper

MIX
Papier aus verantwortungsvollen Quellen
Paper from responsible sources
FSC® C105338

If you have any concerns about our products,
you can contact us on
ProductSafety@springernature.com

In case Publisher is established outside the EU,
the EU authorized representative is:
Springer Nature Customer Service Center GmbH
Europaplatz 3, 69115 Heidelberg, Germany

Printed by Libri Plureos GmbH
in Hamburg, Germany